EXPLAINING THE EV

How do we make sense of complex evidence? What are the cognitive principles that allow detectives to solve crimes and lay people to puzzle out everyday problems? To address these questions, David Lagnado presents a novel perspective on human reasoning. At heart, we are causal thinkers driven to explain the myriad ways in which people behave and interact. We build mental models of the world, enabling us to infer patterns of cause and effect, linking words to deeds, actions to effects, and crimes to evidence. But building models is not enough; we need to evaluate these models against evidence, and we often struggle with this task. We have a knack for explaining, but less skill at evaluating. Fortunately, we can improve our reasoning by reflecting on inferential practices and using formal tools. This book presents a system of rational inference that helps us evaluate our models and make sounder judgments.

DAVID LAGNADO is Professor of Cognitive and Decision Sciences in the Department of Experimental Psychology, University College London (UCL). He has written more than 100 articles and co-authored a textbook on the psychology of decision-making. He has worked with US intelligence, the UK government and various legal and financial institutions, looking at methods to improve reasoning and decision-making.

EXPLAINING THE EVIDENCE

How the Mind Investigates the World

DAVID A. LAGNADO

University College London

CAMBRIDGE
UNIVERSITY PRESS

CAMBRIDGE
UNIVERSITY PRESS

University Printing House, Cambridge CB2 8BS, United Kingdom

One Liberty Plaza, 20th Floor, New York, NY 10006, USA

477 Williamstown Road, Port Melbourne, VIC 3207, Australia

314–321, 3rd Floor, Plot 3, Splendor Forum, Jasola District Centre, New Delhi – 110025, India

103 Penang Road, #05–06/07, Visioncrest Commercial, Singapore 238467

Cambridge University Press is part of the University of Cambridge.

It furthers the University's mission by disseminating knowledge in the pursuit of education, learning, and research at the highest international levels of excellence.

www.cambridge.org
Information on this title: www.cambridge.org/9781107006003
DOI: 10.1017/9780511794520

© Cambridge University Press 2022

First published 2022

A catalogue record for this publication is available from the British Library.

Library of Congress Cataloging-in-Publication Data
NAMES: Lagnado, David A., 1962– author.
TITLE: Explaining the evidence : how the mind investigates the world / David A. Lagnado.
DESCRIPTION: Cambridge, United Kingdom ; New York, NY : Cambridge University Press, 2022. | Includes bibliographical references.
IDENTIFIERS: LCCN 2021019468 (print) | LCCN 2021019469 (ebook) | ISBN 9781107006003 (hardback) | ISBN 9780521184816 (paperback) | ISBN 9780511794520 (epub)
SUBJECTS: LCSH: Evidence–Psychological aspects. | Reasoning (Psychology) | Judgment. | Cognition. | BISAC: PSYCHOLOGY / Cognitive Psychology & Cognition | PSYCHOLOGY / Cognitive Psychology & Cognition
CLASSIFICATION: LCC BF761 .L34 2022 (print) | LCC BF761 (ebook) | DDC 153.4/3–DC23
LC record available at https://lccn.loc.gov/2021019468
LC ebook record available at https://lccn.loc.gov/2021019469

ISBN 978-1-107-00600-3 Hardback
ISBN 978-0-521-18481-6 Paperback

For Tracy

Contents

List of Figures		*page* viii
List of Tables		xii
Preface		xiii
Acknowledgements		xviii
1	The Cliff Death	1
2	Models in Mind	14
3	Causal Modelling	32
4	Thinking beyond Biases	74
5	Expert Reasoning in Crime Investigation	112
6	Questions of Evidence	132
7	Competing Causes	156
8	Confirmation Bias: The Good, the Bad and the Ugly	172
9	Telling Stories	186
10	Idioms for Legal Reasoning	210
11	Causal Reasoning in a Time of Crisis	265
References		282
Index		299

Figures

2.1 Visualization of the location of the projectile in the body *page* 15
2.2 Verification of the suspect's statement 15
2.3 Schematic diagram of a hierarchical knowledge system 27
3.1 Causal graph for barn fire model 38
3.2 Predictive inference in the barn model 50
3.3 Diagnostic inference in the barn model 51
3.4 Explaining away in the barn model 52
3.5 Interventions in the barn model 55
3.6 The difference between doing and seeing 56
3.7 Intervention to avoid confounding 57
3.8 Counterfactual inference in the barn model 61
3.9 Graph showing the causal Markov condition 64
3.10 Causal model of Chicago barn fire 65
3.11 Chicago barn model after updating given evidence
 of the barn fire 67
3.12 Causal model of the broader Chicago fire 68
4.1 False-positive scenario 79
4.2 Benign cyst scenario 81
4.3 Causal models for double test example 83
4.4 Causal Bayes net for forensic process 91
4.5 Causal Bayes net for forensic process including possible
 alternative causes and errors 92
4.6 Three simplified models of the forensic process 93
4.7 Causal model of the conjunction of *Motive* and *Killing* 98
4.8 Estimating number of paths in a structure 101
5.1 The data-frame theory of sensemaking 115
5.2 Simple causal model explaining the observed injuries in the
 abuse frame 119
5.3 Causal model with alternative explanations 120
5.4 Self-solvers versus whodunit structures 123

5.5	Process model of 'whodunit' murders	124
6.1	Common-effect model	148
6.2	Common-effect model for DNA match	149
6.3	Causal model of testing reliability	152
6.4	Extended causal model for DNA evidence	153
6.5	Extended causal model of witness testimony	154
7.1	GSR model for the Jill Dando case	161
7.2	GSR model with probabilities	162
7.3	Two possible causes of the positive test in the explosives case	163
7.4	Zero-sum reasoning in test selection	164
7.5	Causal Bayes net of abuse case	167
7.6	Probability tables (CPTs) for each variable showing participants' mean estimates	168
7.7	Inference in abuse model – *Step 1*	168
7.8	Inference in abuse model – *Step 2*	168
7.9	Inference in abuse model – *Step 3*	169
7.10	Inference in abuse model – *Step 4*	169
7.11	Participants' mean probability ratings of the two possible causes after each item of evidence	169
8.1	Different models for independent and dependent evidence	182
9.1	Causal model of the prosecution account of the injuries to Christopher	188
9.2	Prosecution account of the injuries to Harry	188
9.3	Causal model of the defence account of the injuries to Christopher	189
9.4	Causal model of the defence account of the injuries to Harry	189
9.5	Abstract episode schema	198
9.6	Three stages of the Story Model	199
9.7	Central story for mock jurors choosing first-degree murder	202
9.8	Causal model of the 'first-degree' murder story	204
10.1	Example of a Wigmore chart	213
10.2	Evidence idiom	217
10.3	Combining multiple items of evidence	218
10.4	Two alternative causes of the same evidence	220
10.5	Explaining away idiom applied to Vole blood evidence	221
10.6	Evidence-reliability idiom	223
10.7	Alarm model	224

10.8   Model of independent witnesses of the same event   225
10.9   Belief updating when all three witnesses report
       the same thing   226
10.10 Eyewitness testimony unpacked   227
10.11 DNA evidence unpacked   229
10.12 Updating the DNA model   230
10.13 Basic opportunity model   232
10.14 The opportunity prior idiom   234
10.15 Opportunity model for bar theft   235
10.16 Three nurses motive model   236
10.17 Updated model based on motive evidence   237
10.18 Modelling motive and intention   238
10.19 Modelling Emile Gourbin's motive and intention
       for killing Marie Latelle   239
10.20 Model of fight between Johnson and Caldwell   240
10.21 Modelling propensity   241
10.22 Updated propensity model for (a) low prior convictions
       and (b) high prior convictions   242
10.23 Prior convictions as evidence of both propensity and
       low credibility   242
10.24 Dependence between two items of evidence   243
10.25 Models of (a) independent versus (b) dependent evidence 244
10.26 The difference in updating the models given
       (a) independent and (b) dependent evidence   245
10.27 Dependence between positive ID and confession evidence   245
10.28 Deception model with CPT for witness testimony   247
10.29 Deception model   248
10.30 Deception model with separate evidence   249
10.31 Alibi idiom model with CPT for alibi node   251
10.32 Alibi model combined with CCTV evidence   252
10.33 Alibi model. (a) With prior probabilities. (b) Updated
       probabilities when suspect gives alibi   252
10.34 Alibi model. (a) Updated probabilities with alibi
       and CCTV evidence. (b) Updated probabilities with
       CCTV only   253
10.35 Model with alibi and CCTV   254
10.36 Model for *Witness for the Prosecution*   256

10.37 Model of the Barry George case   260
11.1 Simplified causal model for diagnosis of covid-19   268
11.2 Causal model of confounding   270
11.3 Models of collider bias   271
11.4 Graphic depicting the consensus public health view
      shortly after the first lockdowns were imposed   275
11.5 Competing counterfactual models   275
11.6 Model for inferring covid status given a test result   277

Tables

3.1 Conditional probability table (CPT) for the *Detector* variable   *page* 41

3.2 Conditional probability table (CPT) for the *Sprinkler* variable   43

3.3 Conditional probability table (CPT) for the variable *Fire* with parents *Match* and *Lightning*   43

3.4 Conditional probability table (CPT) for the variable *Barn burns* with parents *Fire* and *Sprinkler*   44

3.5 Pearl's causal hierarchy   49

4.1 One example of the common-cause scenario   86

5.1 Assertions of data-frame theory   114

8.1 Taxonomy for confirmation bias   173

10.1 Updating the *Witness for the Prosecution* model   257

Preface

'The Murders in the Rue Morgue', Edgar Allan Poe (1841)

Who can resist a murder mystery? Whether it's a classic detective novel or a psychological thriller, we rise to the challenge of the whodunit, revelling in the twists and turns, the false leads and the surprise denouement. And despite their tragedy, we are fascinated by real-life crime stories, when evil characters do bad things to good people. In this book I will explore another mystery: how do we – with our limited-capacity minds – manage to tackle such puzzles? This mystery is remarkable but often passes unnoticed. We take our inferential skills for granted. But, if you stop to think, it's amazing that we can formulate – let alone solve – such complex problems. How do we generate hypotheses, weigh up evidence and draw sensible conclusions? How do we leap from a smattering of clues – a bloody razor, uprooted hair, a body shoved up a chimney – to conjure possible causes of a crime scene we have never witnessed before? Even the ability to come up with the *wrong* answer is a feat worthy of awe.

To see how the mind works its magic, we must look beneath the surface, at the cognitive machinery that impels us. Firstly, we are causal thinkers, driven to explain the myriad ways in which people (and things) behave and interact. Who killed the daughter? Why was her body rammed up the chimney? Why was no money taken? To answer such questions we build *mental* models – crude models 'in the mind' that we can probe and manipulate, allowing us to explain what we have observed, to predict what happens next and to imagine how events might have been different. These models enable us to reason about intricate patterns of cause and effect, linking words to deeds, actions to effects and crimes to evidence. They allow us to dig deeper into human behaviour, helping us to understand rather than just describe what we witness.

But building models is not enough, especially if we are trying to solve a crime or find someone guilty. We need to support our models with evidence, and this adds another layer of complexity. We must evaluate how well the evidence fits our favoured account as compared to other possibilities and also assess the quality of the evidence itself. Who was the source of the blood? How reliable was the blood test? Can we trust what the witnesses say? How do we factor these concerns into our overall judgment? To make things even harder, those closely involved in a crime often have motive to deceive us. Is the accused giving an honest account or lying through his teeth?

Despite being adept at creating mental models to explain events, we find evaluating these models much harder. We can readily devise an elaborate story of how a suspect might have committed the crime and yet struggle to produce convincing evidence for this version of events. We have a knack for *explaining*, but less skill at *evaluating*. And sometimes a compelling narrative can outstrip the evidence, with disastrous consequences.

Fortunately, all is not lost. We can improve our reasoning, learning to evaluate our hypotheses with consistency and balance. And there are tools to support us. I will present a system of rational inference that can help us build better models and make sounder judgments.

Structure of the Book

I use crime investigation as a lens through which to explore the principles of evidential reasoning. My premise is that we use the same forms of reasoning, whether we are solving crimes, diagnosing diseases or dealing with everyday concerns. But I focus on legal cases because they provide engaging examples – where bad reasoning can have serious costs.

Each chapter starts with a different crime case, showing how investigators, legal experts or jurors have grappled with difficult and often contentious questions. The cases highlight important principles of reasoning which are not restricted to legal settings but apply to any sphere where people must use evidence to draw conclusions.

Chapter 1 traces a crime from the discovery of a body to the verdict of a court, exposing the challenges faced by decision-makers at each step of the process. How do we generate initial hypotheses from sparse information? How do we develop our hypotheses as we gather new evidence? How do we make sense of a large body of conflicting evidence to reach a final decision?

The next two chapters make the case for the critical role of causal models in reasoning. Chapter 2 focuses on the models we manipulate in our heads and on our impressive capacity to reason about new situations (even the terrible scene at Madame L'Espanaye's apartment!). But how do we know when our causal reasoning is good or bad? Chapter 3 introduces the causal modelling framework, showing us how to draw rational inferences from evidence. In Chapters 4 and 5 we look at how people reason and make judgments under uncertainty, with Chapter 4 focusing on people tackling small-scale problems in the lab and Chapter 5 switching to the expert reasoning of detectives solving murder cases.

Our focus then shifts to evidence evaluation. Chapter 6 looks at the legal concept of evidence, while Chapter 7 explores the subtleties that arise when people assess competing causes of the same evidence. Chapter 8 examines the strategies that people use to gather and interpret evidence, focusing on classic confirmation bias.[1] Chapter 9 then looks at how people construct stories to make sense of complex evidence, using the well-known Sally Clark case.

In Chapter 10, I present a Bayes net approach to modelling legal cases and suggest that this method could be used as a training tool to improve inferential reasoning in the legal domain. Note that this is a more technical chapter than the others and can be skipped by those not wanting the nitty-gritty details. But I do recommend reading the Agatha Christie story and looking at the proposed Bayes net.

Chapter 11 summarizes the key messages in the book by applying them to our thinking during the coronavirus crisis. I show how many of the concepts – from psychology and formal modelling – recur in expert and lay reasoning during the pandemic. I argue that the danger of jumping to

---

[1] Confirmation bias occurs when we gather and interpret evidence according to our prior expectations or preferences. Sometimes this is a reasonable strategy but in other contexts it can lead to biases. Again the murders at Rue Morgue provide a neat example. The police collect and evaluate evidence under the (very reasonable) assumption that the murderer is human. But in this peculiar case this assumption is misleading.

premature causal claims, without careful evidence evaluation, is particularly rife in situations of radical uncertainty. But causal thinking is also an essential tool for dealing with such crises.

Who Is This Book for?

This book is for anyone interested in evidential reasoning – how people reason about evidence and how this reasoning can be improved using formal models. Several disciplines are straddled in the book, so I hope it appeals to students from psychology, crime science, law, computer science and beyond. Ideally, I'd like to encourage the crossing of discipline boundaries: for example, introducing psychologists to legal decision-making, law students to causal modelling, and computer scientists to modelling of legal cases. More ambitiously, I hope the book might be of interest to expert decision-makers outside academia, such as crime investigators, forensic scientists and criminal lawyers.

The book is aimed at students and researchers, and I introduce all necessary technical concepts as the book progresses. It only presupposes some basic probability theory. I actually think that an introduction to causal modelling is a nice route into probabilistic thinking because (as I claim in the book) we are better attuned to causal rather than statistical reasoning. To accompany the book the website www.explainingtheevidence.com provides additional learning materials, including an introduction to probability theory and models of all the Bayes net examples to download and explore.

What This Book Does Not Cover

Human reasoning admits of many levels of explanation. In this book I focus on the cognitive level, how individual minds represent and reason about evidence, with little discussion of the broader social context of reasoning, and nothing on the lower-level neuroscience. Partly this is due to lack of space, but I also feel that the cognitive level is the natural starting point, indispensable for seeing how all the other levels fit together. Neither do I cover the broad literature on the non-cognitive factors – such as emotions and prejudice – that undoubtedly influence legal decision-making. Again, I believe that understanding the cognitive perspective is a precursor to seeing how these other factors might distort and bias our reasoning.

Two Senses of Why

A central theme in the book is that we are better at explaining than evaluating. This can be a slippery distinction to grasp because the two activities are so closely linked – we use evidence to build and revise our models, and we use our models to look for evidence. One way to think about the distinction is to see these activities as responses to two different types of why-question. Carl Hempel (1965) distinguishes between *explanation-seeking* and *reason-seeking* why-questions. The former question asks us why things in the world happen as they do, whereas the latter asks for the justifying grounds to support our claims. For example, when a husband is accused of killing his wife, we can ask why he would do it – what would be his motive for such a crime? To answer this question we point to his violent nature and the fact that his wife wanted to leave him. But we can also ask why we should believe that he did it – how strong is the evidence? Here we point to forensics, CCTV footage or witness testimony.

The two activities are closely interwoven, especially if we don't know the truth of the things we are trying to explain. We use evidence to generate our explanations, and our explanations in turn guide our search for evidence. But they answer distinct questions – *explaining* is about what happens (or happened) in the world, whereas *evaluating* is about our reasons to believe these claims. And our cognition seems more geared towards the former than the latter – or so I shall argue in this book.

Acknowledgements

The seeds of this book were planted a long time ago, when I worked on the project 'Evidence, Inference and Enquiry' under the expert guidance of Philip Dawid, David Schum and William Twining. Around the same time Judea Pearl's book on causality was stirring up cognitive science, and I was fortunate to work with Steven Sloman, applying these new ideas to human reasoning. My next big step came when I started collaborating with Norman Fenton and Martin Neil, who taught me the art and science of modelling legal cases. This led to a six-month stint at the Newton Institute in Cambridge, where I benefitted from discussions with many people, including Richard Gill, Bill Thompson, Leila Schnepps, Julia Mortera, Anne Ruth Mackor, Christian Dahlman, Marjan Sjerps, Charles Berger, Jacob de Zoete, Floris Bex, Henry Prakken, David Bentley, Pat Wiltshire, David Balding and Paul Roberts.

Another key step was working with the Bayesian Argumentation via Delphi (BARD) team on an IARPA-funded project on collaborative Bayesian reasoning; I learned a huge amount from Ulrike Hahn, Kevin Korb, Ann Nicholson, Erik Nyberg, Toby Pilditch, Stephen Dewitt, Marko Tesic, Nicole Cruz, Kirsty Philips, Saoirse Connor Desai and Alice Liefgreen. We even had some laughs along the way.

My colleagues at UCL have (often wittingly) been sounding boards for many of the ideas in this book; in particular, I would like to thank Christos Bechlivanidis, Adam Harris, Nigel Harvey, Ruth Morgan, David Shanks, Marteen Speenkenbrink, Cheryl Thomas, and all members of the Causal Cognition lab, including special guests Marius Usher, Samantha Kleinberg, Jonathan Livengood and Katya Tentori. Special thanks also to my PhD students, past and present, who have helped shape my thinking and my tea-drinking: Neil Bramley, Tobias Gerstenberg, Alice Liefgreen, Milena Nikolic, Nadine Smit, Erica Yu, Paul Troop, Lara Kirfel, Tamara Shengelia, Claire Machan, Matija Franklin and Cristina Leone.

Many colleagues went beyond the call of duty and gave me feedback on the book itself. I'm extremely grateful to Neil Bramley, Sam Dupret, Toby Pilditch, Nichola Raihani, Tracy Ray and William Twining for commenting on various chapters, and to Christos Bechlivanidis, Nancy Cartwright, Philip Dawid, Norman Fenton, Martin Neil, Magda Osman and Marion Vorms for enduring the whole book! I shudder to think how things would have turned out without their help and advice. Thanks also to Cambridge University Press – Janka Romero, Emily Watton and Hetty Marx – for their help and infinite patience, to Cara Chamberlain for precision copy-editing, Melanie Gee for forensic indexing and Vinithan Sethumadhavan for putting it all together.

Many thanks to my family and friends for encouragement and moral support, including my nephew Isaac (aged $11\frac{3}{4}$) who read the first chapter and said it was very boring.

Finally, this book is dedicated to my wife Tracy, for making it all worthwhile.

The Cliff Death

A woman is found dead at the foot of a cliff. Dashed against the rocks. Her body lodged in a crevice ten metres from the cliff face. The cove is a local beauty spot but also a notorious suicide location.

I presume you are already speculating about what happened. Did the woman jump or was she pushed? If she was pushed, who did it and why? You need more facts to draw any firm conclusions, but your mind has been triggered into action. There is a problem to solve. You make a few tentative inferences. Her death was probably caused by the fall. But why did she fall? Perhaps she slipped while walking near the cliff edge. Unlikely but not impossible, especially if it was dark and the path unsafe. Or she might have jumped; in which case what drove her to suicide? But maybe she wasn't alone. She could have slipped during an argument with someone. More sinisterly, she might have been deliberately pushed. But why? Who would do such a thing?

Given what little information we have, suicide seems most likely. After all, at a location like this, suicide is more common than murder. But hang on – the body landed ten metres from the cliff face. How could a woman jump that far away from the cliff edge?

Whatever your perspective – whether you are hearing about a real case or reading a crime novel or watching a TV drama – you cannot resist speculating, trying to build up a picture of what happened and why. If you were an investigator, these conjectures would guide your decisions – telling you what evidence to search for, what forensic tests to carry out, and whom to trace and interview. As an armchair detective, they help you make sense of the unfolding narrative, telling you what to expect next and how to interpret new information.

Even with the slenderest of evidence we generate feasible causes – slipping, pushing, jumping – and causes of these causes – accident, suicide, murder. These are only guesses, not yet deserving the name of theories.

But they are a necessary start to enquiry. We need some initial frame, however skeletal, to guide our investigation.

It's amazing how readily we generate explanations. The hypotheses we create, even at this early stage in an enquiry, are often plausible and relevant. We are blessed with the ability to construct *causal models* and to simulate possible sequences of events. We can imagine a body being thrown from a cliff and landing some distance from the cliff face, or a man plotting to murder his partner, simulating the ways in which he might carry this out. Our causal imagination allows us to explore a rich world of possibility and conjecture.

In this chapter I use the cliff death to introduce the main questions to be addressed throughout the book. How do people build explanations from sparse information? How do investigators and lawyers construct a case against a suspect? How do jurors decide a legal case given a mass of complex and confusing evidence? While the expertise, knowledge and experience of these decision-makers vary widely, I will argue that they all use the same core reasoning principles and share similar strengths and weaknesses.

Let us return to the cliff death. You learn more details.[1]

The woman was twenty-four. Engaged to her boyfriend for three years, but dissatisfied with the relationship. She was seeing a psychiatrist due to bouts of depression. Her boyfriend worked for a notorious businessman, and both men were under investigation for an insurance fraud. The woman knew about the fraud, and this was another reason for tension in their relationship. The police focus their attention on the victim's partner. The boyfriend has an alibi – he was chauffeuring his boss that afternoon and then spent the evening at home alone. But two witnesses contradict his account. The owners of a local cafe near the cliff claim to have seen the woman with her boyfriend and another man that afternoon. Moreover, the police believe that the woman's body landed too far from the foot of the cliff for the woman to have jumped, even with a run-up. They think she must have been thrown.

The discovery of the woman's body was bizarre. Late that night the boyfriend drove to see his girlfriend's father and brother, saying that she had not returned home and he had a sense that she was in the cliff area (where they often used to go for picnics). The boyfriend was in a panic.

---

[1] This case is loosely based on a real case that took place in Australia, simplified and amended but retaining most of the key points: http://en.wikipedia.org/wiki/Death_of_Caroline_Byrne

Together they drove to the cove, and saw her car parked near the path to the cliff. They searched along the cliff top, and suddenly the boyfriend claimed to spot her body down on the rocks. It was pitch dark, and the others could not see anything. But later that night the police discovered the body in the exact location the boyfriend had indicated. How had he known that she was there?

Now you have more substance upon which to theorize. A mixture of facts, claims and counterclaims. You seek a story that makes sense of the evidence but also fits with your presumptions about human behaviour. There are several candidate stories. She might have committed suicide due to depression and a failing relationship. She might have gone walking alone on the cliff and slipped. She might have argued with her boyfriend and fallen during a heated row. She might have been killed by her boyfriend because she knew too much about his business scam. These are just a few possibilities that come to mind – we are incredibly adept at generating stories.

No single story emerges as a clear winner. Each explains some of the evidence but also makes claims that go beyond the known information. And some stories seem inconsistent with the available evidence. For example, the suicide story is supported by the girlfriend's depression but not by the location of the body. The murder story explains the location of the body (and the boyfriend's knowledge of this), but there is little evidence of his motive, beside the fact that his girlfriend knew about his business fraud. Stories project a coherent picture of what happened but can be severely under-determined by the evidence. They also ignore questions about the reliability and quality of the evidence. How credible are the various witnesses? At least one witness must be mistaken or lying, because the cafe owners and the boyfriend assert contradictory things. How reliable is the police's claim about the trajectory of the fall? What about the claims regarding the woman's history of depression or the boyfriend's business dealings? These are key questions, yet initial stories of what happened assume the truth (or falsity) of the content of such claims and do not represent the reliability of the testimony itself.

Our propensity for telling stories and our facility for causal explanation go hand in hand. Each story represents one unique causal sequence – crafted from our causal knowledge but adapted to the specifics of the case. All stories end with the same effect – a dead body beneath the cliff – but differ in the route taken and the assumptions made.

From the wealth of possible stories, two dominate the enquiry: the police's story of murder and the boyfriend's story of innocence. You may feel this tension too – vacillating between murder and suicide as you strive for a single coherent view.

Given the police's goals, it is inevitable they focus on stories that implicate the suspect. This dictates their evidence gathering: interviewing the boyfriend, scrutinizing his alibi, examining his movements on the day in question, sieving his life for cues about his character and motives. Given our goals as interested observers – trying to figure out what happened without a duty to control crime – we are less committed to finding the boyfriend guilty. But we are still driven to find a narrative explanation of the death, and a story that leads from an evil man to the murder of a young woman is compelling in its own right.

Despite the police's focus on the boyfriend, they also explore the possibility of suicide. They gather details about the girlfriend's history of depression, interviewing her doctor as well as family and friends. Finding out that her mother had committed suicide a few years before lends support to the possibility that her daughter was suicidal too. They examine the girlfriend's relationship with the boyfriend. Was it failing and about to end, as some of her friends claimed? Establishing problems in the relationship plays a dual role – it seems to reinforce the suicide story, but it could also be taken to support the murder story by giving the boyfriend a motive. The police also bring in forensic experts to re-examine the body's location in relation to the cliff edge. How feasible is it that she jumped unassisted?

In theory this process of accumulating evidence and revising hypotheses could continue indefinitely, but pressures of time and cost set practical limits. A turning point is reached when the investigators decide if they have sufficient evidence to prosecute the suspect. If so, they shift from an open-ended investigation to case construction – building a case against the suspect that will stand up in court. This is a 'meta-level' decision – at a higher level than simply deciding what evidence to pursue or updating one's beliefs in possible stories. It involves assessing the overall weight of the evidence gathered thus far, and whether it is suitably convincing to push ahead with a prosecution.[2] This kind of meta-level decision is prevalent in everyday reasoning too. We decide whether we have enough information to justify our claims, to stick our necks out and defend a position. If so, we then adopt a tighter confirmatory strategy: we seek to bolster our favoured story and defend it in the face of possible objections.

[2] In the United Kingdom this corresponds to a decision made by the Crown Prosecution Service on the basis that a successful conviction is more likely than not and in the public interest.

In the case of the cliff death, the police take several months before deciding that they have enough evidence to prosecute the boyfriend. He is charged with murder and retained in custody. The police switch to building a legal case against him. They seek to elaborate a story that will be convincing in court – a story that captures the what, the how and the why of the death. Evidence-gathering does not stop but takes on a different focus. The aim is to produce evidence that will satisfy legal requirements and hold up in court, to present a prosecution case that proves the suspect's guilt and rebuts the defence case.

The police fixate on the story of a possessive and devious boyfriend throwing his girlfriend from the cliff. This theory provides the frame for further search and analysis. They enlist experts on 'fall dynamics' to reinforce the conclusion that she was thrown from the cliff. In doing so, they anticipate that the defence will produce their own experts who will claim that the woman jumped to her death. They also intensify the hunt for evidence that refutes the boyfriend's alibi, knowing that this will be a key point of contention in the courtroom. New evidence is interpreted to fit with theory. Thus, when a new witness claims to have seen the woman arguing with her boyfriend on the evening of her death, this is taken as strongly incriminating, reinforcing that the boyfriend had motive and opportunity, and showing that he was lying about his alibi. Similarly, when two fishermen near the cliff claim to have heard a piercing scream at about midnight, this is taken as confirmation that she was thrown.

In building a case against the suspect, the police and prosecutors anticipate and attempt to defuse the defence case. In counterpoint, the defence team seeks to attack the anticipated[3] prosecution case and ideally provide an alternative story. In the case of the cliff death the defence has a clear-cut alternative – death by suicide. This account needs to be tailored to the available evidence and bolstered by any new evidence the defence can find. From a legal viewpoint, the defence is not compelled to present an alternative story, but it will often enhance their case. So, the defence usually has two lines of approach: to seek evidence that undermines the prosecution case and (perhaps independently) to seek evidence that supports their own story.

Fast forward one year. The boyfriend appears in court charged with murder. In a pre-trial hearing the judge has decided what evidence is

---

[3] Rules on disclosure mean that shortly before the trial the defence will know what evidence the prosecution will present. Also, the prosecution is informed about aspects of the defence case, such as whether they are presenting an alibi defence.

admissible. He rules out evidence that the boyfriend drew substantial amounts of money from his girlfriend's account after she had died. This is deemed unfairly prejudicial against the defendant. The prosecution and defence teams have prepared their arguments, and their respective witnesses and experts are lined up to give evidence. The stage is set for the centrepiece of the criminal justice system – a trial by jury.[4]

Now imagine you are a juror in the trial. Together with your fellow jurors you must decide whether the suspect is guilty or innocent. Not just to form an opinion but to make a choice with life-changing consequences. This is an enormous responsibility. And if you are a typical juror you will have no training in law, no expertise in formal reasoning or forensic science, and no prior experience of jury service. Nevertheless, you are required to be a 'fact-finder' – to use only the evidence presented in court, combined with your common sense and everyday knowledge, to decide whether the suspect is guilty of murder. The judge will guide you in this task by providing instructions about the law and about how to deal with certain types of evidence. The judge will even summarize the case for you, outlining the key points to consider. But the ultimate decision will be yours.

This is a huge and multifaceted task. You will be presented with a complex mass of information: a tangled web of evidence, testimonies, claims and counterclaims. You will hear arguments from prosecution and defence, and both parties will call on a succession of witnesses (as well as exhibits such as videos, photographs and diagrams). The witnesses will vary in their credibility. Some will appear trustworthy and competent; others will appear dishonest or incompetent. These witnesses will be aggressively cross-examined, testing the consistency of their accounts and exposing the frailties of human perception, memory and integrity. Expert witnesses will also give evidence, their testimony couched in scientific terms and focused on subtle forensic details. This will add rigor to their claims, but you as a non-specialist might struggle to grasp or evaluate their arguments. How does a non-expert decide between two experts who state opposing opinions?

Uncertainty is pervasive – with regard to both the reliability of evidence itself and the implications that the evidence has for key hypotheses. You can doubt the credibility of a witness report but also be uncertain about

---

[4] Trials by jury are actually quite rare, even in the United Kingdom and the United States, and some countries do not have them at all. However, they play a key role in discussions of fact-finding, and all the legal cases in this book were decided by a jury.

the implications of that report even if it were true. Dealing with probabilities rather than certainties is crucial to the fact-finding process. But it is also incredibly taxing. This difficulty is compounded by the intricate interrelations between evidence and hypotheses. Rarely does a single fact speak directly to the ultimate hypothesis – each fact or supposition is like a thread in a spider's web, drawing strength from surrounding or supporting items. Even so-called direct evidence, such as an eyewitness to the crime itself, depends on the credibility and reliability of the eyewitness. And circumstantial evidence is by definition indirect and dependent on other facts. It is this complex network of facts that dictates the overall 'force' or weight of the evidence against the accused. Eventually you must combine your understanding of the law with your judgment about what happened and decide if you are *sure* of the prosecution charge.[5]

Returning to our court case. The prosecution argues that the boyfriend deliberately killed his girlfriend. He is portrayed as a nasty piece of work: controlling and exploitative, and eager to make money quickly. She was kind and caring, from a wealthy family. They had been together for three years, but the relationship was souring, and he became angry and possessive. Amongst his nefarious dealings, he was involved in a major insurance fraud with his boss. She found out about the fraud and threatened to tell the police. This strained the relationship further. He drove her out to the cove area to try to resolve things, but they had a heated row. In a fit of anger, he threw her from the cliff to her death.

The prosecution calls on numerous witnesses to support this story. The two cafe owners testify that they saw the couple together near the cliff. A local artist testifies that he saw the couple arguing later that evening on the path to the cliff edge. All three witnesses seem highly credible. The prosecution also calls several witnesses to discredit the boyfriend's alibi. A key witness is the boyfriend's boss. In his police interview the boyfriend had claimed not to have gone to the cliff area that day. He said he was chauffeuring his boss in the afternoon, and they had a late lunch together. But his boss testifies that he had lunch with someone else that day and does not recall seeing the boyfriend. Given his shady business reputation, the boss does not seem a credible witness; however, it is unclear why he would falsely undermine his employee's alibi. Overall, these witnesses serve to establish that the boyfriend had the opportunity to commit the crime. They also bring into question his honesty in the police interview.

---

[5] Courts in the United Kingdom no longer ask for 'proof beyond reasonable doubt'; instead judges ask the jury to be 'satisfied that they are sure' before they convict (Crown Court Compendium, 2020).

The prosecution argues that the boyfriend was motivated both by anger at her wanting to leave him and by the fear that she would betray him to the police. To support this claim, they call several witnesses who confirm the girlfriend knew about the insurance fraud and that the relationship was in decline. Numerous witnesses also testify to the kind and caring nature of the girlfriend, and the possessive and aggressive nature of the boyfriend.

Two fishermen testify that they heard a scream at midnight – a woman's voice that was clearly distressed. Several witnesses testify that they were with the boyfriend at the cliff top during the search for his girlfriend. According to them, he claimed to see her body down on the rocks, despite the fact that it was very dark and they could not see anything. The implication was that he already knew she was there.

Finally, the prosecution calls a forensic expert in fall dynamics. He argues that the location of the body was too far from the cliff face for a woman to have jumped unassisted. He refers to several experiments he has conducted, involving policewomen either jumping or being thrown into a swimming pool in order to establish the maximum distance they could travel. He concludes that the victim must have been forcibly thrown.

The defence team cross-examines the prosecution's witnesses at several points, aiming to rebut their claims and cast doubt on their credibility. The reliability of the cafe owners' testimony is probed: they are both shown to have shaky memories for the details of the day in question, and they both admit to only seeing a couple who 'looked like' the couple in question. Moreover, their initial identification was based on looking at a photograph of the boyfriend rather than a proper identity parade. The forensic expert is also questioned about the validity of his swimming pool tests. How well can such tests capture the reality of a body thrown from a cliff edge?

The defence then calls their own witnesses, designed to undermine the prosecution's murder story and support a story of suicide. The girlfriend's doctor testifies that for several years her patient had suffered from bouts of depression, including a severe episode one week before her death. The doctor referred her to a psychiatrist, but the appointment was on the day that she went missing. It is also established that the girlfriend's mother had committed suicide five years earlier, and the girlfriend herself had taken an overdose one year later (although her father claimed this was a cry for help rather than a serious suicide attempt).

An expert witness directly rebuts the claim that the woman's body was thrown from the cliff. He has conducted his own experiments, suggesting that the woman could have jumped given a sufficient run-up. The expert also highlights inaccuracies in the police's estimated location of her body and argues that the body might have landed closer to the cliff edge than previously claimed.

Crucially, the defendant himself does not take the stand. He exercises his right not to give evidence. He therefore foregoes the chance to defend himself from the prosecution accusations but also avoids exposing himself to cross-examination. He cannot give his own version of events, but he is also protected from having his story scrutinized and potentially undermined.

The prosecution and defence give their closing speeches, summarizing their respective stories and pointing to the main flaws in the opposing accounts. The prosecution restates the story it told in the opening address and argues that the defence has presented nothing to undermine this story. For them a key point is that the boyfriend knew the body's location on the rocks, despite the darkness and the inability of anyone else to make out a body. How else would he know this, unless he had been there when she was thrown? They also emphasize their expert's claim that the woman must have been thrown, and the inconsistencies and lies in the defendant's police interview. They note that the defendant failed to address these inconsistencies, despite having the opportunity to give his own version in court.

The defence argues that the prosecution has not proved its case and that there are numerous reasons for reasonable doubt. They reiterate the unreliability of the witnesses who claim to have seen the couple arguing. They point to the lack of a compelling motive for the murder and the inconclusiveness of the expert's opinion about the body's fall. Most importantly, they argue that the prosecution cannot conclusively rule out the possibility of suicide. Indeed, the girlfriend's heavy depression, her previous attempt and the mother's suicide all support this story. Not only has the prosecution failed to eliminate suicide as a possibility but, the defence contends, it is the most plausible explanation based on the totality of the evidence.

Finally, the judge sums up the case and instructs the jury. He tells them that the burden of proof lies with the prosecution: they need to prove that the boyfriend murdered his girlfriend; the defence does not need to prove that he is innocent. The judge cautions them not to read too much into the claim that the defendant gave a false alibi in his police interview. Even if the jury believes that the boyfriend did lie, this is not automatically evidence that he is guilty. Only if the jury is sure that there is no innocent reason for the defendant's lies should they draw inferences about his guilt. One possibility here is that the boyfriend was in fact at the cliff top with his girlfriend, but she fell accidently. In his panic the boyfriend lied to police, saying he was not there, to avoid being accused of killing her. The judge also warns of the fallibility of eyewitness testimony, especially after a long period of time, when memories fade and are subject to bias.

Crucially, the judge instructs the jury that the defendant has a right to remain silent, and his failure to give evidence should not be used against him. What are you to make of this instruction? Why would an innocent man not seek to defend himself? Isn't it natural to infer that he must have something to hide, that he is afraid of being exposed by the prosecution? As with the question about his false alibi, there might be good reasons why he prefers to remain silent, even if innocent. Perhaps he is afraid that he will come across badly to the jury or that earlier misdemeanours will be used against him. Somehow you must balance the possibility of these innocent reasons against the inference that he has something to hide.

When summing up, the judge outlines the key points and highlights the strengths and weaknesses of either side's arguments. He focuses on a puzzle in one of the prosecution's main arguments. They contend that the reason the boyfriend accurately located the body when he claimed to see it from the cliff top was because he had thrown the body earlier that night. However, this argument is predicated on the fact that it was too dark for anyone to see the body from the cliff. But, given this darkness, how would the boyfriend have seen the exact positioning of the body, even if he had thrown it? The judge raises this point but does not offer a conclusion, leaving it as an issue for the jury to consider.

As a juror you hear all this evidence and argument over a protracted period. The case might last several months. It is a challenge to keep track of all the information: the stream of testimonies and cross-examinations, the cut-and-thrust of debate and counterargument, the legal rules and instructions. Moreover, at the outset you were explicitly told not to speculate or form any judgment until the end of the trial. But how can you resist? Is it humanly possible to hold back from speculation and judgment as the case progresses? Indeed, is it even desirable to withhold judgment, given that our minds are so carefully set up for sequential exposure to information? Memory is a cumulative and constructive process – we adapt and build on previous knowledge to make sense of new information. Without this capability we would struggle to remember anything at all, let alone understand and interpret the evidence in a meaningful way. But, as the legal strictures implicitly acknowledge, it is also dangerous to form opinions or interpretations too quickly, before the whole of the evidence has been presented and all parties have had their say.

At this point you might have a rough idea of whether you would vote guilty or not guilty. But you might still be wondering about several issues and how they fit together to determine a verdict. These questions have probably plagued you as you have been sitting through the trial (or reading through the chapter). If you are a jury member you will get the opportunity to discuss these questions with your fellow jurors. As a non-juror following the case, you might deliberate by yourself (or perhaps with other colleagues). Thinking more deeply about the case and taking various viewpoints on the problem can greatly improve your understanding and final decision.

The jury now retire behind closed doors to consider their verdict. Outside of fiction, films and TV dramas, little is known about the inner workings of the juror room. Each juror will have their own viewpoint, their own interpretation of the evidence, their own preferred story or stories about what happened. They must discuss these views together, debate the pros and cons of both sides and ideally converge upon a single group decision. Taking twelve individuals with different views and expecting a consensus to emerge seems a leap of faith. But perhaps the process of deliberation, suitably conducted, allows dissent and divergence to enhance the delivery of a good decision. Just as an individual reasoner can benefit greatly from adopting various viewpoints, seeing both sides of the argument, appreciating the ambiguity and incompleteness of the evidence – so too can a jury benefit from the diverse opinions and arguments of the individual jurors. On the other hand, groups can promote their own distinctive biases – groupthink, the pressure to conform, and over-dominant members can all conspire to make the jury's decision less than the sum of its parts.

The jury gives its decision. After one week of deliberation it reaches a unanimous verdict – the boyfriend is guilty. The judge sentences him to 17 years in prison. This takes into account mitigating factors because the judge believes that the murder was not premeditated but occurred in a fit of anger and aggression. But this is not the end of the process. An appeal is launched.

1.1   Explaining versus Evaluating

My focus in this book is on *evidential* reasoning: we are faced with a problem that cannot be solved automatically, and we must generate hypotheses, weigh evidence and revise our hypotheses as new information emerges.

One recurring theme is the triumph of *explaining* over *evaluating*: while we are adept at generating models to explain evidence, we are less capable at evaluating these models against the evidence. We can reason *from* evidence, but not so readily *about* the evidence or about the relation between our model and the evidence. Both tasks are hard, but in different ways, and each calls on different skills.

1.1.1 *Explaining – Reasoning from the Evidence*

The cliff death example shows how we strive to explain the world, especially when confronted with something puzzling or unusual. It need not be a dead body, but anything that stirs our mind into action. We seek to understand what has happened by constructing models, scenarios and stories. This requires creativity and invention: we cannot simply retrieve a pre-configured pattern because each problem case is unique. Instead we draw on our causal knowledge to build something afresh.

We have a gift for creating novel hypotheses. We might not produce *good* explanations (at least not initially), but we create the raw materials to work with. We get the engine started. This requires a flexibility of mind well beyond the smartest computer, no matter how rich its database of facts and laws. Hearing about the cliff death, we readily devise accounts of what might have happened: perhaps he threw her off the cliff in a fit of rage, or she jumped while severely depressed, or she slipped and fell. Each version explains the evidence in a different way, but each has its own internal logic. And if we were to encounter new facts, no doubt we could re-shape our stories to make sense of these too. We are blessed (and sometimes cursed) with a novelist's instinct for narrative and coherence.

1.1.2 *Evaluating – Reasoning about the Evidence*

Whereas our explanatory aim is to build models of the world, our evaluative aim is to appraise these models in light of the evidence. Here we must reason *about* the evidence, evaluating how well it supports our hypotheses as compared to other alternatives, and assessing the quality and reliability of the evidence itself. In the cliff death, for instance, we must evaluate the competing claims of prosecution and defence, as well as any alternative accounts we construct ourselves. We must assess a range of witness testimonies and expert reports, evaluating their relevance, strength and reliability. The difficulty of this task is magnified by the myriad interrelations between hypotheses and evidence, where the impact of one element often depends on several other elements. Finally, we must integrate everything to reach a decision or verdict.

The challenge of evaluation is daunting, and it's not surprising that people find it so hard. Many shortcomings have been catalogued: people focus on a single story and neglect alternatives; they search for evidence to support their hypotheses and downplay contrary evidence; they fail to scrutinize their sources of evidence; they misinterpret statistical argument. In legal cases these shortcomings can lead to serious miscarriages of justice. I will discuss these blind spots in later chapters.

That we struggle is not newsworthy, but the devil is in the details. Identifying when and why we go wrong is essential for improving our reasoning. It's not that we lack basic reasoning competence; our aptitude for causal, social and common-sense reasoning is impressive. Why do we find evidence evaluation so hard?

One reason is that there is a tension between *explaining* and *evaluating*: the very capacities that allow us to weave coherent stories can impair our ability to evaluate them. We are geared towards discovery and explanation, building crude but effective models to make sense of the world. We rely on educated guesswork, simplifying assumptions and heuristics. Our inferences often involve rough-and-ready simulations rather than careful calculations. This allows us to generate fertile hypotheses, to fill gaps in our evidence and to explore new paths of inquiry. But what makes us strong also makes us weak. While the art of explaining requires us to go beyond logic and probability, evaluating evidence requires the rigor that only logic and probability can bring. And the simplifying heuristics that enable us to invent and explore can compromise the accuracy of our evaluations.

Fortunately things are not as bleak as they seem. It's not that we are incapable of evaluating evidence; the picture is more nuanced. Studies of lay reasoners suggest a continuum of competence – from *satisficers*, who stick with a single story, to *evaluatists*, who successfully coordinate theory and evidence (Kuhn, 2001). And people can shift towards the more competent end of the spectrum. Better reflection on our inferential habits, together with training in probabilistic reasoning, can help us in this journey. I will introduce formal tools – causal modelling (Chapter 3) and Bayes nets (Chapter 10) – designed to improve our inferences and decisions.

Finally, I expect you want to know what happened in the appeal? We are curious creatures who seek to resolve tension and uncertainty. The boyfriend spent three years in jail before he was acquitted on appeal. The judges ruled that there was 'insufficient evidence beyond reasonable doubt' that he murdered his girlfriend and that the jury's verdict in the trial was not supported. But I expect you are still not fully satisfied. What you really want to know is what *actually* happened on the cliff that night.

CHAPTER 2

Models in Mind

If the organism carries a 'small-scale model' of external reality and of its own possible actions within its head, it is able to try out various alternatives, conclude which is the best of them, react to future situations before they arise, utilize the knowledge of past events in dealing with the present and the future, and in every way react in a much fuller, safer, and more competent manner to the emergencies which face it.

The Nature of Explanation, Kenneth Craik (1952)

2.1   The Fight

A father argues with his son. As the row escalates, the son shoots his father in the stomach. The father dies from internal bleeding. Was the shooting manslaughter or murder? The son claims he did not intend to shoot his father, that the gun fired accidently as he fell backwards when his father pushed him. The police investigate his claim by reconstructing the incident.[1]

Using a specialized computer program, investigators build a 3D model of the victim's body, incorporating the medical evidence to reveal the bullet's trajectory through the victim's stomach. The bullet entered on the left side of the abdomen and lodged in the right pelvic bone (Figure 2.1), taking a downward-angled path (assuming the victim was standing upright when shot). Next the police stage a physical reconstruction of the incident, with an actor taking the role of the father and the suspect himself acting out what he claimed happened. Investigators use photographs of this re-enactment to help build a fuller 3D computer model of the situation, including the possible movements and interactions of the father and son. They use this model to reconstruct and explore the shooting incident (Figure 2.2).

---

[1] This scenario is based on Buck, Naether, Räss, Jackowski and Thali (2013).

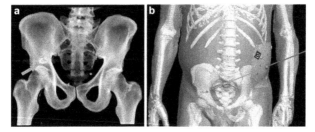

Figure 2.1   Visualization of the location of the projectile in the body. (a) The projectile was situated in the pelvis bone (white arrow), as visible in the CT image. (b) 3D model of the external and internal body, generated from CT and photogrammetry data.
(Adapted from Buck et al., 2013)

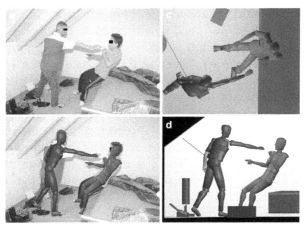

Figure 2.2   Verification of the suspect's statement. (a) Photograph of the gunshot, taken during an on-site reconstruction and representing the suspect's statement. (b) Positioning of the 3D models of the victim and suspect, according to their positions on the photograph. (c) Visualization of the victim–suspect configuration from a top view. (d) Visualization of this configuration from a lateral view. It is clearly visible that the shot could not be possible in this configuration.
(From Buck et al., 2013)

The model shows that the actual bullet trajectory does not match the son's claims, even under plausible variations of the model parameters, such as whether the father was upright or bent over. The model also allows investigators to explore which configurations of the father–son interaction best fit the bullet's trajectory. They identify three 'probable' configurations, which are played as video clips to the court. The court concludes that the son was upright when he fired the gun, contradicting his account of the shooting. The son is convicted of murder.

Despite what we see on TV programs such as *Crime Scene Investigation* (CSI), this example is not (yet) typical of crime scene investigations. But the method of drawing inferences through reconstruction that it exemplifies is pervasive. Investigators seek to explain the past by building models that reconstruct critical events; they use a range of modelling devices, including re-enactments, scale models,[2] physical experiments and computer models (Chisum & Turvey, 2011; Shaler, 2011).

The main reason to introduce this example, however, is not to chart the future of crime investigation but to propose an analogy between the use of computer models by investigators and the way in which the human mind uses internal models to think and reason. The key idea is that when we reason about the world we too use models to reconstruct and explore what could have happened. We build *mental models* to capture key features of the world, to envisage possible scenarios and to generate explanations. For example, to assess the son's claim that the gun fired as he fell backwards, we construct a crude mental model of the fight between father and son, comparing the expected trajectory of the bullet if the son is falling back versus standing upright. While our mental models and simulations differ in many respects from the computer models used by the investigators, we follow the same basic logic. By constructing and manipulating models of the crime situation, we can make a range of inferences about what happened, testing out various claims and establishing the most likely sequences of events.

In this chapter I argue that mental models are central to how we reason – not just as an optional add-on, but as the very engine of inference. This idea is not new. Kenneth Craik (1952) was an early advocate for mental models, and psychologists have developed the notion in various guises, applying mental models to logical reasoning (Johnson-Laird, 1983, 2010),[3] physical reasoning (Gentner & Stevens, 1983; Hegarty, 2004)

---

[2] For example, bullet trajectories are also reconstructed using physical models such as trajectory rods or even plastic straws.

[3] Johnson-Laird's mental model theory was initially applied to deductive reasoning but was extended to probabilistic and causal reasoning. Central to this approach is the claim that people construct mental models to represent logical possibilities and make inferences by examining these models, looking for implications and counterexamples. Model theory has exerted a huge influence on the psychology of reasoning but is now supplanted by probabilistic approaches to reasoning (Hahn, 2020; Oaksford & Chater, 2007). Most crucially for our purposes, model theory lacks the machinery to capture key elements of causal inference because of its grounding in logical relations and possibilities. Knowing that X causes Y tells us much more than what possibilities to represent; it

and language (Zwaan, 1999). While endorsing many of the insights from this prior work, I present a conception of mental models rooted in causality and incorporating ideas from formal causal modelling (see Chapter 3). I will also draw on emerging research in cognitive science that places causal models at the heart of cognition (cf. Danks, 2014; Glymour, 2001; Gopnik & Schulz, 2007; Rehder, 2017; Sloman, 2005; Sloman & Lagnado, 2015; Waldmann, 2017).

2.1.1   Modelling Systems

To create internal models, we need a model-building system. In our crime example investigators used a 3D modelling program to construct and explore a range of different scenarios. Our own reasoning likewise relies on a model-building system (or suite of systems) with the capacity to represent a vast range of situations and interactions. When thinking about the altercation between father and son, we can envisage many possible scenarios and explore different conjectures about what happened. Our model-building toolkit allows us to maintain generic models (what typically happens in a fight) and also to generate specific scenarios (what happened in *this* fight). Underpinning this capability are our intuitive theories and assumptions, which provide the grammar for generating new models (Tenenbaum, Griffiths & Niyogi, 2007). We discuss this hierarchical system in more detail in Section 2.4.1.2.

2.1.2   Simulation, Not Pictures or Videos

To propose that we reason by simulating mental models is not to claim that we simply use mental images or run movies in our heads. While imagery can play a role in inference, it is not the primary engine of thought, even when we solve visuospatial problems (Johnson-Laird, 2006; Shepard, 1978). Just as a 3D modelling package does not operate directly on images or videos but uses an underlying computer program to generate and manipulate these images, so the mind uses an internal modelling system to predict and infer how things behave in the world. This modelling system can also produce mental images to support reasoning, but this is in addition to the core inferences it performs.

---

tells us what happens if X changes, what will happen if we act on X (or Y), what would have happened if we had not done X and so on. We need a theory that captures causal structure, not just logical structure.

In our crime example, to model the interaction between father and son, the investigators took photographs of the re-enacted fight, which were encoded into the computer program. Digitalized information from these photos was used by the program, but its computations did not involve operations on the photos themselves. Likewise, when we ourselves imagine the fight, we might draw on the photos (or mental images based on these photos) to inform our own internal models. But our subsequent mental simulations do not operate directly on these images, even though we might generate novel images as products of our thinking. It is the underlying modelling system that does the core inferential work (the heavy lifting).

The distinction between simulation and the mere use of images and animations has a parallel in legal contexts. When considering computer-generated evidence, the law distinguishes between 'animation' and 'simulation', with a higher bar placed on the admissibility of the latter. Animations are typically used as a visual aid to enhance the presentation of witness testimony, such as providing a visual animation of what a witness claims to have seen. While simulations can also result in videos presented in court, they differ in that they seek to reconstruct events and draw inferences based on scientific analysis of the situation. Thus 'the computer itself is the expert' (Schofield, 2016). Applied to the human context, our internal mental models are used for simulation, not just animation.

How is this simulation achieved? In the case of the computer program, we know the answer. The modelling software is explicitly designed to replicate (to an approximate degree) the properties and dynamics of real-world objects. Crucially, the software encapsulates the relevant physical laws (again to an approximate level, possibly using shortcuts and simplifications), which are encoded in the programming language. The user specifies settings and parameters to capture the specifics of the scenes or interactions they wish to explore, and then the model simulates possible futures based on these settings. If the program is well designed, the model's predictions will mimic (to a certain degree of fidelity) how these scenes and interactions would play out in the real world. For example, a program for modelling human posture would not allow unnatural or impossible positions.

In the case of the human mind, we are still in the dark as to the exact mechanisms at play. But my proposal is that the mind also uses a modelling system to simulate real-world phenomena. Modelling systems encapsulate our knowledge and assumptions about how the world works and allow us to simulate future and past events. Again, the critical factor is that our mental models somehow mimic the structure and dynamics of the real-world situations they seek to model.

2.2 The Dimensions of Our Mental Models

What aspects of the world do our mental models seek to capture? Although the make-up of our models will depend on our inferential goals, which are many and diverse, core features recur and provide the building blocks for our everyday thinking.

2.2.1 Causality

Crucially, our mental models must capture the causal structure of the world, at least in key respects for which we use these models. We need *causal* representations: mental models that we can manipulate such that transformations on these models reflect how the world would change (or would have changed). Such 'working' models support the kind of reasoning crucial for our success and survival in the world. They allow us to predict the effects of events or actions taken: what happens if a person is pushed backwards, if a gun is fired at close range, if a bullet ruptures the stomach? They help us diagnose causes of observed effects: what started the argument between father and son, what made the gun fire, why did the father die? They also allow us to answer counterfactual what-if questions: what would have happened if the father had not pushed the son, if the son had not had a loaded gun, or if the emergency services had arrived straight away?

Causal mental models can address these questions, with the quality of their answers depending on how well the models capture the real-world system to be modelled. There is plenty of room for error here because our models can be naïve, biased or misguided. But even to be capable of addressing such questions is already a huge achievement. These questions cannot be answered by a system that only uses images, videos or 3D physical models, nor by inferential systems based purely on associations, probability or logic. We need a system capable of causal reasoning, a modelling system that encapsulates causal knowledge and simulates according to causal rules.

Fortunately, our causal models need not reproduce the detailed causal mechanisms at play in the world; they can be more abstract and schematic, perhaps only capturing the main input–output relations. Thus, we can model the shooting incident without going into details of the gun's firing mechanism or the physiological details that lead to death from internal bleeding. Despite their schematic nature, our causal models can still mirror the key relations between shooting and dying, between intentions and actions, which are critical for attributing causality in this context. We also have the capability to use a 'zoom lens' approach – unpacking the causal mechanisms in greater detail if we have suitable causal knowledge and the situation demands. A doctor thinking about the father's death can represent it not only as a tragic consequence of the relation between shooting and killing but also as a detailed causal process from a bullet entering the stomach to death by internal bleeding.

One stand-out feature of causal modelling is the capacity to address novel questions – to predict the consequences of actions or events never taken (or imagined) before. We can use our knowledge of how a system typically works to make predictions about a new configuration of causes. These novel predictions can range from minor changes to what we have previously experienced – such as predicting what would happen if we changed the mass of an object – to more radical changes – such as what would happen if gravity were suspended. We explore these novel possibilities by making the requisite changes to our model and mentally simulating the consequent behaviour. In essence, our modelling system allows us to try things out 'in our imagination', just as a modelling program allows us to try things out virtually. Counterfactual thinking is a special case of this ability. To infer what would have happened if things had been different, we 're-play' a counterfactual world in which we implement the relevant changes to predict what would have happened instead.

In sum, the value of trying things out in the mind – forethought – is a cornerstone of causal thinking. Moreover, it involves active manipulation of our mental models rather than simply playing out pre-stored animations or images. We are actors in our simulative thinking, not passive observers.

2.2.2 Objects, Events and Agents

To achieve our inferential goals, our models cleave the world in myriad ways. We track objects, events and processes, seeking to model how things change or unfold over time. We construct models that aim to reveal the mechanisms by which things work, from the crude machinery of a mousetrap to the intricacies of a clock. Building models of physical systems is a central part of cognition. But equally important is our ability to build models of the social world, tracking the behaviour of agents and groups, and their interactions. We readily construct models to explain and predict the behaviour of other people, inferring their hidden mental states, dispositions and characters.

Legal investigations are heavily geared towards human behaviour – people acting or being acted upon, witnesses seeing and reporting things, suspects being examined and interrogated – with the ultimate goal of identifying criminal acts and assigning responsibility. Profiling is a paradigmatic example, where experts seek to infer the psychological make-up of a criminal based on cues about their behaviour. Likewise, in everyday contexts we are often *intuitive profilers* – looking to build latent models that explain other people's actions and behaviour – and *intuitive prosecutors* – looking to assign responsibility for misdemeanours (Alicke, Mandel, Hilton, Gerstenberg & Lagnado, 2015; Tetlock, 2002). In such contexts our mental models offer assumptions and theories about the internal drivers of people's actions and how these might play out in specific circumstances. As I shall discuss in Section 2.3, our folk theories of physics and human behaviour form the basis for our mental modelling system. They allow us to generate plausible models attuned to the vagaries of everyday life.

2.2.3 Spatiotemporal Framework

Just as we use external models such as maps, floorplans and timelines to assist us in our reasoning, so our mental models encode relevant spatiotemporal properties of the world. This information will vary in its level of detail, according to the needs of our modelling. A schematic representation of the layout of a house might suffice if we want to know how many rooms it has, whereas a more detailed plan including details about the location of windows and doors might be needed if we are investigating a burglary.

Our mental models can represent spatial and temporal properties of the world without replicating these exact same properties in the model. The spatial layout of a room can be modelled using vectors of numbers (or patterns of neuronal firings). What is key is that the modelling system replicates the relational structure of the room layout in such a way as to allow for productive inference. For example, we model the room layout so that we can draw inferences based on the positioning of the door, windows and furniture. We know that the bed was not blocking the door, for instance, and can use this fact in subsequent inferences. The same applies to representing temporal properties: the order or timing of events need not be modelled by the exact timing of elements in the modelling system so long as the appropriate relational structure is maintained for inferential purposes.

2.2.4   Explanatory Models

Closely tied to the causal nature of our mental models is their explanatory function. We build models not only to predict and infer but also to help us explain and make sense of what has happened (Lombrozo, 2012; Woodward, 2003). By constructing a causal model, we do not simply give a particular account of what actually happened but also create a flexible vehicle for exploring a range of hypothetical questions and alternative possibilities. This flexibility serves two purposes. As an investigative tool, such models allow us to infer what we would expect if a certain hypothesis was true or false, and thus what evidence to look for. For example, using our model of the fight between father and son, we can infer what bullet trajectory would be expected if the son's claim was true. But causal models also serve as a basis for explanations. Once we decide upon a particular version of what happened, we can use our model to explore how things might have been different under a range of different possible settings (Woodward, 2003), thus gaining a deeper understanding of what actually happened. For instance, exploring the conditions under which the son would still have shot his father (would he still have shot him even if he had not been pushed?) gives a better understanding of why things happened as they did. In short, a mental model, even of a specific situation, gives us the power to explore what-if questions, both to help establish what actually happened (by suggesting lines of potential evidence) and to explore what would have happened, thus giving us an understanding of why.

2.3   Simplified Models

Our mental models of the world are idealized and incomplete. We focus on some aspects of the problem domain while ignoring others, depending on the purpose and goals of our modelling. For example, a mental (or computer) model of the father–son fight can ignore many details of the crime scene, such as the colour of their clothing and the length of their hair. By leaving out irrelevant features, we can concentrate our resources on the elements that matter.

A workable model does not reproduce things exactly but provides a sketchpad for us to explore possibilities and draw inferences. Working models sacrifice fidelity for ease of use and manipulation. When we represent the fight between father and son, we don't model every facet of their movements. Too much detail would overwhelm any attempt at simulating the fight and would in any case be superfluous. Instead, we aim to capture the critical 'moving parts' germane to our inferential goals, often in rough outline only (more akin to a cartoon than a faithful reproduction).

Our models simplify and distort. To ease computation, they are based on assumptions that might not represent actual laws or structure in the real world. For example, in modelling the shooting incident we assume that bullets travel in straight paths (and are not affected by gravity), even though this might not hold for longer distances. Likewise, we make simplifying assumptions about the dynamics and collisions of objects, just as programmers of modern video games employ 'hacks' to make their physics simulations appear realistic to human users (Battaglia, Hamrick & Tenenbaum, 2013; Rule, Tenenbaum & Piantadosi, 2020; Ullman, Spelke, Battaglia & Tenenbaum, 2017).[4]

Simplification is indeed essential to cognition. By using simpler and sparser models we overcome our limited cognitive resources and the computational complexity of the problems we face. Even everyday problems can involve numerous variables, straining the limits of working memory and computation. The role of simplifying assumptions is even more critical when we model complex systems with many interacting elements, such as social interactions that unfold over time (as in a typical crime).

Using idealized models is a virtue, not just a necessity. Simpler models are often exactly what is needed to satisfy our inferential goals, and more complex models would be inappropriate. If we want to know whether the son was falling down when he shot his father, we do not care about the exact dimensions of the room or the lighting or the location of the windows. Instead, we focus on critical factors such as the trajectory of the bullet and the positioning of the men; tracking other details would be beside the point of our enquiry.

More generally, our models should be pitched at the right level for our enquiry, and this sometimes mandates simpler rather than more complex models. Our models should strive to focus on *difference-makers* – those

---

[4] While both computer programmers and our own mental modelling rely on idealizing assumptions, the extent to which these involve the same assumptions is an open question. Nonetheless, cognitive scientists have developed plausible ideas about human modelling by looking at how programmers approach the same sorts of problems, especially in the video game industry, where the aim is to replicate things from the perspective of a human user.

factors that capture the key causal relations to support our inferences. Elements or details that make no difference to our enquiry can be safely ignored (Strevens, 2008).

Using abstract models also promotes learning and generalization. Abstraction allows us to recognize new patterns in repeated experiences and helps us transfer our knowledge to new situations. Classifying past episodes of car thefts in terms of general patterns of offending is more useful than storing every detail of each past incident. By using abstract models based on prototypical patterns of behaviour, we are better poised to understand how things work and to generalize to new cases.

2.3.1   The Dangers of Idealized Models

While simplified and idealized models are inevitable, they can lead to oversight and bias. We might omit crucial details or make unrealistic assumptions, and therefore risk drawing faulty conclusions. For example, when modelling the father–son fight, the positioning of some objects in the room might make a big difference to how we interpret the combatants' movements. A trip over the carpet could be mistaken for a lunge. Likewise, if our model of their mental states during a fight neglects their heated emotions, this could distort our inferences too.

To make matters worse, we are often unaware of how schematic our mental models are, even for things we engage with regularly. Thus, people show an 'illusion of explanatory depth', overestimating how well they understand a range of devices and natural phenomena, such as sewing machines, ballpoint pens and earthquakes. Asked to explain how these systems work, people struggle to unpack the mechanisms involved and only then realize how shallow their knowledge really is (Keil, 2003; Rozenblit & Keil, 2002; Sloman & Fernbach, 2018).

Here people seem to confuse functional knowledge of the causal system – how to use it – for deeper mechanistic knowledge – how it works. We might know how to operate a sewing machine but lack deeper knowledge of its mechanics. We also tend to assume that the ability to visualize and mentally animate something corresponds to understanding how it works. But for complex systems, this capability need not translate to deeper knowledge of the underlying mechanics. We might be able to mentally replay the visual aspects of the needle and thread in the sewing machine without knowing how these components work together. These findings emphasize the schematic nature of our mental models. But they also reiterate the key role of causal models in how we reason: these models often provide us with functional mastery even if we lack deep mechanistic knowledge.

The illusion of explanatory depth can arise in investigative and legal contexts too. For example, legal cases often hinge on complex scientific evidence, such as DNA and fingerprint analyses. But jurors usually only have a naïve understanding of the causal processes behind such evidence and are thus less aware of the potential errors that can occur in testing (Koehler, 2016). Likewise, when presented with eyewitness testimony, jurors lack knowledge of the complex processes underlying human perception and memory, and are thus less likely to see shortcomings in such evidence (Wells & Olson, 2003). In both contexts, over-simplified causal models can lead people to neglect potential errors and thus over-weight the probative value of the evidence (see Chapter 4).

2.4 Modelling Systems

While mental models allow us to represent and reason about a vast range of events and processes, it is the modelling *system* that allows us to create and adapt these models. Like the computer programs designed for crime scene analysis, our mental modelling system can produce a huge variety of models tailored to our inferential needs. For instance, we can generate a model of the father–son fight but adapt this model in innumerable ways, perhaps adding another agent or new furniture, or changing the layout of the room. To achieve this feat, we need a system that captures the general features and properties of the things we want to model, as well as the laws that govern their behaviour.

In the case of the computer program, the relevant knowledge is pre-programmed into the system, allowing it to deliver simulations that reflect (within certain limits of fidelity) real-world dynamics. For the human mind this knowledge is acquired through interactions with the world, whether through learning across the lifetime of an individual or through adaptation across our evolutionary history. The key difference with the standard computer program is that our minds have developed modelling systems that encapsulate knowledge of the world without requiring an intelligent programmer to set things up for us.

How does the human mind achieve this? How does it organize its knowledge to support flexible inference as new situations and problems arise? Psychologists have proposed various cognitive architectures (Anderson, 1996; Laird, 2012; Rogers & McClelland, 2004), but an emerging view is that people use *intuitive theories* of the world, focused on broad domains such as physics, biology and psychology (Carey, 1995; Gerstenberg & Tenenbaum, 2017; Gopnik & Wellman, 2012). These intuitive theories are analogous to scientific theorizing in certain respects, but they are based upon experience and common sense rather than advanced scientific knowledge.

2.4.1 Intuitive Theories

Intuitive theories propose causal explanations for how the world works and a blueprint for predicting and imagining new phenomena. Theories involve an interrelated body of concepts that systematize our knowledge and assumptions. These concepts operate at several levels of abstraction, from generic principles to specific hypotheses, giving order and coherence to the multifarious patterns of data we observe. Like scientific theories, our intuitive theories present an overarching framework to guide the way we learn and reason, and are also open to revision and change. Several features mark out intuitive theories as a distinctive approach to modelling the world.

2.4.1.1 Latent Causes

Intuitive theories shape and interpret our evidence. Rather than simply correlate and organize our experiences of the world, they posit latent causes that generate these patterns. Such causes are often hidden or unobservable, and form part of a richer set of assumptions about the inner workings of the world. In the case of our intuitive psychology, for instance, we interpret people's overt behaviour by positing hidden mental states, such as beliefs and desires, that cause (and explain) their actions. Thus, in the patricide case, we might assume that father and son argued due to differing opinions, and that when the son shot his father this was driven by specific mental states, such as anger and an intention to kill. Indeed, the key courtroom debate hinges on identifying the son's state of mind prior to shooting his father. And, in general, much of the drama and controversy in legal cases revolves around inferences about the mental states – intentions, beliefs and plans – of key protagonists, whether they are defendants, victims or witnesses.

2.4.1.2 Hierarchical Structure

Intuitive theories have a hierarchical or multi-layered structure (Gerstenberg & Tenenbaum, 2017; Tenenbaum et al., 2007). At the highest level are the abstract principles and concepts that provide the

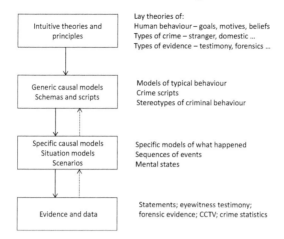

Figure 2.3   Schematic diagram of a hierarchical knowledge system, showing both top-down and bottom-up inference.

'language' for the models and hypotheses at lower levels (Figure 2.3). This language includes an ontology of the types of entities and properties in the domain, and the causal laws and relations that govern their dynamics and interactions. Ideally a small set of laws captures a vast array of possible behaviours, reflecting the productive nature of higher-level theories and allowing them to generate hypotheses and models at lower levels. These laws help construct and constrain plausible hypotheses at lower levels, from generic models of what typically happens to more specific models of particular situations. These situation-specific models in turn act as explanations for actual (and possible) observations, predicting the kinds of evidence we would expect if specific hypotheses were true.

Our intuitive psychology fits this template. It has a rich ontology of mental states and processes – such as beliefs, desires, intentions, planning and reasoning – which underpin a huge range of observable actions and behaviours. Generic causal principles are assumed to govern how these states combine and interact, yielding schemas that can be applied to specific contexts and situations. Thus, one standard principle is that intentional actions are caused by combinations of beliefs and desires; another is that new beliefs can be formed by a process of inference. Such causal templates can be pieced together to construct 'mental' networks, and hence allow us to explain complex social interactions between agents. This intuitive 'theory of mind' also introduces recursive structures, allowing us to represent how one agent might reason about another agent's mental states. For example, we might speculate that the father got angry due to his son's attitude, and in response the son thought that his father was too controlling and told him so, which upset his father further, and so on until the argument escalated into a heated row. To generate such an account, we must model each agent's mental states, including how each agent reasons about the other agent's mental states (Stuhlmüller & Goodman, 2014). This recursive reasoning is a key feature of our intuitive theory of mind and often essential in legal cases.

2.4.1.3   A System for Inference and Learning

Another distinctive feature of intuitive theories is that they provide a system for updating one's view of the world. This applies both to revising lower-level models and to revising higher-level principles and laws, which constitute the model-building system itself.

The first type of learning occurs when we construct specific models to explain patterns of evidence and then update these models as new evidence emerges. On the intuitive theory framework this process involves a combination of both top-down and bottom-up inference: our specific models and hypotheses (at the intermediate level) are constrained top-down by our high-level causal knowledge and bottom-up by the observed data itself. As new information arrives we revise our models further, guided both by the new evidence and our generic knowledge. This interplay between theory and data is characteristic of both science and everyday learning (Koslowski, 1996; Oldroyd, 1986). When things go well, plausible and well-supported hypotheses emerge from this iterative process; but things do not always go well.

This iterative process applies to many investigative contexts. On arriving at a potential crime scene, investigators construct various possible models of what has happened, based on the evidence at the crime scene and other known details of the case. These initial models are guided by both generic knowledge and expertise (top-down) and by case-specific details (bottom-up). For example, when police investigate the father–son shooting, they will use higher-level theories about the typical causes of domestic shootings as well as forensic evidence found at the crime scene. The investigation is a dynamic process: more refined models are proposed as new evidence is discovered, and these models in turn can suggest new evidence to look for. Models are revised not only as evidence is gathered but also as police reason about the case, perhaps via mental simulations and hypothetical reasoning. We will discuss this process of investigative reasoning in Chapter 5, in the context of data-frame theory (Klein, Phillips, Rall & Peluso, 2007).

The second type of revision is more substantial. It involves changes to the higher-level system that produces our specific models and hypotheses: revisions to the principles or causal laws used to generate these models, or to the ontology of entities and properties that provide the language for these hypotheses. Such changes can arise through experience or instruction. For instance, investigators solving high-volume crimes (such as house burglaries or car theft) develop higher-level causal structures to capture the typical patterns of offender decision-making. These 'crime scripts' serve as top-down schemas that are applied to new cases (Cornish & Clark, 2014).

2.4.1.4 The Challenge of Scaling-up

So far the intuitive theory framework has mainly been explored using small-scale problems with well-defined hypothesis spaces and neatly structured hierarchies. Questions remain as to how such an approach scales up to the large and messy problems faced in many real-world contexts. For example, crime investigators often have to make sense of a vast number of interrelated variables, drawing on diverse and possibly conflicting higher-level principles. Even reasoning about our simple fight scenario draws on principles from intuitive physics, physiology, psychology and social cognition. The details of how someone combines and uses this cross-cutting knowledge have yet to be worked out.

Just as we must simplify our mental models, so we must use simplified and heuristic modelling systems. In a sense, using a hierarchical structure is already a simplifying strategy, allowing us to generalize and make faster inferences but risking over-generalizations such as biased stereotypes. We don't yet know what simplifications or heuristics might be used, or how they might manifest in our model-building and inferences.

Irrespective of these open questions, the intuitive theory approach delivers several key insights. It tells us how a mental modelling system could work in principle, with our mental models guided and constrained both by higher-level knowledge and by observed data, allowing for productive and creative inference. Even if our own inference system does not replicate neat hierarchies of theories and models, the framework still tells us what kind of architecture might underpin successful learning and reasoning.

2.4.1.5   Some Potential Dangers of Using Intuitive Theories
A modelling system that incorporates higher-level knowledge reaps many
benefits. As in science, intuitive theories promote flexible and creative
model-building, and unify disparate phenomena under common principles. But this top-down guidance and flexibility can also magnify biases.
We give two examples here which are particularly relevant to investigative
reasoning.

First, when a higher-level theory is flawed, this creates more problems
than simply holding a specific flawed belief because it introduces biases
into how we gather and interpret new evidence, with the potential for a
snowball effect on our other inferences and beliefs. For example, a mistaken theory about the behavioural signatures of serial killers can lead to
biased search and evaluation of evidence, and thus unsafe inferences about
a range of cases. Second, theories grant us more flexibility to deal with
complex patterns of data and therefore increase the risk of adapting our
models to fit the facts, even in light of anomalous data. With a richer
palette of theories, we have more scope to accommodate disconfirming
evidence, by introducing auxiliary or ad hoc hypotheses. The capacity to
protect a favoured hypothesis is especially dangerous in criminal investigations, for instance, when police explain away evidence that does not fit
their targeted suspect. In such cases there is a fine line between explaining
an anomalous piece of evidence and using an ad hoc hypothesis to save a
poorly supported account. Our facility for generating novel explanations,
underpinned by higher-level principles, is a double-edged sword here.

Both of these dangers are recognized in the psychological literature,
often under the umbrella term of *confirmation bias* (Nickerson, 1998). We
discuss this multi-faceted bias in detail in Chapter 8. These dangers also
highlight a more general theme that I reiterate throughout the book – that
people readily generate plausible models of the world but often struggle to
evaluate these models against the evidence. How would this contrast
between our abilities to explain and evaluate fit into the intuitive-theory
framework?

In later chapters I will argue that, just as we have higher-level principles
for constructing models of the world, we need higher-level principles for
evaluating our own reasoning. These meta-level principles would allow us
to critically assess our methods and use of evidence, taking into account
the robustness and consistency of our inferences, the credibility and
reliability of our evidential sources, and the soundness of our evidence-
gathering and evaluation. It's not that we don't have any such principles,
but they are often piecemeal and poorly developed. In short, to improve

our evaluative reasoning we need to think critically about our own model-building, and, where needed, employ formal methods to correct and improve our strategies and habits.

2.5   Summary

We started the chapter with an example of investigators building a 3D computer model to solve a crime. We drew a parallel between their use of modelling techniques to infer what happened – was it manslaughter or murder? – and how the human mind builds mental models to make sense of the world. We explored the key dimensions of these models and how they are generated from modelling systems that draw on higher-level intuitive theories and assumptions. We also highlighted the idealized, abstract and heuristic nature of this modelling, both as born of necessity due to our cognitive limits but also as a virtue for making inferences commensurate with our needs.

CHAPTER 3

Causal Modelling

I now take causal relationships to be the fundamental building blocks both of physical reality and of human understanding of that reality, and I regard probabilistic relationships as but the surface phenomena of the causal machinery that underlies and propels our understanding of the world.

Causality, Judea Pearl (2009)

3.1 The Great Chicago Fire

Puzzles about cause and effect persist even centuries after the critical events have taken place. The Great Chicago fire provides a notorious example. It burned for two days in 1871, destroying many houses and buildings, and killing hundreds of people. The causes of the fire have been intensely debated, spawning many books and articles. Most agree the fire started in a small barn owned by the O'Leary family, located in the poorer suburbs. But controversy surrounds who or what started the fire in the barn.

3.1.1 Mrs O'Leary and Her Cow

The dominant story, now part of folklore, points the finger at Mrs O'Leary. It is alleged that, on the evening of the fire, she was milking one of her cows in the barn, and the cow knocked over a kerosene lantern. Given the abundance of dry hay and wood, the barn set alight, and the fire spread rapidly to neighbouring houses. Mrs O'Leary repeatedly denied this story, claiming she was in bed when the fire started; moreover, a journalist later claimed he had invented the story to sell more newspapers. But this account has persisted nonetheless.

3.1.2 Daniel 'Peg-Leg' Sullivan

Daniel 'Peg-Leg' Sullivan was one of the first people to raise the alarm about the fire. He too became a chief suspect, albeit 100 years later. In the official fire investigation Sullivan testified that he had seen the barn on fire and tried in vain to extinguish the flames before seeking help. But years later an insurance expert re-examined the case, arguing that this testimony was riven with contradictions. According to Bales (2002), it was Sullivan himself who had started the fire: he had been smoking his pipe in the barn and had accidently set fire to the hay. However, there is no direct evidence to incriminate Sullivan, and 100 years on he is unable to defend or explain his testimony.

3.1.3 Gamblers in the Barn

Another account, also turned into a book (Wykes, 1964), was that a group of gamblers, including Mrs O'Leary's son, were shooting craps that night in the barn, and one of them knocked over a lantern. As with the story of O'Leary's cow, this account is not implausible but has virtually no evidence to support it.

3.1.4 Meteorite Theory

It isn't only humans or cows that have been blamed for the disaster. Some have claimed the fire was started by a meteor shower due to the break-up of the comet Biela. This claim was (supposedly) supported by the occurrence of several other fires near Lake Michigan that day, with the meteorite shower invoked as a common cause of all of them (although dry and windy conditions meant that independently started fires in the area were not uncommon). The meteorite theory, popularized in yet another book (Waskins, 1985), also suffers from the inconvenient fact that nobody reported seeing a comet in the sky that night.

3.1.5 The Puzzle Remains

These theories are four of the most popular explanations of the fire. Other stories abound, including that the fire was caused by an act of terrorism due to a communist plot, by partygoers needing a drink of milk or by the spontaneous combustion of the hay. Despite so many proposals, from the mundane to the bizarre, the true causes of the fire remain a mystery.

Taking a broader view, one can also ask why a fire in a small barn led to so much destruction throughout Chicago. Here the tales of Mrs O'Leary or Peg-Leg Sullivan are insufficient. What was it that allowed a small fire to spread so readily? The answers to this question are generally agreed upon. The spread of the fire was promoted by the dry season (there had been a drought), high winds, and wooden buildings. It was also exacerbated by the slow and inadequate response of the fire-fighters. The confluence of these factors spread the fire, turning it from a minor domestic event to a major event in history.

This is a common theme in analyzing major events and disasters, where the larger event is triggered by a smaller event – such as the death of Mark Duggan starting the London riots in 2011,[1] or the assassination of Archduke Ferdinand starting the First World War, or the killing of George Floyd in 2020 sparking huge protests in the United States and beyond. How critical was the minor event? Was the larger event a 'disaster waiting to happen', where some triggering event was inevitable? Or was the triggering event a crucial factor, without which the ensuing events would never have happened? Taking the broader view also highlights the context-dependent nature of causal enquiry. We don't search merely for physical causes but for reasons and lessons too. The killing of George Floyd was not just a question of the death of one man; it raised much broader political and social questions.

The puzzle of the Chicago fire remains to this day. As recently as 1997 the Chicago city council officially exonerated Mrs O'Leary and her cow, shifting the focus onto Daniel Sullivan. Indeed, this introduces another layer of intrigue: how do we evaluate the panoply of different reports and accounts, taking notice of the various motives and intentions behind them – to sell a good story, to settle an insurance claim, to blame an adversary and so on? We raised such evaluative questions in Chapter 1 and will return to them in later chapters. The Chicago fire exemplifies this struggle, with two parallel but intertwined enquiries. On the one hand, an investigation focused on what happened during a period of a few hours on the night of 8 October 1871; on the other, an enquiry about the strength of evidence for the rival claims, which in this case stretches from 1871 to the present time (perhaps including this current chapter as part of that thread!). In short, as well as the puzzle of what actually happened back in 1871, we have the challenge of assessing a multitude of conflicting accounts from witnesses and journalists spreading over many years: the dual problems of explaining and evaluating writ large.

---

[1] https://en.wikipedia.org/wiki/2011_England_riots

3.2 Formal versus Mental Causal Models

While we might not know enough to decide what actually happened in Chicago that night, we possess the mental tools to understand the numerous stories on offer, however bizarre and far-fetched. We can reason about these alternatives, exploring their antecedents and implications – if Mrs O'Leary had started the fire, why did she return to bed without trying to put it out or raising the alarm? – and imagining ways in which things might have been different – what if the emergency services had acted more swiftly? We have the conceptual apparatus to model these putative events and processes, applying our generic knowledge (about fires and people) to the particulars of the case in order to construct plausible (and sometimes implausible) explanations. At the heart of this ability is our capacity to construct and reason with *causal models* – these are the representational vehicles that allow us to express our knowledge of the world, to reason about possibilities, to anticipate the future and infer the past, and to assign responsibility and blame.

3.2.1 What Is a Causal Model?

Up until now we have talked loosely about *causal models*. But the term covers several related concepts. At their core, causal models are representations of causal systems in the world. A causal model aims to capture how a system works, how it changes over time and how it responds to interventions. By necessity these models are simpler and more abstract than the systems they represent; but, critically, they aim to mirror key causal features of the real world.

We must distinguish *mental* causal models from *formal* causal models. The former are psychological constructs, part of the cognitive machinery with which humans represent the world. The latter are mathematical objects, part of a formal system or framework also used to represent the world. In this chapter we will introduce a framework for representing causality – *causal Bayes nets* – that will help us model many of the investigative and legal cases discussed throughout the book.

This framework performs several key roles. First, it provides formal tools to help us think and reason about causality. It helps us articulate our causal claims, clarify our assumptions, and explore their logical and probabilistic implications. Second, it plays a crucial role in the psychology of causal reasoning. Having a formal system is invaluable for appraising and improving people's intuitive inferences, and causal Bayes nets are standardly used as a baseline in causal cognition. Third, it serves as a guide to how the human mind itself might carry out such reasoning (Danks, 2014; Glymour, 2001; Gopnik & Schulz, 2007; Rottman & Hastie, 2014; Sloman, 2005; Sloman & Lagnado, 2015; Waldmann, 2017).

To elaborate on the third point, the framework suggests how intelligent agents (like us) might build internal models to represent and reason about the world. Such an approach has value even if it turns out that the mind reasons according to different principles. Indeed, we have learned a lot about human causal reasoning by comparing it to the dictates of the formal framework. On the one hand, people deviate from its prescriptions. We use impoverished models and simplifying heuristics, often essential to overcome the large computational demands placed on us (see Chapter 4). But, on the other hand, people's causal models are in some respects richer than the formal models, by including spatiotemporal information, mechanisms and narrative structure (Sloman & Lagnado, 2015).

3.3 Introduction to Causal Bayes Nets

A causal model[2] is a highly schematic representation of a real-world system; it aims to capture how the system works, how its elements combine and interact, and what would happen if we intervene to change things. A causal model has both a qualitative and a quantitative side. The qualitative component is a *causal graph,* which depicts the causal relations between events or features of the system, without specifying their strength or direction. It fits with the qualitative nature of much of our everyday causal knowledge, where we might know that one thing influences another, but not much more. The quantitative component gives us richer information, specifying the sign and strength of these relations, and how multiple causes combine to produce their effects.

Causal modellers divide the world into variables and links. Variables describe those features of the system that we want to include in our model, and can represent a range of entities, such as events, properties and propositions. Each variable can take multiple possible states (or values), but only one state can be true at any one time.[3] One can think of a variable

---

[2] My presentation draws on Pearl (1988, 2009), Fenton and Neil (2018), Halpern (2016) and Woodward (2003). I have simplified things and avoided technical details to make it accessible to a general audience. By happy accident I have blended Pearl's sprinkler example with Halpern's forest fire.

[3] More formally, each variable has a set of possible values that are exhaustive (one must be true) and mutually exclusive (only one). Variables can be discrete or continuous; for most of the models in this book we use binary variables that take one of two possible values, such as true or false.

as a question, and each of the states of the variable as possible answers. For example, we will use a variable to represent whether or not a fire occurs, with possible states of 'yes' or 'no'. Often our task is to infer the states of some variables (our hypotheses) given our knowledge of the states of other variables (our evidence). If we don't know the value of a specific variable, we can assign each possible value a probability and update these probabilities as we get new evidence.

Before tackling the Chicago fire, we will start by modelling the causes of a typical barn fire. We will skip forwards 150 years and look at a modern barn, complete with a fire detector and sprinkler system.[4] To keep our example simple, we will consider just two possible causes of a fire: someone drops a match (*Match*) or lightning strikes the barn (*Lightning*). Many other causes are possible, but we will keep things simple for now. We will distinguish between the fire starting (*Fire*) and the barn burning down (*Barn burns*); we will also include whether the detector is triggered (*Detector*) and whether the sprinkler activates (*Sprinkler*). All of these variables are binary, taking values of either true or false.

The glue that holds a causal model together, and gives it meaning and power, are the connections between variables. These are captured by a *causal graph*, where nodes correspond to variables, and arrows (or directed links) between variables correspond to causal relations. An arrow from X to Y represents the claim that X is a *cause* of Y. The graph for our model of the barn fire is shown in Figure 3.1. The following causal relations are assumed: both dropped matches and lightning strikes can start fires, a fire can cause the barn to burn down and also trigger the detector, the detector triggering can activate the sprinkler, the sprinkler activating can prevent the barn burning.

The absence of links also captures key assumptions in our model. For example, the absence of a link from *Fire* to *Sprinkler* assumes that the fire has no direct effect on the sprinkler, but can only influence it indirectly, by triggering the detector. Similarly, there are no links from *Match* or *Lightning* to *Barn burns*, as we assume that they can only burn down the barn by starting a fire.

Let's introduce some causal network terminology. If X causes Y, and there are no intermediate variables, then X is a *direct cause* of Y; otherwise, X is an *indirect cause* of Y. So *Lightning* is a direct cause of *Fire* and an indirect cause of *Detector*, *Sprinkler* and *Barn burns*. The direct causes of a variable are also known as its *parents*, and the direct effects of a cause are known as its

---

[4] We will return to model the specifics of the Chicago fire in Section 3.10.

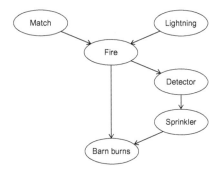

Figure 3.1   Causal graph for barn fire model.

children. Whether a cause is direct or indirect is relative to the model. For example, by adding the new variable *Smoke* in between *Fire* and *Detector*, *Fire* is no longer a direct cause of *Detector*, but an indirect cause via *Smoke*.

3.3.1   Defining 'Cause'

What is meant by 'cause' here? We adopt a pragmatic notion, based on the idea that causes are potential handles for changing the world (Woodward, 2003). Roughly defined, *X* causes *Y* if there is a possible manipulation of *X* that would change *Y*, given certain settings of the other variables in the model. This definition needs some unpacking.

Take the causal link from a dropped match to fire: *Match* → *Fire*. It asserts that there is a possible intervention on the status of the variable *Match* – for instance, making it *true* that someone drops a lit match, which would change (in this case, increase) the probability of a barn fire. Whether a fire actually occurs depends on various other factors, including the settings of other variables and background conditions. These factors are often unknown, and thus probabilities are used to quantify our uncertainty about their status and the subsequent outcome. So the causal link from dropped match to fire represents a capacity or tendency, not a guarantee; this is characteristic of most everyday causal claims.

This conception of cause captures some key intuitions about causality. It highlights the role of causal knowledge in helping us to decide how to act effectively in the world. By knowing what causes what, we can better plan and act in order to achieve our goals. It also marks a crucial asymmetry in the causal relation, whereby causes are potential means to manipulate (or change) their effects, but not vice-versa.

The notion of cause used here is broader than our everyday usage of the term. It includes as causes both positive and negative factors. Thus, we include the sprinkler as a cause of the barn burning down, even though it reduces the probability of this happening. The broader notion also allows for factors that contribute but are not alone sufficient for the outcome. Any factor that raises (or lowers) the probability of the effect can be included as a cause, even if it only enables or inhibits the outcome.

3.3.2   *Causes versus Background Conditions*

When we build a causal model, we must take some background conditions for granted. While not explicit in the model, they involve crucial assumptions that operate behind the scenes. For example, our current model does not represent whether oxygen or fuel is present, yet both are needed for a fire to start. Likewise, neither weather conditions nor the physical make-up of the barn is included, yet both would affect whether the barn burns down. Our choice of which factors to include as variables depends on the goals and context of our enquiry. Thus, oxygen is typically pre-supposed when investigating a barn fire, but it might be made explicit when investigating a fire in a chemical laboratory.

Our goals also dictate the level of detail at which we specify our models. Often a causal link between two variables is a placeholder for a more complex mechanism, which could be decomposed into finer-grained variables and links. For example, the *Detector → Sprinkler* link could be unpacked to include details about how the detector activates the sprinkler, inserting intermediate variables to represent the internal workings of the system. This finer detail might be needed if we are investigating possible faults in the system. Choosing the right level of grain for a causal model is both art and science (Halpern, 2016). The level of detail should be tailored to the inferential needs of the modeller. The capacity to zoom in or out of a situation to identify a causal model at the right level of grain is a critical feature of both the causal modelling framework and the human mind itself.

3.4   The Quantitative Component

The graph tells us which variables are causally connected, giving us a map of the structure. But by itself the graph tells us nothing about the sign or strength of these relations, nor how multiple variables combine. The 'how' of the causal model is given by the quantitative component, which tells us how each variable is influenced by its direct causes. This requires a set of functions, one for each variable, which specify how the value (or the probability) of that variable depends on the values of its parents (direct causes). For variables with no parents, their states (or probability distributions across these) are assigned exogenously, from outside the model, using background knowledge. Crucially, the quantitative side of a model allows us to make probabilistic inferences, updating the probabilities of the variables in our model given new evidence.

On the *causal Bayes net* approach[5] each variable in the model has a conditional probability table (CPT), which specifies the probability of the effect variable, given each possible configuration of its direct causes. We will first show how this works for variables with a single causal parent, then move to variables with multiple causes.

3.4.1   Simple Cause-Effect Link

Consider the single link: *Fire → Detector*. To quantify the relation between these two variables, we must specify the probability of each value of the effect variable (*detector, ~detector*) given the possible values of the cause variable (*fire, ~fire*).[6] Because both variables are binary, we only need two conditional probabilities:

- The probability that the detector triggers, given that a fire starts: *P(detector | fire)*
- The probability that the detector triggers, given that no fire starts: *P(detector | ~fire)*

The CPT for the *Detector* variable is shown in Table 3.1. Here we assume that if a fire starts, the probability that the detector is triggered is high (95%), but we allow for a small probability that it does not trigger (5%). Perhaps the sensor is defective, or the battery is flat. We also assume that without a fire the probability that the detector triggers is low (5%). The CPT thus captures two sources of uncertainty: that the detector might

[5] Pearl (2009) presents an alternative *structural model* approach, where relations between variables are captured using deterministic structural equations, with uncertainty incorporated via probabilities for background conditions. Pearl argues that this more expressive formalism is required for counterfactual analysis. But here we use causal Bayes nets, which are more appropriate for modelling evidential reasoning (Fenton & Neil, 2018).

[6] We use lowercase variable names for the values of the variable. For example, *Fire* = true is denoted by *fire*, and *Fire* = false is denoted by *~fire*, where the symbol ~ represents 'not'.

Table 3.1 *Conditional probability table (CPT) for the* Detector *variable.*

	Fire = true	*Fire =* false
Detector = true	*95% (true positive)*	*5% (false positive)*
Detector = false	*5% (false negative)*	*95% (true negative)*

Note that because *Detector* is a binary variable, and the total probability across all values of a variable must sum to one: $P(\sim detector \mid fire) = 1 - P(detector \mid fire)$; $P(\sim detector \mid \sim fire) = 1 - P(detector \mid \sim fire)$

trigger even if there is no fire (false positive), and that it might not trigger despite a fire (false negative).[7]

The CPT has a dual role here: on the one hand, it captures the strength of the causal link; on the other, it tells us the degree of support that evidence of the effect provides for the hypothesized cause. In this simple case, this degree of support is given by the *likelihood ratio (LR)*, which is the ratio of the two conditional probabilities in the CPT:

$$LR = \frac{P(detector \mid fire)}{P(detector \mid \sim fire)}$$

This ratio shows us how much to update our prior belief in the causal hypothesis (*fire*) given evidence about the effect (the *detector* triggers). Here we need to use Bayes's rule (see Box 1), which tells us to update our beliefs in proportion to the strength of the evidence.

Quantifying the link *Detector → Sprinkler* requires a similar CPT (see Table 3.2). Here again we use illustrative probabilities. We assume that the mechanism connecting the detector to the sprinkler usually works well: if the detector triggers, the probability of the sprinkler activating is high (95%); if it does not trigger, the probability is low (5%).

3.4.2 *Variables with Multiple Causes*

When an effect variable has multiple parents, the CPT encodes how these causes combine to generate the effect. In our model the variable *Fire* has two possible causes, *Match* and *Lightning*. The CPT for *Fire* therefore requires four conditional probabilities, one for each configuration of its causes (see Table 3.3). Here we assume that lightning has a stronger propensity to cause a fire than a dropped match. For example, we suppose

---

[7] In this example we assume the error rates are equal (at 5%), but they can differ.

BOX 1 Bayesian Updating

Bayesian updating is a formal method for updating one's beliefs given new evidence.[8] Starting with our *prior* belief in a hypothesis H, $P(H)$, we use Bayes' rule to compute our *posterior* belief given evidence E, $P(H|E)$:

$$P(H|E) = \frac{P(E|H).P(H)}{P(E)}$$

In simple cases[9] we can use the odds[10] version of Bayes' rule, obtained by dividing $P(H|E)$ by $P(\sim H|E)$:

$$\frac{P(H|E)}{P(\sim H|E)} = \frac{P(E|H)}{P(E|\sim H)} \times \frac{P(H)}{P(\sim H)}$$

This reformulates Bayes' rule such that our new belief in the hypothesis is the product of our prior belief and the LR:

Posterior Odds = Prior Odds × Likelihood Ratio

We thus compute our new belief in the hypothesis by multiplying our prior belief by LR. If LR > 1, we increase our belief; if LR < 1 we decrease our belief; and if LR = 1, we do not change our belief. The magnitude of change is directly proportional to the LR.

In other words, our belief in hypothesis H is revised in proportion to how strongly H predicts the observed evidence as compared to its alternative ($\sim H$).

Let's apply this to the *Fire* → *Detector* model. Suppose our prior probability for fire is 1% (odds of 1:99). We observe that the detector is triggered (*Detector* = true). The LR for this new evidence is calculated from the CPT in Table 3.1:

$$LR = \frac{0.95}{0.05} = 19$$

To compute our posterior belief in fire we can use the odds version of Bayes' rule:

Posterior Odds = Prior Odds × LR = 1:99 × 19 = 19:99

---

[8] It is based on work by Bayes (1763) and Laplace (1812); see McGrayne (2011) for the history, and Stone (2013) for a gentle introduction.
[9] When we have two mutually exclusive and exhaustive hypotheses, H and $\sim H$.
[10] Odds provide an alternative means to express probabilities. The odds ratio for hypothesis H is the probability of H being true divided by the probability of H being false: Odds = $P(H)/1 - P(H)$.

Therefore:

$$P(Fire \mid Detector) = 19/(19 + 99) = 0.16$$

Thus, observing that the detector was activated should increase our belief in fire from 1% to 16%. In very simple cases we can update probabilities by hand, but typically we will need to use Bayes net software.[11]

Table 3.2 *Conditional probability table (CPT) for the* Sprinkler *variable.*

	Detector = true	Detector = false
Sprinkler = true	95%	5%
Sprinkler = false	5%	95%

Table 3.3 *Conditional probability table (CPT) for the variable* Fire *with parents* Match *and* Lightning.

	Match = true		Match = false	
	Lightning = true	Lightning = false	Lightning = true	Lightning = false
Fire = true	90%	50%	80%	5%
Fire = false	10%	50%	20%	95%

that the probability of a fire given lightning, but no dropped match, is 80%, and that the probability of a fire given a dropped match, but no lightning, is 50%. We also assume that if both occur, the probability of fire is higher (90%) than for either cause alone, and if neither occurs, the probability of fire is lower (5%) than for either cause alone. The exact numbers do not matter as much as this relative ordering.

The variable *Barn burns* also has two possible causes: *Fire* and *Sprinkler*. But in this case one of these causes, *Sprinkler*, is preventative. The CPT has four conditional probabilities, as shown in Table 3.4. We assume that if a

[11] Once the number of variables increases, Bayesian computations are too difficult to calculate by hand. The development of efficient algorithms was a breakthrough in making probabilistic inference feasible, even for large interconnected networks (Pearl, 1988). Bayes net software is now readily available. The models in this book were constructed using Agenarisk and are available to download at: www.explainingtheevidence.com.

Table 3.4 *Conditional probability table (CPT) for the variable* Barn burns *with parents* Fire *and* Sprinkler.

	Fire = true		Fire = false	
	Sprinkler = true	Sprinkler = false	Sprinkler = true	Sprinkler = false
Barn burns = true	10%	90%	0%	0%
Barn burns = false	90%	10%	100%	100%

fire does not start, then the barn will not burn down, irrespective of whether the sprinkler activates. If a fire does start, then we assume a high probability that the barn will burn down if the sprinkler doesn't operate (90%), and a low probability if it does operate (10%). Again, the precise probabilities are not as important as their qualitative pattern: here they effectively tell us that the barn is only likely to burn down if a fire starts *and* the sprinkler system does not work.

3.4.3　Functions for CPTs with Multiple Causes

As the number of causes increases, the number of possible states for the effect grows rapidly, so filling out CPTs becomes an onerous task. However, we can simplify this task by using one of various *combination functions*. These functions capture distinctive ways in which multiple causes combine to generate an effect, and we can use our domain knowledge to decide which function to apply. The key idea is that, rather than explicitly specify the full CPT, we use a function that determines the probability of the effect for any combination of its parents. Two common functions are the *noisy-OR* and *noisy-AND*.

3.4.3.1　Noisy-OR Function

The *noisy-OR* is a probabilistic version of the logical *OR* gate. In a logical *OR* the effect occurs if at least one of the causes is present. In a *noisy-OR*, the probability of the effect is raised if one of the causes is present, and it rises further with each additional cause. A classic application of the *noisy-OR* function is in medical diagnosis, where there are several possible causes of a symptom, each of which generates the symptom via a separate mechanism.

The *noisy-OR* function yields the probability of the effect as a function of the strengths of each of the causal parents, plus a 'leak' value for the probability of the effect if none of these causes are present. The strength of each cause is given by the conditional probability of the effect when only that cause is present and is thus independent of the presence of the other causes.[12] In our barn model we use a *noisy-OR* for the CPT for *Fire,* thus assuming that a dropped match or lightning each has an independent influence on the probability of fire.[13]

3.4.3.2 Noisy-AND Function
The *noisy-AND* is a probabilistic version of the *AND* operator. Each causal parent must be present for the effect to occur; but, even if all causes are present, there is still some probability that the effect will not occur. Our CPT for *Barn burns* approximates a *noisy-AND* function: the barn is only likely to burn down if the fire starts (*Fire* = true) and the sprinkler system fails (*Sprinkler* = false).

3.4.3.3 Other Functions
Other functions include a linear additive combination – where the strengths of each cause add together – and non-linear functions such as the *X-OR* – where each cause on its own increases the probability of the effect, but together they reduce it. Selecting the right function requires some prior knowledge about how the causes in question typically combine (Danks, 2018; Griffiths & Tenenbaum, 2009).

One advantage of using a function is that we don't need to store CPTs for combinations that we rarely encounter; instead we can compile the CPT when the need arises (Pearl, 1988). For example, one might have an estimate for the probability of fire given a dropped match, and separately for fire given lightning, but not have a pre-stored estimate for fire given both occur. The *noisy-OR* allows us to estimate this 'on the fly', based on the separate probabilities that we already know. This capability proves extremely useful in modelling novel cases, where disparate causes combine, leading to configurations never experienced before.

---

[12] For effect E, and two possible causes A and B (with strengths S_a and S_b), and leak strength S_l:
$$P(E \,|A\&B) = 1 - ((1 - S_a) \, (1 - S_b) \, (1 - S_l))$$

[13] If instead we believed that the two causes combine synergistically, we would not use the *noisy-OR,* but would assign a higher probability for the fire given both causes.

3.4.4   A Broader Definition of Cause

Characterizing the quantitative component of the model in terms of functional relations between variables suggests a broader definition of cause: X is a direct cause of Y if it is part of the function that determines Y. Pearl and colleagues give a nice analogy:

> A variable X is a cause of a variable Y if Y in any way relies on X for its value ... think of causation as a form of listening; X is a cause of Y if Y listens to X and decides its value in response to what it hears. (Pearl, Glymour & Jewell, 2016)

Thus, the causal relation admits of two complementary readings – on the one hand, an active notion of cause as something that changes its effects; on the other hand, a passive notion, as an effect's responsiveness to its causes. Both map onto important intuitions about causality and evidence, and we will explore their interrelations in subsequent chapters.

3.5   Building Larger Models

To scale up to larger models, we apply the same basic principles. Each variable in a model has its own CPT: for variables with causal parents in the graph (*endogenous* variables), the CPT is a function of its parents; and for variables without parents (*exogenous* variables), the CPT is simply its prior probability. Any larger model is constructed by combining three basic structures: a causal chain, common cause, and common effect.

3.5.1   Causal Chain

In a chain structure, $X \rightarrow Y \rightarrow Z$, the causal influence from X to Z is mediated by Y. Thus Z is a function of Y alone, and its CPT only relates to possible states of Y. For example, consider the chain:

Lightning $\rightarrow$ Fire $\rightarrow$ Detector

Here there is no direct arrow from *Lightning* to *Detector*. *Lightning* only affects *Detector* indirectly, via its effect on *Fire*. Thus, *Detector* only needs to 'listen to' the possible values of *Fire*. This structure often promotes efficient inference. For example, if we know there is a fire, the probability of the detector triggering does not depend on whether lightning struck – it would be the same if a match was dropped or if there was some other cause of the fire.[14] In general, when assessing the probability of an effect variable we only need to look at its immediate causal parents.

3.5.2 Common Cause

In a common-cause structure, $X \leftarrow Y \rightarrow Z$, a single cause has several different effects. Each effect has its own CPT that quantifies the relation between the cause and that specific effect. For example, consider the model:

Sprinkler $\leftarrow$ Detector $\rightarrow$ Alarm

The variable *Detector* has two effect variables, *Sprinkler* and *Alarm*. The causal link from *Detector $\rightarrow$ Sprinkler* represents a distinct causal mechanism from *Detector $\rightarrow$ Alarm*, and each effect has a separate CPT to quantify these relations. Both *Sprinkler* and *Alarm* 'listen to' the status of *Detector*. This means that *Sprinkler* and *Alarm* will be correlated even though they have no direct causal link. Knowing about one can tell us something about the other. Thus, hearing the alarm makes us predict that the sprinkler will activate. However, this correlation disappears if we already know that the detector has activated. This information blocks any extra inference from the alarm to the sprinkler, because we know the status of the detector, which fully determines the probability of the sprinkler.[15]

3.5.3 Common Effect

In a common-effect model, $X \rightarrow Y \leftarrow Z$, there are multiple causes of the same effect. In this case Y is a function of two causes, X and Z. For example, consider the model:

Match $\rightarrow$ Fire $\leftarrow$ Lightning

The common effect *Fire* listens to both *Match* and *Lightning*, and thus both are included in its CPT. Note that, although *Match* and *Lightning* are not causally connected, if we know about the status of *Fire*, they become

---

[14] Technically, *Lightning* is *probabilistically independent* of *Detector* conditional on *Fire*. And more generally, for a chain, $X \rightarrow Y \rightarrow Z$, X is independent of Z conditional on Y.

[15] *Sprinkler* is *probabilistically independent* of *Alarm* conditional on *Detector*. And more generally, for $X \leftarrow Y \rightarrow Z$, X is independent of Z conditional on Y. Note that the chain structure and the common cause thus both share the same conditional independence relation.

correlated. In this case, knowing there was no lightning increases the probability of a dropped match.[16] This is an example of explaining away, which we discuss below.

These three structures are the building blocks for any causal model. Any graph can be decomposed into some combination of these structures; knowing which to apply can greatly simplify our inferences.

3.6   Using Causal Models for Inference

Causal models allow us to make inferences about the world. We use them to tackle a variety of questions of increasing sophistication. Pearl (2018) presents a three-level hierarchy (see Table 3.5) that encapsulates three main types of cognitive activity – seeing, doing and imagining – which he terms the 'ladder of causation'. These levels map onto increasingly richer ways of representing causality, and more complex types of reasoning. We will illustrate each level of the hierarchy using the barn fire model. We also add another activity, *supposing*, which is often key in investigative contents, and which operates mainly at level 1.

3.6.1   Inference from Observations

At the first level of the hierarchy is inference from observation: how should we update our beliefs if we *observe* the values of some subset of variables in our model? There are a few subtypes of inference here.

3.6.1.1   Predictive Inference

In predictive inference we reason *forwards* from causes to effects. Indeed, even before we acquire any evidence, the parameterized causal model already carries out predictive inference, using the prior probabilities for each exogenous cause, and propagating this probabilistic information through the network. This gives us a prior probability distribution across all the variables in our model. This initial distribution is already useful, telling us what events are expected (or unexpected) given typical background conditions.

---

[16] *Match* is *probabilistically dependent* of *Lightning* conditional on *Fire*. And more generally, for $X \rightarrow Y \leftarrow Z$, X is dependent on Z conditional on Y. Note that this pattern is exactly opposite to the pattern for the other two structures.

Table 3.5 *Pearl's causal hierarchy, with fire examples added in final column.*

Level	Typical activity	Typical question	Examples	
1) Association	Seeing	How would seeing X change my belief in Y?	What does a symptom tell me about a disease?	What does an alarm tell us about a fire?
2) Intervention	Doing Intervening	What if? What if I do X?	What if I take aspirin? Will my headache be cured?	What if we install a smoke detector? Will a fire be prevented?
3) Counterfactuals	Imagining Retrospection	Why? Was it X that caused Y? What if I had acted differently?	Was it the aspirin that stopped my headache? Would Kennedy be alive had Oswald not shot him?	Would this fire have been prevented if we had installed a smoke detector?

Adapted from Pearl (2018).

Let's assign priors to the two exogenous variables in the barn model. We assume a prior probability of 10% for *Match* and 1% for *Lightning*.[17] Once we set these priors, the network structure and CPTs determine probabilities for all other variables in the model. These probabilities are computed via Bayesian updating, in this case generating the probabilities 'forward' from the priors (see Figure 3.2a). Given the low priors, the probability of a fire is also low (10%), as are all the other downstream variables. In particular, the probability of the barn burning is only 2%.

The main exemplar of forward reasoning, however, is when we know that a specific cause has occurred and use the model to update the probabilities of its effects. Updating the direct effects is straightforward because this is given by the CPT itself, which specifies the probability of the effect for each configuration of its causal parents. Updating the probabilities of indirect effects is slightly more complicated, as it involves a chain of such inferences.

---

[17] As mentioned before, these are illustrative probabilities. We could use databases on barn fires to get more realistic estimates, but these can involve very low probabilities, making it harder to follow the key computations. None of the reasoning principles are affected by using rough estimates, and usually it's the comparative values that matter most. Readers are encouraged to download the models and try out their own estimates.

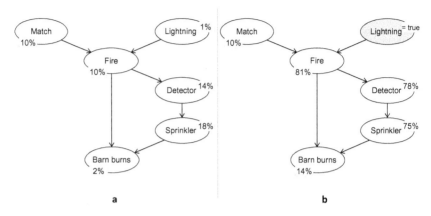

Figure 3.2   Predictive inference in the barn model. (a) Model with prior probabilities for each variable. (b) Model with updated probabilities given *Lightning* = true. Note that grey nodes represent variables that are assumed or observed to be true.

Suppose we observe that lightning strikes the barn (see Figure 3.2b). This is our new evidence, and we thus assign *Lightning* = true (100%). Given this new setting, the probability of a fire jumps up (81%), as does the probability that the detector is triggered (78%) and hence that the sprinkler is activated (75%). Finally, the probability of the barn burning is now 14% – up from its prior value of 2%, but still relatively low because of the high probability that the sprinkler is activated.

3.6.1.2   Diagnostic Inference

Diagnostic inference involves inferring the probabilities of the potential causes given evidence of the effects.[18] Reasoning *backwards*, from effects to causes, is pervasive in investigative as well as everyday contexts. We have already seen a simple example of this – see Box 1 – showing how Bayes' rule is used to update our prior belief in the cause given the strength of the new evidence.

  Suppose we observe that a fire starts (*Fire* = true). Intuitively this should raise the probabilities of each of its possible causes, but by how much? Here Bayesian updating tells us that our new probabilities are a function of the prior probabilities and the strengths of each of the causes. The prior probabilities of *Match* and *Lightning* are 10% and 1% respectively.

---

[18] Note that this is not always the same as inferring that a specific cause, if true, actually caused the outcome in question. In some cases, it is possible for several causes to be present, and the question of which actually caused the outcome (or how much each cause contributed) is an issue for further debate (see Halpern, 2016, and Section 3.11).

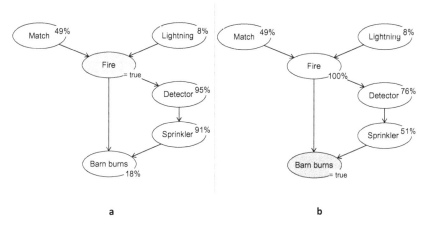

Figure 3.3   Diagnostic inference in the barn model. (a) Model with updated probabilities given *Fire* = true; (b) Model with updated probabilities given *Barn burns* = true.

Assuming a *noisy-OR* function, the strength of each cause depends on the probability of the effect given that cause in isolation (and also taking into account the 'leak' strength for unspecified causes). Here the strengths of *Match* and *Lightning* are 50% and 80% respectively, and the leak strength is 5%. These settings give us posterior probabilities of 49% for *Match* and 8% for *Lightning* (see Figure 3.3a). So even though *Lightning* is the stronger cause, *Match* is still more likely given the evidence, because its prior probability was higher.

Diagnostic inference is readily extended to situations where we only get evidence about downstream effects of the potential causes. In such cases we must make a sequence of Bayesian updates as we trace back from the observed effect to the putative causes. For example, suppose we observe that the barn has burned down (*Barn burns* = true). Given only this evidence, we can update all the other variables in the model (see Figure 3.3b). In this case, *Fire* is 100% because it's a necessary condition for the barn to burn. Thus, both *Match* and *Lightning* retain their probabilities from the previous example. But the probabilities for *Detector* (76%) and *Sprinkler* (51%) are both lower than before. This is because, while the fire raises their probabilities (predictively), the barn burning down decreases the probability of *Sprinkler* and thus *Detector* (diagnostically). This example shows how new evidence sometimes generates *both* predictive and diagnostic reasoning (and these can work in opposite directions).

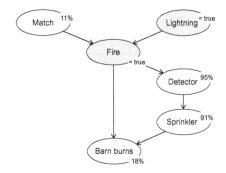

Figure 3.4   Explaining away in the barn model: the probability of *Match* is reduced back
almost to its prior probability given that *Lightning* = true.

3.6.1.3   Intercausal Reasoning

Another key pattern of inference is *intercausal* reasoning – when evidence
about one possible cause of an observed effect changes the probabilities of
alternative causes. For example, suppose we observe the barn is on fire, and
then find out that lightning has struck the barn. How should this affect
our belief in other possible causes? This depends on how these causes
combine. With a *noisy-OR* (and other similar functions) we get a distinctive pattern of inference termed *explaining away*: evidence about one cause
reduces the probability of the other causes.

It is easiest to see how this pattern of inference works by breaking it into
two steps. First, we observe the effect (the fire), which raises the probabilities of both causes. Second, we find out that lighting has struck the barn
(see Figure 3.4). This reduces the probability of a dropped match to 11%
(almost back to its prior of 10%). The fire is sufficiently explained by the
lightning, so evidence for the dropped match has been *explained away*.

This pattern of inference holds even when we only have uncertain
evidence about the effect. For example, if we know only that the barn
has burned down, then finding out that lightning struck the barn will still
explain away the dropped match.

Explaining away is a special feature of causal Bayes nets and is hard to
capture with purely logic-based reasoning systems (Pearl, 1988). It is a
commonplace inference in legal contexts, where prosecution and defence
attempt to rebut each other's arguments by introducing alternative
accounts to explain away the evidence proffered against their side. We
discuss this pattern of inference in detail in Chapters 7 and 10.

3.6.2 Suppositional Reasoning

Causal models are not just devices for updating our beliefs in light of new evidence; they also provide a medium for asking what-if questions. Such imaginative thinking allows us to explore the consequences of our nascent hypotheses, testing them against what we already know, and opening new lines of inquiry. While Pearl's hierarchy focuses on what-ifs that involve counterfactuals (at level 3), we can also ask 'what-if' at the level of seeing or doing.

Inference by supposing works in a similar way to inference by observation: we assign values to one set of variables and see how this changes the probabilities of the other variables. The crucial difference is that no new evidence is actually acquired, and we only make inferences 'as-if' specific variables were true or false. Thus, our new probabilities are conjectural, showing us what to expect if such-and-such were true. This capability is extremely useful, allowing us to explore the implications of different possible causes.

Are there tell-tale signs of an intentionally set versus an accidental fire? Both might involve the dropping of a match, but with arson we would expect the presence of an accelerant or other accompanying factors. Our causal model is readily extended to capture such possibilities, adding variables to represent the act of arson and its characteristic network of causes and effects. The extended model can then be used for what-if inferences, helping us decide what aspects of the case to investigate further.

3.6.3 Inference from Interventions

Another key purpose for constructing causal models is to help us act more efficiently: to control and change things to suit our goals. We want to know how things will change if we intervene on a causal system, rather than just observe it. In the context of barn fires, we want to know how to reduce or prevent these fires – for example, how to stop careless smoking and the discarding of cigarettes or matches, how to improve the safety of electrical devices, how to fireproof materials and objects in the barn, and so on. To achieve these aims we must ascend to level 2 in Pearl's hierarchy: from seeing to doing.

What makes causal models special, and distinguishes them from purely probabilistic models, is that they allow us to answer questions about interventions. Causal models tell us what will happen if we take actions that change the system we are acting upon. They provide 'oracles for intervention'. To achieve this, Pearl (2009) introduces the *do-operator*, which specifies how our model should be changed given our interventions. It gives us a formalism to predict the consequences of our actions, including those never taken before.[19]

In the real world we often intervene by changing one element of a causal system and observing the consequences. In the causal modelling framework this is mirrored by intervening on the corresponding variable in our model and updating our beliefs about the other variables. Crucially, this intervention can change the structure of the model.

Consider first a fragment of the barn fire model:

Fire → Detector → Sprinkler

Ordinarily, when we observe that the detector is triggered, we increase the probability of a fire, and of the sprinkler being activated (this is level 1 inference). But suppose instead that we decide to activate the detector ourselves. Perhaps we want to check if it is working properly, and therefore decide to pump smoke into the sensor. Intuitively, this intervention should not change the probability of fire. However, we would still expect the sprinkler to be activated.

The causal framework captures this kind of inference using the do-operator. This involves setting the intervened-on variable to a specified value (*Detector* = true), removing any arrows leading into that variable (in this case the arrow from *Fire* to *Detector*), and then using Bayesian updating on the resulting model (in this case updating the probability of *Sprinkler*).

Crucially, by using the do-operator we have changed the original model, and hence the inferences that it mandates. Formally, the probability of fire given that we ourselves activate the detector, $P(\text{fire} \mid \text{do}(\text{detector}))$, is very different from the probability of fire given that we observe that the detector is triggered, $P(\text{fire} \mid \text{detector})$. In the former case, the probability of fire remains at its prior value, $P(\text{fire} \mid \text{do}(\text{detector})) = P(\text{fire})$, whereas in the latter case it increases, $P(\text{fire} \mid \text{detector}) > P(\text{fire})$.

More generally, intervening to set a variable to a specific value entails suspending the causes that usually determine the value of this variable.[20]

---

[19] There are alternative approaches to modelling interventions in the Bayes net formalism (see Dawid, 2020), but Pearl's is the dominant approach in the literature.

[20] Formally, interventions can be represented either by 'surgically' removing incoming links to the intervened-on variable or by adding a new variable to the model to represent this new function. The latter method is more general, as it allows for probabilistic interventions that are not guaranteed to

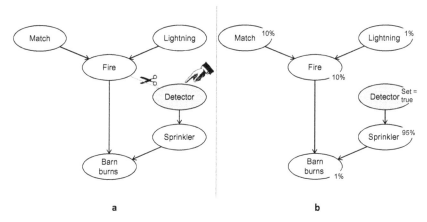

Figure 3.5   Interventions in the barn model. (a) Intervening to set *Detector* = true and thus cutting link from *Fire* to *Detector*. (b) Updating the probabilities in the model after the intervention.

Its value is no longer a function of its causal parents, but is determined solely by our intervention. Moreover, such an intervention is assumed to be *modular:* it does not disrupt other links in the model. In particular, outgoing links from the intervened-on variable remain as they were prior to the intervention. In short, our intervention creates a new model, and it is this modified version that is used for inferring the probabilities of the other variables (using standard Bayesian updating).

Let's illustrate now with the entire barn fire model. Here again suppose that we intervene to trigger the detector ourselves. We thus modify the model: the arrow from *Fire* to *Detector* is cut because *Detector* is no longer a function of *Fire* (see Figure 3.5a). However, this intervention does not disrupt any other links in the model.

We now revise the probabilities of the other variables using Bayesian updating (see Figure 3.5b). Although the *Detector* is set to 100%, the probability of *Fire* does not change from its prior value. After all, we have triggered the detector, so we should not attribute this to a fire. This means that the probabilities of *Match* and *Lightning* also remain at their prior values. By contrast, the downstream variables change. The probability of *Sprinkler* increases to 95%, but the probability of *Barn burns* decreases to

---

set the intervened-on variable to a certain value. For example, suppose we test the detector by holding a lit cigarette underneath its sensor. This intervention is not guaranteed to trigger the detector, although it will raise the probability that the detector activates.

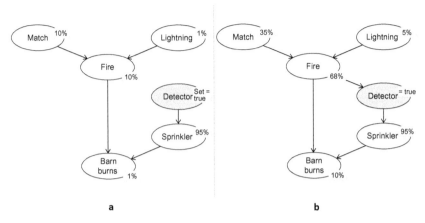

a   b

Figure 3.6   The difference between doing and seeing. (a) The updated barn model if we
intervene to set *Detector* = true. (b) The updated model if we simply observe that
Detector = true.

1% (lower than its prior value). This is because while the probability of fire
stays at its prior value, the sprinkler has an increased probability of
activating (due to our action).

The difference between seeing and doing is stark here. Consider what
happens if, rather than setting it ourselves, we see that the detector has
triggered. In this case the model structure would not change (see
Figure 3.6b), and the updated probabilities would be very different. Now
the probability of *Fire* is 68%, and both *Match* and *Lightning* increase
accordingly. The probability of *Barn burns* also increases from 1% to 10%.
Confusing observation and intervention can have disastrous consequences.

3.6.4   Using Interventions for De-confounding

We have shown how interventions are modelled in a simple example, but
the same logic applies to a host of real-world contexts. Indeed, interventional thinking is the cornerstone of experimental methodology and testing, allowing us to identify causal relations even when confounding
threatens. Thus, to establish that X causes Y, it is not enough to show
that increases in the probability of X are correlated with increases in the
probability of Y, because both X and Y might be effects of a common cause
Z (see Section 3.7.2). One way to establish a causal link is to perform an
intervention on X, to see if Y changes, ruling out the possible confounding
effect of Z.

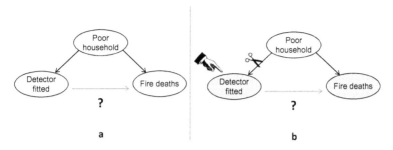

Figure 3.7   Intervention to avoid confounding. (a) Causal model of relations between poverty, smoke detectors and fire deaths. (b) An intervention to provide households with detectors, irrespective of level of poverty, tests whether detectors reduce fire deaths.

For example, to assess the efficacy of smoke detectors in preventing fire deaths, observational studies must deal with many confounding factors, such as poverty and education (see Mierley & Baker, 1983). While there is a statistical correlation between households having a smoke detector and lower fire deaths, it is possible that detectors do not reduce fire deaths, but both factors are effects of a common cause. Perhaps poorer households cannot afford to install smoke detectors and are also at greater risk of fire because of the quality of their property (see Figure 3.7a).

One way to test the causal claim is to conduct an experiment, where smoke detectors are given to households selected at random, and fire deaths are measured (see Figure 3.7b). By intervening to give households fire detectors, the causal link from poverty to detector is cut. A reduction in fire deaths among those receiving smoke detectors is therefore evidence that a causal link exists because it cannot be explained by confounding factors such as poverty (Gorman, Charney, Holtzman & Roberts, 1985).

But, having used causal knowledge to identify the potential confounder, we can also *simulate* the effect of the intervention by using the original observational data refined by information about the confounder, and then applying the do-operator. Here again the contrast between seeing and doing is critical – the latter helps us rule out confounding factors, taking advantage of level-2 thinking.

3.6.5   Intervening in Investigative and Legal Contexts

At first sight it might seem that interventional reasoning is irrelevant to investigative or legal reasoning. Such enquiries are typically focused on what has happened in the past, and thus the question of what will happen if we intervene on the system seems moot. But, in fact, interventional thinking is relevant in several ways.

First, even when our enquiries focus on what happened in the past, they often hinge on testing claims or facts through experimentation. Thus, when a building burns down, and the causes of the fire are sought, it is common to conduct experiments to test different accounts of what happened. For example, consider the tragic fire in Grenfell Tower, London, in 2017.[21] One focus of the investigation was on the flammability of the cladding on the outside of the tower block. Empirical testing of the cladding showed that it was highly flammable. This finding was a serious warning about future fire hazards, but it also suggested that the cladding on the Grenfell tower block caused the fire to spread and resist containment. The basic principles of intervention are here used to establish a causal claim – that the cladding is highly combustible and promotes the spread of fire – which is then applied to the specific case under investigation.

Second, interventions can play a role in the process of acquiring and evaluating evidence itself. Although the archetypal characterization of the investigator is as a careful observer of people and crime scenes, an investigator is also an active participant, intervening on the post-crime world to reveal its secrets. While unable to intervene on the past, on the story of the crime itself, investigators can intervene in the causal processes that unfold post-crime, and which are critical for generating evidence

This is most clearly seen when investigative actions disrupt the normal course of events and lead to distorted inferences – for example, when a suspect is forcefully interrogated to yield a confession, or when evidence is planted to falsely incriminate the suspect. Likewise, in the courtroom, lawyers will cross-examine witnesses, and their line of questioning is often an intervention into the typical processes whereby people give accounts of what they saw or did. Such actions are interventions on the typical causal processes that link people to events. Thus, the fact-finder must take care to avoid mistaking information that is the product of an intervention, such as bribing the suspect to extract a confession, rather than a 'pure' observation (the suspect confesses because he is guilty). These kinds of intervention are best represented as additional variables in the causal model, and thus the intervention becomes part of the broader causal model.

Third, interventions are a critical precursor to the use of counterfactual thinking and assignments of causation. In order to figure out what would

---

[21] https://en.wikipedia.org/wiki/Grenfell_Tower_fire

have happened if someone had acted differently – and thus to assign responsibility and blame – we must replay the past while making specific interventions on our causal models. Did the cladding make a difference to the spread of the fire? To address this question, we need to know whether the fire would still have occurred, even if the building had not used cladding. This requires that we intervene on our model of the actual fire by removing the cladding and counterfactually inferring the probability of the fire spreading given this change. Here the findings of actual experiments can inform our investigations and help determine whether the cladding was a crucial element in the fire.

3.7 Reasoning about Counterfactuals

Counterfactual thinking is pervasive in legal and everyday contexts. But from a theoretical viewpoint it presents various puzzles. As lay people, we generate and evaluate counterfactuals with ease, but it's not clear *how* we achieve this – how we represent and reason about worlds that have not occurred, while maintaining plausibility and consistency. Moreover, up until recently, counterfactuals have eluded formal analysis, and were deemed too metaphysical for use in scientific or statistical reasoning.

The causal modelling framework offers a novel approach to counterfactuals, building on the notions of causal models and interventions. It proposes a formal procedure for evaluating them, and hints at how people might achieve this using their own mental causal models. The capacity to support counterfactual inference is a unique feature of causal models, and takes us to the highest level in Pearl's hierarchy.

By definition, counterfactuals invite us to consider what would have happened if certain things had been different (contrary to the 'facts'). Would Y still have occurred if X had not occurred? Often, these *what-if* questions concern human actions: what would have happened if they had done this rather than that? But they also apply to natural events: would the fire still have spread if the wind had not been so strong?

To address even a simple counterfactual query requires several components: we need a causal model of the system in order to describe how it changes in response to interventions, we need to assign values to this model to capture what actually happened, we need to introduce our counterfactual suppositions by making specific changes to the actual world, and finally we must somehow replay this counterfactual world to see what else changes.

Counterfactual reasoning takes us to level 3 in Pearl's hierarchy. To formalize inference at this level, Pearl (2009) uses *structural causal models*, which provide a more expressive form of representation than causal Bayes nets. Both approaches use graphs to represent qualitative causal relations; but, rather than conditional probability tables, structural models use deterministic structural equations to capture the functional relations from causes to effects, with uncertainty introduced via error variables (which are not usually represented in the graph itself).[22] These error variables correspond to exogenous background factors that are not explicitly modelled, but might disturb the relation between cause and effect (e.g., triggering the effect without the specified causes being present, or preventing the effect despite the causes being present).

Because we focus on causal Bayes nets throughout the book, we will not give details of the formal machinery behind structural models (see Halpern, 2016; Pearl, 2009). However, we will still try to give an intuitive sense of how counterfactuals can be modelled.

3.7.1   The Three Steps of Counterfactual Inference

Suppose we have a causal model and a specific set of values or probabilities for its variables. In particular, we know that $X =$ true and $Y =$ true. What would the probability of Y have been, if X had been false? This counterfactual query is evaluated using three steps:[23]

1   *Abduction*: Update our belief in what actually happened using the current evidence.
2   *Action*: Modify the causal model by *intervening* to set $X =$ false, thus removing any incoming links into X.
3   *Prediction*: Use the modified model to compute the counterfactual probability of Y.

Pearl (2009, p. 37) characterizes these steps as follows:

> In temporal metaphors, Step 1 explains the past in light of the current evidence e; Step 2 bends the course of history (minimally) to comply with the hypothetical antecedent X = x; finally, Step 3 predicts the future (Y)

---

[22] For example, in a structural model of our barn example, the variable *Fire* is a deterministic function of its direct causes (*Match* and *Lightning*) and an error variable that captures background factors such as unspecified alternative causes of the fire (e.g., electrical faults) or preventative factors (e.g., extreme dampness).

[23] This definition is adapted from Pearl (2009, p. 206, theorem 7.1.7).

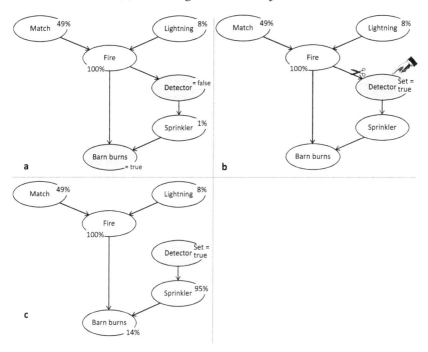

Figure 3.8   Counterfactual inference in the barn model. (a) Step 1 – update probabilities of the variables given the stated evidence (*Detector = false*, *Barn burns* = true). (b) Step 2 – modify the model by intervening to set *Detector* = true, thus removing the link from *Fire* to *Detector*. (c) Step 3 – counterfactual inferences based on Bayesian updating of the new model.

based on our new understanding of the past and our newly established condition, X = x.

Let's apply this procedure to the barn fire example. Consider a situation where we know that the detector was not activated, and the barn burned down. Our counterfactual is: *Would the barn still have burned down if the detector had activated?*

To address this question, we start with step 1 (abduction) and update our beliefs given our evidence about the actual situation. The current evidence (*Detector = false*, *Barn burns* = true) permits us to draw further inferences about the actual state of the world. We use Bayesian updating to revise our beliefs (see Figure 3.8a). In particular, the probability of fire increases to 100% (without a fire the barn cannot burn down), and the probabilities of dropped match (49%) and lightning (8%) both increase (as possible causes of the fire).[24] Given that the detector did not trigger, and the barn burned, the probability that the sprinkler activated is very low (1%).

Now we proceed to step 2 (action). The counterfactual asks us to imagine that the detector was triggered. We thus intervene on our model to set the detector to true (do(*Detector* = *true*)). As we saw above, this creates a new model in which the incoming link from *Fire* to *Detector* is removed.[25] Our intervention has thus changed the structure of the graph (see Figure 3.8b).

Finally, in step 3 we update the probabilities of the variables in this new model (see Figure 3.8c). Since we have removed the link from *Fire* to *Detector*, we do not change the probability of *Fire*, which remains at 100%. Note that this is the probability it had in the actual world, given the evidence. The causes of fire also retain their actual values from the pre-intervention situation. However, the counterfactual intervention to trigger the detector changes our beliefs about its causal descendants. In particular, the probability that the sprinkler activates increases (95%), and as a consequence the probability that the barn would have burned down is low (14%).

Given a causal model, the three-step process thus allows us to address counterfactual queries. What's special about this approach is that it tells us what changes and what stays the same when we shift (via our hypothetical intervention) from the actual situation to the counterfactual situation of interest. The causal model dictates that variables that are causally upstream (ancestors) of the intervened-on variable will not change from their pre-interventional values, whereas those downstream (descendants) can change, depending on the functional relations in the model. In our example, we used the given evidence to update the probability of fire to 100%, and this was carried over to our counterfactual world; but the actual probability of the sprinkler operating was not carried over – it was changed by our counterfactual intervention.

A useful metaphor here is that to compute a counterfactual we 'rewind' the world back to the point at which the counterfactual antecedent is imagined, and then replay the situation forward, potentially changing the values of the downstream consequences of this intervention. This has

---

[24] In the structural model we would also update the background variables. For example, based on the fact that the barn was on fire, we would infer that the background conditions were suitable for a fire to occur (e.g., oxygen and fuel were present) and there were no countervailing conditions (e.g., no dampness or rain), and similarly for the other background variables in the model.

[25] In the structural model approach this corresponds to replacing the equation for the intervened-on variable with a constant value, in this case setting *Detector* to take the value 'true'.

suggestive parallels with psychology models of mental simulation and how people engage in counterfactual thinking (see Chapter 4).

Note that in order to handle counterfactuals, structural causal models must make various assumptions about the nature of the background variables and what might or might not change as a consequence of hypothetical interventions.[26] The quality of our counterfactual inferences thus depends heavily on the quality of our causal assumptions, which ideally we would justify with other knowledge or evidence.

3.8 Summary of Using Causal Models for Inference

All these types of reasoning figure prominently in investigative and everyday contexts, with the causal modelling approach providing a unifying framework. The power of this approach is that, given a causal graph and a set of parameters, we can in principle compute the probabilities of any chosen variables, conditional on knowing (or assuming or setting) the values of any other set of variables. Such updating of our beliefs given new evidence lies at the heart of evidential reasoning.

Moreover, even without precise parameters, causal models can still play a crucial role in reasoning. The causal graph stipulates a set of probabilistic dependencies and independencies that hold irrespective of the exact parameters or functional forms between variables. These qualitative probabilistic relations give us crucial information about what is relevant to what, and how these relevance relations can change conditional on what we know. We will explore this aspect of causal Bayes nets in Chapter 6, arguing that they provide a formal underpinning to legal notions of relevance.

3.8.1 *Causal Relations versus Probabilistic Dependence*

A crucial feature of the causal framework is that it not only distinguishes causal relations from probabilistic dependence but also shows how these two concepts are interconnected.

---

[26] On the structural approach the background variables are crucial because they are updated based on what happens in the actual world, and then these values are carried over to the counterfactual world. One potential difficulty (see Dawid, 2000, 2021) is that the exact specification of these background variables is left unmodelled and is underdetermined by the domain variables in the causal model. This leaves open the question of how we justify one background specification over another.

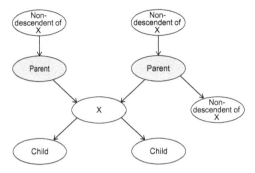

Figure 3.9   Graph showing the causal Markov condition. The parents of variable X screen off X from all variables in the model except X's descendants. In other words, X is conditionally independent of its non-descendants *given* its parents.

3.8.1.1   How They Differ

Whereas causal links represent our assumptions about stable relations in the world, probabilistic relations reflect our uncertainty about the world, and can change according to what we know. Thus, variables that are not causally connected can still be correlated conditional on our knowledge of other variables in the model (when conditioning on a common effect), and variables that are causally connected can become independent given knowledge of other variables (when conditioning on the intermediate variable in a chain). In both cases the causal relations between variables remain constant, but the probabilistic dependencies change according to one's knowledge of other variables. We will examine such patterns of dependence, and how they affect our judgments of evidential relevance, in later chapters.

3.8.1.2   How They Relate

Each causal graph implies a particular set of probabilistic independencies, which hold irrespective of the exact parameters or functional forms. We have seen how the three basic structures entail specific conditional independence relations. More generally, causal Bayes nets encapsulate the *causal Markov condition*. This states that if we know the direct causes (parents) of a specific variable X, then knowledge of any other variable (except X's descendants) gives us no new information about the probability of X. The parents of X 'screen off' X from all other variables in the model, except X's descendants (see Figure 3.9). This condition is invaluable for compact representation and efficient inference. Rather than storing the

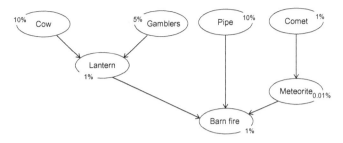

Figure 3.10   Causal model of Chicago barn fire.

entire probability distribution for a set of variables, the causal graph allows us to generate any parts of this distribution as needed. Informally, the condition captures an essential aspect of evidential reasoning, the ability to simplify inference by screening out irrelevant factors.

3.9   Revisiting the Chicago Fire

The causal modelling framework applies both to generic systems – such as the typical causes of a barn fire – and to specific situations – such as the possible causes of *this* particular barn fire on *this* occasion. When constructing specific models, variables are tailored to the case in hand, allowing us to incorporate critical and possibly unique features of the situation.

Let's build a causal model of the Great Chicago fire. We will keep it simple, basing it on the main components outlined in Bales (2002). First, we focus on the question of what caused the fire in the O'Leary's barn, and then look at the broader Chicago fire. We consider three possible causes of the barn fire – a knocked-over lantern (*Lantern*), Dan Sullivan's pipe (*Pipe*) and a meteorite hitting the barn (*Meteorite*); two possible causes of the lantern being knocked over – Mrs O'Leary milking her cow (*Cow*) and the rowdy gamblers (*Gamblers*); and one possible cause of the meteorite – a comet in the sky above Chicago that night (*Comet*).

The causal graph connecting these variables is shown in Figure 3.10. It also captures our assumptions about which variables are *not* directly connected. Thus, the variable *Comet* has no direct link to *Barn*, and is only indirectly connected via *Meteorite*. Likewise, there are no direct links from *Cow* or *Gamblers* to *Barn*, thus assuming that the cow (or the gamblers) can only cause the fire by knocking over the lantern. Any of these assumptions could be relaxed by adding extra links, although this would make the graph more complicated. Here there is a trade-off between fidelity and use: on the one hand, we should avoid adding links that would at most have a minimal influence; but, on the other hand, we don't want to omit links that might represent a substantial influence.

What about the quantitative side of the model? To parameterize the model we need priors for each of the exogenous causes and CPTs for the other variables. We will use rough figures for illustrative purposes, but these could be made more realistic by consulting records and reports about the activities and habits of the people involved. In the case of the Chicago fire most of this information is probably lost, so we would still be restricted to coarse estimates.

We start with the functions that connect causes to their effects. We assume that *Cow* and *Gamblers* combine via a *noisy-OR* function to determine the probability of *Lantern*. Therefore, we only need to provide strength parameters for each cause. Here we assume that knocking over a lantern is more likely to occur when rowdy people are gambling (10%) than when the cow is being milked (5%). We also assume that the three possible causes of the barn fire – *Lantern*, *Pipe* and *Meteorite* – combine via a *noisy-OR* function. Here we assume that a barn fire is most likely if hit by a meteorite (50%), less likely if a lantern is knocked over (20%), and even less likely if someone smokes a pipe (5%). We also need to quantify the link from *Comet* to *Meteorite*. We assume a low probability (1%) that a meteorite hits the barn if the comet is present, and zero probability if the comet is not present.

Finally, we need priors for each of the exogenous causes, using background knowledge from the case: that Mrs O'Leary occasionally milked her cows at night (10%), that Sullivan occasionally smoked his pipe in the barn (10%), and that gambling in the barn occurred less frequently (5%). We assign a lower probability to the comet being in the sky above Chicago that night (1%). Note that the relative values of the priors are more important here than their exact absolute values.

These estimates are for probabilities *prior* to the evidence, and hence prior to taking into account the fact that there was a barn fire, and also prior to the large quantity of evidence produced in the investigation and subsequent reports. It is worth noting that getting prior estimates is often difficult because of the threat of 'hindsight' bias – people find it hard to suppress what they already know about what did happen (Roese & Vohs, 2012).

We now have a fully parameterized model and can use it for inference. We know (of course!) that there was a fire in the barn that night. By setting the observation that *Barn* = *true*, we can use Bayesian updating to revise our probabilities for the other variables. The results of this computation

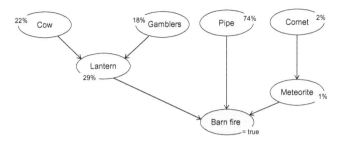

Figure 3.11   Chicago barn model after updating given evidence of the barn fire.

are shown in Figure 3.11. All of the possible causes of the fire have increased in probability, with Sullivan now the most probable culprit (74%), followed by the cow (23%) and then the gamblers (18%). Finally, the meteorite theory has barely increased (2%).

Without taking the exact figures too seriously, the process of updating the model highlights several points:

- *Inference depends on priors and causal strengths.* The posterior probability for each cause depends on both its priors and its causal strength. Thus, although the priors for *Pipe* and *Cow* are equal, the stronger and more direct causal connection from *Pipe* to *Barn* means that it has a higher posterior. Also, despite the causal strength of *Meteorite* → *Barn* being high, the very low prior for *Comet*, and the weakness of the *Comet* → *Meteorite* link, keeps this cause very improbable compared to the other possibilities.
- *Causal assumptions greatly simplify the inference problem.* By having a sparsely connected graph and assuming *noisy-OR* functions, only a few probabilities are needed to yield a fully parameterized model.
- *Amenability to sensitivity analysis.* Given the model it is easy to adjust estimates to see how these changes would affect our conclusions: for example, what happens if we assume a much higher prior for the comet? We can also explore the impact of adding or removing causal links. Thus, the model can be seen as a template for exploring possibilities rather than yielding a fixed judgment.

3.9.1   Introducing Other Evidence into the Model

Despite making some progress, this causal model is only the starting point for our enquiry about the causes of the Chicago fire. It is a sketch of the main causal claims, a first draft that needs to be fleshed out and tested by

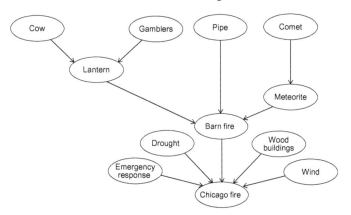

Figure 3.12   Causal model of the broader Chicago fire.

evidence. And this process is dynamic: as evidence is recruited for our causal claims, these claims will be revised, enriched, qualified, rejected and replaced.

The Chicago fire presents a twofold challenge here: the reported evidence is vast but of low quality. It suffers from a glut of unreliable testimonies and rumours, but with very few hard facts behind this deluge of information. Fake news and misinformation dominated the story from the outset. So how should we proceed? How should we integrate evidence into our causal models?

As well as modelling our hypotheses about what happened, the causal framework allows us to model the evidence for these claims. We can represent evidential reports as *effects* of the hypothesized events they are supposed to support. We shall discuss this causal notion of evidence in Chapter 6. By modelling evidence using causal models, we can also account for the reliability and credibility of evidence. This approach fits neatly with the notion of causation as 'listening' – the evidential variables 'listen' to their causal parents, acting as witnesses to these causes.

3.9.2   The Broader Chicago Fire

For completeness we extend our causal graph to include the broader Chicago fire. What were the factors that allowed a small barn fire to grow into a citywide inferno? Based on the historical evidence, we add several variables to our model (see Figure 3.12): the buildings were made of wood (*Wood buildings*), the city had experienced a drought (*Drought*), strong winds were present (*Wind*), and emergency services responded slowly (*Emergency response*). Historical accounts suggest that many of these variables were true, but for a thorough analysis we could instead add evidential nodes to infer their probabilities. However, even if we accept their truth, we can still use the model for counterfactual reasoning, helping us to decide questions of responsibility and blame.

For example, according to Bales (2002), a fireman involved in fighting the fire claimed: 'it was a nasty fire, but not a particularly bad one, and with the help of two more engines we could have knocked it cold.' With a suitably detailed causal model of the fire, we could assess the plausibility of such a claim. Would the disaster have been averted if the emergency services had sent more engines, or responded more quickly? To address these questions, we follow the three steps of counterfactual inference. First, updating our model based on the known evidence (for example, given the rampant fire we infer that background conditions were conducive); second, intervening on the model by adding extra engines or making the response more rapid (note that these interventions would not change upstream causes, such as the initial fire in the O'Leary's barn). Finally, we use the modified counterfactual model to infer how things would have been different. Thus, our causal model can be used to infer likely causes given the evidence, and to address counterfactual queries.

3.10 From General to Singular Causation

We have seen how to build a causal model of a specific situation, and how causal variables are updated given new evidence. But there is a critical element missing from the analysis so far. Even if we manage to ascertain the values of all the variables in our model, we are still not guaranteed an answer to the ultimate question of what caused what. This is because the causal links in our model (even when variables are attuned to the specifics of the situation) still represent *potential* rather than *actual* causal relations. A direct link from X to Y states that changing X would lead to changes to Y, under some background settings. It does not (yet) state that X actually caused Y on this occasion, even if we know that both X and Y occurred.

For example, in our model of the Chicago fire, the link from *Barn* to *Chicago fire* states that a fire in the barn is a *potential cause* of the Chicago fire, but does not stipulate that the barn fire *actually caused* the Chicago fire. We know the barn fire and the Chicago fire both occurred, but this does not guarantee that the one caused the other, and this singular claim cannot be read off from the model. After all, it is possible that the Chicago fire was started by some other cause (or causes) not represented in our model. Moreover, even if we include all possible causes in the model, we still might not be able to give a definitive answer to our causal question. Two or more potential causes might be present, either of which could have caused the fire, and yet the causal model by itself cannot tell us which actually caused the fire, or if both contributed.

In many cases this is not too problematic. We know that X is the only possible cause of Y and that both have occurred, so we can infer that X caused Y. We strike a match, and light the candle, confident that the lit match caused the candle to light. But sometimes we are not in such a privileged position, especially in contested legal cases, where many factors are unknown or hidden from view.

A pragmatic approach to this problem is to enrich the model, adding more details about the processes that link putative causes to their outcomes. In particular, one might create finer-grained causal chains by adding variables intermediate between cause and outcome. For example, to connect the barn fire to the Chicago fire one might add intermediate variables, such as the path (or paths) taken by the fire as it spread across the city. And one might do the same thing with other putative causes, such as the possible paths emanating from a different fire in the city that night. The aim here is twofold: not only to strengthen the case for a particular causal chain by revealing the finer-grained process that connects cause to effect, but also to identify any 'gaps' in this putative process, thereby ruling out possible causes. For example, discovering that the barn fire failed to spread to any neighbouring houses would have ruled it out as the cause of the Chicago fire, and shifted the focus to alternative causes.

Such strategies have practical bite and are often critical in causal investigations. By creating a richer and more specific causal model we generate more evidential tests for the different possible pathways from causes to effects. Indeed, in some cases we might be able to rule out all feasible alternatives, so that only one possibility remains. But enriching a model does not always solve our problem, namely, to establish whether X caused Y on this particular occasion. Sometimes it merely shifts the key causal question to a finer-grained level. We are still left with the question of how to move from a potential causal relation to an actual causal claim. Here again, the causal model alone does not answer this question. Something more is needed.

3.10.1   *Problem of Actual Causation*

Exploring the problem of *actual causation* takes us beyond the scope of this book. But we will briefly show how it is addressed within the causal modelling framework (see Halpern, 2016; Halpern & Pearl, 2005).

The causal modelling approach takes a counterfactual approach to defining actual causation. Roughly, X caused Y if the following two conditions hold:[27]

- *Necessity*: In a world where both X and Y have occurred, if X had not occurred, then Y would not have occurred.
- *Sufficiency*: In a world where neither X nor Y has occurred, if X had occurred, then Y would have occurred.

The *necessity* condition corresponds to the but-for test used in legal contexts: *but for* the defendant's action, the adverse outcome would not have occurred. This condition alone is known to be both too liberal (letting in too many events as causes) but also sometimes too strict (ruling out events that are causes). Here the sufficiency condition helps to correct some of these problems, and is by itself an important condition. These conditions can also be given a probabilistic interpretation (see Pearl, 2009).

We will give a few examples based on the barn fire. Consider a case where someone drops a match and the barn catches fire and burns down. Did the dropped match cause the fire? In the simple case (where no other causes were present) the dropped match is both necessary and sufficient: if it hadn't been dropped then the fire would not have occurred; and in a world where there was no dropped match or fire, intervening to drop a match would have led to a fire.

But consider a trickier case, where lightning strikes the barn at the same time as the match is dropped.[28] Now the necessity condition might not be met – for example, if the barn would still have caught fire if the match had not been dropped, because the lightning would have set it alight. This is a case of over-determination – where two (or more causes) occur, and each would have been sufficient on its own for the effect to occur.

There are various ways to address this classic problem. One approach is to test the conditions under a contingency in which we intervene to remove the lightning (Halpern, 2016; Halpern & Pearl, 2005). In this possible world the dropped match satisfies both conditions: without the lightning, the dropped match is both necessary and sufficient. The lightning is also ruled a cause because, under the contingency where no match

---

[27] Note that this is not intended as a reductive definition of causation: after all, we need to use causal knowledge to help us decide the truth of the counterfactuals.

[28] A more realistic example is when two marksmen shoot the victim at the same time, and either shot was sufficient to kill the victim. See Lagnado, Gerstenberg and Zultan (2013) for a causal model of a real case.

is dropped, the lighting is now necessary and sufficient for the fire. Both these judgments fit with our intuitions.

Another tricky case is pre-emption. For example, if a match is dropped and lightning strikes, and each event sets a different part of the barn on fire. Either would be sufficient to burn down the barn, but it is the fire started by the dropped match that burns it down first. Here the fire started by the dropped match 'pre-empts' the fire started by the lightning. Intuitively we want to say that the dropped match burned down the barn, not the lightning, while accepting that the barn would still have burned down if the match had not been dropped (due to the fire started by the lightning).

Handling both types of case is difficult, and various solutions have been proposed, usually involving further constraints on the counterfactual conditions, but with no consensus on the right approach. However, whatever the solution, the problem clearly highlights the need for careful causal modelling. Moreover, these problems are not just philosophical puzzles, but raise serious concerns in legal contexts (see Lagnado & Gerstenberg, 2017; Stapleton, 2008). And counterfactual notions of necessity and sufficiency are also used in recent medical diagnosis systems (Richens, Lee & Johri, 2020) and computer fault diagnosis (Beer, Ben-David, Chockler, Orni & Trefler, 2012).

3.11   How the Causal Modelling Approach Helps Us with Our Enquiries

First and foremost, causal modelling gives us a powerful tool to enhance rather than replace human reasoning. It does not (by itself) give us definitive answers to our enquiries, but it provides a rigorous framework to explore possible answers. It helps us lay out our causal knowledge, forcing us to make our assumptions explicit – specifying what is connected to what and quantifying these relations where possible. It helps us build exploratory causal models to tweak and test, to update and revise as new information comes to light.

Moreover, a causal model is not simply a heuristic aid to reasoning, such as a mind map or argument diagram. The modelling framework provides a computational tool for drawing sound inferences given our assumptions. As with formal logic, the correctness of the probabilistic conclusions is guaranteed *if* we accept the premises and assumptions (model and parameters). And this scales up. Even for more complex models, with many interconnected variables, the same rules of Bayesian updating can be applied to deliver valid probabilistic inferences. Which means that the main debate can shift to the viability of these assumptions – such as the acceptability of the causal relations and their strengths, and the plausibility of prior probabilities.

The output of these formal computations can sometimes surprise us. Even if we have supplied the model and probabilities, the Bayesian machinery might deliver consequences that go against our intuitive judgments. In such cases we have two choices: to accept and try to understand seemingly counter-intuitive results, or to reconsider our prior assumptions. Either route advances how we understand and reason about a difficult problem.

3.12 Summary

Starting with the Chicago fire, I have introduced the basics of causal modelling. This framework allows us to represent our causal claims using graphs, and it captures the different types of causal inference: ascending Pearl's ladder from reasoning about observations, to reasoning about interventions, to counterfactual reasoning. The framework serves several purposes. It gives us a tool to help analyze investigative and legal cases, clarifying and improving our own understanding of these problems (see Chapters 6 and 10). It also allows us to assess the quality of other people's reasoning, whether they are legal decision-makers or participants in psychology experiments (see Chapter 4). Finally, while not proposed as a fully descriptive model of human inference, it serves as an inspiring guide to how intelligent agents (like us) might represent and reason about the world.

CHAPTER 4

Thinking beyond Biases

There appear to be many situations in which questions about events are answered by an operation that resembles the running of a simulation model ... A simulation does not necessarily produce a single story, which starts at the beginning and ends with a definite outcome. Rather, we construe the output of simulation as an assessment of the ease with which the model could produce different outcomes, given its initial conditions and operating parameters ... The ease with which the simulation of a system reaches a particular state is eventually used to judge the propensity of the (real) system to produce that state.

'The Simulation Heuristic', Kahneman and
Tversky (1982a)

4.1 Introduction

A jogger is found dead in an isolated country lane. He has been shot in the head and is propped up against a fence. On the ground by his left hand is a gun. Was he murdered or did he shoot himself? The man was killed by a single shot, fired from the discarded gun. Fingerprint experts find a mixture of prints on the gun, suggesting it was handled by several people. It's impossible to get any distinct prints from the trigger, but the victim's prints are found on the top of the gun barrel. The police consider several ways in which these prints could have been left – by the victim pushing the gun away, by the gun being placed in his hand, by him firing the gun. They conclude that the prints are unlikely to have arisen from the man firing the gun himself.

Given this evidence, do you think murder or suicide more likely? Intuitively the evidence suggests murder. After all, the print evidence supports the hypothesis that he did not shoot himself. But this inference would be too quick. We must also consider the base rates of the possible causes. Shootings are rare in isolated countryside lanes, whereas suicides are more prevalent (but still unlikely). However, even if we have some knowledge of the base rates, it is not trivial to combine them with the fingerprint evidence to yield a posterior belief. Strictly, we should use Bayes' rule (see Chapter 3), but this is difficult to apply in such situations.

A simpler strategy is to prefer the cause that best explains the evidence – which cause would make the pattern of prints most likely? Murder or suicide? And here the police rely on mental simulation – the position of the prints is unlikely to have arisen from the man himself firing the gun, and more likely if we suppose that someone else pulled the trigger. These inferences depend on the police's imagination and experience of similar shootings, not on explicit Bayesian reasoning.

4.1.1 Principles of Intuitive Judgment

In this chapter we explore psychological research on how people make intuitive judgments under uncertainty. Here we focus on studies conducted on lay people in the psychology lab, whereas in Chapter 5 we will look at studies of experts in real-world contexts. We also focus here on small-scale judgment problems, deferring large-scale legal problems until Chapter 9.

Drawing together several threads from previous research, I offer five key principles:

- *Causality*: People construct causal mental models to infer, explain and evaluate. These models are developed from intuitive theories, tailored to the problem context. These are *working models* that support various forms of reasoning, including prediction, diagnosis, and what-if reasoning.
- *Simulation*: Inference is often driven by simulating causal models; this forms the basis for probability judgments and model appraisal. Simulation is not a mere 'rule of thumb' heuristic, but part of the fabric of reasoning.
- *Simplify*: People simplify both models and inference. They use schematic models and approximate inference, often focusing on a single model at a time. These strategies involve inevitable trade-offs between fidelity and efficiency, and sometimes lead to biases.
- *Specificity*: Despite the use of schematic models, people also aim for specific scenarios tailored to the case at hand; these are concrete and vivid, striving for a singular picture of what has happened. For larger-scale problems these scenarios are combined to form narratives and stories.
- *Sampling*: People sample from memory and the world, and also use causal models to generate samples of events and processes; while there

are dangers of biased sampling, it is often an efficient trade-off for reasonable decision-making.

I also add a bonus principle – which only applies occasionally:

- *Reflective*: People have the capacity to reflect on their models and inferential practices, but this is not automatic and often needs to be encouraged. Metacognition allows us to distinguish theory from evidence and helps us avoid or correct for biases induced by our heuristic strategies.

These principles operate together and involve synergies and trade-offs. Thus, the need to simplify often drives the other principles, but is sometimes in tension with them. Together these principles allow people to make plausible inferences and decisions, despite problem complexity and uncertainty. Some biases are inevitable, but, by seeing how and why people falter, we can help mitigate these shortcomings.

4.1.2 Reframing Heuristics

The notion that people use *heuristics* rather than optimal methods is commonplace in psychology (Kahneman, 2011). But the concept is heavily theory-laden, with proponents shaping it to their needs. Simon (1956) introduced heuristics to denote non-optimal strategies in problem-solving, mainly focusing on problems of search. Kahneman and Tversky (1982b) cast heuristics as cognitive shortcuts or 'rules of thumb', and accentuated how they often lead to biased judgments. In contrast, Gigerenzer and Todd (1999) recast them as essential tools for good decision-making, with different heuristics adapted to different types of task environment. More recent approaches in cognitive science see heuristics as rational trade-offs, optimal relative to our bounded cognitive resources (Lieder & Griffiths, 2020).

I too seek to reframe heuristics in a more positive light, as flexible strategies attuned to the complex problems we face. These strategies deserve careful analysis, to show how they function in the context of a broader cognitive framework (Griffiths, 2020). Moreover, I would argue that causal thinking and simulation are not heuristics in themselves, but fundamental components of how we reason. We might require heuristic methods to help build models and draw inferences, but causal thinking and simulation are the bedrock of cognition, not optional tools or shortcuts. This reframing suggests new approaches to how reasoning might be improved, by building on our core competencies in causal reasoning to address limitations in evidence evaluation.

4.2 Causal Models in Judgment and Reasoning

Causal inference is a basic capacity of the human mind that shapes much of our reasoning. The heuristics and biases framework (Kahneman & Tversky, 1982a) also accords a role to causal thinking, but portrays it as a shortcut that can lead to biases rather than a core facet of reasoning.[1]

> In the context of explanation and revision, the strength of causal reasoning and the weakness of diagnostic reasoning are manifest in the great ease with which people construct causal accounts for outcomes which they could not predict, and in the difficulty that they have in revising uncertain models to accommodate new data. It appears easier to assimilate a new fact within an existing causal model than to revise the model in the light of this fact. Moreover, the revisions that are made to accommodate new facts are often minimal in scope and local in character. (Tversky & Kahneman, 1982, p. 126)

Here is one of the studies that Tversky and Kahneman use to illustrate this claim. Participants are presented with a short description of a graduate student (Tom) and told it was written by a clinical psychologist on the basis of projective tests. The description mentions not only Tom's high intelligence, need for order and moral sense, but also his lack of creativity or empathy for others. Asked to predict his area of study, most choose computer science or engineering over social sciences or education. But participants also agree that such projective tests are a poor source of information for predicting choice of profession.

Next, it is revealed that Tom is enrolled in a training program for special-needs education. Participants are then asked to explain the relation between Tom's personality and his choice of career. They thus face a conflict between the short description (which suggests a socially awkward and unempathetic character) and the fact of his chosen subject area (which suggests a caring and empathetic character). Rather than question the validity of the short description, most participants explain the conflict by referring to selected aspects of the description (his deep moral sense) or reinterpreting reasons for Tom's choice of subject (such as positing his need for dominance). This is striking because participants accepted that

---

[1] Indeed, Kahneman (2011) casts causal thinking as a system-1 process – rapid, automatic and intuitive – whereas I would argue that it cuts across the system-1 versus system-2 distinction.

the description was an unreliable guide, and yet retained the model in the face of contradictory data. Tversky and Kahneman (1982) conclude that 'responses illustrate both the reluctance to revise a rich and coherent model, however uncertain, and the ease with which a model can be used to explain new facts, however unexpected' (p. 128).

Their claim fits a central theme of this book – that causal thinking can trump evidence evaluation. But we must avoid the trap of over-focusing on negative side-effects. Causal reasoning is a basic and essential capacity; without it people could not make sense of evidence at all. To fully understand human reasoning, we need to examine (and give credit to) our model-building capacities, as much as we scrutinize the biases that sometimes follow.

4.2.1   Causal Models Applied to Probability Judgments

The advent of causal Bayes nets (Pearl, 2009) sparked a renaissance in causal cognition, providing a formal framework against which to appraise human judgment, and a guide to the kinds of representation and inference needed for normative inference. A wealth of research shows that adults and children are capable of distinctively causal reasoning – including interventional and counterfactual inferences (Danks, 2014; Gopnik & Schulz, 2007; Rottman & Hastie, 2014; Sloman, 2005; Sloman & Lagnado, 2015; Waldmann, 2017). Moreover, while human inference is not perfectly consistent with the framework, it fits well with its qualitative principles.

This causal framework has also been applied to people's intuitive judgments of probability. We will look at empirical studies that suggest a *causality-first* approach, whereby people build causal models of the problem situation, which in turn shape their judgments.

4.2.1.1   Base-Rate Neglect?

One prominent bias identified by the heuristics and biases approach is *base-rate neglect,* where people ignore or under-weight the prior probability of a hypothesis when assessing the impact of an evidential test. This kind of problem has been extensively studied with lay people as well as experts such as clinicians and judges. While debate goes on as to why, and under what conditions, people neglect base rates (Barbey & Sloman, 2007), the tendency persists across a range of problems.

Using the causal model framework, Krynski and Tenenbaum (2007) offer a novel analysis of the problem. They argue that rational inference in such contexts depends crucially on the causal structure of the problem, and thus comparing people's inferences to purely statistical norms is not appropriate. Different causal models prescribe different inferences. To solve such problems, people must construct suitable causal models and parameterize them correctly. Krynski and Tenenbaum argue that base-rate neglect arises when participants struggle to map the available statistics onto their causal model; but if participants were assisted in achieving the correct mapping then their inferences would be closer to the correct answers.

The authors explore several types of judgment problem, but we focus on the mammogram problem. Here participants are told that a woman has a routine screening for cancer (with a low base rate), and she receives a positive mammogram. They are told the true-positive and false-positive rates for the mammogram, and asked for the probability the woman has cancer based on this test result.

We represent this with a two-node causal model (see Figure 4.1), with three parameters:

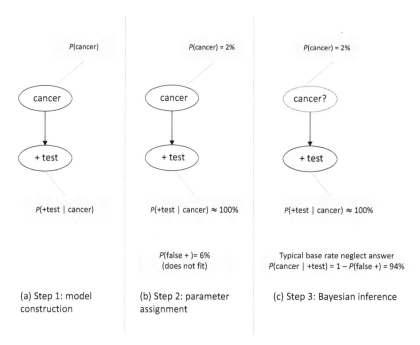

Figure 4.1   False-positive scenario.
(Adapted from Krynski & Tenenbaum, 2007)

- *prior probability* – base-rate of the disease, *P(cancer)*
- *true-positive rate* – probability of positive test given cancer, *P(+test | cancer)*
- *false-positive rate* – probability of positive test given no cancer, *P(+test | ~cancer)*

Given evidence of a positive test result, we can use Bayes' rule[2] to compute the *posterior probability* of the disease:

$$P(cancer \mid +test) = \frac{P(+test \mid cancer) \cdot P(cancer)}{P(+test \mid cancer) \cdot P(cancer) + P(+test \mid \sim cancer) \cdot P(\sim cancer)}$$

Given the probabilities in the example in Figure 4.1:[3]

$$P(cancer \mid +test) \approx \frac{.02}{.02 + (.06 \times .98)} \approx 0.25$$

Krynski and Tenenbaum (2007) propose that people follow a three-step process:

1   Construct a causal model of the situation,
2   Assign parameters to the model, and
3   Compute the posterior probability for the target variable using Bayesian inference.

Applied to the mammogram problem, people first use their real-world knowledge to build a simple causal model where *cancer* is a cause of positive mammograms (step 1). Next they attempt to parameterize the model with the statistics supplied in the problem (step 2). While the base rate of cancer – *P(cancer)* – and the true-positive rate – *P(+test | cancer)* – fit naturally onto the model, participants are expected to find it harder to incorporate the false-positive rate, as it has no clear place in this simple model. Due to an incompletely parameterized model, therefore, participants will struggle with Bayesian inference (step 3). Instead, they resort to simpler computations, such as subtracting the false-positive rate from the true-positive rate, or simply reporting the true- or false-positive rate alone (see Figure 4.1).

   To test their analysis, Krynski and Tenenbaum (2007) developed a novel version of the mammogram task that clarified the causal model

---

[2] See Chapter 3 for details about Bayes' rule. Here we use the standard form of Bayes' rule with the denominator expanded using the law of total probability:

$$P(+test) = P(+test \mid cancer) \cdot P(cancer) + P(+test \mid \sim cancer) \cdot P(\sim cancer)$$

[3] *P(cancer)* = .02; *P(+test | cancer)* ≈ 1; *P(+test | ~cancer)* = .06

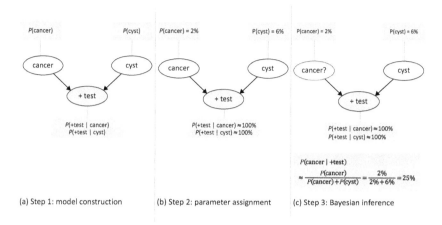

(a) Step 1: model construction   (b) Step 2: parameter assignment   (c) Step 3: Bayesian inference

Figure 4.2   Benign cyst scenario.[4]
(Adapted from Krynski & Tenenbaum, 2007)

underlying the problem and provided statistics that mapped more readily onto this model. Participants were told about an explicit alternative cause for the false-positive result – a benign cyst. Now the correct model is a common-effect structure with two possible causes (*cancer* and *cyst*) of positive mammograms (see Figure 4.2). Participants are also given the base rate for cysts (rather than a false-positive rate), which is more readily mapped onto the causal model. Based on these changes they were expected to give more accurate answers because the model is easier to parameterize and thus more amenable to Bayesian inference.

In this new version of the problem the conditional probability of the positive test given either cause is roughly one; therefore in step 3 participants only need to combine the priors for each cause, which simplifies the Bayesian computation. This amounts to treating the causes as deterministic and accounting for uncertainty in terms of the prior probabilities of the possible causes.[5] However, to make the problem more comparable to the standard base-rate problems, the authors also used a revised version where the conditional probability of +*test* given *cyst* was substantially less than one. This probability needed to be factored into the Bayesian

---

[4] Note that the Bayesian inference in step 3 assumes that there are no other major causes of the positive test result aside from cancer and cyst (see Chapter 7 for discussion of this assumption in a legal context).
[5] This is a common and useful strategy in evidential reasoning. It was also adopted in the police reasoning in the jogger example at the start of this chapter.

computation, thus making the causal version more equivalent to the standard problem.

In both versions of the problem more people gave the correct solution in the causal format than the standard version (up from 20% to 40%). Thus, instances of base-rate neglect were reduced. The authors take this as evidence that, when statistics can be properly incorporated into people's causal models, Bayesian inference is improved.

Various studies have followed up on this work, suggesting a more nuanced picture. One caveat is that the extent to which people benefit from the causal format depends on their numerical abilities (McNair & Feeney, 2015), with only higher-ability participants giving more correct responses. This suggests that the causal format helps people represent the problem and parameterize the model, but only those with higher numerical capabilities can then complete step 3 and compute the correct Bayesian answer. A related issue is that while the causal format helps people avoid base-rate neglect, it is not clear they achieve this through improved *Bayesian* inference.

Hayes and colleagues explored these issues, using think-aloud protocols to probe people's reasoning processes (Hayes, Ngo, Hawkins & Newell, 2018). They showed that while people's probability estimates were closer to the normative answer with the causal format (with less overestimation), the number of correct answers did not substantially increase. This suggests that, although the causal format might have helped people incorporate the false-positive rate into their reasoning, it did not (by itself) promote Bayesian inference. Instead, the think-aloud reports revealed that people used a variety of non-Bayesian reasoning strategies to complete the task. Thus, giving people a better causal model of the task reduced the overestimation typical of base-rate neglect, but did not thereby shift people to become fully Bayesian reasoners. This finding fits with another set of studies (Hayes, Hawkins & Newell, 2016) showing that the causal format helped people consider alternative causes of the test results, but it did not thereby facilitate exact Bayesian inference.

4.2.2   Using Causal Models to Tackle Independent versus Dependent Evidence

Using the causal framework allows us to see how people handle the question of dependent versus independent evidence. Hayes and colleagues explored how lay people integrate multiple tests to make a diagnosis in the mammogram problem (Hayes, Hawkins, Newell, Pasqualino & Rehder,

2014). The novelty in their task was that the patient had two separate mammograms in a single session, each test carried out on a separate scanning machine. The instructions clarified that the second test was performed irrespective of the first test result, and that each machine produced its results independently. Crucially, the problem was presented in either a non-causal or causal frame. In the *non-causal framing,* alongside the base rate of cancer (2%), participants were given the true-positive rate (80%) and false-positive rate (15%) for the test. In the *causal framing* they were told about an alternative cause of a positive mammogram – a benign cyst – with a base rate of 30%, and were given the conditional probability of a positive test given a cyst (50%), which equates to a false-positive rate of 15%. In each condition participants judged the probability of cancer, given one positive test, and also two positive tests.

Based on the causal model framework, Hayes et al. (2014) predicted that participants would construct different models for the non-causal versus causal frames, and thus interpret the two positive results differently. When no alternative cause is provided, participants would treat each positive result as an independent piece of evidence, assuming that false positives would be due to separate random factors for each test machine (see Figure 4.3a). In contrast, when an alternative cause is provided, participants would attribute false positives to this common cause and thus

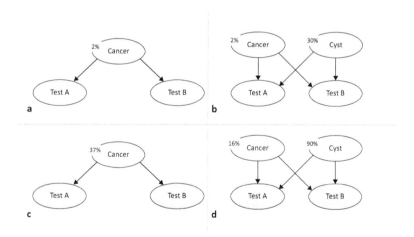

Figure 4.3   Causal models for double test example. (a) Model with only cancer as explicit cause of test results. (b) Model with both cancer and cyst as explicit causes of test results. (c) Updated probabilities for cancer-only model. (d) Updated probabilities for cancer and cyst model.

treat the two test results as dependent pieces of evidence (see Figure 4.3b). Therefore, in the non-causal condition participants would substantially increase their judgments of the probability of cancer from one to two tests because it's unlikely that random factors would lead to two false positives (see Figure 4.3c), whereas in the causal condition there would be a smaller increase because the benign cyst is the best explanation for the two positive results (see Figure 4.3d).

These predictions were confirmed. In the non-causal condition, participants increased their probability judgments of cancer from one to two tests, whereas in the causal condition there was only a minimal increase. In short, without a specific alternative cause, participants assume the positive mammograms give independent and hence stronger evidence for cancer than when they have a specific alternative cause that renders the test evidence dependent.

These studies show that people use causal models to make sense of the problem, and that these models can determine whether they treat evidence as independent or dependent. Moreover, people follow the qualitative norms of causal Bayes nets and assign higher probability to the cancer hypothesis in the independent rather than the dependent case. Note that their probability judgments were still higher than predicted by normative Bayesian updating, suggesting that they used a simplifying strategy rather than fully Bayesian computations.

Overall, then, having an appropriate causal representation of the judgment problem can improve people's probabilistic updating, but does not seem to achieve this by triggering Bayesian calculation. Causal thinking might help us reason better, but it does not overcome our shortcomings in precise probabilistic computation. Nonetheless, this line of research clearly shows the crucial role of causal models in probability judgment.

4.2.3   Causal Structure Trumps Statistical Information

Further support for the causality-first thesis is given by Bes, Sloman, Lucas and Raufaste (2012). They defend an *explanation-based* account of how people use causal structure to shape their probability judgments, which they contrast with standard Bayesian inference.

> The explanation-based hypothesis proposes that people construct explanations of data and these explanations then serve as the basis of judgment without further regard to the statistics on which they are based. The hypothesis assumes that an explanation is constructed from prior knowledge about causal mechanisms that posits some combination of causes,

enablers, disablers, and preventers to describe how the data were generated. This explanation serves as a summary representation of the data but can take a life of its own if the data are not entirely consistent with it. This view suggests that people will make judgments based on qualitative causal structure that encodes explanatory relations and will neglect the original data. (Bes et al., 2012)

One consequence of this view is that people with different causal models can generate different probability judgments, even when given exactly the same statistical information. Another is that ease of explanation will shape people's probability judgments, with higher conditional probability estimates given to more plausible causal accounts.

Bes et al. (2012) make three key predictions:

- *Chains stronger than common causes.* The conditional probability of one event (B) given another event (A) will be judged higher when there is a direct causal path linking these two events, such as in a chain ($A \rightarrow C \rightarrow B$), rather than when these two events are indirectly linked via a common cause ($A \leftarrow C \rightarrow B$). This is because an explanation of B given A is easier to construct when their connection is mediated by a directed sequence of cause-effect links, than when there is no causal path from A to B, and thus two separate causal paths need to be combined into an explanation.
- *Predictive stronger than diagnostic.* The conditional probability of B given A will be judged higher when A is a cause of B (a predictive inference) than when B is a cause of A (a diagnostic inference). This difference is due to predictive inference being aligned with the direction of causal explanation (and also possibly because diagnosis is typically a more complex judgment).
- *Direct path stronger than mediated path.* The conditional probability of B given A will be judged higher when there is a direct link between A and B ($A \rightarrow B \rightarrow C$), rather than when it is mediated by another variable ($A \rightarrow C \rightarrow B$).

These predictions were tested in several experiments, using plausible but fictitious scenarios involving three factors. Participants were always presented with the same statistical information about the correlations between factors, but, according to condition, were given different causal structures to account for the data (see Table 4.1).

In all experiments the explanation-based predictions were supported. Despite being presented with identical statistical data, people gave higher conditional probability judgments for causal chains versus common-cause

Table 4.1 *One example of the common-cause scenario.*

Presentation of three variables	Recently, some researchers have revealed the existence of a statistical relation between muscle tone, level of magnesium and quality of sleep.
Statistical correlation (presented either as verbal summary or in trial-by-trial format)	In 40% of people, muscle tone, level of magnesium and quality of sleep are all high. In 40% of people, muscle tone, level of magnesium and quality of sleep are all low. In 20% of people, those variables have different levels: some are high whereas others are low.
Causal model	The researchers found an explanation of the existence of this statistical relation: An increase in the level of magnesium leads to an increase in the quality of sleep. An increase in the level of magnesium leads to an increase in muscle tone.
Diagram	This explanation can be represented by the following diagram:

Evidence	Mary, 35 years old, has good quality of sleep.
Probability judgment	According to you, what is the probability that Mary has good muscle tone?

From Bes et al. (2012).

structures, for predictive versus diagnostic chains, and for direct versus indirect chains. These results held irrespective of whether participants received the statistical information in summary format or experienced the data in a trial-by-trial fashion.

In sum, people's probability judgments were heavily shaped by their assumed causal models, with structural features of these models dictating the magnitude of their estimates. These findings fit with previous research showing that people use initial causal models to interpret incoming statistical data, rather than learn purely from data in a bottom-up fashion (Dennis & Ahn, 2001; Lagnado, Waldmann, Hagmayer & Sloman, 2007; Waldmann, 1996).

The idea that people's judgments are influenced by ease of causal explanation fits with sense-making theories (see Chapter 5) and the Story Model of legal decision-making (see Chapter 10). In the latter case the explanation-based thesis is pitched at a more holistic level – where people construct stories to explain large bodies of evidence – rather than at the level of individual items.

Overall, across various studies we have seen not only the key role of causal thinking in probability judgment, but also that human inference is not perfectly captured by Bayesian algorithms.

4.3   Mental Simulation

By building causal models, humans are able to simulate possibilities – assessing the consequences of imagined actions and the plausibility of explanations, and exploring what-if questions. I will argue that mental simulation is a core facet of the mind; it is constitutive of reasoning rather than being a shortcut or rule of thumb.

4.3.1   Simulation: Heuristic versus Basic Mechanism for Thinking

The idea that people reason by simulating mental models arises in many areas of psychology, including physical reasoning (Gentner & Stevens, 1983; Hegarty, 2004), logical reasoning (Johnson-Laird, 1983, 2010), social reasoning (Wells & Gavanski, 1989) and expert decision-making (Klein, 2017). The idea has been rejuvenated in recent cognitive science, inspired by the notion that the mind uses generative models to simulate physical systems (Battaglia et al., 2013; Lake, Ullman, Tenenbaum & Gershman, 2017).

Kahneman and Tversky (1982a) see mental simulation as one of several short-cut heuristics by which people make intuitive judgments. Thus, people judge the probability of events by how easily these events can be simulated from a causal model; they also compare the *ease of simulation* of different possible outcomes starting from different initial settings of their models. Such mental simulations are used for a range of judgments, including prediction, probability estimation, and counterfactual and causal judgment.

On their view, simulation is an intuitive process that often leads to biased judgments. But this perspective underplays the positive role of simulation in human thought. Our ability to simulate possibilities is an incredibly powerful feature of cognition, enabling successful common-sense and expert reasoning (Klein, 1999). Rather than a crude heuristic, simulation is better seen as a sophisticated capability of human cognition (Gerstenberg, Goodman, Lagnado & Tenenbaum, 2021; Gerstenberg & Tenenbaum, 2017).

Consider Kahneman and Tversky's (1982a) example of using simulation to predict what will happen if civil war breaks out in Saudi Arabia. Even for an expert with vast data and state-of-the-art computational methods, the problem is hugely complex. It requires rich knowledge of many socio-political factors – including details about the situation in Saudi Arabia at that time – and general assumptions about how groups and factions behave and interact. A near-omniscient intelligence would struggle here, let alone a human reasoner with limited resources. And yet people somehow make judgments in such cases, and experts often reach reasonable estimates and predictions (Tetlock & Gardner, 2016). To simulate possibilities people must construct scenarios that abstract from huge amounts of information to yield a manageable number of variables and parameters. Abstraction and simplification are essential to getting anywhere, with a necessary trade-off between fidelity and workable models.

In addition, the 'what-if' nature of the question introduces a counterfactual dimension that goes beyond simple prediction:

> Note that this simulation exercise differs from mere prediction, because it involves a specified initial state, which may diverge more or less from current reality. The assessment of remote contingencies, in particular, involves an interesting ambiguity: What changes should be made in one's current model before the 'run' of the simulation? Should one make only the minimal changes that incorporate the specified contingency (e.g., civil war in Saudi Arabia), subject to elementary requirements of consistency? Or should one introduce all the changes that are made probable by the stipulation of the condition? In that case, for example, one's model of the political system would first be adjusted to make the civil war in Saudi Arabia as unsurprising as possible, and the simulation would employ the parameters of the revised model. (Kahneman & Tversky, 1982a, p. 202)

We must decide what to 'carry over' from the actual world to our hypothetical scenario: which variables are kept at their actual values and which are allowed to vary according to the 'running' of the simulation? We presented a formal approach to this problem using causal models in Chapter 3. Note that in the current example the supposition of civil war might not be modelled as a strict intervention that sets 'civil war' without changing other antecedent events. Instead, it could involve several ways in which civil war might break out and then seeing how these different models play out. And a final estimate might require averaging over these possibilities.

The key point is that simulation can involve a suite of complex inferences – prediction, diagnosis, what-if reasoning and counterfactuals. While it is inevitable that people use approximate processes to make such judgments, this does not relegate simulation to a mere heuristic. Rather it is a core mental capacity that is part of the fabric of thought itself.

4.3.2 Simulation in Diagnostic Reasoning

We simulate events to help us predict and plan for the future, but we also simulate events to infer what has happened in the past. Given a pattern of observations, we attempt to construct a causal model that explains this pattern – a model that would make the data likely or expected. We test the plausibility of a model by 'running' it forwards in our mind, seeing how readily it recapitulates the observed data. On this view we do not directly infer the probability of a hypothesis from the data but do so indirectly by assessing how readily the hypothesis would generate the data.

Simulating from cause to effect comes naturally: it mirrors the direction in which events occur in the world, and it harnesses our low-level brain machinery, which is forward-looking and geared towards prediction. It allows us to compare different possible causes of a pattern of evidence and identify which cause best predicts the evidence. Returning to our example of the jogger death: the police analyzed the prints on the gun by assessing how likely the print pattern was given different possible scenarios – the jogger shot himself alone, someone else shot the jogger, someone else forced the jogger to shoot himself, and so on. The investigators mentally simulated each cause to assess how readily it would generate the actual pattern of prints.

But, as we have seen, this process is only the first step in diagnostic inference. It tells us how likely the evidence is given each cause, but does not tell us what we really want to know – which cause is most likely? Here we must use Bayesian updating, weighting the likelihoods of each cause with their respective priors. This step is trivial if we assume causes have equal priors: the most likely cause is the one which makes the evidence most likely. However, with unequal priors we must make an additional computation, and this gets more difficult as the number of causes increases.

It is thus not surprising that people are generally better at predictive rather than diagnostic reasoning. Moreover, as Kahneman and Tversky (1982a) suggest, people tend to use *ease of simulation* as a proxy for a probability judgment. That is, when inferring the most likely cause of an outcome, people instead make the easier judgment of which cause brings about the effect most readily (given their mental model). While this form of 'attribute substitution' is efficient, it can lead to characteristic errors. As we saw in the jogger case, the police concluded that the jogger did not shoot himself because it was easier to explain the prints if someone else had shot him. But this analysis ignores the priors of the causes (or assumes equal priors for each cause), and in this case the priors favoured suicide over murder. By jumping straight from likelihood to posterior, the analysis also makes it difficult to incorporate new evidence (such as finding out that the man was clinically depressed).

A similar oversight occurred in the analysis of the father–son fight presented in Chapter 2. In that case investigators concluded that the son had intentionally shot his father because this supposition made the bullet trajectory most probable. But here again this judgment ignores the priors and other relevant evidence. Despite these dangers, mental simulation is a powerful tool; it helps us make probabilistic inferences, to conduct 'what-if' analyses and envisage counterfactual worlds.

4.4   Simplifying Strategies

Reasoning about real-world problems is hard: we must build causal models, assess the evidence and pull it all together to make informed judgments. These demands multiply as the size of the task grows, as we conduct new tests, gather new evidence, revise our models and re-interpret the evidence. I defer discussion of how people solve large legal cases until Chapter 10. But even small-scale problems present a challenge. A 'simple' crime – with a single perpetrator and victim, and a few pieces of evidence – is already sufficiently complex to tax our capacity for representation and inference.

There are many ways to simplify a problem. Here I argue that once we accept the key role of causal thinking and simulation, we can better identify the strategies that people might adopt. Indeed, by using causal models people already engage in a simplifying process: taking advantage of independence assumptions that greatly reduce storage and processing demands. Nonetheless, causal models with multiple variables still present a challenge. How do people simplify their models to make inference tractable?

4.4.1   Singular Models

One robust finding is that people tend to consider only one model at a time (Dougherty, Gettys & Thomas, 1997; Evans, 2007; Johnson-Laird,

2006). This is usually explained by our limits in working memory and the serial nature of explicit reasoning. While reasoners can construct several models of a situation, they are restricted to simulating or evaluating these models sequentially (Klein, 2017). Comparing different models makes strong demands on memory because the evaluation of one model must be stored in order to compare it to another model (Evans, 2007). Likewise, when learning causal models from data, people tend to maintain only one model at a time, adapting their favoured model in a piecemeal fashion to fit with new evidence (Bramley, Dayan, Griffiths & Lagnado, 2017).

4.4.2 Pruning Networks

Even when focusing on a single model, people still confront a tough task, often needing to draw inferences from a complex web of variables. I propose that people prune their causal networks in systematic ways to allow for simulation and inference. Variables and links are removed or collapsed, but not at random; in pruning a model people strive to preserve its meaning and coherence.

To take a forensic example, consider the problem of inferring the guilt of a suspect from trace evidence. This often amounts to pursuing the following chain of inference (Koehler, Chia & Lindsey, 1995):

Reported match ⇒ True match ⇒ Source ⇒ Present at crime scene ⇒ Guilt

While Koehler presents this as a sequence of inferences, we will recast it as a causal Bayes net, using the model to represent the forensic process itself (see Figure 4.4). We replace the inferential arrows with causal links, thus 'reversing' their direction. Using this model, inference can go in either direction: from causes to effects (predictive inference) or effects to causes (diagnostic).

This causal model captures key steps in the process from a potential crime to the report of a trace match, and also identifies points at which errors can intrude. Here the causal chain can be read as a series of if-then claims: if the suspect committed the crime, then expect his DNA at the crime scene; if his DNA is at the crime scene, then expect a match in the

Figure 4.4   Causal Bayes net for forensic process.

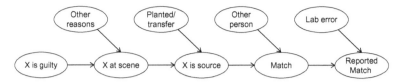

Figure 4.5   Causal Bayes net for forensic process including possible alternative
causes and errors.

forensic test; if a match, then expect the report of a match. Each link will have a strength quantified by the parameters in the model, which in turn depend on unmodeled factors such as possible disrupting factors or alternative causes (see Chapter 3).

The chain of inference in legal cases usually moves from evidence (effects) to crime (causes). Starting from a *reported* match by a forensic expert, one infers that there is a *true* match. This inference is not guaranteed because reports are sometimes mistaken (for example, due to lab errors). But typically a reported match greatly raises the probability of a true match. Next, from a true match one infers that the suspect is the source of the trace. Again, this is not guaranteed; the actual source might be someone else with the same profile as the suspect (usually the probability of this is very low, so this step is considered relatively secure). From the suspect being the source, one infers that he was present at the crime scene; this too is uncertain because his DNA might have been left by someone else (through secondary transfer or being planted). Finally, from the suspect's presence at the crime scene one infers his guilt. Needless to say, this inference is also uncertain: the suspect might have been at the crime scene for innocent reasons. These alternative factors are made explicit in the causal model in Figure 4.5.

While this network still suppresses some details, it provides a relatively complex model of the causal process from crime to forensic report.[6] Most importantly, it identifies different types of error that can intrude in the forensic process. People are known to prune or collapse aspects of this chain, and thus overlook potential sources of errors. In particular, when

---

[6] Note that decisions must be made about the level of grain of the causal model, choosing variables that are critical to the investigative process. Also, decisions must be made about which variables to link: for example, in this model we have assumed that the alternative factors are independent of whether the suspect is guilty – e.g., no link from 'guilt' to 'secondary transfer/planting'. But we might instead believe that planting of DNA evidence is more likely if the suspect is innocent, in which case we should insert a link. By adding extra variables or links we might make the model more accurate, but we will also make inference harder.

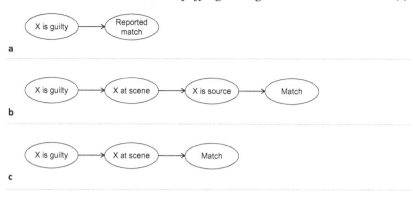

Figure 4.6   Three simplified models of the forensic process.

people operate with overly simplified models they often overestimate the power of forensic evidence (Fenton & Neil, 2018).

The crudest form of pruning is to use a mental model that only represents 'guilt' and the reported match, with a direct link between them (see Figure 4.6a), thus ignoring many of the possible errors in the forensic process (or grouping them together as one collective error). This can lead people to overestimate the probative value of a reported match (Koehler, 2016). Such a simplification is more likely to occur when the chain is part of a bigger model: for instance, when people take the validity of a DNA match for granted, and then combine it with other (weaker) evidence to prosecute a suspect. This strategy is particularly dangerous when a case is primarily built around forensic evidence.

A less crude simplification is to assume that the reported match is a true match (see Figure 4.6b), effectively ignoring the possibility of lab errors or flawed reporting. This is a common oversight (Koehler, 2016), and also leads to overestimating the probative value of match evidence. Again, it will be more pernicious if the truncated chain is part of a bigger case against the suspect. Another possibility is to omit the variable that represents whether or not the suspect is the source of the DNA (see Figure 4.6c), effectively ignoring the possibility that the suspect's DNA might have been deposited via secondary transfer or planting.

Alongside these pruned models are various shortcuts that people use when required to make probabilistic inferences. Note that it is often hard to tell if people are working from a pruned model or using a more complex model but employing shortcuts that under-weight some of these components. For example, empirical research shows that when people evaluate

DNA match evidence, they do not sufficiently adjust for lab error rates (Koehler, 2016). But it is unclear if they use a pruned model, or make the wrong computations, or possibly both.

4.4.3   Assuming Independence of Evidence

Another way to prune one's model is to treat separate items of evidence as independent. This yields a common-cause model, where the target hypothesis is a parent of each individual item of evidence, but with no links between these items of evidence. Such a model, known as a naïve Bayes model, greatly simplifies computation, as each item of evidence has a separate impact on the hypothesis, depending on its individual strength (see Chapters 6 and 10 for details).

However, evidence is often interrelated, not independent. In legal domains witnesses might collude, and an investigator might share critical evidence (see Chapter 8); in medical domains symptoms are often correlated, and in everyday situations people draw information from interconnected sources. Ignoring dependencies between evidence can lead to serious errors. Notorious cases include Roy Meadow's expert testimony in the Sally Clark trial – where he erroneously assumed that two SIDs deaths in the same family could be treated as independent, leading him to vastly underestimate the probability of her two babies dying from SIDs (see Chapter 9) – and *People* v. *Collins* – where an expert incorrectly assumed that the probability of the suspect having a moustache was independent of him having a beard.

More generally, numerous studies in psychology and decision-making have shown that people simplify causal models when drawing inferences (Fischhoff, Slovic & Lichtenstein, 2013). This often leads to people overestimating the probability of a target hypothesis because the uncertainty of the intervening steps is ignored (Gettys, Kelly & Peterson, 1973; Schum, 2001).

4.4.4   Summary

We have only touched the surface of research showing that people simplify their models and their inferences, often in response to processing limitations. Crucially, people do not simplify at random, but prune their models to support inference and simulation. We are forced to simplify, and often reduce our models in reasonable ways, but there is always the risk of error. We will see more examples of this strategy in Chapters 7 and 9.

4.5 Specificity

People tend to prefer explanations and inferences that are specific. While our generic models are schematic, we use this knowledge to build more specific models tailored to the case at hand. We often take an 'inside view' on a problem – focusing on the specifics of the particular case rather than more abstract information about typical cases (Kahneman, 2011). In legal contexts people want individualizing information – evidence linking the suspect to the crime rather than merely putting them in a class of possible suspects (Wells, 1992). We also like vividness and detail, even when this is not critical to solving the problem (Bechlivanidis, Lagnado, Zemla & Sloman, 2017; Heller, 2006).

These more specific mental models – *situation models* or *scenarios* – are the bread and butter of everyday thinking and legal reasoning (van Koppen & Mackor, 2020). They also underpin our ability to understand language (Zwaan & Radvansky, 1998) and make sense of events (Radvansky & Zacks, 2014). For larger problems people weave scenarios together to construct stories (see Chapter 9).

This drive for concrete scenarios makes sense. By creating a more specific model we make it more *informative*, and thus more useful and testable. When the police build a profile of the perpetrator of a crime, they aim to add details (often without strong evidence) to generate new paths of enquiry. For example, conjecturing that the perpetrator is a local white man in his thirties is more informative than simply conjecturing that he is a man. It narrows down the field of possible suspects and suggests further hypotheses to test. Hence the allure of psychological profiling, where experts posit particular characteristics of the perpetrator to help push the investigation forward.

But this drive for specificity comes with its dangers. More specific hypotheses are more likely to be false than their less specific superordinates. The conjecture that the perpetrator is a local man is more likely to be false than the conjecture that he is a man. Thus, narrowing the grain of a hypothesis invokes a trade-off between informativeness and accuracy. People are sensitive to this trade-off (Yaniv & Foster, 1995), but often reduce accuracy in favour of a more informative hypothesis or claim.

The hunt for the Yorkshire ripper, Peter Sutcliffe, provides a striking example (Bilton, 2012). Police were searching for a serial killer who had murdered more than 10 women. They had a glut of information and were tracking and interviewing several possible suspects. However, based on a recorded phone message, purportedly from the killer, they assumed that he had a strong Wearside accent. This hypothesis was overly specific and misdirected the enquiry. The phone message turned out to be a hoax, and Sutcliffe had no such accent; he was eventually arrested, but only after he had committed more murders.

A more subtle danger is that by focusing on the specifics of a single model, we might ignore relevant distributional data about similar cases, neglecting the 'outside view'. For example, when estimating the completion time of a new project (such as building a hospital or writing a book) people tend to focus on properties of the particular project and fail to situate it within a broader class of projects, which would often yield a more realistic estimate – usually much longer (Buehler, Griffin & Ross, 1994; Tversky & Kahneman, 1973). Similarly, when predicting whether a criminal is likely to re-offend, in addition to details peculiar to the individual, accuracy can be improved by using recidivism rates for similar offenders (Redmayne, 2012). Rational judgment requires a balance of both specifics and broader-level knowledge.

4.5.1   Conjunction Effects

Related to the dangers of specificity is the infamous conjunction error (Tversky & Kahneman, 1983). Here is a crime-related version.[7] Participants are given a short profile of Mr P: he owns an import-export company based in New York, frequently travels abroad, and was once convicted of smuggling precious stones and metals. He is currently under police investigation. Participants are then asked to rank the probability of several statements, including:

Mr P killed one of his employees (B)
Mr P killed one of his employees to prevent him talking to the police (A&B)

People rank A&B as more probable than B, but by the laws of probability a conjunction cannot be more probable than one of its conjuncts: $P(A\&B) \leq P(B)$.[8] Adding a conjunct makes the claim less probable. Indeed, there are many other reasons why Mr P might have killed his employee, such as revenge or self-defence, so adding a specific motive makes the statement more precise but also less probable.

---

[7] The best known version is the Linda problem in which people are given a short profile of Linda as a young woman concerned with issues of discrimination and social justice, and must then judge how likely she is to be a 'feminist bank teller' or a 'bank teller'.
[8] By the laws of probability: $P(A\&B) = P(B) \cdot P(A \mid B)$; therefore $P(A\&B) \leq P(B)$.

Conjunction errors occur across a range of problem domains, including medicine, law and finance (Tentori, Crupi & Russo, 2020). Moreover, these errors persist even when people bet according to their beliefs, and thus lose money by violating this basic rule of probability. Tversky and Kahneman (1983) explain such errors in terms of attribute substitution: people answer a hard question (how probable is *A&B*?) by using a more readily accessible judgment. In the case of Mr P, people find it more natural to assess the probability of the effect (killing the employee) given the cause (to prevent him talking to the police), rather than the conjunctive probability of both effect and cause. The claim that Mr P's employee was threatening to talk to the police gives Mr P a motive, and thus better explains why he killed the employee. Moreover, the stronger the cause-effect relation, the greater the incidence of conjunction errors (Crisp & Feeney, 2009).

Tversky and Kahneman (1983) warn us of the dangers of scenario-based thinking:

> A detailed scenario consisting of causally linked and representative events may appear more probable than a subset of these events. This effect contributes to the appeal of scenarios and to the illusory insight that they often provide. The attorney who fills in guesses regarding unknown facts, such as motive or mode of operation, may strengthen a case by improving its coherence, although such additions can only lower probability. (p. 308)

While they emphasize the dangers of bias, scenario-based thinking is critical to enquiry. It allows us to generate plausible models and explanations, and to estimate the probabilities of events. Building informative models might run the risk of conjunction errors, but this is an inevitable side-effect of conjecture and exploration. By adding an extra component to our model, we open up new routes for confirming our target hypothesis. For example, by adding a motive to the Mr P story, we can look for new evidential support for the motive, which would then (indirectly) also support the claim that he killed his employee. We show this by constructing a simple Bayes net model, with three variables: *Motive, Evidence of motive*, and the hypothesis that Mr P killed his employee, *Killing* (see Figure 4.7).

While it's true that the probability of the conjunction '*Motive* and *Killing*' is lower than *Killing*, if we find evidence for motive we increase the probability of *Motive* and thereby increase the probability of *Killing*. So, although adding *Motive* to our model makes it less probable overall, new evidence of motive increases the probability of the hypothesis we really care about – is Mr P guilty?

Figure 4.7   Causal model of the conjunction of *Motive* and *Killing*.

Such model-building and evidence-gathering is the basis of investigative reasoning (see Chapter 10 for details of how to use Bayes nets in this way). Thus, building up a scenario that explains the evidence, and also predicts new evidence, is crucial. Indeed, establishing motive is a critical facet for understanding a crime, and is often a priority in crime investigations (see Chapter 5, also Liefgreen, Yousif, Keil & Lagnado, 2020). But the same argument applies to other aspects of a crime, such as propensity, opportunity, capability and means (see Chapters 6 and 10). By positing one of these factors and then finding evidence for it, we indirectly confirm our target hypothesis about who committed the crime.

This example highlights the usefulness of enrichening one's model so that it can be tested by new evidence. By formulating more specific models we make our theories more testable – whereas leaving them non-specific makes them less open to testing. Naturally we will encounter a trade-off as to how specific we should make our models. This question will often be dictated by the goals of our enquiry. For example, in a murder enquiry we want our model to be specific enough to satisfy the requirements of legal proof but not so specific that we risk making our model improbable.

4.5.1.1   *Specificity and Simulating*
People's preference for specificity also links with the use of mental simulation. When people use simulation for physical reasoning, they make better inferences when key aspects of the mechanism are represented (Hegarty, 2004). For example, when solving problems about the rotation of interlocking cogwheels, people perform better when the teeth of the cogwheels are represented. Similarly, in more complex contexts such as reasoning about a crime, adding key details about the causes of a crime make it easier to mentally simulate the effects (Heller, 2006). Therefore, if people are using ease of simulation as a proxy for probability, then a more specific model will be judged more probable than a less specific one.

We might also expect limits to the benefits of specificity. Too much detail, especially causally irrelevant detail, could make the simulation harder to run, and thus reduce the ensuing probability judgments. As with the accuracy–informative trade-off, one would thus expect a simulation–specificity trade-off too. The ability of our minds to zoom in and out at various levels of detail suggests that we can negotiate these trade-offs, although it's an open question how well we do this.

4.5.2 Summary

Our drive for building specific models is a reasonable strategy. It helps us to explain the evidence, to explore new lines of enquiry and to simulate more easily. These benefits come with costs: more specific models are less likely to be true – trading accuracy for informativeness – and they sometimes close off viable paths of enquiry. But, overall, the capacity to build informative models is a price worth paying.

4.6 Sampling

Pollsters draw on samples of voters to predict the results of elections, and psychologists test samples of people in order to draw inferences about the whole population. In both cases the difficulty (or impossibility) of testing everyone is overcome by basing one's judgments on subsets of responses. If the sampling is done right, then we can draw remarkably accurate inferences from even small subsets; but if our samples are biased and unrepresentative, our inferences can be misleading.

The idea that people sample the environment to make judgments has a long history in psychology, often drawing on concepts from statistics. Most psychologists agree that sampling allows us to overcome computational demands and complexity, but they differ as to how rational or successful these methods are. I will argue that sampling is often an efficient method for making judgments, but we must tolerate the inevitable uncertainty in our judgments and be aware of possible biases in our sampling methods.

We will focus mainly on how people use sampling to make judgments of probability or frequency. It's useful to distinguish two broad categories of sampling:

- *Sampling from the mind*: drawing samples from our memory or constructing examples from our knowledge
- *Sampling from the world*: drawing samples from the external environment

Which is more common, death by homicide or death from diabetes? Death from a plane crash or death from DIY projects? Most people judge the more eye-catching deaths as more common, and in general overestimate the frequency of extreme and vivid events (Lichtenstein, Slovic, Fischhoff & Combs, 1978).

This distortion can arise at either stage of the process, from sampling the world or from sampling the mind, or both. Much of our information about extreme events comes from media reports, and these sources have a vested interest in over-representing striking events (such as murders and plane crashes) while under-representing mundane events (such as deaths from diabetes or asthma). Thus, our exposure is often a biased sample from the real world. Yet even when we are exposed to representative samples, our memory can itself be biased. We still selectively remember the gruesome events over the pallid ones. Thus, the samples we draw from memory are rarely a representative sample of what we are exposed to.

The dangers of non-representative sampling are well known. In statistical contexts, random sampling is often used to address this problem, but this is less feasible (or even desirable) in everyday contexts. When we seek to estimate a frequency or probability, we seldom sample at random but instead seek information we consider most relevant to address the question. Our sampling is oriented towards things we care about. Non-representative sampling is the norm, not the exception.

4.6.1   Sampling the Mind

Tversky and Kahneman (1973) proposed that people estimate frequencies and probabilities using the *availability heuristic*. The key principle is attribute substitution: to judge the probability or frequency of an event, people assess 'the ease with which instances come to mind'. Despite the simplicity of its formulation, the heuristic covers several different operations. It applies both to the recall of instances (e.g., how often can you recall deaths from homicide?) and to the generation of possible instances (e.g., how many paths can you imagine from A to B?). And it need not involve actual recall or generation but can rely on you assessing the ease with which these operations *could* be performed.

Availability is often an ecologically valid cue to frequency because frequent events are typically experienced more often than infrequent events. But availability can also mislead us, in particular when events are vivid, dramatic or emotionally charged (see Kahneman, 2011). Thus, extreme events such as plane crashes or homicides are more readily available than less noteworthy ones such as deaths from diabetes or asthma.

The main evidence for the availability heuristic comes from judgment biases. From Tversky and Kahneman's (1973) original studies onwards, researchers have argued that this heuristic is responsible for a wide range of misestimates of frequency. For example, under timed conditions people generate far more words of the form '——ing' than '———n-' even though the first class is a subset of the second (Tversky & Kahneman, 1983). Moreover, when one group estimates how many words in a novel have the first form, and another group estimates how many have the second form, estimates are much higher for the first form. This suggests that people rely on the ease with which they can retrieve instances to make their judgments. Probing memory with '——ing' is more effective than '———n-'. Note also that people judge the more specific set as more frequent than the less specific superordinate set, committing a conjunction error.

In another paradigm, people are shown two structures (A and B) and asked to estimate the number of possible paths from top to bottom (see Figure 4.8).

People find it easier to visualize paths in structure A than structure B, and hence judge that A contains more paths than B. But, in fact, both structures have the same number of paths: structure A has 8^3, and structure

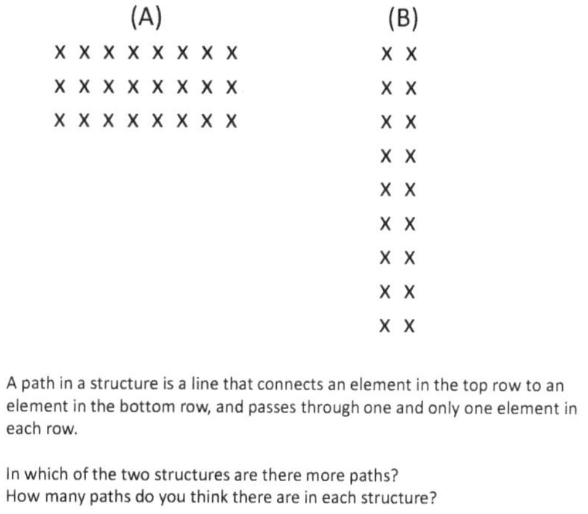

```
        (A)                    (B)
    X X X X X X X X          X X
    X X X X X X X X          X X
    X X X X X X X X          X X
                             X X
                             X X
                             X X
                             X X
                             X X
                             X X
```

A path in a structure is a line that connects an element in the top row to an element in the bottom row, and passes through one and only one element in each row.

In which of the two structures are there more paths?
How many paths do you think there are in each structure?

Figure 4.8   Estimating number of paths in a structure.
(Aadapted from Tversky & Kahneman, 1973)

B has 2^9, both equal to 512. Tversky and Kahneman suggest several reasons for this preference. First, the most salient paths are the columns, with A having more than B (8 versus 2). Second, crisscrossing paths are more distinctive in A than B; paths in A share on average about 1/8 of their elements, whereas paths on B share 1/2. Third, paths in A are shorter than in B. Overall, then, people use the ease of visualization to judge path frequency.

While the availability heuristic has been applied to a huge range of domains, it serves mainly as a descriptive label rather than as an explanation. Psychologists use it to cover a range of distinct mental operations in one brush stroke, typically as a placeholder for a memory or judgment bias. But it is seldom given a deeper analysis in terms of more precise cognitive or computational models.

4.6.1.1   New Sampling Approaches

The idea that people sample information to overcome their cognitive limitations has been revitalized in recent cognitive science, inspired by sampling methods from statistics and machine learning. Under suitable conditions these methods approximate Bayesian inference, but in other contexts they can lead to biases. However, although error-prone, these methods are recast as rational relative to the broader decision-making context (see Lieder & Griffiths, 2020). Without going into details, I give a flavour of the ongoing research in this area.

Recent sampling approaches are based on two key ideas – that people encode probabilistic information about the world using generative models, and that they can simulate these models to produce samples of events or examples. These samples can then be used to estimate the probabilities or frequencies of real-world events (Sanborn & Chater, 2016). For example, suppose you are playing a game of darts. To estimate the probability that you will hit the bullseye, you use an internal 'dart-throwing' model, which incorporates your skill and previous experience, as well as factors such as the distance and size of the board. This model allows you to generate a sample of dart throws and outcomes, from which you can estimate the probability of hitting the bullseye. For example, you might base your estimate on the proportion of simulated throws that hit the bullseye.

Crucially, if sampling is unbiased then as the number of samples increases, inference will approximate the probability distribution implicit in the model. But with a small number of samples your estimates can be inaccurate. For example, if you only generate a few samples from your internal model you might misestimate the chances of hitting the bullseye.

The standard view here is that small samples lead to biases; thus, Kahneman (2011) portrays sampling via availability as an irrational and risky mental shortcut. Resource rational approaches offer an alternative take (Lieder & Griffiths, 2020). Lieder and Griffiths argue that sampling is rational relative to the resource limitations of the decision-maker. Moreover, they show that for simple decision problems it is rational to use just one or a few samples, once we factor in the cost of sampling (Vul, Goodman, Griffiths & Tenenbaum, 2014). This follows because in certain contexts the cost of extra sampling – in terms of effort and time – can outweigh the benefits in accuracy that more samples would bring.

In a similar vein, Lieder, Griffiths and Hsu (2018) argue that over-weighting extreme events – a classic symptom of the availability heuristic – can be recast as a rational strategy for decision-making relative to our limited resources. They introduce a *utility-weighted* model for memory-based decisions. The key idea is that people do not encode all events equally but weight them according to perceived importance. Our memories prioritize extreme events (such as a murder or a lottery win) over mundane events (such as going to the shops). When people judge event frequency, they are more likely to sample extreme events from memory and thus overestimate the probability of these events. This memory bias is rational relative to the costs of ignoring high-impact but low-probability outcomes. Lieder et al. (2018) use this model to explain a range of memory and decision-making phenomena, including framing effects and preference reversals.

Resource rational approaches have been applied to a range of heuristics in decision-making (Lieder & Griffiths, 2020). While it's too early to tell how effectively these approaches capture human behaviour, they are attractive because they offer a unified framework for both normative and heuristic models of inference.

4.6.1.2 *Sampling and Simulating from Internal Models*
Most of the work on sampling has focused on relatively simple problems, such as estimating frequencies or deciding between a few options. But sampling methods hold promise for more complex inferences. As noted above, a key claim of the sampling hypothesis is that people use internal generative models to produce samples for inference. These probabilistic models aim to capture contingencies and propensities in the real world, and by sampling these models we can draw more complex inferences (Icard, 2016).

To illustrate, consider a medical diagnosis example (similar to the mammogram problem discussed above) with two possible causes of a positive test. The key idea here is that people, through instruction and experience, can build a generative model that incorporates the strengths of these causes and the priors of the diseases. This model can then be used to generate samples, each sample simulating the profile of an individual patient. If the sample size is large enough, sampling will approximate the underlying probability distribution. Moreover, the model can be used to answer specific questions, such as probability of a disease given a positive test, by selecting profiles with a positive test and computing the proportion of these with the disease.[9]

One drawback with this particular sampling method is that if the outcomes of interest are rare, then we need a very large sample to address our questions. For instance, for rare diseases most of our simulated patients will be disease free and will test negative. And this problem will magnify for larger models. To overcome this limitation a more efficient sampling method would be needed.

Indeed proponents of the sampling hypothesis have explored a variety of sampling methods, each with their own trade-offs in terms of accuracy and efficiency (Icard, 2016). In some studies people's inferences appear to fit with a specific method, although it's still an open question exactly what sampling strategies people are using, and how this can be established empirically.

For example, in the medical diagnosis problem, one approach would be to sample *conditional* on each disease being present, rather than starting by sampling from the prior for each disease. This approach effectively ignores the priors (or treats them as uniform), and thus would lead to the typical judgment biases observed in these diagnosis problems. The strategy is also very similar to how people actually sample information in this kind of problem (Fiedler, Brinkmann, Betsch & Wild, 2000). This suggests that while people are indeed sampling, they might not use a procedure that approximates Bayesian inference in this case. Nonetheless, the sampling hypothesis, and the various sampling strategies available, opens up new possibilities for analyzing human judgment.

4.6.1.3 Sampling Causal Links
In addition to making inferences by sampling within a single model, sampling approaches can also be used to update our models in light of new evidence. For example, Bramley et al. (2017) explored how people learn causal models by repeatedly intervening on a causal system made up

---

[9] This procedure is called rejection sampling (Devroye, 2006).

of several variables. As well as showing that people tend to maintain and test only one causal model at a time, Bramley et al. proposed that people update their model through sampling. Each time people encounter new evidence they sample close variations of their current model (e.g., adding or removing a link), and only update the model if the new proposal better explains the current evidence. Overall, people were conservative in their model changes, tinkering rather than making radical changes, but they still did a good job of uncovering the correct model after sufficient trials.

Although Bramley et al. only looked at causal systems with a small number of variables, the strength of the sampling approach they propose is that it can scale up to larger structures. But we still don't know how people build and test models in such situations. It's likely that they combine sampling approaches with other simplifying strategies.

4.6.2 Sampling the World

People are consigned to draw samples from the world too, seldom having complete information before they need to make a judgment or decision. Many of the same questions arise as with mental sampling: what are the risks of relying on small samples; are our sampling strategies biased; and, if so, how damaging are these biases for effective decision-making? But the process of sampling from the world also introduces novel issues.

One notable addition is that we are not merely observers of information but also creators, often intervening in a situation to gather data or evidence.[10] While this can be advantageous, allowing us to probe behind our observations to uncover causal relations,[11] it can also produce side-effects that undermine our judgments. Thus, sometimes the act of sampling changes the behaviour we are trying to learn about. For instance, a bullying boss who questions his employees about whether or not he is intimidating would most likely acquire a distorted sample of responses. Likewise, a police interrogator using coercive interview tactics can interfere with the evidence-gathering process and get a false confession.

The key point is that the very act of sampling can sometimes disturb the system under study, for good or for bad. How well do people deal

---

[10] Perhaps this also arises in mental sampling – for example, when we probe our memory or simulate our mental models, do we potentially distort the system we are trying to learn about? Motivated reasoning might be a case of this – where our desired outcomes change the structure of our models.

[11] See discussion of intervention-based inference in Chapter 3.

with this possibility? Research findings are mixed: in some contexts people can use knowledge that they are intervening to better learn about a system (Sloman & Lagnado, 2015), but in other cases they also show a poor awareness of the confounding effects of their own sampling actions (Kuhn, 2012).

Even if our sampling does not change the system under study, it can still introduce subtle biases that are easy to miss. We rarely gather a random sample of the population or system we seek to understand, and our sampling methods can be biased in various ways. This includes selection bias, where we focus only on the subset of the population we wish to draw inferences about (our target), and ignore the contrast class. But this means that we only learn about features that are associated with the target set rather than those that distinguish that target from other people. A notorious example is given by the profiling of so-called 'serial nurse killers', where investigators only sampled the characteristics of convicted nurses, but not those of non-convicted nurses (Gill, Fenton, Neil & Lagnado, 2020; Yardley & Wilson, 2016). Without the comparison class we have no way of knowing if these features are diagnostic. Worse still, even with a comparison class we have no guarantee that these features are causally relevant to being a serial killer.

A more subtle bias occurs when our sampling process is shaped by our ongoing evaluations. For example, in a social context we seek to interact with people whose company we expect to enjoy. To gain an impression of new colleagues we sample from their behaviour. Colleagues who give a good initial impression are more likely to be resampled compared to those who give a poor impression. But consequently we are less likely to correct a false-negative impression than a false-positive impression (Denrell, 2005; Denrell & March, 2001). Thus, by sampling according to previous interactions, we risk introducing a bias into our search. Note that this locates the human bias not with sampling per se, but with the lack of awareness of how our sampling creates a biased sample.

4.6.2.1 Naïve Sampling
Overall, empirical work on people's sampling gives mixed findings: sometimes they are accurate and sometimes they are biased. Fiedler and colleagues seek to reconcile this tension, proposing that people are *naïve intuitive statisticians*, capable of estimating frequencies from samples, but also naïve in taking samples at face value (Fiedler & Juslin, 2006). They argue that judgment biases arise not because people misprocess the samples they have, but because they fail to correct for biases in their sampling

methods. Fiedler calls this *metacognitive myopia* – a failure to recognize and correct for biases induced by the external sampling process.

Fiedler, Walther, Freytag and Plessner (2002) give a real-world example from the murky world of lie-detection. They show that police and lawyers mistakenly endorse the accuracy of polygraph lie-detectors based on flawed validity studies. These studies focus on cases that confirm the polygraph test – i.e., when a suspect confesses after receiving a positive test – but they exclude cases that might disconfirm the test. This is because if someone fails the test but does not confess, there is no follow-up to show the suspect is innocent, so the false-positive rate is unknown. Moreover, it's possible that someone who fails a test might give a false confession. The police and lawyers therefore suffer from metacognitive myopia – they do not see the inherent bias in these studies and do not correct for the missing data. And this is not a one-off example – experts in other forensic domains are prone to similar errors (see Chapter 8).

Applying their approach to judgmental biases, Fiedler et al. (2000) argue for a naïve sampling account of base-rate neglect. People are given tasks such as the mammogram task (Section 4.2.1.1) but are allowed to sample case files rather than read summary statistics. People's judgments are compared in two key conditions: (1) one group sample by *predictor* – they select files denoting either positive or negative mammogram results and find out whether the patient has breast cancer; (2) the other group sample by *criterion* – they select files denoting whether or not a patient has breast cancer and find out whether the patient has a positive or negative mammogram.

Fiedler et al. (2000) conjectured that people would be relatively accurate samplers – in terms of estimating the proportions in their samples – but would be poor at noticing or correcting for the potential bias in criterion sampling. This is exactly what they found. Predictor-based samplers were accurate in their judgments of the probability of cancer given a positive test, whereas criterion-based samplers overestimated that probability. This can be explained by the latter choosing roughly equal numbers of cancer and no-cancer files, and not appropriately factoring in the low base-rate of cancer.

In related work, Hogarth, Lejarraga and Soyer (2015) distinguish between the learning setting – in which people acquire their samples – and the decision setting – where they apply this knowledge. They highlight the problem of a mismatch between the two settings – so-called 'wicked' environments – where the acquired samples can lead to poor judgments. They also argue that one route to improving judgment is to structure the learning setting to better match the decision setting. Hogarth and Soyer (2011) show that people avoid biases like base-rate neglect when they can sample from the posterior distribution.

In these experiments people were explicitly given the results of the sampling, so there was less need to rely on memory-based sampling. But it is natural to extrapolate these findings to memory-based judgments too. For example, encouraging mental sampling by predictor rather than criterion should lead to more accurate judgments.

4.6.3 Summary

People sample information, whether to assess frequencies and probabilities, or to simulate inferences to avoid difficult analytic computations. Building on ideas from Tversky and Kahneman, more recent theorizing aims to flesh out broad concepts such as availability within a computational framework, which takes seriously the trade-off between accuracy of beliefs and efficiency of decision-making. We have also broached the concern that even when people are accurate at processing samples, they often lack the metacognitive insight to see that their sampling procedures might be biased and need correction. This fits with the more general claim that people often struggle to evaluate their own reasoning processes.

4.7 Metacognition

As well as our capacity to reason about the world, we are (sometimes) able to reason about this reasoning – to reflect on the aptness of our mental models and assumptions, our methods of model-building and evidence-evaluation, and the rigour of our inferential practices. Such *metacognition* is critical for learning, allowing us to select suitable strategies, monitoring and revising them as needed (Flavell, 1979; Perfect & Schwartz, 2002). It is also crucial for avoiding or correcting biased reasoning, helping us recognize and adjust for limitations and distortions in our mental models.

Metacognition is a hallmark of sophisticated reasoning, but it does not come easily. Our default is to reason about the world *through* our mental models, not to reason about the models themselves; mental models are like lenses through which we see the world, and not typically the objects of our attention (Horst, 2016). The transparency of our mental models accounts for why everyday reasoning often appears so seamless, but it also suggests why we are susceptible to certain cognitive biases. If we don't 'see' the mental models that our inferences depend on, we are less likely to notice when they are flawed or inadequate. For example, base-rate neglect is pernicious because people do not realize that they have omitted crucial information from their model, such as the base rates of hypotheses or alternative causes of the evidence (Krynski & Tenenbaum, 2007). To overcome complexity, we use simpler models and heuristic inference, but we are often unaware of the trade-offs and compromises these incur.

Moreover, the intuitive theories and assumptions that underpin our mental models are often implicit, and thus hard to scrutinize and evaluate. This problem is magnified because our theories also shape how we evaluate our models against evidence, and can thus spawn a self-supporting cycle, such that biases are repeated and re-affirmed.

4.7.1 Coordinating Theory and Evidence

Metacognition is crucial for how we test our theories against evidence. For Kuhn (1989, 1991, 2000) the ability to coordinate theory and evidence is the cornerstone of good reasoning, and hinges on the capacity to reflect on our own thinking:

> This development is metacognitive, as well as strategic. It requires thinking about theories, rather than merely with them, and thinking about evidence, rather than merely being influenced by it, and, hence, reflects the attainment of control over the interaction of theories and evidence in one's own thinking. (Kuhn, 1989, p. 674)

To properly evaluate a theory or model we must be able to represent the theory separately from the evidence, making it an 'object of cognition' in its own right, and assessing whether it is supported or falsified by the evidence. This portrayal of good reasoning sets high standards, and reasoners can fall short. Kuhn (1991) explores how people assess causal theories in everyday domains, such as the causes of unemployment, recidivism and educational failure. She shows that people often fail to scrutinize their own beliefs. They meld theory and evidence into scripts about 'how things happen', confuse explanations for evidence, and struggle to deal with contrary evidence. For example, when asked to produce evidence for a causal claim, such as why ex-convicts re-offend, many participants simply elaborate their pet theory rather than give supporting evidence. People's fusion of theory and evidence also inhibits their ability to consider alternative theories or counterevidence. Once they have a script for why convicts re-offend, this seems to block off alternative accounts. Kuhn and colleagues have extended this framework to jury decision-making, with similar findings (see Chapter 9).

The problem of theory–evidence coordination fits with a central thesis of this book, that people are better at explaining than evaluating. But with a few qualifications. First, even when people *do* differentiate theory from evidence, the task of evaluation is still demanding. Second, people often lack evidence to support their causal claims; but, even so, elaborating an explanation has benefits (Brem & Rips, 2000). For example, unpacking a possible mechanism can deepen our knowledge of why things might happen and open novel avenues for enquiry. Third, it is not always easy to separate theory and evidence. Even in science, our observations are theory dependent (Hanson, 1958), and in legal cases parties often dispute what the 'evidence' is (see Chapter 5).

Despite the challenges, people can improve their meta-reasoning skills. They can learn to scrutinize their arguments and consider alternative theories and counterevidence (Kuhn, 2008, 2017). Various methods help, including instruction and training (see Chapter 10), and using self-explanations (Chi, De Leeuw, Chiu & LaVancher, 1994) and tools (Royce, Hayes & Schwartzstein, 2019). Furthermore, biases in probabilistic reasoning can be reduced with suitable aids (Mandel & Navarrete, 2015; Operskalski & Barbey, 2016). The social process of arguing also plays a crucial role (Mercier & Sperber, 2011, 2017). Indeed, the jury system forces people with differing perspectives to discuss the evidence and converge on a joint verdict. And group deliberation has been shown to improve the quality of reasoning in legal cases (McCoy, Nunez & Dammeyer, 1999).

In sum, while our modelling system is primarily set up for reasoning about the external world, with extra support we can be encouraged to reflect upon and improve our reasoning.

4.8 Summary

In this chapter we have looked at how lay people reason and make judgments under uncertainty in small-scale problems. I identified five main principles – causal thinking, simulation, simplifying, specificity and sampling – that summarize a broad range of empirical findings. I also argued that these principles – especially the use of causal thinking and simulation – are the very fabric of human thought and not an optional add-on or rule of thumb. We have also discussed some of the difficulties that people experience when evaluating their own reasoning processes. In Chapter 9 we will show how these difficulties also arise in legal decision-making.

CHAPTER 5

Expert Reasoning in Crime Investigation

'We have facts', they say. But facts are not everything – at least half the business lies in how you interpret them!

Crime and Punishment, Fyodor Dostoevsky (1866)

5.1 Introduction

A couple notice that their baby is bleeding from his mouth. They are puzzled because the child had not fallen or knocked himself. Concerned, they take the baby to hospital. Doctors examine the baby and detect bruises on his body. This raises suspicions, so they conduct further tests, including an X-ray to test for fractures. The radiologist reports the presence of fractures to the child's ribs. The police are brought in; based on the medical evidence the couple are charged with child cruelty. The parents protest their innocence; they don't understand why their child is bleeding, nor why he appears to have bruises and fractures. But the family court rules it a case of abuse. They place the child into care, and a criminal case is launched against the parents.

While preparing for the court trial, the defence team explore other possible causes of the bleeding and bruises. Knowing that these symptoms can be caused by certain medical disorders, the baby is tested for a variety of conditions. The tests reveal that the baby suffers from a rare blood disorder that causes spontaneous bleeding and bruising. He also has a vitamin D deficiency that can cause infantile rickets. These findings are sufficient to explain all the child's symptoms, without recourse to positing abuse.

The prosecution team prepare their case against the parents. They recruit an expert radiologist to confirm the X-ray findings. However, after examining the X-rays he questions the validity of the previous report and doubts whether there were any fractures in the first place. The case collapses, and the couple are acquitted. But their child has been in adoption for several years, and they must fight to get him back.

In Chapters 2 and 4 we focused on how lay people reason, identifying several core principles. But how does this compare to experts such as crime investigators solving complex and high-stakes problems? In this chapter we look at naturalistic decision-making (NDM), which studies how experts, such as fire-fighters, military commanders and nurses, make decisions in real-world settings (Klein, 2017, 2008; Zsambok & Klein, 2014).

First, I will outline data-frame theory (one of the main approaches in NDM) using the child abuse example. Next, I present observational studies of real murder investigations, which reveal how detectives 'in the wild' combine common-sense principles and specialist knowledge to solve cases. These findings are further supported by experimental studies on detectives. Finally, I will argue that most of the naturalistic research on crime investigation focuses on how investigators *explain* evidence, but gives us few details about how investigators *evaluate* complex evidence.

5.1.1 From Lab to Real World

A common complaint with experimental psychology is that it studies people in artificial conditions using oversimplified problems, and hence its findings cannot be generalized to real-world contexts. This view is unnecessarily pessimistic, as many findings initially developed in the lab translate to everyday contexts, and experimental paradigms are becoming more closely adapted to real-world tasks. But there is a grain of truth in the complaint, insofar as many studies of human reasoning focus on isolated aspects of inference, without looking at how these parts fit together in service of a broader goal. A related complaint is that experimental studies are usually based on *lay people*, and thus might not generalize to *expert* decision-makers. We might learn how jurors reason, but what about crime investigators, lawyers and judges? Naturalistic decision-making addresses these shortcomings by studying experts in situ, while they tackle high-stakes problems. Here we will focus on the most clearly articulated version of NDM, the data-frame theory of sensemaking (Klein, 2008, 2017).[1]

5.2 The Data-Frame Theory

Central to data-frame theory is the idea that people explain events by imposing structure on what they experience, as well as adjusting these

---

[1] This approach is also closely related to the notion of sensemaking in organizations introduced by Weick (1995).

structures in light of their experiences. Thus, a dynamic interplay emerges between the *data* we experience and the *frames* we use to interpret this data. This cyclical conception of cognition draws on earlier ideas in psychology (Neisser, 1976) but is applied to larger-scale and deliberative reasoning, rather than perception-action cycles. Data-frame theory (Klein, Phillips, Rall & Peluso, 2007) sets out a broad vision of the interplay between cognitive structures and data, and how this shapes people's reasoning in complex real-world environments. Its key claims are shown in Table 5.1.

First let us clarify some terminology:

- The notion of 'frame' covers explanatory structures such as causal models, scripts and stories: structures that organize, connect and filter the data in question. In our example of suspected child abuse, the initial frame was the hypothesis of child abuse, which explained the observed symptoms and suggested critical future actions. By contrast there was the 'accident' frame, which gave a very different explanation of the same symptoms.
- The notion of 'data' is also wide ranging, including observations, statements and evidence. In the abuse case the initial data were the symptoms presented by the child, such as the bleeding to his mouth and marks or bruises on his body, and the parents' claims that they had not hurt the child or observed any accidents. Later data included the X-rays and the results from the medical tests.

Table 5.1 *Assertions of data-frame theory.*

Assertion	Example from child abuse case
The frame is inferred from a few key anchors	'Child abuse' frame inferred from the bleeding and bruises
The inferences used in sensemaking rely on abductive reasoning as well as logical deduction	Abuse provides an abductive inference that explains the bleeding and bruises
Sensemaking usually ceases when the data and frame are brought into congruence	The family court decision
Experts reason the same way as novices but have a richer repertoire of frames	Doctors and family lawyers used their expert frames
Sensemaking is used to achieve a functional understanding – what to do in a situation? – as well as an abstract understanding	Decision whether to take the child from his parents
People primarily rely on just-in-time mental models	The doctors and family court used mental models that did not include the possibility of genetic disorders

Adapted from Klein et al. (2007).

Crucial to the data-frame approach is the principle that data are not purely perceptual or experiential givens, but are interpreted using a frame. This highlights the symbiotic relation between data and frame, and also shows how data involves a degree of abstraction essential for its use in reasoning, but which also risks oversimplification and distortion. For example, whether or not the marks on the child's body are classified as bruises depends on the frame adopted. The abuse frame takes bruises as data, whereas a different frame might take the marks as the data, and the bruises as inferred. Similarly, the statements made by the parents are interpreted against a frame which includes assumptions about their honesty and reliability. This lends a degree of contextuality to data: it is seen through a lens, and its meaning changes according to the lens employed.

5.2.1 Interplay between Data and Frame

The interplay between data and frame is multi-faceted (see Figure 5.1). The key operations are:

- *Questioning a frame* to identify inconsistencies, judge plausibility and assess the quality of the data

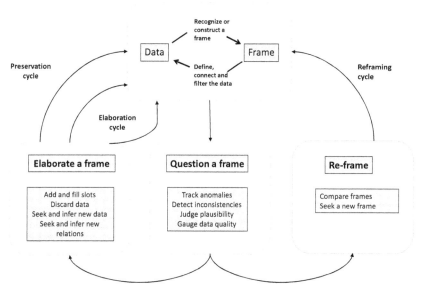

Figure 5.1   The data-frame theory of sensemaking.
(From Klein et al., 2006)

- *Elaborating a frame* to add new variables, gather new data and relations, and possibly discard some data
- *Reframing*, which involves comparing frames and seeking new frames

In our example, the hospital staff constructed an abuse frame to make sense of the bleeding and bruises. This frame was further tested by taking X-rays to look for fractures. The radiologist interpreted the X-rays as showing the presence of prior fractures. This new data reinforced and elaborated the abuse frame, and the police deemed it sufficient to make a charge of abuse against the parents. Protestations by the parents were dismissed, and indeed their inability to present an alternative account of the injuries strengthened the frame: if there was no accident then abuse was more likely.

Once the parents were charged, the defence team raised questions about the abuse frame, proposing an alternative 'innocent' frame. On this account the medical evidence was explained by innocent causes: the bleeding and bruising due to a blood disorder, and the apparent fractures due to rickets from a vitamin deficiency. These explanations were subjected to medical tests, and both were confirmed.

Now we have two competing frames, representing the positions of prosecution and defence. The prosecution tried to bolster their frame by re-affirming the X-ray results; but instead this test produced an anomalous result, with the independent pathologist questioning the existence of fractures. At this point the case collapsed. The Crime Prosecution Service (CPS) made an explicit comparison between frames, judging that the abuse frame was no longer sustainable and that the evidence better supported the innocent frame. Note that a wholesale switch in frames is not essential for a legal case to collapse; it could have been that the prosecution lacked sufficient evidence to make a case, even if suspicion still remained about the parents. But in this case the decision was clear cut, and the innocent frame was accepted by all parties.

5.2.2 *Cognitive Operations in Sensemaking*

The data-frame theory identifies several cognitive operations involved in sensemaking (which map neatly onto the principles we presented in Chapter 4).[2] Crucially, a frame is built from only a few key anchor points, and this core is then used to acquire new data. Frames are based on causal

---

[2] In particular, they map onto the use of causal models, simulation, simplification and specificity.

factors, and inference involves mental simulation, 'running' the assembled frame to envisage how things might unfold, or how events might have been caused (Klein, 2017). The details of how mental simulation is achieved, from a computational or psychological viewpoint, are not typically elaborated, but the role of causal models is critical. Moreover, the theory emphasizes the use of 'just-in-time' mental models. These models are incomplete and schematic, built from local cause-effect relations based on fragmentary knowledge of the system and tailored to the specific situation, in contrast to comprehensive models of the whole system. Just-in-time models do not relate to time pressure per se, but to constructing a model *as and when* it is required for inference, rather than using a fully comprehensive model, which would be unwieldy and often unnecessary.

Just-in-time models are used by both experts and novices. While experts draw on a richer seam of knowledge and a broader range of frames, they still employ just-in-time models to reason with specific cases. This is particularly apparent in contexts, such as crime investigations, where knowledge relevant to the specific case needs to be assembled anew rather than retrieved wholesale from a database of similar problems. Overall, just-in-time models are efficient for many tasks, but, as with any heuristic approach, they risk oversimplification.[3]

These cognitive operations readily apply to the abuse case. The abuse frame was generated from just a few anchor points, with bleeding and bruising serving as initial data. The X-rays were then taken to confirm this frame. The decision to call in the police was based on a just-in-time model rather than a comprehensive model of the possible causes of the symptoms (which would have included genetic and other medical conditions). Moreover, this decision is readily supported by mental simulation, and the ease of imagining how acts of abuse would lead to the observed injuries.

5.2.3 Functional Goals of Enquiry

Sensemaking is also tied to functional goals, such as what decisions or actions need to be taken in the problem situation. Thus, the abuse frame used to interpret the child's injuries endorsed specific actions and decisions: the decision by the hospital to contact the police, the police's decision to charge the parents, and the court's decision to put the child

---

[3] Also see our discussions of the use of simplified and idealized models in Chapters 2 and 4.

in adoption. And the functional side can itself direct and shape how data and evidence are interpreted. For example, once the parents were under suspicion of abuse, the functional goal of presenting a legal case against them guided the gathering of suitable evidence.

According to the data-frame theory, sensemaking usually stops when data and frame are brought into congruence. This is highlighted as a positive feature because it gives investigators a stopping rule (Klein et al., 2007); but it also has a potential downside because it risks halting an enquiry prematurely. In our example, the initial abuse frame showed a close fit between data and frame, and this might have inhibited the search for alternative accounts or new evidence. The general problem is that data and frame can be in harmony even though the frame is incomplete or flawed. Addressing this problem requires meta-level assessment of how good the data-frame package is when judged from the 'outside'.[4] Have we got sufficient and high-quality data, have we rigorously tested our hypotheses, have we explored alternative frames? These probes go beyond mere data-frame alignment, drawing on higher-level principles of evaluation. This is not to say that the data-frame approach can't be supplemented by such meta-level principles, but these evaluative issues are not spelt out in any detail.

5.2.4 Abductive Reasoning

Another feature of data-frame theory is the emphasis on *abductive reasoning* rather than deductive inference. Here abductive reasoning involves generating a hypothesis that would, if true, explain the evidence (cf. Peirce, 1931).[5] For example, on observing bruises and bleeding, the doctor posits abuse as a plausible explanation. This is not a deductive inference: the symptoms might be caused by other things. Abductive inference is closely related to causal inference: we need to generate a causal hypothesis that fits with our causal knowledge of the world, and which satisfies certain hypothetical and counterfactual relations. By inferring abuse as a possible cause, we assume that if abuse had happened, it *would have* led to these injuries. We also assume that if there had been no abuse, then the injuries would have been unlikely. Such inferences are captured by the causal modelling framework introduced in Chapter 3. From a psychological

---

[4] Judged from a perspective that is not simply a different frame, but from a meta-perspective on the robustness of the data-frame package.
[5] 'Abduction is the process of forming an explanatory hypothesis' (Peirce, 1931).

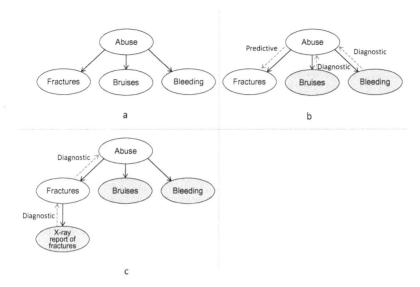

Figure 5.2 Simple causal model explaining the observed injuries in the abuse frame. (a) Model prior to evidence. (b) Model given evidence of bruises and bleeding. (c) Model given additional evidence of fractures. Note that grey nodes represent variables which are observed to be true.

perspective abductive inferences rely on our background causal knowledge, which we combine with the specific details of the evidence to generate one or more plausible explanations. This is what we have previously termed 'explaining' (see Chapters 1 and 2), which we have argued is a special feature of human reasoning.

More generally, much of the expert reasoning studied in NDM is causal reasoning, where experts use their causal models for prediction, diagnosis and imagining what if. Although not explicitly discussed in the context of data-frame theory, the causal modelling approach introduced in Chapter 3 provides a useful framework to apply here, both as a normative benchmark to assess quality of reasoning, and also as a guide to the mental structures that people might use.[6]

To show how causal modelling might be applied, let's revisit the child abuse case. Consider a simple causal model (Figure 5.2a), which depicts abuse as a potential cause of fractures, bruises and bleeding. Initially the doctors observe bleeding and bruises (Figure 5.2b), which both raise the

---

[6] See Chapter 3 for more discussion of the benefits of a formal causal framework.

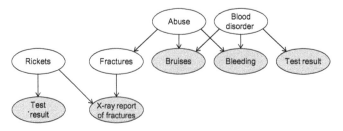

Figure 5.3   Causal model with alternative explanations. Blood disorder explains bleeding
and bruises, and rickets explains fractures.

probability of abuse (via diagnostic inference); this in turn raises the probability of fractures (via predictive inference). The X-ray report (of fractures) further raises the probability of fractures, and hence also increases the probability of abuse (Figure 5.2c).

At this point the defence introduces the blood disorder as an alternative explanation of the bruises and bleeding, which is supported by the positive test result (Figure 5.3). Thus, the evidence for abuse is explained away by the blood disorder, and the probability of abuse is reduced. Finally, rickets is suggested as an alternative explanation for the X-ray report, and this hypothesis is supported by a positive test for rickets. Thus, rickets explains away the X-ray report (as evidence for fractures), which in turn further reduces the probability of abuse.

We have presented the sequence of causal inferences as qualitative changes in belief, but it is straightforward to use specific probabilities and show how things change quantitatively (see Chapter 7). The key point here is that the causal models allow us to represent a range of inferences in a formal framework. This framework serves as a normative guide and standard against which to compare human inference. And psychological studies using this abuse case suggest that people build similar models and update them roughly in line with normative expectations (see Chapter 7; Shengelia & Lagnado, 2020).

Moreover, this example shows the importance of representing evidential reports (e.g., the X-ray report), as well as the events they are supposed to be evidence for (e.g., the presence of fractures). We will argue in the next chapter that modelling evidence is critical for proper theory evaluation. But this can lead to more complex models, and hence it is not too surprising that people (even experts) might oversimplify (see Chapter 4, also Chapters 7–9).

5.2.5 Expert versus Novice Reasoning

One standout feature of data-frame theory is its focus on expert reasoners. How do they differ from novices? According to NDM, although experts perform better in their specialist domains, both experts and novices use the same reasoning strategies (Klein, 2017). Both seek to explain things by building and simulating causal models. Experts differ from novices in having specialist knowledge and a wider repertoire of frames to draw on. This allows them to generate richer causal models that are better adapted to the problems in their domain. Experts also have specialized routines, such as procedures, checklists and guidelines. While this makes decision-making more efficient, it doesn't guarantee that experts are immune to oversights and errors.

Given these findings, Klein et al. (2007) argue that the main way to improve our reasoning is to acquire a better repertoire of domain-relevant frames, rather than changing how we reason per se. However, there seems to be room for improving our reasoning too, beyond just acquiring more domain knowledge. Presumably training in formal methods, such as probabilistic thinking, gives people better evaluative tools, not just a richer or wider repertoire of frames. Indeed, these evaluative skills are domain independent, applying across diverse subjects. We will discuss methods to improve evidential reasoning in Chapters 9 and 10.

5.2.6 Summary

We have taken a short tour of the data-frame theory of sensemaking. Its key claim – that experts reason by building and simulating causal models – fits closely with the model-building approach presented in Chapter 2. While data-frame theory introduces a broader notion of frame, the model-building approach is more explicit about the role of intuitive theories as generators of causal models, and introduces a hierarchical structure for learning and inference. Both approaches also emphasize the simplified and just-in-time nature of people's causal models, which is backed up by the empirical research we explored in Chapter 4.

5.3 Expert Reasoning in Crime Investigations

Sensemaking is vital in crime investigations, where the police actively develop and test hypotheses, gathering and interpreting complex evidence in a dynamically unfolding enquiry. Such enquiries throw up a distinct set of challenges: investigators must decipher the complexities of human behaviour and also assimilate information from human sources of varying credibility and reliability, some of whom actively seek to mislead the investigation (Ormerod, Barrett & Taylor, 2008).

5.3.1   Process and Structure in Murder Investigations

A unique window into crime investigation is given by Martin Innes (2003), who conducted fieldwork studies of UK police detectives as they investigated and solved murders. Crime investigations have distinctive high-level goals: to determine whether a crime has been committed (and if so what), to identify the perpetrators, and to gather evidence suitable for proving a case.[7] These goals are shaped by legal concerns, such as what constitutes a crime and what counts as relevant and admissible evidence. Thus, investigators do not seek just to determine what happened, but also to establish whether any actions were unlawful, and to build an evidential case against the suspects. To address these goals, investigators use a repertoire of sensemaking skills, including constructing case narratives using crime typologies and legal scripts.

While murder enquiries differ along many dimensions, Innes (2003) identifies some common themes. To start with, the police distinguish between *self-solvers* and *whodunits*, which represent two archetypal forms of investigation, differing in terms of their stages, availability of information and decision-making demands (see Figure 5.4).[8]

5.3.1.1   Self-solvers
At the routine end of the spectrum are *self-solvers*. A suspect is identified early in the process, and the bulk of the enquiry focuses on assembling a strong evidential case against them.[9] Self-solvers benefit from rich information at an early stage, including witness testimonies and forensic

---

[7] Definition of a crime investigation in Criminal Investigations and Procedures Act 1996: 'An inquiry to ascertain if an offence has been committed, to identify who is responsible, and to gather admissible evidence to be placed before a judicial authority'.

[8] Strictly, self-solvers and whodunits represent endpoints on a spectrum, with intermediate and hybrid cases that include elements of both; but the majority of investigations analyzed by Innes fell into one of these two categories.

[9] Some cases where a suspect is identified early on can still be complex – for example, when there is doubt over whether the suspect intentionally killed the victim, or whether a crime was committed at all. An infamous example is the Oscar Pistorius case, where there was no doubt that he shot his girlfriend, Reeva Steenkamp, but considerable debate about whether he knew it was her at the time of the shooting. Nonetheless, Innes's analysis suggests that early identification of the suspect is usually a critical factor in investigations.

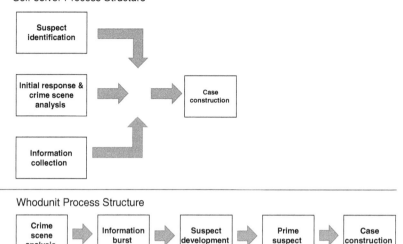

Figure 5.4   Self-solvers versus whodunit structures.
(Adapted from Innes, 2003)

evidence – hence the emphasis by investigators on the 'golden hour' for gathering crucial evidence before forensic traces decay and memories fade. Several investigative activities occur quickly and in parallel: crime scene analysis, information gathering and suspect identification. Given this initial phase, subsequent decision-making is focused on extending the evidence to show exactly how the suspect committed the offence, and on making a strong case that will stand up in court.

5.3.1.2   *Whodunits*

At the challenging end of the spectrum are *whodunits*. These are rarer cases where no suspect is identified in the early stages, and the initial evidence gives no clear indication of potential suspects. A classic example of a whodunit is the murder of Jill Dando, who was shot dead outside her London flat in 1999 (for details see Chapter 7). Despite a huge police investigation, no suspects were identified for over a year.

As with self-solvers the first phase involves gathering information from the crime scene. Routine methods[10] play a central role, including forensic

---

[10]   Proactive versus passive methods: www.app.college.police.uk/app-content/investigations/investigation-process/#instigation

examinations, door-to-door enquiries, examining CCTV footage, taking statements from witnesses and so on. One focus is to acquire information about the victim by interviewing family, friends and colleagues. This is critical to building a victim profile, including their history, character, habits and movements prior to death. For Jill Dando, as she was a TV celebrity, all her movements prior to the crime were well documented, and her colleagues and friends easy to trace. Nothing turned up in any of these searches.

Such information helps police infer possible motives for the murder and to identify any people with opportunity to commit the offence. In tandem, police seek to construct a profile of the perpetrator, based on characteristics of the crime (possibly including a modus operandi). In the case of Jill Dando's murder, the nature of the crime suggested a hired hitman, and considerable initial effort focused on this line of enquiry.

The search strategies in the early phases of a whodunit are more diverse than in self-solvers, with a consequent 'information burst' once parallel lines of enquiry deliver results. This raises the problem of sifting through masses of information to isolate what is relevant, with many false trails possible (see Figure 5.5). Managing a complex body of information is a key component of such investigations. In the Jill Dando case, there was a vast amount of information, and it was only when police were sifting through earlier calls to the police that they were alerted to the strange behaviour of Barry George, who subsequently became a suspect.

The intermediate stage involves developing a clearer vision of the perpetrator and the crime. As more information is gathered about details of the perpetrator, so the suspect population is narrowed. This process

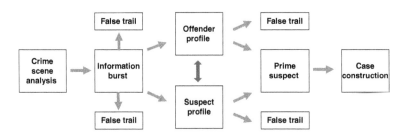

Figure 5.5   Process model of 'whodunit' murders (adapted from Innes, 2003). Note that 'offender profile' pertains to details gathered about the actual perpetrator, whereas 'suspect profile' relates to details about the suspect under investigation.

involves attempts to rule in or eliminate potential suspects from the enquiry. Statements from suspects are scrutinized and tested, and their backgrounds studied for any connections with the victim.

Identifying a prime suspect is a turning point in the enquiry, shifting to a positive search strategy focused on uncovering evidence that directly incriminates the suspect. The suspect is now the central focus: how they are connected with the victim and the crime scene, what their movements were prior to the crime, what their prior history is, and so on. Thus, Barry George's life was investigated in minute detail, with many aspects seen as fitting the picture of a local loner obsessed with the victim. His prior conviction for sexual assault and other misdemeanours fuelled suspicions against him.

Here hypothetical reasoning is pervasive. Suppose the suspect committed the crime: what else would we expect to have occurred, and what evidence would confirm this? Interviewing suspects and testing their claims are often imperative, and rely on tacit knowledge of intuitive psychology and explicit interrogation techniques. How can the suspect's story be refuted? Are there inconsistencies in their account, and how can these be exposed? Indeed, Barry George's police interviews were replete with inconsistencies, as well as his failure to remember exactly where he was at the time of Dando's shooting.

The reasoning process in whodunits is also characterized by *iterative looping*: 'Detectives are continually engaged in the process of reinterpreting and reframing established knowledge in the light of new information' (Innes, 2003). As new information arrives investigators need to rethink and rework their assumptions and knowledge, assembling and refining plausible models of the crime. This reframing and revision are typical of sensemaking (as depicted in Figure 5.1).

5.3.1.3 Case Construction

The final phase in the enquiry is *case construction* against a specific suspect. In the UK the decision to charge is made by the CPS, based on two key criteria: whether the evidence is strong enough so there is a 'realistic prospect of conviction' and whether the prosecution is in the public interest. Once a suspect is charged the process of case construction is accelerated. Information is structured to build an *evidenced case narrative*: a story that explains how (and ideally why) the suspect committed the crime, and is supported by a body of evidence. In constructing a strong narrative, further evidence is often sought to firm up and fill in gaps in the prosecution account, to anticipate attacks from the defence team, and to disconfirm the defendant's expected account. Crucial here is ensuring that the prosecution narrative fits with the legal demands of the case: the relevance and admissibility of the evidence and proof of the legal requirements of the offence.

Evidence is the lifeblood of any enquiry, essential to developing and testing nascent hypotheses, and to supporting more mature theories at the case-building stage. It is broadly divided into 'softer' types – such as witness testimony – and 'harder' types – such as forensic evidence (including DNA, fingerprints, gunshot residue, blood traces). For example, the gunshot residue found on Barry George's coat, which matched gunshot residue found at the crime scene, was crucial to his being charged. It linked him to both crime and victim.

In line with data-frame theory, evidence is rarely 'given', but is interpreted against background knowledge and assumptions, and defined relative to a hypothesis or narrative. Questions can thus be asked of the reliability and credibility of evidence, by probing the source or method by which it was produced. Even forensic evidence such as DNA involves an interpretative frame and assumptions that are open to scrutiny and debate. For example, once Barry George was convicted, the probative force and reliability of the gunshot residue evidence was heavily contested, eventually leading to a successful appeal.

5.3.1.4   Lines of Enquiry and Chronologies

Innes identifies a range of cognitive skills and tools that investigators use to achieve their goals. One key organizing theme is a *line of enquiry* – a proposal about some aspect of the case with a corresponding set of actions and evidence-seeking activities. A line of enquiry is a dynamic frame, which is elaborated as new information arises. Not simply a hypothesis about the state of the world, but also a program for acquiring new information. Complex cases stimulate multiple lines of enquiry, possibly examining a range of different suspects or theories; thus, resources are often stretched. But the official dictate is to consider 'all reasonable lines of inquiry'[11] to avoid fixating on only one suspect or account.

A chronology or timeline is a crucial tool too, both in the active stages of the investigation and when preparing a case for court. Detectives conceive of

---

[11] 'In conducting an investigation, the investigator should pursue all reasonable lines of inquiry, whether these point towards or away from the suspect. What is reasonable in each case will depend on the particular circumstances' (Code of Practice issued under section 23(1), CPIA).

murder as a temporally extended episode, and construct timelines to organize information about a case, aiming to capture the sequence of actions and
events as they unfolded before, during and after the crime. These stages map
onto typical kinds of activity, and yield distinctive types of evidence:

- *Prior to the crime*: The precursors of the crime, including history and
  timelines of perpetrator/suspects and victim; questions of motive,
  intent and planning; prior interactions between suspects and victim;
  prior character of suspects and victim, their dispositions, habits, criminal records and so on.
- *Immediately before the crime*: Events and activities leading up to the
  crime, focusing on the behaviours of suspects and victim; questions of
  opportunity and capacity; provoking or triggering conditions.
- *During the crime*: How the crime was carried out, focusing on questions
  of means and manner; interactions between perpetrator and victim.
- *After the crime:* The aftermath and events following the crime, including the behaviour of the suspect: fleeing the crime scene, disposing of
  weapons or clothes.

Note that a chronology is not the order in which evidence is gathered or
hypotheses are developed, but the (assumed) sequence of events as they
actually happened. Nonetheless the chronology provides a useful device for
organizing evidence according to whether it speaks to events that occurred
prior to, during or after the crime incident. A chronology also stimulates
inference. It helps identify gaps in the assumed sequences of events, suggesting
new hypotheses or sources of evidence to explore. It can also help expose
inconsistencies in a witness's testimony. For example, Barry George provided
inconsistent timings for his activities and whereabouts at the time Jill Dando
was murdered, and this was considered a key strand of evidence against him.

   Timelines often combine with information about spatial location. Thus,
when investigators seek to establish whether a suspect had the opportunity
to commit the crime, proximity to the crime scene is crucial (see our
discussion of opportunity evidence in Chapter 10). Time and place can
also combine to generate new lines of search. For example, tracking the
location of a suspect's mobile phone at different times allows investigators
to build a model of the possible routes taken by the suspect, and thus
identify new locations to search for evidence.

   Chronologies therefore play both an organizing and an inferential role
in enquiries. Accordingly, investigators must use mental models capable of
representing events in time and space, at varying levels of resolution, and of
capturing the dynamics needed for spatial- and temporal-based reasoning.

These models need not be highly accurate, but should be sufficient to predict or imagine paths of agents through varying environments.

One way for the human mind to achieve this is by mental simulation (as discussed in Chapters 2 and 4). We construct surrogate mental models or maps to capture the relevant spatiotemporal relations in the real world, and run simulations that mimic the trajectories expected in the real-world environment. Crucial here is not the high resolution of the modelling, but that it captures the key relations needed for inference. To model the timings and paths taken by a person as they walk from A to B, and to establish if they had enough time to do something, only requires a good-enough model.

Chronologies also help investigators develop stories or theories of the crime. By causally connecting the actions and events in a timeline, a temporal sequence is transformed into a narrative. Narratives are central to crime investigations. They come in many different forms, but all aim to describe and explain what has happened (for more on stories see Chapter 9). Crime narratives are usually oriented around a central protagonist (the perpetrator) – with specific goals, beliefs and desires – who engages in a sequence of actions and interactions, culminating in the fatal interaction with the victim. The narrative often includes a moral evaluation of the perpetrator, and aims to assign responsibility and blame. Investigators construct narratives by drawing on various sources of information, including case-specific details, causal knowledge and assumptions about human behaviour, schemas about typical story structures, and templates and stereotypes about types of crimes and perpetrators.

5.3.1.5   Crime Typologies

Despite the near infinite variety of ways in which murders occur, they tend to fall into a small number of categories, characterized by the context and the perpetrator's motives and reasons for committing the crime. These categories are used by the police and supported by empirical research. Innes (2003, 2007) extracts the following crime typologies:

- domestic homicides
- confrontational homicides
- criminal cause homicides
- sexual murders
- child murders
- stranger murders
- serial murders

Each category yields a distinctive frame for making sense of the crime. Confrontational homicides, for instance, typically occur in public – triggered by a dispute between young men – and often follow a stereotypical sequence of events; they likewise suggest a specific set of investigative actions to gather evidence. Barry George fell into the category of a 'stranger murder', and stimulated the search for evidence that he was obsessed with Jill Dando from a distance.

By using a crime type as a guiding frame, investigators can make better sense of the mass of complex evidence they acquire, which is often equivocal and uncertain. The crime type provides a blueprint that helps investigators construct specific narratives tailored to the details of the crime. The narrative is shaped in order to present a strong and persuasive case – to convince other decision-makers, such as the CPS, that there is sufficient evidence to prove the case. Here the communicative and persuasive goals of a narrative come to the fore, and decision-making is heavily influenced by compelling aspects of the narrative, sometimes at the expense of careful evidence evaluation (see Chapter 9). In the case of Barry George, the evidence was weak and poorly evaluated, but the prosecution built a persuasive narrative.

In addition to crime typologies, investigators draw on prior experiences of crimes, using previous cases to draw analogies and similarities for the current case. This strategy requires the learning of higher-level theories in order to connect the individual cases and identify common features worth exploring further. For example, the notion of a deluded loner who murders the object of their obsession might be acquired through knowledge or experience of previous cases, and applied to a new case that meets some of these criteria (as with Barry George).

In sum, Innes (2003, 2007) portrays investigators as active sensemakers, using abductive inference and common-sense reasoning to build case narratives, drawing on prior experience and domain knowledge about how and why murders are committed, including assumptions about types of crimes and perpetrators. They also use legal scripts to guide and frame their enquiries and interpretation of evidence.

5.3.2 Experimental Studies of Detectives

While these fieldwork studies reveal sensemaking at a coarse grain, experimental studies of detectives (although rare) show finer-grain aspects of sensemaking at work, including the use of mental models and simulation. Barrett (2009) studied how UK detectives reasoned as they solved vignette-based crime cases. The detectives combined common-sense reasoning with specialist knowledge and assumptions. They actively developed situation (causal) models to explain the evidence, and to suggest new hypotheses to test. For instance, they simulated different ways in which a perpetrator might have attacked the victim, or different routes he might have taken before and after the crime. They also used mental simulation to explore the consequences of possible investigative actions: for example, envisaging what would happen if the police circulated a partial description of the offender, and inferring how this might lead to a quick arrest or overload the enquiry with possible suspects. Detectives also used legal scripts about typical crimes to help direct their hypotheses and assess the evidence. When the events matched a well-defined legal script, then evidence was interpreted in light of this frame, whereas when there was no clear match with a legal script they speculated with less convergence. These findings support the conclusions of Innes's fieldwork, and the key principles of data-frame theory.

5.4   Evaluating the Evidence

These studies emphasize the key role of sensemaking in crime investigation. But there is less discussion of the details of evidence evaluation. While testing and evaluating hypotheses are acknowledged as core activities, no analysis is given of exactly how these activities are tackled or achieved. Most of the focus is on how investigators construct causal models and use these to simulate events and explain evidence, but much less on the appraisal of these models given the evidence. The key focus is on *explaining*, not *evaluating*.

How do investigators approach evidence evaluation? This task goes beyond abductive inference; it involves assessing the quality of the evidence and how well that evidence supports the proposed hypotheses. And it presents substantial challenges when enquiries are complex and there is a mass of conflicting evidence.

Investigators must assess the strength and quality of evidence, both to update their hypotheses and to guide their search for new evidence. How significant is this DNA evidence? What does this blood spatter tell us about the crime? How believable is this witness? Who should be interviewed first? What forensic tests should we prioritize? Such questions require judgments about the potential value of evidence. How would this information, if obtained, improve our knowledge of the case? And as the enquiry progresses, investigators must integrate the whole body of evidence to judge how strong a case is overall, deciding whether they have sufficient evidence to prosecute.

Despite its importance, there is very little empirical work on how expert investigators negotiate these issues. They clearly have competencies in evidential reasoning, but the cognitive details are unknown. We will look at formal approaches to evidence evaluation in Chapters 6 and 10; in future research it would be intriguing to see how well these approaches map onto the intuitive processes used by crime investigators in the wild.

5.5   Summary

In this chapter we looked at how crime investigators reason when solving crimes. I presented the data-frame theory of sensemaking, which emphasizes the interplay between our cognitive frames and the data used to support them. Experts, like lay people, reason by building and simulating causal models. But experts differ in having better specialist knowledge and a wider repertoire of frames, such as legal scripts and crime typologies, which allow them to build richer models. Finally, I argued that most research on crime investigation focuses on how investigators explain evidence, but it gives us fewer details on how they evaluate complex evidence.

CHAPTER 6

Questions of Evidence

*Questions of evidence are continually presenting themselves to every
human being, every day, and almost every waking hour, of his life . . .
Whether the leg of mutton now on the spit be roasted enough, is a
question of evidence . . . which the cook decides upon in the cook's way,
as if by instinct.*

'Rationale of Judicial Evidence', Jeremy Bentham (1843)

6.1 Introduction

To set the stage for our discussion of evidence let us visit a notorious crime
from the last century. The case is notable because it was solved by the
famous French detective Locard, who pioneered the use of forensic science. Locard also introduced the principle that 'every contact leaves a
trace', now adopted as a guiding maxim in forensic investigations.

The crime took place in Lyon, France, in 1912. Marie Latelle and Emile
Gourbin were young fiancés, soon to marry. Tragically, Marie was found
strangled at her parents' country house. Emile was arrested on suspicion of
her murder. He was an obvious suspect: jealous and possessive, known to
be provoked by Marie's flirting. But Emile appeared to have a strong alibi.
On the night of Marie's death, he claimed to be with friends several miles
from the crime scene. Under interview, his friends testified they were with
Emile until about 1 am, drinking and playing cards, and then they all
retired to bed. The doctor's report, however, showed that Marie was
murdered at midnight, which appeared to rule out Emile.

Locard was summoned to solve the case. He examined Marie's neck, and
detected scratches. Checking Emile's hands, he found traces of pink face
powder under his fingernails. Locard then examined the face powder from a
box belonging to Marie: it matched the composition of the powder from
Emile's fingernails. Moreover, it was a unique combination of elements:
custom-made for Marie by a local pharmacist. Confronted with this

132

evidence, Emile confessed to the crime. He admitted to meeting Marie that night. She had refused to marry him, and in a rage he had strangled her. He also admitted to fabricating his alibi. Unknown to his friends he had set the clock forward one hour during their evening of heavy drinking. When they retired to bed, he slipped away before midnight to meet Marie. Emile's careful plan to fabricate an alibi was to prove his downfall. This act was used as evidence that the murder was premeditated rather than a crime of passion.

In this chapter we switch our focus to evidence evaluation. I will examine the concept of evidence as used in legal investigation – and the key factors of relevance, strength and reliability – arguing that a purely probabilistic conception is insufficient. We will see that questions of credibility and reliability can become complex, requiring us to identify the causal processes that generate the evidence. I then propose a causal conception of evidence, grounded in a formal causal framework.

6.2 Evidence – General Principles

The notion of evidence is critical in many specialist domains, including law, medicine, science, intelligence analysis and history (Anderson, Schum & Twining, 2005). It is also a crucial concept in everyday reasoning and argument, where people use or present evidence for or against a claim. In discussing the notion we draw heavily on the legal domain, where it has received careful scrutiny and analysis; but many of the key features, contrasts and subtleties carry over into everyday reasoning. Indeed, we can learn much about the psychology of evidential reasoning by exploring parallels with the concept of evidence in legal contexts.

6.2.1 Evidence Is Relational and Contextual

One crucial feature of evidence is that it is relational: it is 'about' something. It indicates or points to another proposition or claim (Achinstein, 2001; Hacking, 1975). For example, spots are evidence of measles, smoke is evidence of fire, and blushing is evidence of embarrassment. This 'pointing to' relation is underpinned by some causal relationship: spots are a sign of measles because measles cause spots, smoke is a sign of fire because fire causes smoke, and blushing is a sign of embarrassment because being embarrassed causes blushing. Note that these relations are uncertain – fire is not guaranteed to cause smoke, and one can be embarrassed without blushing – but even a defeasible relation is sufficient to ground the 'pointing to' relation. And evidence can point to the falsity rather than the truth of a proposition. While dark clouds support the hypothesis of rain, clear skies would support no rain.

Similarly, in the legal context evidence points to key elements of the case that need to be established or proved. An eyewitness's claim that she saw the suspect kill the victim, and the traces of the victim's blood on the suspect, both point towards the hypothesis that the suspect committed the crime, whereas the suspect's claim that he was not at the crime scene points to his innocence. And causal assumptions again underpin these evidential relations: the suspect committing the crime (if true) is a potential cause of both the witness's testimony and the traces of blood, whereas his innocence (if true) would be a cause of his protestations (although these might alternatively be caused by his desire to evade punishment).

6.2.2   Ambiguity of Evidence

In general usage the term 'evidence' is ambiguous and has several interrelated meanings. A key distinction is between:

- *Evidence as a tangible object or report*; as something that is collected, discovered or presented during the investigative or legal process; this might be tangible evidence such as physical traces, or testimonial evidence from a witness – for example, the marks on the victim's neck, or the witness's testimony that she saw the suspect at the crime scene.
- *Evidence as the events or properties that are supposed to hold true,* such as a sequence of events in the course of the crime. These 'evidentiary facts' are usually inferred from the tangible objects or testimonial reports – for example, the presence of the suspect at the crime scene, or the fact that the victim was strangled.

Confusing these two senses can be dangerous. The report of an event must be separated from the event reported (Schum, 2001). This applies both to testimony and forensic evidence. For instance, we must distinguish the testimony of Gourbin's friends (that they were with him at midnight) from him actually being with them at midnight. In this case their testimony was based on the false belief that the clock was accurate. Similarly, in forensic analysis we should distinguish the scientist's report from the facts reported, thus separating Locard's report that the powder found under Gourbin's fingernails matched Marie Latelle's face powder, from the fact of an actual match. While inferring the latter from the former seems secure, we must not ignore the possibility of errors in the testing or reporting.

Sometimes there is genuine dispute about what is 'evidence' – one side might claim there is tangible evidence, such as bruises on a body, and use this to infer abuse, whereas the other side might claim there is only tangible evidence of marks on the body, and dispute the inference to bruises.

Any analysis of evidence, whether in law or everyday reasoning, needs to consider questions of relevance, reliability and probative force (Schum, 2009)

6.2.2.1 *Relevance*

Evidence is vital to any enquiry but only if it is *relevant* to what we seek to establish or prove. Relevance is a prerequisite for admissibility in law (Dennis, 2007), and for effective reasoning in any domain, including science, medicine, history and everyday life. But while it is a truism that evidence should be relevant to our inferential goals, assessing relevance is by no means trivial. It depends on what else we know or assume about the case in hand, on our models of how the world works in general, and on our specific models of what might have happened in particular. For example, Emile Gourbin's admission that he put the clocks forward is relevant to the question of whether he planned to kill Marie, but only against the background that he intended to fabricate an alibi. Likewise, the rarity of Marie's face powder is only relevant to Emile's guilt given that traces of the powder were found under his fingernails.

Perhaps surprisingly the law offers only minimal guidance on the question of relevance, seeing it as a matter of common-sense logic and experience (Roberts & Zuckerman, 2010). What legal guidance there is, is often couched in qualitative probabilistic terms. Thus, a highly influential definition states:

> The word 'relevant' means that any two facts to which it is applied are so related to each other that according to the common course of events one either taken by itself or in connection with other facts proves or renders probable the past, present, or future existence or non-existence of the other. (Stephen, 1948)

Federal rules of evidence give a closely related definition: evidence is deemed relevant if 'it has any tendency to make a fact more or less probable than it would be without the evidence.'[1]

---

[1] Federal Rule of Evidence 401.

The key idea looks simple enough – that evidence is relevant to a hypothesis if it changes the probability of the hypothesis in question. It also corresponds to the qualitative notion of confirmation standard in philosophy of science (Howson & Urbach, 2006), whereby evidence E supports hypothesis H if the probability of H given E is greater than the prior probability of H. In particular:

- E confirms H if $P(H|E) > P(H)$
- E disconfirms H if $P(H|E) < P(H)$
- E is neutral for H if $P(H|E) = P(H)$

While the probabilistic conception of relevance looks straightforward, it glosses over several tricky issues. Before addressing these, we outline the related notion of probative strength.

6.2.2.2 Strength of Evidence

It is not enough to have relevant evidence; we also need to assess its strength. Even without precisely quantifying strength, we need at least a rough comparative sense, to differentiate weaker from stronger evidence. For example, witness testimony that the suspect was at the crime scene 10 minutes before the crime took place is usually seen as stronger evidence that the suspect committed the crime than testimony that the suspect was there two hours before the crime took place.

The law also requires some notion of probative value or strength. In both UK and US law, evidence is deemed inadmissible if its prejudicial effect is likely to outweigh its probative value. Therefore, a rough assessment of probative strength is needed when a judge considers the admissibility of evidence. But, aside from these minimal requirements, questions of probative value are mainly left to the fact-finder, with no clear guidance from the law as to how these questions should be addressed.[2]

In contrast, questions of evidential strength are actively debated in forensic science. The dominant approach is the *likelihood framework*,[3] which proposes that the strength of evidence is measured by the likelihood ratio (LR):

---

[2] Bentham heroically proposed the notion of a 'thermometer of persuasion', whereby probative force is assessed by the degree to which a judge is (or ought to be) persuaded by the evidence given his knowledge of the common course of events and circumstances (for discussion, see Twining, 1985).

[3] This is advocated in the United Kingdom (see Royal Statistical Society guidelines) and Europe (ENSFI guidelines). But see Fenton and Neil (2018) arguing that the likelihood ratio only gives a valid measure of evidential support in simple cases where our hypotheses are mutually exclusive and exhaustive (see also Chapter 7).

$$LR = \frac{P(evidence \mid prosecution\ hypothesis)}{P(evidence \mid defence\ hypothesis)}$$

For example, suppose that Bill is accused of a crime, and blood belonging to the perpetrator is recovered from the crime scene. The blood type has a 1 per cent prevalence in the general population. Bill also has this blood type. What is the strength of this evidence for the hypothesis that the blood belongs to Bill? According to the LR approach, we compare two probabilities:

- *P(Blood match | Bill is source)* – the probability of the blood match, given that the blood at the scene comes from Bill, which we estimate as very high (close to 1)
- *P(Blood match | Bill is not the source)* – the probability of the blood match, given that the blood does not come from Bill, which we estimate as 0.01 (based on the prevalence of the blood type in the population)

$$LR = \frac{P(Blood\ match \mid Bill\ is\ source)}{P(Blood\ match \mid Bill\ is\ not\ source)} \approx 100$$

In words, the match evidence is about 100 times more likely if the blood came from Bill rather than someone else.[4] These values are often translated into verbal descriptions to make them easier to communicate to non-experts.[5]

6.3 Challenges Faced by Probabilistic Approaches

Despite the apparent simplicity of a probabilistic approach, it conceals a range of difficult questions, both theoretical and practical. One question is how we should interpret the term *probability* in definitions of relevance or probative force. Various notions of probability exist, but no single account covers all the uses to which probability is put (Gillies & Gillies, 2000). Broadly speaking these interpretations divide into *objective* accounts – where probability is a property of the world (such as a relative frequency or propensity) – versus *subjective* accounts – where probability is a measure of our epistemic uncertainty. The problem is that neither type of account

---

[4] We have kept things simple here – assuming that the blood definitely belongs to the perpetrator and that there are no errors in testing the blood at the crime scene or Bill's blood. Adding these details, which often arise in real cases, increases the complexity of an LR analysis (see Fenton & Neil, 2018; and Chapter 10).

[5] For some dangers with using verbal labels, see Martire, Kemp, Watkins, Sayle and Newell (2013).

on its own seems sufficient to ground a sensible definition of relevance or probative strength.

One shortcoming of using an objective notion is that it would restrict judgments of relevance and probative force to contexts with well-defined statistical frequencies, and thus exclude most types of evidence, including qualitative forensic evidence, as well as witness testimony, confessions and alibis. But this departs from both legal and common-sense practice, where reasoning and judgment are regularly couched in probabilistic talk. Even more problematic, an objective notion cannot capture the key concept of relevance used in investigative or legal contexts. According to the legal definition, evidence is relevant to a hypothesis if it *changes* the probability of that hypothesis, *making* it more or less probable. But evidence cannot change the objective probability of the hypothesis in question; at most it changes our beliefs about whether this hypothesis is true or false. For example, testimonial evidence about a claim (that the suspect committed the crime) does not *change* anything about what actually happened; it changes our beliefs about what happened. We acquire evidence to know more about the world, but our evidence does not change the facts we are enquiring about.

This suggests that relevance (and strength) should be defined in terms of epistemic or subjective probability, since it reflects whether (and how much) we should change our beliefs in what happened. But a purely subjectivist notion of probability seems inadequate too, because it appears to allow too much leeway in people's judgments, and does not place suitable constraints to ensure our judgments are reasonable or warranted. Presumably evidence is not relevant to a hypothesis merely because it changes someone's beliefs – what if this change of belief is irrational or biased? It should change them for good reasons (or at least for what look like good reasons given what is known at the time).

In short, the notion of probability used to judge relevance and strength, while reflecting our epistemic uncertainty, needs to place some rational constraints on our beliefs. Our judgments must be grounded or warranted in some way, and open to critique and revision. The nature of this grounding is a controversial subject, but we advance some suggestions in Section 6.4.

Linked to this theoretical problem is a practical one. How is a probabilistic conception of evidence to be used in practice? What guidance does it provide for evaluating evidence in order to advance our enquiries? Taking a probabilistic definition at face value, we need to assess (at least) two probabilities – for example, on the likelihood ratio approach we must assess both $P(E \mid H)$ and $P(E \mid \sim H)$. Here again the question arises of what we should base our judgments on: while in some forensic contexts we have statistical information to help us, in other contexts, when we have qualitative evidence such as witness testimony, arriving at precise probability estimates seems much harder. The answer is not to fixate on probability as a measure of something objective in the world, but as a measure of our uncertainty – which is often qualitative and comparative rather than precisely quantitative. But this does not mean it has no grounds – we can often draw on our expertise, experience and causal knowledge to ground our judgments. What's key is that these judgments are not *merely* subjective, and are open to critique and improvement.

Finally, the probabilistic definition of relevance by itself seems overly simplistic, and it's unclear how it deals with complex cases. We are rarely faced with just one hypothesis and one item of evidence, so we need to scale up the definition to apply to more complex structures, involving multiple interconnected hypotheses and pieces of evidence. Assessing the LR in a complex structure is non-trivial. And we often have to deal with non-exhaustive (and possibly non-exclusive) sets of hypotheses, which makes the relation between evidential support and LRs more subtle. We address this issue in Section 6.4 and in Chapter 10.

6.4 Credibility and Reliability of Evidence

So far we have focused on the relationship between evidence and hypothesis. But, in order to assess how well evidence supports a hypothesis, fact-finders must also address questions about the credibility of the source of the evidence. Is the witness honest? Did she get a good view of the incident? Can she accurately remember what she saw? Simply put, credibility modulates the degree to which an evidential report accurately represents the hypothesis at which it is aimed. Lack of credibility can severely downgrade the probative force of witness testimony, making it unsafe to rely on for subsequent inferences.

The terms *credibility* and *reliability* are often used interchangeably, but in legal contexts credibility is usually reserved for questions about the honesty or veracity of a witness, whereas reliability concerns questions about the witness's accuracy. For example, whereas Emile Gourbin's testimony about his whereabouts at midnight was dishonest, the testimony of his friends was honest but inaccurate.

While such judgments seem effortless, they often involve complex patterns of reasoning. We must infer the witness's beliefs and intentions, their reasons for giving the testimony that they do, and the relation of that testimony to the other evidence presented in the case. Thus, we must deal with several unknowns simultaneously, interpreting what is claimed under various different suppositions (about the witness's honesty and accuracy). This requires mastery of an intuitive theory of mind (he's saying X because he believes X), and recursive or nested inferences (he's saying X because he thinks it will convince me that X).

Despite this complexity (or maybe because of it) in legal proceedings the evaluation of credibility is typically left to people's common sense. Exceptionally, the judge gives specific directions to the jurors, or an expert on memory is called upon (to warn against known biases in eyewitness testimony). But mostly lay people are entrusted with assessing another person's credibility, and indeed this is a cornerstone of the jury system.

6.4.1 Testimonial Evidence

The paradigm case of testimonial evidence is when a witness makes a specific claim about something they have observed 'first hand', such as a witness report that she saw the suspect loitering at the crime scene. Witness testimony can be evaluated along several dimensions (Schum, 2009):

- Credibility
  - Is the witness telling the truth?
  - Does the witness have a motive to lie?
  - Is the witness in general trustworthy?
- Reliability
  - Perceptual – did the witness accurately observe what happened?
  - Memory – did the witness accurately recall what happened?
  - Belief – are there cognitive biases that shape their testimony?
  - Context – are there external factors that shape their testimony?

Credibility often hinges on the witness's underlying reasons for saying what they did. Naturally, the accused has a motive to lie, as do his family and friends. But testimony from partial witnesses should not be fully disregarded. Sometimes they tell the truth, and, if not, discovering a lie can tell us something important about the accused's guilt (see Chapter 10 for an analysis of when adverse inferences can be drawn from a fabricated alibi). Detecting deception is a difficult task, and often requires additional inferences about the motives behind a witness's claims (see Chapter 10 for a simple model of deception).

Assessing reliability also involves complicated inferences. A witness's accuracy depends on a range of cognitive and situational factors, which operate at various stages in the process from when the events were (allegedly) observed through to the testimony given in court. These stages roughly divide into the phases of perception, retention and recall. Consider a witness who claims to have seen the suspect leaving the crime scene. The witness's ability to perceive the events in question depends on her observational sensitivity: was her eyesight good, was she paying attention, what did she expect to see, and so on; and external conditions such as the duration of the events, the time of day, whether her view was obstructed, and her distance from the events. Then there is the intervening period before the witness is questioned, during which time memories are known to decay and to be sensitive to intrusions. Perhaps the witness discusses the incident with other witnesses and is influenced by their accounts. Then the police interview, and the task of identifying the suspect from a line-up, videos or photos. These procedures are also known to create biases, especially if the identification process is poorly designed (Wells & Olson, 2003). Finally, when the witness testifies in court, and is cross-examined, another set of factors can distort her testimony, such as leading or intimidating questioning, thus further compromising her reliability.

At each stage of the testimony process, therefore, many factors influence and possibly undermine the witness's reliability. And the same applies to other forms of testimony, such as confessions (where coercive interview techniques can lead to false confessions) and jail-house informants (where the motives of the informant are highly suspect). These situations all serve to highlight the complexity behind judgments of credibility and reliability, and the need to examine the dynamic process that produces witness testimony.

6.4.1.1   Tests of Credibility

Legal theorists have proposed various tests for assessing credibility (Bingham, 2006; Eggleston, 1978):

- *Plausibility*
  - How plausible or probable are the events claimed by the witness? An extraordinary claim, which defies the common course of events, should reduce the witness's credibility.
- *Consistency*
  - Is the witness's account internally consistent?
  - Is the witness's account consistent with testimony from other witnesses, or with other agreed facts in the case?

- *Credit/demeanour*
  - o The *credit* of the witness – both general factors about their char-
       acter, and their credibility on issues not directly relevant to the
       case. Credit is usually established during the presentation of testi-
       mony and under cross-examination.
  - o The demeanour of the witness when giving evidence or answering
       questions.

These tests make intuitive sense. In particular, probing a witness's account
to test for its consistency with other testimony and evidence in the case is a
crucial part of fact-finding. And cross-examination is a powerful tool to
generate new evidence, both about what happened and the credibility of
people's accounts.

   But such testing is non-trivial. The different tests interact in complex
ways: for example, to assess the consistency of one witness's testimony with
that of other witnesses, whose credibility is also under examination, requires
a parallel evaluation of several moving parts. And while examining the credit
of a witness extends the net of relevant evidence, it also adds to the
complexity of the chains of inference. Finally, judgments of consistency
require holistic assessments across a network of interconnected claims.

6.4.2   Physical Evidence

In some ways assessing the reliability of physical evidence is more straightforward because it does not rely solely on the testimony of a witness and
inferences about hidden mental states. Nonetheless, questions about its
reliability still involve a complex set of issues. It will be presented and
interpreted by someone (usually an expert), and often involves a method of
analysis that is not open to immediate scrutiny.

   Three main factors arise in assessing the reliability of evidence:

- *Authenticity* – is the item of evidence really what it is claimed to be? Is
  this the gun that shot the fatal bullet? Is this blood-stained shirt from
  the victim? Is this DNA from the crime scene, or was it deposited at the
  lab? The chain of custody of the evidence is crucial here, and any
  breaks in this chain can cast doubt on its authenticity.
- *Integrity* – how well preserved is the sample? Has there been decay,
  contamination or interference?
- *Accuracy* – how reliable is the method or procedure that produces the
  evidence? This applies both to general concerns about the method
  (e.g., bite-mark or hair analysis have poor reliability) and also possible
  errors in the application of the method in a specific case.

Forensic evidence in particular presents several challenges (Banks, Kafadar, Kaye & Tackett, 2020; Murrie, Gardner, Kelley & Dror, 2019; Saks & Koehler, 2005). Most kinds of trace evidence – DNA, fingerprints, gunshot residue, fibres, soil and pollen – require complex analyses using methods and technologies that go well beyond common-sense knowledge. Such evidence is interpreted and presented by experts, and it is hard for a non-expert to assess the validity or reliability of their analyses. For example, DNA evidence is the product of an extensive testing process, and its interpretation requires sophisticated statistical analyses which are inscrutable to non-experts (and sometimes use complex algorithms that are hard to scrutinize even by experts). DNA analyses also involve various assumptions that are impossible for a non-expert to evaluate, but which can be critical to the reliability of the test results.

The situation is even worse with other forms of forensic evidence, where the reliability of the methods is unknown, even by the forensic practitioners who employ them. Many kinds of forensic analysis still lack validation and operate with assumptions that are questionable and non-scientific, notorious examples being bite-mark and hair analyses.[6] Hence, when presented in court, forensic evidence has huge potential to mislead. The significance and strength of evidence is often exaggerated, and the reliability of a method left unquestioned, with little acknowledgement of the possible errors. A striking example is the once-standard practice in hair analysis of reporting that hairs taken from the defendant are indistinguishable from those left by the offender, based on intuitive comparisons by an 'expert' but with no firm scientific basis for this judgment. These judgments might convince fact-finders (and judges) but in fact have very little probative value.

Ideally fact-finders should be given the error rates of the methods, or at least be informed about possible shortcomings and sources of error. Without this information it is impossible for a fact-finder to appropriately assess the reliability of the evidence produced. They are left to rely on their own intuitive judgments of the trustworthiness and competence of the expert, balancing this against the testimony of opposing experts (if available). The severity of these issues is highlighted by the detection of a large number of miscarriages of justice due to flawed forensic evidence (Garrett, 2011; Simon, 2012; Smit, Morgan & Lagnado, 2018; cf. Innocent Project).

---

[6] www.fbi.gov/news/pressrel/press-releases/fbi-testimony-on-microscopic-hair-analysis-contained-errors-in-at-least-90-percent-of-cases-in-ongoing-review

The question of expert evidence deserves mention here. As noted above, when an expert presents evidence, the fact-finder must assess the reliability of this evidence without having sufficient knowledge to critique the content of what is claimed, thus leaving them to rely on other indicators, such as trust of the expert. This holds not only when complex forensic evidence is presented, but also for expert testimony given by psychologists, medical experts and many others. Here again the ordinary fact-finder is hard pressed to assess the reliability of the evidence, and is thus vulnerable to being convinced by authoritative but inaccurate expert opinion (Dror, 2018). The Sally Clark case, discussed in Chapter 9, is a well-known example.

6.4.3   Summary

We have surveyed the challenges and subtleties in evaluating items of evidence: deciding questions of relevance, strength, credibility and reliability. I have argued that a purely probabilistic approach is insufficient; in Section 6.5 I will present a causal perspective on evidence to help us capture the complexity of the evaluation process.

6.5   Causal Model View of Evidence

Locard's exchange principle, that 'every contact leaves a trace', has become a guiding maxim in forensic science. But it also suggests a deeper thesis – that evidence is grounded in causal relations, such that the activities (causes) of interest generate a variety of traces (effects), and the task for an investigator is to infer the likely causes from these traces.

My proposal is that critical events of interest (such as a crime) trigger causal processes that radiate through the environment in myriad ways – by transfer and persistence, via objects and people, through physical and social transmission. These processes leave traces – marks, impressions, memories – which we can use as evidence to help reconstruct the original events. To complicate matters, however, operating in parallel are a host of separate processes that interact and interfere with the phenomena we care about. So the challenge is to sort out the critical causal pathways from the distracting and obfuscating thicket. At an abstract level, then, investigative thinking aims to detect and interpret the traces left by prior events, and causal inference is a vital tool in this endeavour.

Previously I argued that people use causal models to make sense of what has happened, allowing them to construct plausible explanations (see Chapter 2). Here I extend this claim to evidential reasoning, arguing that people also use causal models to help assess the relevance, strength and reliability of evidence. This is not merely a descriptive claim about what people actually try to achieve, but also a prescriptive claim about what we should do: that evidence is best understood and evaluated in a causal context.

I will use the causal model framework (introduced in Chapter 3) to make these claims more formal, exploiting the connection that the framework forges between causal structure and probabilistic dependence.

6.5.1 Relevance

While contemporary accounts of relevance focus on probabilistic criteria, we have seen that this alone is not sufficient. We want a criterion that supports both qualitative and quantitative evidence, and gives some guide to how people should reason about evidence. Intriguingly, an earlier definition of legal relevance given by Stephen (1876) was also couched in causal terms:

> Facts, whether in issue or not, are relevant to each other when one is, or probably may be, or probably may have been – the cause of the other; the effect of the other; an effect of the same cause; a cause of the same effect: or when the one shows that the other must or cannot have occurred, or probably does or did exist, or not; or that any fact does or did exist, or not, which in the common course of events would either have caused or have been caused by the other.

As well as proposing that relevance depends on causal relations, Stephen's definition clarifies that one fact A is relevant to another fact B, not only if B causes A, but also if it is connected to A via a less direct causal connection, such as when A and B have a common cause or a common effect. In the spirit of this approach, I propose a conception of relevance couched in the causal model framework, using the connection it forges between probabilistic dependence and causal structure:

> Evidence E is relevant to Hypothesis H if E probabilistically depends on H, relative to a causal model M (and some setting of the variables in that model).

This definition makes relevance relative to a causal model.[7] It captures both 'direct' cases – where H is a cause of E – and 'indirect' cases – where

---

[7] For a related perspective on evidential relevance, which casts it as a three-place relation between an evidence claim, a hypothesis and an argument, see Cartwright and Hardie (2012).

H is connected to *E* via an indirect path. It is consistent with probabilistic notions of relevance, but also applies to more complex contexts.

Three key features of this definition are:

- It is based on qualitative causal structure, and thus judgments of relevance can be made without knowing or estimating probabilities, and without specifying the exact functional relations between variables.
- It depends on the settings of other variables in the model, which allows for relevance of evidence conditional on what else is known or assumed in the case.
- By making relevance relative to a causal model, it allows for debate about what constitutes an acceptable causal model, with the possibility of justifying this choice through argument and evidence (for instance, based on accepted empirical knowledge and generalizations).

The proposal also fits nicely with the informal definition of cause from Pearl et al. (2016), that one variable (*H*) is a cause of another variable (*E*), if *E* 'listens to' *H* in order to decide its value (see Chapter 3).

To see how this proposal works, I illustrate with a few simple examples. First, consider 'direct' cases, where there is a causal path from *H* to *E*. A clear-cut paradigm is the single-link model:

$$H \rightarrow E$$

For example:

Measles → Spots
Suspect strangled victim → Powder match

H is a (potential) cause of *E*, thus *E* probabilistically depends on *H*. Hence *E* is relevant to *H*, because knowing the truth or falsity of *E* changes the probability of *H*. For example, the presence of spots is relevant to whether someone has measles because it changes the probability of measles. Likewise, finding the victim's face powder on the suspect's hands is relevant to whether he strangled the victim because it raises the latter probability.

Single-link models are naturally extended to causal chains, where there are one or more intermediate variables on the causal path from *H* to *E*.

$$H \rightarrow X \rightarrow E$$
Exposure → Measles → Spots
Suspect wanted to kill victim → Suspect strangled victim → Powder match

Here *E* depends on *H*, via the intermediate variable *X*, and is therefore relevant to *H*. For example, the presence of spots is relevant to whether someone has been exposed to the measles virus because it changes the probability of the person having measles, which in turn changes the probability of exposure. Likewise, finding the victim's face powder on the suspect's hands is relevant to whether he wanted to kill the victim because it changes the probability he strangled her, and thus the probability he wanted to kill the victim.

In all these cases there is a causal path from hypothesis to evidence, and hence the evidence is relevant to the hypothesis. Note that according to the causal model framework, knowledge of an intermediate variable (X) would screen off E from H, thus rendering E and H conditionally independent. Does this make E irrelevant to H? If X is an accepted fact, then, on this model, E no longer contributes anything to H. But note that if the truth of X is disputed, E would be relevant to H. Also, the simple model itself might be disputed: it might be argued that there is a causal connection from E to H that does not go via X, in which case E is relevant to H despite knowledge of X.

More subtle cases arise when there is no causal path from H to E, but the variables are connected through an indirect path. There are two basic structures in which this can occur: common causes and common effects.

In a common-cause model, one variable C causes both E and H:

$E \leftarrow C \rightarrow H$
Fever $\leftarrow$ *Measles* $\rightarrow$ *Spots*
Evidence $\leftarrow$ *Motive* $\rightarrow$ *Crime*
Report $\leftarrow$ *Jealous* $\rightarrow$ *Crime*

On this model, E is relevant to H due to its connection through C. For example, evidence of spots is relevant to whether someone also suffers from a fever. This is because knowing about the spots changes (raises) the probability of measles, which in turn changes (raises) the probability of fever. Similarly, evidence that a suspect has a motive for a crime is evidence that he committed the crime because the motive is itself a contributing cause of the crime. Applied to the Gourbin case, evidence that Gourbin was jealous was relevant to whether he killed Marie because it gave him a motive (raising the probability that he carried out the crime).

Finally, we have a common-effect structure, where two variables have no direct links between them, but they share a common effect. For example, suppose that measles and allergy are causes of spots (see Figure 6.1a). Prior to knowing someone has spots, these two causes are independent, and thus knowing someone has an allergy is irrelevant to knowing whether she has measles (and vice-versa).

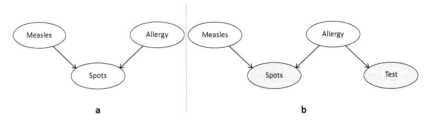

a   b

Figure 6.1   Common-effect model. (a) Measles and allergy are independent. (b) Measles and allergy become dependent conditional on evidence of spots, and a test for the allergy is then relevant to whether someone has measles.

However, once we know a person has spots, then measles and allergy become dependent. Knowing or getting evidence about one can change our probability in the other. Thus, evidence about the result of a test for the allergy is relevant to whether the patient has measles (see Figure 6.1b). More specifically, a positive test would increase the probability she has an allergy, and thus reduce the probability of measles (explaining away the spots as evidence for measles); in contrast a negative test would increase the probability of measles (see Chapter 3, Section 3.6.1.3).

To take the crime example, suppose that a forensic lab claims that the suspect's DNA matches the profile found at the crime scene, but the defence team question the significance of this report on the basis that the forensics lab might have made an error. The claim of a lab error is connected to the claim that the suspect was at the crime scene via the common effect of the DNA match (see Figure 6.2). In this case, evidence that the lab used a faulty process is relevant to whether the suspect was indeed at the crime scene. For example, perhaps the examiners used the same lab to test both the suspect's DNA and the DNA from the crime scene, thus increasing the risk of contamination.[8]

Such cases can appear counter-intuitive, because variables that are causally unrelated become relevant to one another given some information about their common effect. This magnifies with more complex networks of hypotheses and evidence, where relevance switches according to what else is known in the network. Indeed, people seem better attuned to evidence when it is a causal consequence of the events under investigation, and find more remote and indirectly connected evidence harder to

[8] Standard forensic practices should avoid this type of error, but it does sometimes happen. For example, see www.manchestereveningnews.co.uk/news/greater-manchester-news/forensic-procedures-criticised-as-man-wrongly-799500

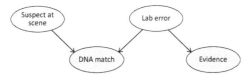

Figure 6.2   Common-effect model for DNA match. Evidence of a lab error is relevant to whether the suspect was at the scene, given the DNA match.

evaluate. From a formal viewpoint, however, the criterion of relevance is naturally scaled up to complex structures (Pearl, 2009; see Chapter 3).

6.5.2   *Strength of Evidence*

The causal model framework also provides a means to quantify the strength of causal links between variables – and thus evaluate the probative force of individual items of evidence – as well as a method for integrating these individual judgments into holistic judgments for all (or any subset) of the evidence.

Consider first the ideal case where we have a fully parameterized causal model; that is, all the variables in the model have fully specified probability tables (see Chapter 3). Here we can compute the posteriors for the hypotheses of interest given any set of evidence.

But getting a complete set of parameters is itself a challenge. Sometimes we might have information from empirical databases, such as in medical domains with established risk factors, incident rates of diseases, conditional probabilities of symptoms given diseases, and test error rates. But in legal and everyday contexts we often lack relevant statistical information, and must use estimates based on common sense and experience. Here is where the causal approach gets its bite because we can apply our causal knowledge to help quantify the links, despite the lack of pre-given probability information.

Rather than leave common experience as a black box (as is standard in legal discussions), it can be unpacked using insights from causal modelling. The key idea is that fact-finders can use their knowledge to help estimate the strengths of the links between variables in their models. Causal knowledge can help us parameterize our models in various ways.

6.5.2.1   *General-Level Causal Knowledge*

Experience and instruction give us rich general-level causal knowledge of the physical and social world. In particular, we encode stable estimates of the powers and tendencies of causes to produce their effects and can transport these estimates to new circumstances. When we build models of specific situations, we can draw upon this knowledge to estimate the strengths of causal links, and thus quantify (roughly) strength of evidence. For example, knowing that X is a potent cause of Y, and Y is rarely caused by anything else, we can assign a high value to the evidential support that Y provides for X. In contrast, if A is a rare and weak cause of B, then B provides only weak support for the presence of A. The more refined our measures of causal strength between variables, the more precise our assessments of evidential force; but even rough comparisons can be incredibly useful.

6.5.2.2   Specific Causal Factors

Moreover, we can use this world knowledge, plus case-specific details, to identify causal factors that might enable or disrupt the causal connections from hypothesized events to evidence. These 'disturbance' factors are key to predicting the consequences of causes (Pearl, 2009), but they also help us judge how strongly the observed evidence supports the hypothesized causes. For example, knowing that viewing conditions were extremely good makes it more likely that a witness accurately reports what she saw, and thus her report provides stronger evidential support for her claim. In contrast, knowing that conditions were very poor reduces the probative force of her testimony.

The ability to generate alternative causes of the observed evidence is also crucial for evaluating strength of evidence: the stronger (and more prevalent) the alternative causes, the weaker the support provided by the observed evidence for our target hypothesis. Adopting a causal framework is a natural way to incorporate the influence of alternative causes.

Indeed, the need to assign strength to links can often be side-stepped by generating causal explanations that perfectly predict the evidence, thus shifting the focus onto estimating the prior probabilities of these alternative causes. For example, consider the jogger example from Chapter 4. The police observed a pattern of fingerprints on the gun, and came up with various hand positions that could have caused this pattern. Essentially they assigned a probability of one to the observed pattern *given* each plausible position. So their judgment of which cause was most likely, given the evidence, reduced to a comparison of their priors.

In sum, by viewing evidence against a causal backdrop, we have a wider range of information to help us refine and quantify our judgments of evidential strength. Moreover, basing our judgments on causal knowledge makes them more objective in the sense of appealing to features of the external world to ground such judgments, but retains an inevitable 'subjective' element insofar as people make these judgments relative to their own causal knowledge and beliefs. While the use of causal models makes evidence evaluation more feasible, it still allows for the intrusion of systematic biases into human evaluations – indeed, it potentially explains some of these biases (see Chapters 4, 7 and 8 for examples).

6.5.3 Reliability and Credibility

Taking a causal perspective on evidence also illuminates how to evaluate reliability and credibility. Here again we construe evidence as the result of a complex set of causal processes emanating from the events of interest but interacting with other processes that enhance or disrupt their observed effects. The factors that dictate reliability and credibility of evidence are thus also potential causes – enabling, inhibiting or alternative causes – that modulate the resultant reports or testimony, and thus affect their evidential value.

6.5.3.1 Physical Evidence

We identified three factors in assessing the reliability of physical evidence – authenticity, integrity and the accuracy of the methods – and all involve causal processes. The chain of custody of evidence, such as preserving a gun or jacket found at the crime scene, is a causal process through which the identity of objects must be tracked (from crime scene to police lab to court), and protected from interference. Similarly, trace evidence (blood, hair, DNA, GSR) gathered at the crime scene, or sampled from the suspect, must be preserved for examination, introducing a causal process with multiple possibilities for disruption and contamination. In all such cases, the probative value of the evidence can be moderated (or undermined altogether) by causal factors that intervene on the path from discovery to evaluation.

6.5.3.2 Reliability of Testing Procedures

Forensic testing is a crucial phase where interfering causes can reduce the strength of evidence by undermining the reliability of the testing procedures. Consider a case where an athlete's blood is tested for the presence of a specific illegal drug. We start with a simple model:

Drug → *Test*

This model represents a single causal link between two variables: the presence (or absence) of the drug causes a positive (or negative) test result. But as with all forensic tests the drug test is not perfect, suffering from two types of error:

- *False positive* – test result is positive, but the drug is not present
- *False negative* – test result is negative, but the drug is present

Various factors can cause these errors. For example, false positives might be due to other substances in the blood that trigger the test, and false negatives might be due to substances in the blood that mask the presence of the drug. Our knowledge of these factors helps us quantify the evidential value of the test. One approach is to incorporate them into the conditional probabilities for the test, where the false positive corresponds to P(*positive test* | *no drug*), and the false negative to P(*negative test* | *drug*). A likelihood ratio can then be calculated to measure the evidential value of the test. Alternatively, these factors can be represented as specific variables in the causal model, making the causal role of these factors more transparent (see Figure 6.3).

Note that in most of the causal models in this book, we focus just on the factors that lead to false positives because our cases usually involve positive tests or identifications, but sometimes it is important to model the possibility of false negatives – for instance, where evidence that is expected does not appear – and thus analyze the factors that might interfere with the production of the expected evidence.

6.5.3.3 More Complex Models

The use of forensic evidence often involves multiple stages from discovering the trace to analyzing and reporting the evidence. Hence various opportunities arise for the reliability of the evidence to be compromised.

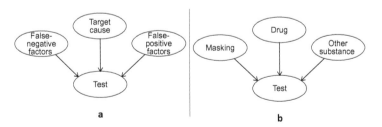

Figure 6.3   Causal model of testing reliability. (a) Generic model of the separate factors that can lead to false-positive or false-negative results. (b) Drug testing example.

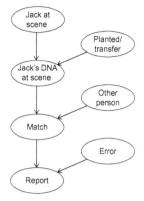

Figure 6.4   Extended causal model for DNA evidence.

The analysis of DNA evidence presents a good example, despite its reputation as a silver bullet in criminal cases.

We have already provided an extended causal model for the case of DNA evidence (see Chapter 4), and we re-use that model here (see Figure 6.4). A match is reported between Jack's DNA and traces found at the crime scene. This report supports the claim that Jack was at the crime scene, but involves a sequence of steps, each of which admits of alternative explanations. Only once we take these factors into account can we assess how probative the reported match is for the hypothesis that Jack was present. Typically, the probability of each error will be low, but they should not be ignored, especially if the DNA is the only evidence in the case. (In Chapter 10 we revisit this model and show how these factors can affect the probability of the hypothesis).

The key point here is that by considering possible interfering causal factors and alternative causes at each stage of the process, we can better assess the overall reliability of the evidence, identifying factors that might compromise its probative force.

6.5.3.4   *Testimonial Evidence*
Modelling the credibility of testimony follows the same principles, except it is often more complex because it requires the modelling of cognitive processes, including people's reasons for providing testimony. We must assess the sincerity and competence of the witness in providing their testimony. As we saw above, testimony can involve complex processes of perception, memory, belief and communication.

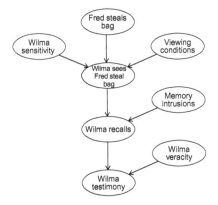

Figure 6.5   Extended causal model of witness testimony.

Consider a situation where a witness (Wilma) claims to have seen the suspect (Fred) steal a handbag from someone in the street.

Fred steals bag → Wilma sees Fred steal bag → Wilma recalls event → Wilma testifies to event

Each of the steps from the claimed event to the witness's testimony admits of alternative explanations (see Figure 6.5). For example, whether or not Wilma saw Fred take the bag depends not only on whether Fred actually took the bag but also on several other factors, including Wilma's capacity or competence to observe this event (her eyesight), and the viewing conditions (did she get a good view, was the street crowded and so on). Likewise, whether she recalls this event accurately depends on the time delay between the incident and the recall, and any intervening events that might disrupt or modify her memory. Finally, when she testifies, the content of her testimony depends not just on what she can recall, but also on her intentions to tell the truth (rather than mislead).

By modelling the causal process from claimed event to testimony we can uncover the factors that might disrupt this process, and thus how the credibility of the testimony might be undermined and its probative force reduced. Or perhaps enhanced, if we can rule out potentially disrupting factors.[9]

---

[9] The approach to testimony is closely related to Friedman's route model analysis (1988) and proposals by Bovens and Hartmann (2002).

6.6 Summary

In this chapter we have examined the legal concept of evidence and the key factors of relevance, strength and reliability. I have argued that a purely probabilistic conception of evidence is insufficient, and presented a causal perspective on evidence. The causal approach provides a unified framework to capture the interrelations between hypotheses and evidence, and helps us to assess probabilistic relevance and strength. This perspective lays the foundation for a principled approach to modelling legal cases, which I develop in Chapter 10.

CHAPTER 7

Competing Causes

In the human mind, one-sidedness has always been the rule, and many-sidedness the exception. Hence, even in revolutions of opinion, one part of the truth usually sets while another rises.

On Liberty, John Stuart Mill (1869)

7.1 The Murder of Jill Dando

The TV presenter Jill Dando was murdered outside her flat in London in 1999. Killed by a single gunshot to the head. Neighbours saw a man in his thirties running from the flat. Gunshot residue was recovered from the scene but no other forensic evidence. Police speculated that it was the work of a hired hitman; but, despite a massive investigation, no progress was made for over a year. Then Barry George entered the frame. A loner with learning difficulties who lived nearby, with a prior conviction for sexual assault. On the day of the crime George had visited a disability centre and taxicab office, and several people reported that he had returned after a few days insisting they give him an alibi. When interviewed George protested his innocence, but he gave an inconsistent account of his movements at the time of the crime.

On searching his flat, police found piles of newspapers, including pictures of Dando and other TV presenters, and magazines about guns. Photos also showed him handling a replica gun. The police were building a case against him, but had nothing to link him directly to the crime. Then they found the 'smoking gun'. Forensic tests on his overcoat revealed a single particle of gunshot residue (GSR) in the coat pocket. This residue matched the GSR found in Dando's hair. George was charged with murder.

In the trial the prosecution portrayed George as a dangerous loner, obsessed with celebrities and firearms. They presented four main lines of evidence: that several witnesses had identified him near the crime scene, that he had lied under interview, that he had attempted to provide a false alibi, and that the GSR evidence linked him to Dando's shooting. The defence questioned the accuracy of the eyewitnesses, and the relevance of his inconsistencies under interview. They also criticized police procedures in handling the GSR evidence, arguing that the coat could have been contaminated with GSR during the police search or subsequent analysis of the coat. The prosecution in turn rejected these claims, arguing that the chances of finding GSR in the coat pocket were very low on any of these 'innocent' explanations, and thus could be discounted. Barry George was found guilty and sentenced to life.

The first appeal was unsuccessful, but a second appeal was launched five years later. Its main basis was new forensic analysis, which suggested the GSR evidence had no probative value because the GSR particle was as likely to have arisen from contamination as from George shooting Dando. The judges accepted this argument and ordered a re-trial. In the second trial the GSR was not admitted, and therefore no evidence linked George to the crime. He was found not guilty.

This case raises questions about the legal process, and the nature of investigative reasoning. We will return to the case to re-examine how the court reasoned about the GSR evidence.

In this chapter we look at subtleties that arise when people evaluate evidence, in particular when they are confronted with alternative causes of the same evidence. I will identify a new fallacy in evidential reasoning – the zero-sum fallacy – and show how both legal experts and lay people are prone to this error. But on the positive side I will also show that people are pretty good at qualitative causal reasoning, despite using simplifying strategies.

7.2 Competing Causes

Investigative reasoning often involves deciding between competing explanations of the evidence. Was the victim murdered or did he commit suicide? Were the fingerprints on the trigger left by the victim or someone else? Is the witness lying or telling the truth? Do the blood test results indicate drug X or drug Y? These decisions are the bread and butter of legal and everyday enquiries. But the notion of *competing* explanations hides various subtleties.

7.2.1 *Competing Explanations Need Not Be Exclusive or Exhaustive*

The archetypal notion of competing hypotheses is that they are *mutually exclusive*, such that the truth of one excludes the truth of the other.

For example, murder and suicide are mutually exclusive hypotheses about someone's death.[1] However, explanations can still compete even if they are not mutually exclusive. For example, the presence of drug X or drug Y in someone's blood can compete to explain a positive drug test, even though both drugs might be present. Finding out that drug X is present reduces the probability of drug Y because it is 'explained away' (see Chapter 3). But at most the probability of drug Y is reduced back to its prior value; it is not ruled out altogether (as it would be if drug X and Y were exclusive). Moreover, if drug X and Y do not predict common evidence, then knowledge of X would not impact on Y, so no competition occurs. Thus, competing but non-exclusive hypotheses sometimes mandate different patterns of inference from exclusive hypotheses.

Competing hypotheses also need not be *exhaustive* – that is, both hypotheses might be false (as compared with exhaustive hypotheses, where at least one must be true). Thus, in our example of the jogger's death in Chapter 4, murder and suicide are not exhaustive hypotheses: the jogger might have been killed accidentally (or killed himself accidentally). Murder versus not-murder would be exhaustive categories, but less helpful because not-murder covers a mixed bag of alternatives.[2] For simplicity's sake, people often treat hypotheses as exhaustive, especially when other possibilities are considered very improbable. Thus, in the police investigation of the jogger's death, the possibility of an accidental killing was not considered. This simplifies subsequent reasoning, but can lead to errors, such as excessive confidence in the target hypothesis and neglect of viable alternatives.

A common assumption is that competing hypotheses are both *mutually exclusive* and *exhaustive*: that is, one, and only one, of them is true. This can greatly simplify inference, making probabilistic computations easier. Hence with only two hypotheses, evidence that raises the probability of one hypothesis automatically lowers the probability of the other, and vice-versa. In such cases the two hypotheses are like opposite ends of a balance, and evidence that speaks for one side automatically speaks against the other. With multiple hypotheses, eliminating one hypothesis means the

[1] One might come up with an imaginative example where someone is *both* murdered and commits suicide at the same time – but for practical purposes these causes of death are treated as mutually exclusive.

[2] More generally, a hypothesis (*H*) and its negation (~*H*) form an exhaustive (and exclusive) pair. But operating with the negation of a hypothesis is often problematic, as it can include a whole range of alternatives, some of which are unknown, and thus assessing the probability of the evidence given ~*H* can be difficult.

probability of the others must increase (although exactly how the probability is redistributed depends on the priors and likelihoods of these
alternatives).

When this assumption holds, it is much easier to assess the impact of
evidence, and the 'balance of evidence' metaphor works well. However,
when competing hypotheses are independent, this metaphor can be misleading and lead to erroneous inferences. Effectively one is reducing a
common-effect structure (where an evidential variable has multiple parents) to a simpler two-node structure (where a single parent has multiple
exclusive and exhaustive states as hypotheses). Such simplifications can
lead to biases in evidential reasoning, as is shown both in real legal cases
and in psychological experiments (see also Chapter 4).

7.2.2   *Hydraulic Causes?*

A classic finding in social psychology is that people treat competing but
independent causes *as if* they were exclusive, inferring that the presence of
one cause discounts the probability of the other (Nisbett & Ross, 1980).
This *hydraulic assumption* (Heider, 1958) has been applied to how lay
people explain human behaviour, and in particular their tendency, when
explaining someone's actions, to appeal to either internal characteristics of
the person or external circumstances (Alicke et al., 2015). For instance,
when inferring why someone has an angry outburst, evidence that he has
an angry disposition will discount the possibility the outburst was due to
an aggravating situation. This tendency is closely related to a preference for
unitary rather than multi-factor causal explanations.

The strong claim that people treat internal versus external causes of
behaviour as hydraulic has been qualified in subsequent research, and in
some contexts discounting has been shown to follow normative principles
(Morris & Larrick, 1995). Nonetheless, the basic phenomenon, that
people make inferences *as if* causes are exclusive rather than independent,
seems robust, and has repercussions for evidential reasoning in general.
A related but more subtle error involves people disregarding evidence that
is equally well explained by two competing causes.

7.3   The Zero-Sum Fallacy

Treating competing causes as hydraulic is akin to assuming that evidence is
a zero-sum resource, such that evidence in favour of one explanation is
evidence against the other. This has the consequence that the same

evidence cannot support both hypotheses, and thus evidence that is equally predicted by two competing explanations offers no support to either. But, as we have shown above, this only holds if hypotheses are exclusive and exhaustive. Applying such zero-sum reasoning in contexts where these assumptions do not hold can be dangerous.

Let us return to the case against Barry George. In the second appeal the defence argued that the GSR evidence had no probative value, partly because there was such a small amount, but also because it was as likely to have arisen from poor police handling procedures as from George shooting Dando. The defence quantified these two probabilities, stating that both were around 1/100. That is:

- $P(GSR \mid George\ shot\ Dando) = P(GSR \mid handling\ errors) = 1/100$

On their analysis the likelihood ratio for the evidence was equal to one, and therefore the GSR had no probative value. This argument was accepted by the judges, and the appeal was successful. A retrial was ordered, in which the GSR evidence was ruled inadmissible; in the second trial Barry George was found not guilty.

Was the court's argument flawed?[3] It assumes that if a piece of evidence (the GSR in the coat pocket) is equally probable under two competing hypotheses, then it cannot support either of these hypotheses. But this only holds if the two hypotheses are mutually exclusive and exhaustive. And this assumption is clearly not met in this case: it is possible that both hypotheses are true, and also that neither is true. Rather than being neutral, the GSR evidence is probative against George (even though it might only be of weak strength).

To see this formally, we can represent the situation using a causal model, with *George shot Dando* and *Handling errors* as two possible causes of the GSR evidence (see Figure 7.1). We assume these two causes are independent. Crucially, since both are positive causes of GSR, and they don't interact in any strange way, then the GSR evidence should increase the probability of both (perhaps not to the same degree; this depends on their relative strengths and priors).

This positive increase for both hypotheses is guaranteed so long as we assume that the causes combine in a straightforward way. More specifically:

---

[3] It is important to note that we are not questioning George's innocence – indeed the case against him was weak on many grounds; but we are raising doubts about the court's argument that the GSR evidence was non-probative.

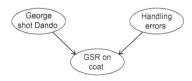

Figure 7.1   GSR model for the Jill Dando case: two possible causes of the GSR.

- If both causes are present, the probability of GSR is greater than if only one cause is present
- If neither cause is present, the probability of GSR is less than if only one cause is present

Given these assumptions, and so long as the priors for the causes are neither zero nor one, it can be shown that the GSR always provides some probative value for *George shot Dando*, such that P(*George shot Dando* | GSR) > P(*George shot Dando*),[4] although this value might be small (depending on what values we assign to the CPTs).

   To further illustrate, consider how this works with some specific numerical values. To parameterize the model we need priors for each cause, and CPTs for the GSR variable. In the appeal, the defence gave values for two of the conditional probabilities:

- P(*GSR* | *George shot Dando*) = P(*GSR* | *handling errors*) = 0.01

We can use the *noisy-OR* assumption to derive the probability of GSR given both hypotheses are true:

- P(*GSR* | *George shot Dando & handling errors*) = 0.02

And let's assume that the probability of *GSR* given neither hypothesis is true is very low:

- P(*GSR* | ~ *George shot Dando & ~ handling errors*) = 0.001

We use uniform priors for the two causes, but, as noted above, the GSR will be probative for *George shot Dando* irrespective of the exact priors (see Figure 7.2a).

   Using these values, the model shows that the GSR increases the probability that *George shot Dando* from 50% to 73% (see Figure 7.2b).

   A key thing to note is that both causes increase in probability given the GSR evidence. So while the GSR discriminates between *George shot*

---

[4] A proof is given in Pilditch, Fenton and Lagnado (2019).

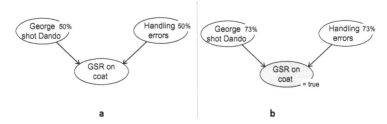

Figure 7.2   GSR model with probabilities. (a) Model with prior probabilities. (b) Updated probabilities given the GSR evidence.

Dando = *true* and *George shot Dando* = *false*, which is the judgment we care about, it does not discriminate between *George shot Dando* = *true* and *Handling errors* = *true*. One reason people might be misled when evaluating the GSR evidence is if they focus on the latter comparison rather than the former. That is, if they mistakenly infer that because the GSR does not discriminate between the specific prosecution and defence accounts, then the evidence is not probative. But this would only hold if the hypotheses were exclusive and exhaustive.

Indeed, the general set-up of criminal trials can encourage such mistaken thinking; the court must decide between the prosecution and the defence accounts, which although usually exclusive are rarely exhaustive. Nonetheless it is common for people to argue using the 'balance of evidence' metaphor, such that evidence for one side is automatically evidence against the other side, and vice-versa. While this approach might work well most of the time, in some contexts it can be seriously misleading.

The reasoning error in the Barry George appeal was committed in the highly charged context of a criminal appeal, involving legal and forensic experts. But it raises an issue that goes to the heart of standard methods for evaluating evidence in terms of likelihood ratios (Fenton, Lagnado, Hsu, Berger & Neil, 2014), and also arises informally in many contexts in which lay people reason about evidence.

7.4   Zero-Sum Thinking in Common-Sense Reasoning

How pervasive is zero-sum thinking in lay reasoning?

Consider the following scenario:

> Ann is suspected of handling explosives. Police use the Griess test for the presence of nitroglycerine on her hands – a standard test for detecting whether someone has handled explosives. Reliable empirical research shows

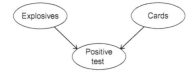

Figure 7.3   Two possible causes of the positive test in the explosives case.

that the probability of testing positive is 95% if someone has handled explosives. However, the test can also give positive results for another reason. Ann claims she was playing cards shortly before being tested. Reliable empirical research shows that the probability of testing positive is 95% if someone has handled cards.

Ann tests positive.

Does a positive Griess test result give any support to the claim that Ann has handled explosives?

Yes/No/ Cannot tell

We presented over a thousand participants with these kinds of scenarios (Pilditch et al., 2019). Their responses were typically spread evenly across the three options (so only about one-third said 'yes'). But the correct response, based on the analysis above, is 'yes'.

Here again the scenario can be captured with a common-effect model (see Figure 7.3), with Ann handling explosives (*Explosives*) and Ann handling cards (*Cards*) as independent causes of the positive test (+*Test*). These causes are non-exclusive (both can be true) and non-exhaustive (there are other possible causes of the positive test result).

The positive test supports the claim that Ann has handled explosives, increasing its probability from whatever its value was prior to the evidence: $P(explosives \mid +Test) > P(explosives)$. This holds true irrespective of the priors one assumes for the causes, and for any reasonable parameterization of the CPT for the test variable.[5] The positive test also increases the probability that she was playing cards: $P(cards \mid +Test) > P(cards)$. But, as pointed out above, while the positive test fails to discriminate between either cause, it does discriminate between *Explosives* = true and *Explosives* = false, which is what we care about in this investigative context.

These findings were robust across different scenarios, and despite instructions that sought to clarify the non-exclusive and non-exhaustive

---

[5] In particular, the result holds if the probability of a positive test is higher when both hypotheses are true than when only one is true, and is lower when both are false (see proofs in Pilditch et al., 2019).

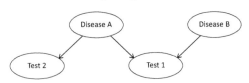

Figure 7.4   Zero-sum reasoning in test selection. Test 1 is more reliable than Test 2.

nature of the two hypotheses. Moreover, when people were presented with
a negative test result, they correctly judged this as disconfirming both
hypotheses, but did not see that if a negative test could disconfirm a
hypothesis, then a positive result should be able to confirm it.

The initial studies focused on people's qualitative judgments of evidential support because we wanted to show that the reasoning errors were not
merely due to problems of computation. Further work has used quantitative versions of the task, giving participants priors for the two hypotheses,
and seeing how these were updated in the light of the test result. When
given priors of 50% for each hypothesis, most participants did not change
their judgments when presented with the positive test evidence, confirming the zero-sum effect in a quantitative setting. However, when given
priors of 10% for each hypothesis, participants did increase the probability
of both hypotheses, but only to a cap of 50%. Thus they still seemed to
treat the hypotheses as exhaustive and reasoned as if the test provided a
fixed sum of evidential support, such that at most each hypothesis could
reach 50% (for similar findings see Tesic, Liefgreen & Lagnado, 2020).

Finally, we also looked at whether zero-sum thinking might influence
people's choice of which new evidential test to conduct (Pilditch, Liefgreen &
Lagnado, 2019). For example, participants were given the task of determining
whether a patient had disease A, and had to choose between an evidential test
(Test 1) that was highly reliable but did not discriminate between diseases
A and B, versus a less reliable test (Test 2) that depended solely on A, and was
not connected with B (Figure 7.4). Across a range of tasks and different
parameter settings, participants showed a marked preference for the less
reliable test rather than the more informative test. Again, this is explained
by zero-sum thinking, and the assumption that a test result (Test 1) which is
equally predicted by another hypothesis (B) provides little support for the
target hypothesis (A).

We thus have converging evidence that lay people make erroneous
inferences when faced with competing but non-exclusive or non-
exhaustive hypotheses. We posit that these errors are based on a miscon-
ception of evidential support as a finite, shared resource across the

hypotheses under contention. This zero-sum notion of support is appropriate only if hypotheses are both exclusive and exhaustive. But, in general, evidential support is not a zero-sum game, and reasoning from this assumption can lead to ignoring valuable evidence. While zero-sum thinking might work as a simplifying strategy in certain contexts, it has adverse consequences if used as a universal rule.

7.4.1 Simplifying and Simulation

How does this error relate to the reasoning principles identified in Chapter 4? It clearly suggests the use of a simplifying strategy. If we assume that competing causes are exclusive (and hydraulic), our inferences become easier, and will often correctly track the qualitative pattern of explaining away. But the error also seems related to the principles of *simulation* and *specificity*. As discussed in Chapter 4, people often use *ease of simulation* to judge how well a causal hypothesis explains the evidence (cf. Kahneman & Tversky, 1982b). Therefore, when we assess the support that evidence E gives to one of two competing causes (A and B), it is natural to compare how well either cause generates the outcome. If they both do so equally well, we rightly conclude that E does not discriminate between them.

But, as we saw above, this comparison does not answer the question of whether E supports A versus its negation ($\sim A$), and this is what we need to know in order to assess the evidential support E provides for A. Using simulation to get the right answer here is tricky, because we need to estimate how likely E is given $\sim A$. This is a harder judgment to make, especially if $\sim A$ covers a range of possible sub-hypotheses. We would need to simulate each, and then compute a weighted average across them. It's not surprising if people instead stick to comparing A and B.

7.5 Scaling up to Larger Structures

So far we have focused on three-variable models, but most evidential reasoning involves larger bodies of evidence. To explore how people deal with competing causes in a more complex case, Shengelia and Lagnado (2020) gave people a streamlined version of the child abuse case (introduced in Chapter 5) and examined how they updated their beliefs as evidence was presented. Participants were first presented with the case background:

> *Background*: A young child was brought to hospital by his parents because they noticed the child had bleeding in his mouth. The parents had no explanation for the bleeding, and said the child had not been involved in an

accident. Doctors suggested two possible causes for the bleeding: abuse and a rare blood disorder. Figures from previous hospital admissions suggest that 1 in 100 children admitted with bleeding to the mouth have been abused by their parents, and 1 in 1000 have the rare blood disorder.

[Note that it is possible that both causes are true: e.g., that a child has been abused and has the disorder; it is also possible that neither is true, and that the symptoms arise due to other causes.][6]

Main Questions:

- What are the chances that the parents abused the child?
- What are the chances that the child has the blood disorder?

After giving their initial probability judgments, participants were presented with the evidence item by item, and made new probability judgments after each item.

Evidence Items (with Probability Judgments Given after Each Item):

- Upon further examination, the doctors noticed bruising on the child. Both abuse and the blood disorder can cause bruises.
- Fractures are a common consequence of abuse, but not of the blood disorder. The hospital radiologist carried out an X-ray on the child. He reported that the X-ray showed fractures.
- Further tests were carried out. The child was tested for the blood disorder, and he tested positive.
- Prior to taking the case to court, an independent expert radiologist employed by the prosecution re-examined the X-ray results and claimed there were no fractures.

The case is sufficiently complex to require various types of inference – prediction, diagnosis and explaining away – yet simple enough to be captured by a causal Bayes net model against which to compare people's inferences (see Figure 7.5).[7]

A distinctive feature of the study is that people needed to update their beliefs about two independent hypotheses – abuse and the blood disorder – and were told that these were neither exhaustive nor exclusive.

---

[6] In our initial study this information was not made explicit, but in subsequent studies it was presented after each question.
[7] Note that in a separate study we asked people to draw their causal models of the case, and most participants constructed the causal graph shown in Figure 7.5.

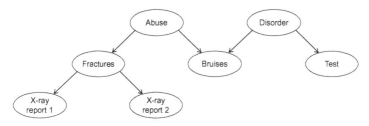

Figure 7.5   Causal Bayes net of abuse case.

We also elicited each participant's estimates of the parameters for the causal model, so we could construct an individualized causal model for each participant. These estimates were elicited as a set of conditional probability questions: e.g., 'If a child has the blood disorder, what's the probability he will test positive?' and so on for each conditional probability. Therefore, rather than rely on externally given probabilities, we used people's own estimates, and thus could evaluate their reasoning according to their own individualized causal models. This allowed us to focus on quality of reasoning, rather than how well people estimate initial probabilities.

The mean probability parameters are shown in Figure 7.6, but note that each participant gave their own individual estimates. We can then use these individualized models to predict what inferences each participant *should* make if they correctly apply Bayesian updating.

From a normative viewpoint the case requires several distinct patterns of inferences. The qualitative side of these inferences is illustrated in Figures 7.7–7.10.

As well as giving qualitative inferences, the causal Bayes net, once supplemented by a set of probabilities, can be used for exact numerical computations too.

7.5.1   Empirical Results

We depict both people's actual judgments, and those predicted by their individualized Bayes net model, in Figure 7.11. The solid lines in the graph show how people updated their beliefs in the hypotheses of abuse and disorder with each new piece of evidence. The dashed lines show the causal model predictions, based on applying Bayesian updating to each participant's prior model.

Several findings emerge from this data. First, participants' judgments fit the qualitative predictions of their own normative models. That is, people

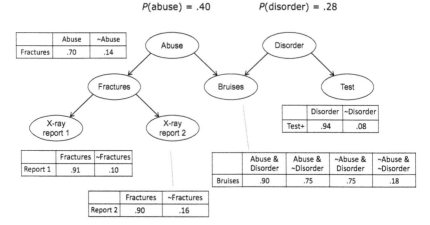

P(abuse) = .40   P(disorder) = .28

	Abuse	~Abuse
Fractures	.70	.14

	Disorder	~Disorder
Test+	.94	.08

	Fractures	~Fractures
Report 1	.91	.10

	Abuse & Disorder	Abuse & ~Disorder	~Abuse & Disorder	~Abuse & ~Disorder
Bruises	.90	.75	.75	.18

	Fractures	~Fractures
Report 2	.90	.16

Figure 7.6   Probability tables (CPTs) for each variable showing participants'
mean estimates.

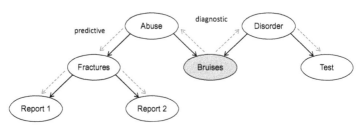

Figure 7.7   Inference in abuse model – *Step 1*: Evidence of bruises should raise the
probability of both abuse and blood disorder – via *diagnostic* inference – and thereby also
raise the probability of fractures (and X-ray reports of fractures) via *predictive* inference.

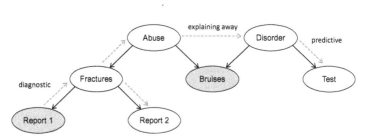

Figure 7.8   Inference in abuse model – *Step 2*: Report 1 of fractures should raise the
probability of fractures, which in turn raises the probability of abuse; this lowers the
probability of disorder via *explaining away*.

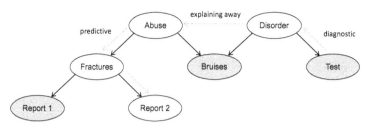

Figure 7.9   Inference in abuse model – *Step 3*: The positive test raises the probability of the blood disorder, which thus lowers the probability of abuse via explaining away; this in turn lowers the probability of fractures.

Figure 7.10   Inference in abuse model – *Step 4*: The second X-ray report (by the expert pathologist) says no fractures, which lowers the probability of fractures, which in turn lowers the probability of abuse and via explaining away raises the probability of disorder.

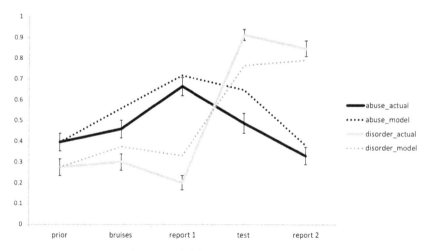

Figure 7.11   Participants' mean probability ratings of the two possible causes after each item of evidence, also compared with the mean of their individualized Bayesian models.

increase their beliefs when the normative model predicts an increase, and decrease their beliefs when the model predicts a decrease. There is one small departure from this, for the very final judgment of the probability of blood disorder, which decreases slightly rather than increasing. Follow-up studies show this is because participants, having found out that the initial X-ray report was unreliable, become slightly more sceptical about the blood test result. Overall, however, people show good qualitative reasoning, successfully navigating predictive, diagnostic and explaining away inferences.

Second, participants did not use the base rates given in background information, but instead introduced substantially higher priors. This highlights the importance of eliciting priors rather than assuming participants accept the stated base rates (as in many previous studies of probabilistic reasoning). It also suggests that people read more into the initial set-up, perhaps judging there is additional evidence to render abuse and blood disorder more likely than the base-rate population statistics.

Third, there are two areas where participants' judgment systematically either under- or overestimate the probative value of the evidence. Thus, given the evidence of bruises, participants under-weight the value of this evidence, and only slightly increase the probability of either hypothesis. This is an example of zero-sum thinking, where evidence that is predicted by competing hypotheses is taken as neutral. In this case, bruises are predicted by both abuse and disorder, so they are not seen as support for either causal hypothesis. Indeed two earlier studies showed *no change* of probability after the bruises evidence; therefore in subsequent studies we added a statement – presented before each probability question – clarifying that the two causes were neither exhaustive nor exclusive. This explicit statement slightly improved judgments, but participants still underestimated the impact of the bruises evidence.

Closely related are several instances of over-weighting: an excessive decrease in the probability of disorder given the first X-ray report, and an excessive increase in the probability of disorder given the positive test, combined with an excessive decrease in the probability of abuse. This shows the other side of zero-sum thinking: treating competing causes as exclusive and thus hydraulic, such that an increase in the probability of one hypothesis reduces the probability of the other more than that mandated by Bayesian explaining away.

Finally, note that despite such over- and under-weighting, by the final judgment people are close to the normative prediction. This shows that errors can cancel each other out across the course of an experiment, so it is important to elicit item-by-item judgments (if possible) to get a more accurate picture of the process of inference, rather than just rely on a single final judgment.

This study shows people's capability to handle complex structure, emphasizing their use of qualitative causal reasoning over exact Bayesian computation. It also highlights the use of zero-sum thinking as a simplifying strategy to make workable inferences. For this problem the exact probabilities did not play a crucial role; thus people's qualitative reasoning led to sensible final answers. We expect that a lot of cases are decided in similar ways, and as long as the exact numbers aren't critical (as might be the case with DNA evidence), people's inferences will not suffer too much from the use of simplifying strategies.

7.6 Summary

In this chapter we explored some subtle errors that arise when people evaluate evidence. In particular, we showed that both legal experts and lay people commit a zero-sum fallacy, whereby they assume that evidence which is equally predicted by competing causal hypotheses has no probative value for either. However, on a positive note, we also found that in a complex legal case people are pretty good at qualitative causal reasoning, despite still endorsing this fallacy. More generally, in line with the principles advanced in Chapter 4, people appear to tackle evidential reasoning by constructing causal models and using strategies that simplify inference.

CHAPTER 8

Confirmation Bias
The Good, the Bad and the Ugly

It is a capital mistake to theorize before one has data. Insensibly one begins to twist facts to suit theories, instead of theories to suit facts
'A Scandal in Bohemia', Arthur Conan Doyle (1891)

8.1 Introduction

Madrid suffered an awful terrorist attack in 2004, when several bombs exploded at the main train station, killing 192 people and wounding many more. Police found a bag of detonators in a van nearby, with fingerprints on the bag. As part of a global investigation the FBI checked the prints on their database and identified 20 possible matches. One of these was Brandon Mayfield, an attorney and ex-military officer living in Oregon, USA. He was a convert to Islam, and had recently represented a client connected to the Taliban. Mayfield became the prime suspect, and fingerprint experts declared that his prints '100% matched' those found on the bag.

The Spanish police disputed the fingerprint match, but the FBI persisted in their claims and arrested Mayfield. The match was 'confirmed' by another independent expert. However, soon afterwards the Spanish police matched the fingerprints to an Algerian suspect based in Spain. Mayfield was freed. He later received $2 million in compensation; the Office of the Inspector General (OIG) (2006) cited 'confirmation bias' as one reason for the error.

8.1.1 Ubiquitous but Multiple Meanings

Confirmation bias, broadly defined, is the selective gathering and weighting of evidence to support a specific hypothesis, and the failure to gather or recognize evidence that counts against that hypothesis (Nickerson, 1998). It is one of the best-known cognitive biases, both inside and outside

Table 8.1 *Taxonomy for confirmation bias.*

	Search	Evaluation	Presentation
Good	Generate *most plausible* hypotheses Choose diagnostic tests that can confirm or disconfirm expectations E.g., Positive test strategy	Strategies that approximate Bayesian updating Appropriate weighting and integration of evidence	Balanced selection
Bad	Generate hypotheses from flawed theories Fail to conduct tests that might support alternatives	Over-weight positive evidence and under-weight negative evidence	Present evidence selectively to support own position
Ugly	Intentionally select and test hypotheses known to be flawed Intentionally ignore alternative hypotheses	Intentionally ignore or underweight disconfirming evidence	Intentionally distort selection – including non-disclosure of counterevidence

psychology. Whether it involves lay people in reasoning tasks, or investigators solving crimes, the bias seems pervasive (Rossmo & Pollock, 2019). However, confirmation bias is really an umbrella term, covering a variety of cognitive strategies, not all of which involve biases (Hahn & Harris, 2014; Klayman, 1995).

To help make sense of a vast field, I will organize the topic according to three stages of enquiry: search, evaluation and presentation. These stages interact, and a typical enquiry will involve interlocking cycles where hypotheses are generated, tested and then adapted, but the rough division maps onto separable phases in a typical enquiry. Cutting across these stages, I identify confirmatory strategies as good, bad or ugly. Roughly, a strategy is *good* if overall it fits with the truth-seeking goals of the enquiry, and *bad* if it undermines these goals (and hence deserves the term 'bias'). *Ugly* is reserved for those strategies that are intentionally misleading: they subvert the goal of truth, but serve the goal of persuading other people. See Table 8.1 for the full taxonomy.[1]

---

[1] To keep things simple I avoid some finer-grained questions, such as whether good strategies are knowingly good, although this is important when we look to improve people's reasoning.

8.2   Search

The first stage of search is to generate plausible hypotheses to explore and test. Although not often discussed in terms of confirmation bias, this stage is a precursor to evidence gathering, and can set up the possibility of bias. What models we construct depends heavily on our goals and our intuitive knowledge and theories. Selectivity is unavoidable – from a huge space of possibilities we need to select a few hypotheses or models to work on. An investigator confronted with a crime will prioritize hypotheses about what happened, who did what, how and why: their hypotheses will be suspect-focused, and based on knowledge about types of crimes, criminal behaviour, and so on (see Chapter 5).

This narrowing of focus is usually a good thing. Our prior expectations help us generate plausible hypotheses to work with, under time and resource constraints. But these benefits depend on the quality of our prior beliefs and assumptions: flawed theories will lead to weak hypotheses, and undermine our truth-seeking goals.

In addition, the tendency to focus on only one or a few hypotheses raises the chance of neglecting better alternatives (Evans, 2007). By itself this might not be too bad, if flawed hypotheses are disconfirmed and we then generate new ones; this is part of the trial-and-error cycle crucial to science. But if the narrow focus is compounded by biased testing and evaluation, flawed hypotheses might be spuriously supported. Even more dangerous is the setting up of a feedback loop, whereby the spurious confirmation of these hypotheses lends support to the misguided intuitive theories themselves. Such negative loops are pernicious, and can occur in real-world cases.

Hypothesis generation can also be ugly, when reasoners intentionally generate hypotheses that suit their own goals: to persuade rather than tell the truth. In such cases investigators push hypotheses that they know to be flawed, and avoid truth-conducive alternatives.

8.2.1   Searching for Evidence

The main focus of research on confirmation bias concerns the search for evidence. How do people decide what tests to conduct, which witnesses to interview, what questions to ask?

Here again people need to narrow the search space, selecting from a wide variety of possible tests and questions.

Ideally, enquirers would adopt an optimal testing strategy – computing how much informational value is expected from each test, and then choosing the test with the highest expected value. But this is a difficult task. They would need to consider the possible outcomes of each test (both positive and negative) and assess how useful each outcome would be – where usefulness is measured in various ways, such as how much impact it has on our beliefs or how much it reduces our uncertainty (Nelson, 2005). The usefulness of a test outcome is closely related to its *diagnosticity*,[2] which is defined in terms of the likelihood ratio (see Chapters 6 and 10); this effectively compares how much more (or less) likely an outcome is if the target hypothesis is true rather than false. Evidence is diagnostic to the extent that it discriminates between the target hypothesis and its alternative. Finally, we must weight the informational value of each outcome by the probability of getting that outcome, combining these assessments to derive an overall expected value for each test.

For example, consider a medical context where a patient has flu symptoms and we must choose between two tests, A and B, to determine if she has a specific virus. To compute the expected value of a test, we need to assess the usefulness of each outcome (positive or negative result). These values then need to be weighted by the respective probability that each will occur. Note that there is a balance here between usefulness and expectedness. When we know the virus is rare, we expect that a positive test is unlikely, and a negative test likely; however, a positive test would be more useful. We need to do these computations for both A and B, and choose the test with highest expected usefulness. No mean feat!

Unsurprisingly, people seldom attempt to compute the expected value of a test, even in domains such as forensics or medicine. The computations are complex, and often require information that is not readily available to the decision-maker. Empirical studies show that while people are sensitive to the diagnosticity of a test outcome – selecting tests that allow for better discrimination between hypotheses – they also tend to rely on simple strategies or heuristics. In some contexts these strategies approximate the optimal procedures, but in other cases they show a clear divergence (Baron, 2004; Coenen, Nelson & Gureckis, 2018; Liefgreen et al., 2020; Nelson, 2005; Oaksford & Chater, 2009; Skov & Sherman, 1986).

8.2.2   *Positive Test Strategy*

People often seek evidence that, if true, would confirm their expectations. They ask questions for which they expect to receive a positive response if

---

[2] Note that diagnosticity alone is not a suitable measure of usefulness, for several reasons (Nelson, 2005): it does not take into account the prior probability of the hypotheses; it can give infinite value to a test outcome that rules out a hypothesis entirely, even if that outcome is incredibly unlikely; it is only defined for a pair of hypotheses.

their hypothesis holds. For example, if the police believe that someone is a drug-user, they look for evidence that would confirm this hypothesis, by testing the suspect's hair or blood for the presence of drugs. Similarly, in the child abuse case discussed in Chapter 5, when doctors suspected the couple of abusing their baby, they looked for evidence of fractures, which they took to confirm the abuse hypothesis. Although commonly held up as a bias, this *positive test strategy* is not by itself flawed, and is often a reasonable strategy for uncovering the truth. Even if the police expect their suspect to test positive for drugs, and the doctors expect to see fractures, the evidence might turn out differently. In fact, in the child abuse case, while the doctors initially reported fractures, follow-up tests by an expert (hired by the prosecution) showed no fractures. Thus, this part of the abuse hypothesis was disconfirmed, despite the experts expecting the test to turn out positive.

Psychological research, mainly using abstract tasks, has found broad support for this positive test strategy (Klayman & Ha, 1987). In the classic 2–4–6 task (Wason, 1960) participants had to identify the rule underlying sequences of triplets of numbers, having been told that the sequence 2–4–6 conformed to the rule. Participants formulated hypotheses about the rule, and then tested these by proposing test sequences, receiving feedback as to whether or not their sequence fit the rule. The actual rule was highly general – any triplet with ascending numbers – whereas participants usually posited more specific rules, such as increases by two. The experimental 'trick' was that these specific hypotheses were subsets of the actual rule, and thus received confirmatory feedback. The key empirical finding was that people generated positive rather than negative tests of their hypotheses: for example, if someone entertained the hypothesis that numbers increased by two, they would propose 1–3–5 or 6–8–10 rather than 6–7–8 or 5–3–1. People often thought they had the right rule, due to these positive tests being confirmed, but they did not try to falsify their rule with a negative test.

While initially cast as a flaw in people's hypothesis testing, a positive strategy is now commonly seen as a reasonable method (Austerweil & Griffiths, 2011; Evans, 1989; Klayman & Ha, 1987; Oaksford & Chater, 2009). In part this re-conception is due to a shift from a normative standard of testing based on falsification (Popper, 1959) to a Bayesian approach (Howson & Urbach, 2006) that allows for confirmation (and disconfirmation). But in addition, Wason's initial studies on the 2–4–6 task were intentionally set up to ensure that using a positive test strategy could not solve the task. Subsequent research shows that in less contrived tasks the positive strategy is often well adapted to the context, and is an effective method (Klayman & Ha, 1987; McKenzie, 2004; Oaksford & Chater, 2009).

However, there are still dangers in sticking to positive tests. For one, as we shall see below, if investigators also overestimate the impact of a positive test outcome, then they will inflate the probability of the target hypothesis. In addition, the efficiency of a positive test strategy depends on the nature of the problem environment: sometimes it can undermine our testing goals. This is because the strategy only exposes our target hypothesis to one type of error: it can show that a positive (predicted) outcome of the hypothesis does not occur. But it cannot reveal another type of error: that a negative (unpredicted) outcome *does* occur.

Suppose the police have a prime suspect for a crime, and are seeking to show that he was at the crime scene. A reasonable strategy is to scour CCTV footage of the crime scene area to see if he appears. This is a positive test strategy – and finding him would confirm his presence at the scene. (Not finding him is less conclusive, especially if CCTV does not cover all of the crime scene and nearby areas). Here a negative test strategy might also be useful – looking at CCTV footage from elsewhere; if he is found, this would rule him out as a suspect. Balancing both types of search is often best.

However, note that in this example there is an asymmetry, because the crime scene area is typically much smaller and easier to search than the area outside the crime scene (which in principle covers a vast area). Given the inevitable limits in the magnitude of the search, the latter search is unlikely to reveal the location of the suspect, even if he was not at the crime scene.

This example highlights a key factor in determining the success of positive testing, termed the *rarity assumption*. If positive outcomes of a focal hypothesis are rare, then positive tests are more effective than negative tests; in such cases, on a Bayesian analysis positive tests are expected to be more informative, and have more potential for falsifying the focal hypothesis (Klayman & Ha, 1987; McKenzie, 2004; Oaksford & Chater, 2009). Translated to our example: searching CCTV near the crime scene is expected to be more informative than searching outside the crime scene; the latter search is unlikely to tell us anything useful, since (given a limited search) we are unlikely to spot the suspect, even if he was indeed outside the crime scene. It would be like looking for a needle in a haystack. However, the situation changes if the suspect claims to have been at a specific site outside the scene. It makes sense to look there. But now we are effectively switching to a positive test of a different hypothesis, which predicts that we should see him at this new site.

In sum, conducting positive tests of our hypotheses need not undermine the rationality of our search, and under suitable conditions this is actually an effective strategy.

8.2.3   What Might Underlie the Positive Test Strategy?

How does the positive test strategy link with other cognitive principles, such as our use of mental models and simulation? Evans (2007) offers an explanation which invokes both:

> when we mentally simulate a possibility, we naturally fill out our mental model with plausible content: what is likely to be the case if the supposition holds. This leads to positive expectations of what should occur and the formulation of positive predictions. (p. 47)

This claim is particularly applicable to the testing of *causal* models. For example, the causal models we use to investigate a crime mainly focus on positive expectations: the presence of a motive, an intention, a weapon, a murderous action, blood spatter, eyewitness accounts and so on. We want a concrete story of what happened, and also seek causal pathways that link the suspect to the crime. This ties in with our use of simulation too: we typically simulate a sequence of active causes and effects. This is not to say that we can't infer or simulate negative predictions too, but they are less readily accessible. Thus, a puzzle such as 'why the dog didn't bark'[3] is held up as a subtle piece of reasoning because it forces us to think of reasons for the absence of an effect.

Given our predilection for plausible causal models, it's not surprising that our hypothesis testing is likewise oriented towards testing for positive effects. We construct a model of what we believe happened, and look for positive effects of this model. We find it less natural to search for causal effects that our model does not predict.

8.2.4   Extremity

As well as preferring questions that are more likely to yield a positive answer, people also prefer tests with more extreme probabilities of giving a positive answer. For example, when seeking to identify an unknown object (A or B) people prefer a test question that has a 90% of being true if A is

---

[3] In the Conan Doyle (1892) story 'Silver Blaze', Sherlock Holmes used the fact that the watchdog did not bark to infer that the dog knew the perpetrator of the crime.

true, and a 50% if B is true, over a question that has a 50% of being true if A is true, and a 10% if B is true (McKenzie, 2006). Both questions are positive tests of A – they are more likely to yield a positive result if A is true – but the first is more extreme than the second.

Again, by itself this preference need not lead to biased beliefs. Although you are more likely to receive a positive answer, this answer is less diagnostic – it will change your belief in the target hypothesis less because it is more expected. In contrast, an unexpected outcome would change your beliefs more, and thus is potentially more useful, but this outcome is also less likely to occur. For example, in the case of identifying the unknown object, the positive outcome is more likely, but will only increase your belief in A from 50% to 64%, whereas a negative outcome would reduce your belief from 50% to 17% (see McKenzie, 2006). Here there is an inevitable trade-off between the usefulness and the expectedness of an outcome (Poletiek, 2001). Expected results don't change our beliefs as much as unexpected results.

However, the preference for extremity (like the positive test strategy) can lead to bias if people fail to evaluate the diagnostic value of the outcomes properly; in particular, if they overestimate the value of a result that supports the target hypothesis and undervalue a result supporting the alternative (we explore an example below).

8.2.5 *Frontrunner Preference*

Most empirical work on evidence search uses binary hypothesis spaces: either a target hypothesis and its negation, or a pair of mutually exclusive and exhaustive alternatives. This restricted format makes it harder to generalize about people's inferences in more realistic problems. Liefgreen et al. (2020) introduce a more complex investigative paradigm – based on crime scene analysis – which allows for more than two target hypotheses (e.g., multiple possible perpetrators of a crime) and evidential tests that can yield more than two outcomes. Given this richer paradigm we show that many people have a 'frontrunner' preference – choosing evidential tests that would maximize the chances of one hypothesis (e.g., one suspect) standing out from the others, even when this is not the best choice according to optimal methods. We also show that people can modulate their strategies according to whether they are conducting a one-off test versus a sequence of tests, and that a poor decision early on in an enquiry can mislead people in subsequent stages. Here the frontrunner preference is not an irrational bias per se. Sometimes it is efficient, but at other times it can lead to sub-optimal search.

We have seen how confirmatory strategies at the evidence search stage can be good or bad, according to the conditions under which they are applied. They can also be ugly: for instance, if investigators wilfully restrict their search to evidence that they know will support their hypotheses, and avoid tests they expect will falsify them. Unfortunately, tales of corrupt investigations are common in the literature (Rossmo, 2008), although there is little empirical work on this question.

8.3   Evaluating Evidence

Another key stage is evidence evaluation – how people assess evidence and use it to update their beliefs. We have already seen in Chapter 4 that people are not perfect Bayesians, instead using various simplifying strategies, and this applies to hypothesis testing contexts too. Of particular danger is when a systematic bias in evaluation interacts with an asymmetric testing strategy.

As noted, search strategies such as the positive test strategy and extremity preference are not intrinsically biased, but can lead to errors if combined with flawed evaluation. Thus, if one adopts a positive test strategy, and overestimates the diagnostic value of positive test outcomes, then a distinct bias towards the target hypothesis will follow. This seems a common error in crime investigations, arguably in play in several high-profile cases, such as the cases of Sally Clark (see Chapter 9) and Barry George (Chapter 7). It also occurs in studies of hypothesis-testing, such as tasks requiring people to identify unknown objects based on shared features; in such tasks people mainly conduct positive tests and often overestimate the value of positive outcomes (Rusconi & McKenzie, 2013). One explanation for this finding is that people assume that a positive test is at least as informative as a negative test, even in cases where the latter has higher diagnosticity (McKenzie, 2006).

A more blatant example is when investigators disregard negative outcomes altogether, and only focus on the positive results. Incredibly this happened in the Mayfield case, where the fingerprint examiners disregarded portions of Mayfield's prints that did not match the prints found on the detonator bag. They tried to explain away the mismatch, arguing it was a composite of two separate prints, but this was a very speculative attempt to preserve their target hypothesis.

More subtle problems arise when investigators use extraneous case information to help them evaluate ambiguous or equivocal evidence. In the Mayfield case, for example, the independent expert who re-examined the prints knew that they had previously been declared a match, and also knew about the other evidence against Mayfield. This information is likely to have biased the expert's own judgment.

Such a possibility is termed 'cognitive bias' in the forensic domain, and has been studied in a range of expert forensic domains, including fingerprint and DNA analyses (Dror & Charlton, 2006).[4] The main finding is that when forensic experts are faced with a difficult analysis, their judgment can be influenced by task-irrelevant information about the case. For example, when fingerprint examiners are asked to make difficult comparisons, they are more likely to declare a match to the suspect if they know about other incriminating evidence, and less likely if they know about other exonerating evidence (Kassin, Dror & Kukucha, 2013; but see also Curley et al., 2020).

The bias here is subtle because, while the extraneous information is irrelevant to the task of assessing the particular evidence item (fingerprint match, DNA, etc.), it is relevant to the truth of the ultimate hypothesis. Thus, a suspect's confession is probative of guilt, and should be combined with the fingerprint evidence when fact-finders make *their* judgment about the overall impact of the evidence. But the forensic expert should not incorporate this extraneous evidence into their own assessment of the fingerprint evidence. Doing so risks double-counting the confession evidence: it now exerts an influence on the fingerprint report too. It also means that the examiner strays outside their area of expertise and beyond the remit of their analysis. For example, a fingerprint expert should not be expected to incorporate evidence about DNA tests, confessions or alibis in their own analysis; the probative force and reliability of this evidence needs to be analyzed separately (ideally by a different expert).

Cross-contamination between separate sources of information is not just restricted to forensic tests, but can occur with other forms of evidence, such as eyewitness testimony, alibis and confessions. For instance, knowledge of a suspect's confession can influence an eyewitness's identification of the suspect. The problem is exacerbated if the same person is involved in several testing stages, and therefore knows the results of prior tests when

---

[4] The work on cognitive biases is rapidly gathering momentum in the legal and forensic domain, and paints a dire picture. However, it's still too early to know the full extent of the problem, without broader psychological studies (cf. Curley, Munro, Lages, MacLean & Murray, 2020). Also, the broad-brush use of terms like 'cognitive' and 'confirmation bias' makes it hard to distinguish between genuine biases and sensible confirmatory strategies. Nonetheless this work raises awareness of the role of cognitive factors throughout the justice system. These have been ignored for too long or treated in a piecemeal and non-scientific fashion.

Figure 8.1   Different models for independent and dependent evidence. In the left-hand model the expert report and eyewitness report are independent sources of evidence; in the right-hand model the expert report is contaminated by knowledge of the eyewitness report.

conducting subsequent tests. It can also occur when different investigators share information about the case, with a knock-on effect throughout the case. This *snowball effect* can lead to investigators over-inflating the strength of the case against a suspect (Dror, Morgan, Rando & Nakhaeizadeh, 2017).[5]

An additional threat is that the fact-finder, who must make a decision based on all the evidence, is unaware of cross-contamination, and treats the different lines of evidence as independent. We have already mentioned the perils of mistakenly assuming independence (see Chapter 4). The key problem is shown using Bayes net models (see Figure 8.1). The actual cross-contamination is captured in the right-hand model side by a link from the extraneous evidence to the expert report, whereas the model tacitly assumed by the fact-finder omits this link (left-hand model). Mistakenly treating evidence items as independent makes us overestimate the probability of the target hypothesis (see Chapter 10 for a quantitative example).

The proposed cognitive bias, then, is compounded by a meta-level 'blind spot' – not realizing (or knowing) that separate lines of evidence are interdependent due to the cognitive biases of the investigators, examiners and witnesses. Presumably this interdependence is easier to detect in some cases, such as when two eyewitnesses collude, but harder to detect when different forensic experts have unintentionally 'colluded'.

[5] Indeed, Scherr, Redlich and Kassin (2020) propose a *multi-stage cumulative disadvantage framework* which tracks how biases and errors can accumulate against innocent suspects as they transit through the criminal system. They argue that confirmatory biases operate at multiple stages of the process, starting from police interviews and interrogations, through to the investigation of forensic evidence, eyewitness accounts and alibis, onto treatment by judges and juries, and continuing in post-trial appeals.

Several approaches seek to address these problems, such as blinding experts to extraneous information, using sequential unmasking of relevant but potentially biasing information, or using case managers to delegate blinded testing (Thompson, 2011). These methods seek to restrict experts to task-relevant information, while allowing that some tasks require a broader use of case information. They also aim to coordinate and distribute forensic analyses to avoid the same person working on several stages – such as gathering forensic evidence from the crime scene (where they will be exposed to a range of other case information) and also analyzing this evidence in the laboratory. For trace comparisons, such as DNA and fingerprint analysis, they recommend elaborate procedures to allow for prior analysis of crime samples before comparing with suspect samples. Properly implemented, these methods should reduce the risk of cognitive bias and snowball effects.

However, these methods cannot correct for biases within the mind of a single individual. When one person alone is responsible for testing and evaluating multiple lines of evidence, an internal 'snowball' effect seems hard to avoid. The fictional detective who solves a case single-handedly will presumably interpret one item of evidence in light of other pieces, and also based on his emerging view of the case as a whole (Thompson, 2011). More generally, in everyday contexts, where individual reasoners gather and interpret evidence by themselves, we would expect similar cascades. Simon, Snow and Read (2004) argue that legal decision-makers are prone to similar coherence effects, whereby they distort the evidence to fit with their emerging hypotheses and decisions (for a discussion of this view, see Lagnado & Gerstenberg, 2017). It remains an open question how pernicious this internal snowball effect might be in our everyday reasoning when confronted with multiple lines of ambiguous evidence.

Finally, what about the dangers of people manipulating this phase of investigation on purpose? Given that legal decision-makers will often be unaware of the possible cross-contamination and biases in evidence evaluation, this seems a natural juncture where unscrupulous parties can take advantage. For example, someone might actively manipulate the extraneous task information given to examiners to make a forensic test turn out as desired, or knowingly present cross-contaminated evidence to the fact-finders as if it is independent.

8.4 Presentation Stage

Presenting evidence, whether to other decision-makers in the investigative process, or to fact-finders in court, is also a key step in an enquiry. People usually need to select a subset of evidence to present from a larger body of evidence, and here too there is scope for confirmatory strategies and biases. A blatant example is when investigators or lawyers present only that subset of evidence that favours their party's interests, and leave out unfavourable evidence. For instance, in the case against Barry George for the murder of Jill Dando (see Chapter 7), the prosecution argued that George was obsessed with Dando, and as evidence they presented numerous newspapers with photos of her, found in his flat. What they failed to make clear was that George hoarded thousands of newspapers, and the police had selected only those that featured Dando. Moreover, she was a huge celebrity at the time and featured regularly in the papers.

Digging a bit deeper, there was some evidence to support the claim that George was obsessed with female TV presenters. But this evidence did not support an obsession for Dando in particular, which is what the prosecution asserted. They selected their evidence to support this contention, and thus misled the jury.

Adversarial contexts encourage the biased selection of evidence. If one of your goals is to persuade others of your viewpoint, it's only natural to accentuate evidence in favour of your account and downplay opposing evidence (unless you can rebut it). Indeed, some psychologists argue that the primary function of reasoning is for us to argue with and persuade others of our own opinions (Mercier & Sperber, 2011). But this does not mean that the standards of good reasoning disappear: the biased selection of evidence still undermines accuracy (whether or not this is your primary goal).

The problem of what evidence to present is acute, even in non-adversarial contexts. How do you select a balanced sample of the evidence, given that random selection is not an option? You need a meta-level strategy – anticipating the best balance of evidence to report, in order to promote accuracy and avoid error. This requires assessing the impact of individual items of evidence, and how they fit together for overall impact. It also requires a model of how you expect your audience to respond to the evidence – how can you change their beliefs for the better? These are complex challenges, and again there is plenty of scope for confirmatory strategies. For example, if one has already over-weighted positive evidence in previous stages, this is likely to be exaggerated in the 'final cut'. This runs the risk of amplifying any prior biases, especially if the audience is blind to earlier phases in the process.

Returning to the legal domain, the challenge of what evidence to present is crucial at several stages of the process, such as when investigators submit a case to the Crown Prosecution Service, and when legal teams present evidence in court. One danger is that the fact-finders will only see a subset of the evidence gathered by either side, and their decision-making depends solely on what they see, with the expectation that this is the best of what evidence there is. While there are crucial rules of disclosure, this does not avoid the problem that the fact-finder receives only a filtered subset of the evidence.

An awful high-profile failure occurred in the Sally Clark case, a mother convicted of killing her two babies, when crucial evidence that one of the babies had an infection was not disclosed by the pathologist (see Chapter 9). But many legal cases also show the dangers when investigators or prosecutors fail to provide a balanced picture of the evidence (Simon, 2012).

8.5   Summary

We have seen that the term 'confirmation bias' covers various strategies that operate at different stages of an enquiry. Despite the term 'bias', these strategies are not always irrational. In some contexts they are reasonable and well-adapted to the goals of enquiry, but in other contexts they can lead us astray. One danger is when investigators fail to realize that their strategies are selective and biased. Without this meta-level insight into the way we gather and evaluate evidence, we risk distorting the impact of that evidence, sometimes with disastrous consequences. Thus, the detectives and fingerprint examiners involved in the Mayfield case, and the police compiling evidence against Barry George, all failed to take a meta-level view of the evidence, mistakenly interpreting it as firm support for their hypotheses.

The difficulty of taking this higher-level view – reasoning *about* rather than *from* the evidence – seems a basic shortcoming in how we evaluate evidence. But it is perhaps understandable given the huge demands that sound evaluation requires. In Chapter 9 we will discuss how people's metacognitive awareness of their use of evidence might be improved.

CHAPTER 9

Telling Stories

*[A story] can only have one merit: that of making the audience want to
know what happens next. 'The king died and then the queen died' is a
story ... A plot is also a narrative of events, the emphasis falling on
causality – 'The king died and then the queen died' is a story. But 'the
king died and then the queen died of grief' is a plot. The time-sequence is
preserved, but the sense of causality overshadows it.*
Aspects of the Novel, E. M. Forster (1927)[1]

9.1 Introduction

Stories are pivotal to how we make sense of the social world. They help us
organize and store rich patterns of experience, explain people's actions and
behaviour, ascribe praise and blame, and persuade others of our view. Legal
contexts provide fertile ground for stories: human actions are usually the
central focus of an investigation or trial, and the prosecution seeks to tell a
story that will convince both judge and jury.

We start the chapter with the Sally Clark case, a terrible miscarriage of
justice that raises many questions about reasoning and decision-making
throughout the legal process. We then present the dominant theory of
juror decision-making – the Story Model – which argues that story
structures are central to how people make sense of complex evidence in
legal trials. I suggest how the Story Model might be augmented with causal
models, and also extended to include evidence evaluation.

9.2 The Sally Clark Case

In legal trials, where evidence is paramount, the drive for a plausible story can
conflict with the need for evidential support. This clash of aims – explaining

---

[1] Forster's use of the term 'story' is idiosyncratic – typically we would include both plot and causality
as part of a story. But it's a nice quote because it emphasizes the role of causality.

versus evaluating – is amplified when a case involves statistical evidence, which is notoriously tricky for people to handle. An example of this conflict arose in the tragic case of Sally Clark. She was the victim of an awful miscarriage of justice: wrongly convicted of murdering her two young children. Her conviction was eventually overturned, but it wreaked irreparable damage to her life and those around her. The case has become an exemplar of the misuse of statistics in a legal trial, but it also reveals the dangers of storytelling and the distortion of evidence to fit a powerful narrative.

9.2.1 Background

Sally and Stephen Clark, both solicitors, were married and lived together in a cottage in Cheshire. Their first son, Christopher, died suddenly at 11 weeks old. Sally was alone with the baby when he lost consciousness; she called an ambulance, but despite her efforts, and those of the emergency services, he could not be revived. The pathologist concluded that he died from a respiratory infection. One year later, the couple's second child Harry, aged 8 weeks, died in similar circumstances. This time the pathologist judged the death suspicious, identifying injuries consistent with shaking. He re-examined Christopher's death and revised his earlier judgment, now claiming this death too was unnatural, with evidence of smothering. Sally Clark was charged with double murder.

9.2.2 The Prosecution Case

At trial the prosecution alleged that Sally Clark had smothered both her children.[2] They relied on several expert witnesses, including the pathologist Dr Williams and Professor Meadow, an expert in child paediatrics. The prosecution argued that neither death was due to SIDS (Sudden Infant Death Syndrome or 'cot death') because both babies had prior injuries. They claimed that the many similarities between the two deaths 'would make it an affront to common sense to conclude that either death was natural, and it was beyond coincidence for history to so repeat itself'.[3] Among these similarities were the facts that both babies had died at similar ages, that both were found unconscious by Sally in the same room and at

---

[2] Shortly before the trial the prosecution changed their account of Harry's death from shaking to smothering. They discovered that the pathologist had erred in preparing slides, and mistakenly claimed that Harry had suffered intra-retinal bleeding, a classic sign of shaking. Without this key indicator death by shaking was considered improbable.

[3] Quote taken from the trial summary in the first appeal, *R* v. *Clark* (2000).

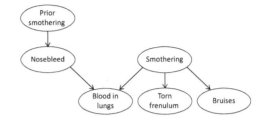

Figure 9.1　Causal model of the prosecution account of the injuries to Christopher.

Figure 9.2　Prosecution account of the injuries to Harry.

the same time shortly after a feed, that Sally was alone with the babies at the time of discovery, and that Stephen was away or due to go away.[4] According to Meadow these similarities pointed to death from smothering.

Crucially, the prosecution argued that both babies had suffered abuse and deliberate harm (see Figure 9.1). In the case of Christopher, Dr Williams presented three distinct medical findings: bruises to the arms and legs, a torn frenulum,[5] and blood in the lungs. The prosecution alleged that these injuries suggested he had been smothered to death. Furthermore, they argued that Christopher's nosebleed 10 days before his death was evidence of a prior smothering attempt.

For Harry, the prosecution presented evidence of prior abuse – injuries to the ribs and to the spinal cord, and death by suffocation – hypoxic damage to the brain and haemorrhages to the eyes and eyelids (see Figure 9.2).

The prosecution also attacked the credibility of Sally and Stephen. For instance, Stephen stated that on the night of Harry's death he had returned home at 5.30–5.45 pm. But taxi records showed that he had returned at 8.10 pm. The prosecution argued that Stephen was lying to protect his wife, minimizing the window of opportunity for Sally to kill her son.

---

[4] How unusual are these similarities? Although the prosecution made much of them (and this was repeated in the first appeal judgment) they seem relatively unsurprising, and would still be expected if Sally Clark had not killed her children but they had died of natural causes.

[5] The tissue between the floor of the mouth and the tongue.

Finally, the prosecution argued that it was incredibly unlikely for two babies in the same family to both die from cot deaths. Meadow gave evidence, based on a large-scale study, that the probability of two SIDS deaths in a family like the Clarks was 1 in 73 million. This figure was reached by squaring the probability of a single cot death (1 in 8,543). Meadow stated that a double SIDS death could be expected only once every 100 years.

9.2.3   The Defence Case

The defence argued that both boys died from natural causes. They gave alternative explanations for Christopher's injuries (see Figure 9.3), and questioned the reliability of Williams's evidence, which rested only on his own judgment and poor-quality photographs. Moreover, they claimed that even if this evidence was genuine, the injuries could have arisen during attempts to resuscitate him or in the post-mortem. However, they did not dispute the bleeding in the lungs, accepting it was consistent with asphyxiation.

The defence experts also disputed the causes of Harry's injuries (see Figure 9.4). They argued that spinal bleeding was a common finding in natural deaths, and that the dislocated rib probably occurred post-mortem. They argued that the evidence for inter-retinal haemorrhages was flawed due to an error in slide preparation by Williams, and that the bleeding in the eyes was a post-mortem effect. They accepted that the pinpoint haemorrhages in the eyelids were consistent with smothering, but argued that this was only a weak indicator. Overall, the defence experts concluded that Harry's death was 'unascertained', but agreed that it was not a case of SIDS.

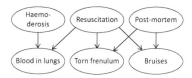

Figure 9.3   Causal model of the defence account of the injuries to Christopher.

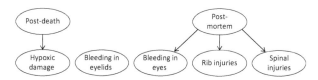

Figure 9.4   Causal model of the defence account of the injuries to Harry.

The defence also countered the claims that Sally and Stephen were unreliable witnesses. Stephen accepted that he had been mistaken in his initial timings, but insisted this was an innocent mistake and not an attempt to mislead the court. The defence argued it was implausible that a father would be so blind in his loyalty as to cover up for a wife who had murdered their two children.

Finally, the defence criticized the statistical evidence. They argued that the 1 in 73 million figure presented by Meadow was incorrect, and underestimated the chances of two cot deaths in the same family. In particular, simply squaring the figure for a single cot death ignored the possibility of familial factors making a family more prone to cot deaths. Despite the ambiguities in the medical evidence, and the misleading statistical evidence, Sally Clark was convicted of murdering her two children. She was sentenced to life imprisonment.

9.2.4   The First Appeal

The conviction was appealed, mainly on the basis that the statistical evidence was misleading. Two key points were made.[6] First, the calculation of the 1 in 73 million figure was flawed because it incorrectly assumed that SIDs deaths in the same family were independent events. This calculation ignored genetic or environmental factors that might predispose a family towards SIDS. The statistic presented by Meadow thus underestimated the chance of two SIDS deaths in the same family.

Second, the prosecution failed to explain how the statistic was relevant to whether Sally Clark murdered her children. By itself, the figure only concerns the probability that a family suffers two SIDS deaths. To make it relevant to whether Sally is guilty, it needs to be compared with the probability that a mother would murder both her children.[7] But the latter probability was not raised in court, despite the fact that even by a rough estimate it is much lower than the stated probability of two SIDS deaths. Without this alternative probability being presented in court, it is possible that the jury committed the prosecutor's fallacy, taking the figure of 1 in 73 million as the probability Sally Clark was innocent. The jury was not warned against this reasoning error, despite it being an acknowledged fallacy in legal cases.

---

[6] See Dawid (2002, 2005).

[7] Actually the court only needed to prove that one child had been murdered, which complicates the probabilistic analysis of the case (see Fenton, 2014).

The court of appeal rejected the first argument stating that the exact figure was irrelevant, since the key argument made by the prosecution was that the chance of two SIDS deaths was extremely low. The court acknowledged the possibility that the statistical figure had a larger impact on the jury than it should have, but concluded that the case against Sally Clark was nevertheless overwhelming, and they dismissed the appeal.

While Sally Clark was in prison, her husband and defence team still worked hard to prove her innocence. The turning point came when they discovered Harry's microbiological tests, showing he had been suffering from a bacterial infection. Numerous independent experts stated that this infection probably caused Harry's death. Incredibly, Dr Williams had known about these results prior to the trial, but had failed to disclose them because he considered them irrelevant. In fact during the trial the jury had asked whether there were any test results for Harry, and Dr Williams had responded that there were no relevant results.

9.2.5   The Second Appeal

In the second appeal the court agreed that Dr Williams's failure to disclose the test results had deprived the jury of crucial evidence. They also criticized Meadow's statistical evidence, arguing that this alone would have provided sufficient grounds for quashing the verdicts. Sally Clark was released.

9.2.6   Postscript

This judgment had a knock-on effect on many other cases in which mothers were accused of child murder, including cases where Professor Meadow had also been a key expert witness. Several convictions were overturned, and Meadow and Williams were both found guilty of serious misconduct. The final tragedy in this case was the death of Sally Clark in 2007. She died from alcohol poisoning, unable to recover from the loss of her children.

9.2.7   Lessons to Be Learned

The Sally Clark case tells us many things. Foremost, it is a tragic story of a mother who loses both her children, and is falsely convicted of murder. The struggle for justice, and her eventual release and exoneration, are overshadowed by the sadness of her consequent death. Second, there are practical lessons to be learned from the case, including the status and remit of expert witnesses. Finally, the case raises many questions about the nature of evidential reasoning, by jurors, lawyers, judges and experts. Indeed many of the themes developed in this book are illustrated by the case and its aftermath.

9.3   Key Lessons for Evidential Reasoning

The Sally Clark case, like most criminal cases, can be analyzed at several levels. At the *macro-level* it involves a conflict between competing stories told by prosecution and defence: a mother who murdered her babies versus an innocent mother struck by extreme misfortune. At the *micro-level* it involves a web of specific hypotheses about what happened, assessments of the medical and testimonial evidence, and interpretations of the statistical information. These levels interact, with narratives guiding the formation of hypotheses at the micro-level, while in parallel these hypotheses inform and revise the macro-level narratives. This dynamic process lies at the heart of sensemaking and data-frame theories of human decision-making (see Chapter 5).

Both levels are crucial for understanding how people reach judgments and how they communicate decisions to other parties in the process. While stories emphasize the holistic nature of a case, specific hypotheses seek to provide the finer-grain detail and explain the evidence.

9.3.1   Stories of the Case

The evidence in this case was complex, with extensive but ambiguous medical evidence, conflicting testimonies from clinical experts, and the notorious statistical evidence. Compounding this were questions about the credibility of both Sally and Stephen Clark, and the reliability and competence of Meadow and Williams. Inevitably the decision-makers in the case – prosecution, defence, medical experts, judge and jury – had to simplify this web of evidence, claims and counterclaims, to draw their own conclusions.

The prosecution presented a simple but powerful story. They portrayed Sally Clark as an unhappy mother, begrudgingly sacrificing her own career, and left alone to cope with a young child. Both deaths were explained according to this template: Sally killed her children and sought to cover up her crimes. This narrative explained most of the medical evidence and also the inconsistencies in Sally and Stephen's testimony; it also seemed to be supported by the statistical evidence, which emphasized the rarity of two SIDS deaths. Sally was thus singled out as the sole protagonist to blame.

The defence presented a very different account – not so much a story as a collection of disparate events that led to the two deaths and the pattern of injuries observed. Sally was cast as a caring and attentive mother, struck by the tragic misfortune of two infant deaths. While no definitive causes of death were identified, the defence invoked a confluence of separate factors to explain the injuries and medical evidence. Rather than assign responsibility to an individual, the deaths were attributed to incredibly bad luck, with perhaps some blame going to the medical pathologist for mishandling the evidence and thus allowing the case to go to trial.

Comparing these accounts is an onerous task. One needs to assess their prior plausibility and coherence, alongside how well each account is supported by the evidence. It's unclear how best to make this comparison, even using Bayesian modelling techniques (Neil, Fenton, Lagnado & Gill, 2019). Each account differs on multiple dimensions, including their coverage of the evidence, their fit with prior causal knowledge, the credibility of the testimony and evidence advanced in their support. They also differ with respect to broader criteria such as simplicity and coherence. For example, the prosecution story centres on a single dominant cause – a mother smothering her children – that generates most of the observed injuries and medical evidence, whereas the defence relies on several separate causes to explain the evidence. The prosecution story is thus simpler and easier to remember and communicate.

Moreover, the defence account seems *ad hoc*, tailored to explain the specific injuries observed (and also over-flexible, in the sense that one could recruit a similar set of causes to explain almost any pattern of injuries). By contrast, the prosecution story appears less ad hoc – the hypothesis of smothering predicts a distinctive pattern of injuries. But note that the actual details of the case complicate this simple picture – there were some injuries unexplained by the smothering hypothesis, and also some injuries expected on the smothering hypothesis but not observed. However, the process of simplification during and after the trial ironed out these inconsistencies.

While simplicity alone might favour the prosecution story, the rarity of a mother killing her children should be taken into account, and balanced against the rarity of two SIDS deaths. One also needs to consider the probabilities of the different causes of the pattern of injuries. These probabilistic evaluations were not handled well in the court case: the prosecution story crowded out a balanced consideration of the statistics, which were distorted to fit the prosecution story.

The first Court of Appeal judgment re-affirmed the prosecution story, while allowing for a few minor changes to the micro-level hypotheses, such as accepting that the statistical evidence had been overstated. The second appeal, however, abandoned the prosecution story altogether. They presented a new story in which Harry died from a bacterial infection, and Christopher's death was also due to natural causes. Meadow and Williams became the key protagonists to blame, and Sally was exonerated.

This story is now the standard version. The case has become a cautionary tale about the misuse of statistics in court, and also the need to validate expert witnesses. These are important lessons, but it is also notable that the central story of the case is now stripped of the complexities of the medical and testimonial evidence, and the inherent challenges in deciding such cases. This highlights a crucial feature of a story structure – its role in simplifying and compressing complex information in service of a central theme or message.

9.3.2   Micro-level Analysis of the Case

While stories drive people's understanding of a legal case, they are integrally connected with the specific hypotheses that subserve them. The Sally Clark case also exposes the challenges of reasoning at the micro-level, and the use of various human reasoning strategies.

9.3.2.1   The Need to Simplify
In tandem with building a cohesive story, which itself is a key simplifying device, various strategies were used at the micro-level. For one, the prosecution framed the case as a dichotomy between murder and SIDS, inviting the inference from not-SIDS to murder. But this framing was misleading, because it ignored other possible causes of death, in particular that one (or both) children died from an unspecified infection. This amounted to treating competing hypotheses as exhaustive, which as we've seen is a common but misleading route to simplifying a decision problem.[8] Some of the medical evidence was also simplified by contracting causal chains, and thus ignoring possible sources of uncertainty; for instance, the prosecution assumed the presence of bruising on Christopher, ignoring the inferential step from marks on the body to bruises.

---

[8] In fact, at the trial both prosecution and defence experts argued against SIDS – as strictly defined – whereas commentaries on the trial usually frame it as a dispute between SIDS and murder.

Most pernicious were the crude mistakes in Meadow's presentation of the statistical evidence: he falsely assumed independence of the deaths, and also invited the prosecutor's fallacy (equating the low probability of two SIDS deaths with the probability of innocence). In hindsight these mistakes seem obvious. But given what we know about how people struggle with probabilistic reasoning, it is not surprising that the jury were misled,[9] especially since the correct way of using the statistics was never presented in court.

Moreover, both Meadow and the judges in the first appeal also subscribed to a qualitative version of the prosecutor's fallacy – drawing on 'remarkable' similarities between the two deaths without considering the prior probabilities of these events, or their conditional probabilities if Sally was innocent. Indeed, none of the similarities seem particularly improbable on the supposition that the children died of natural causes. In short, the need to simplify the case promoted fallacious reasoning, and the jury were not given sufficient guidance to avoid common pitfalls in probabilistic reasoning.

9.3.2.2 Causal Reasoning

The case also illustrates the heavy role of causal reasoning to make sense of evidence. This holds both for the *physical* and *testimonial* evidence. The medical experts explained the children's injuries in terms of causal processes – smothering, resuscitation attempts, post-mortem effects – and also posited disrupting causal factors such as errors in slide preparation. These explanations drew on causal schemas based on medical knowledge and experience.

The parties also invoked psychological causes to explain human behaviour. The prosecution castigated Sally Clark's character, seeking to explain why she would kill her children. They also questioned Stephen Clark's motives (and his desire to protect his wife), seeking to explain why he gave inconsistent testimony. Here the explanations drew on common-sense intuitive theories about people's character, motives and intentions, and were invoked to persuade the jury.[10] But causal schemas are sometimes flawed, even when based on expert knowledge. Thus Meadow's causal theories about child abuse were overly simplistic and wrongheaded.

---

[9] Both types of error are common in lay reasoning (see Chapter 4).
[10] Note the dual role of these explanations – to make sense of evidence but also to persuade others of your account.

Likewise, the prosecution claims about Sally Clark's character relied on speculative stereotypes.

Causal and counterfactual thinking were also crucial to the judgments in both appeals. Judges had to decide whether the omission or mispresentation of evidence *would have made a difference* to the jury's verdict. In the first appeal the judges concluded that improving the presentation of the statistical evidence would not have affected the jury's verdict,[11] whereas in the second appeal a different set of judges argued that the statistical evidence was sufficiently misleading, and would have made a difference. Judges in the second appeal argued that had the jury heard evidence of Harry's infection, this would have affected their decision-making. These conclusions hinge on counterfactual reasoning, which in turn is based on intuitive causal theories, in this context how a jury would react to different evidence presentations.

Finally, most commentaries on the case, whether legal or popular, have relied on causal reasoning to explain why Meadow's statistical argument was flawed. They point to possible causal factors (genetic or environmental) that undermine his assumption of independence. However, the more costly mistake, the prosecutor's fallacy, is less often discussed, presumably because it is hard to explain without introducing probabilistic notions such as prior probabilities, likelihoods and Bayesian updating. This fits with the general idea that people find causal concepts easier to grasp, but struggle with probabilistic computations.

9.3.2.3   *Reliability and Credibility of Evidence*
The case also highlights the two key dimensions of an enquiry – building models to explain the evidence but also assessing the reliability and credibility of the evidence. As noted above, the credibility of Sally and Stephen Clark were crucial elements in the trial. In contrast, both Meadow and Williams were assumed competent in the trial and first appeal, but the second appeal judgment undermined their credibility, as did subsequent medical hearings. Combining these two dimensions is difficult, and here again shortcuts are inevitable, such as taking a binary attitude towards witness credibility (either believing or disbelieving) and expert competence, rather than making graded assessments. This kind of categorical approach greatly simplifies the overall task, but is known to introduce

---

[11] 'In the context of the trial as a whole, the point on statistics was of minimal significance and there is no possibility of the jury having been misled so as to reach verdicts that they might not otherwise have reached' (*R* v. *Clark*, 2000).

errors (cf. Dewitt, Lagnado & Fenton, 2018; Gettys et al., 1973; Johnson, Merchant & Keil, 2020). Once again the building of a story can override the subtleties of assessing reliability and credibility.

In short, the Sally Clark case shows us how stories play a key part in evidential reasoning, and the interplay between macro- and micro-level thinking. It also shows us how a compelling story can dominate and possibly distort the evaluation of evidence. Next we look at a cognitive model of legal decision-making based on storytelling, which supports our intuitive analysis of the Sally Clark case.

9.4 The Story Model of Legal Decision-Making

Everyone agrees that stories are crucial to legal reasoning: investigators use them to structure their enquiries and construct a case against the suspect; prosecution and defence teams use them to present and argue their cases in court, and jurors use them to make sense of the evidence and reach a verdict. But how do people construct and evaluate these stories? The dominant cognitive theory of how people use story structures to make legal decisions is the *Story Model* (Pennington & Hastie, 1986, 1988, 1992).

On the Story Model, jurors construct narratives to organize and interpret the mass of evidence presented in court. These stories draw on causal knowledge and assumptions, including scripts about how people typically think and behave. This knowledge is combined with case-specific information to construct causal *situation models* of what happened, usually based around human agency and social interactions. Jurors select the best story – one that explains the evidence, fits with their ideas about stereotypical stories, and satisfies various criteria such as coherence, plausibility and completeness (see Section 9.4.1). This story is then matched against the possible verdict categories to yield the juror's pre-deliberation decision.

9.4.1 Story Structures

One of the novel claims of the Story Model is that people develop rich narrative-based explanations of the evidence. This goes beyond simple evidence-integration accounts (Hogarth & Einhorn, 1992) where people compute a weighted sum of the evidence for or against the crime hypothesis. Instead, jurors are assumed to construct a story that makes sense of the evidence and supports a verdict in a more holistic fashion. These narrative structures are usually based around the actions of human protagonists, and are generated from abstract templates known as *episode schemas*. These

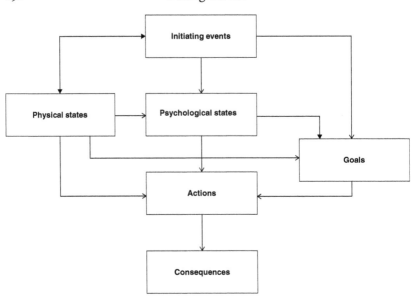

Figure 9.5   Abstract episode schema.
(Adapted from Pennington & Hastie, 1986)

schemas represent event sequences that occur in real-world contexts as well as fictional stories, and can be used iteratively to produce complex actions and narratives (Bennett & Feldman, 1981; Schank & Abelson, 1977). An archetypal episode schema is depicted in Figure 9.5.

This episode schema is centred on the thoughts and actions of a human protagonist. At the top level are a set of initiating events and background physical states; these events cause specific psychological states in the protagonist (e.g., particular beliefs, desires and emotions), and lead him or her to formulate goals and intentions, which, in turn, motivate subsequent actions; these actions, in combination with other physical states, generate consequences. This schema can be embedded in a larger episode, and a story structure is often constructed from multiple embedded episodes.

Applying these schemas to the case-specific information presented at trial, people build a story, or several stories, that aim to make sense of what happened and account for the evidence. Ultimately people seek a story that matches their understanding of the verdict category, and there is interplay between story construction and matching of the story to the requisite verdict categories. The process is depicted in Figure 9.6.

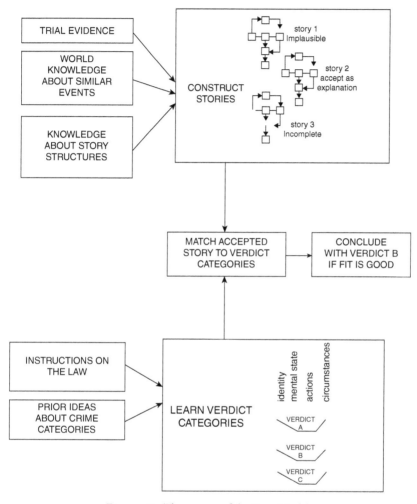

Figure 9.6   Three stages of the Story Model.
(From Pennington & Hastie, 1992)

How do people decide which stories to accept? Stories are evaluated according to three principles: coherence, coverage and uniqueness. The latter two principles are relatively clear cut: better stories cover more of the evidence, and one should have more confidence in a story when it has fewer competitors. The notion of coherence is more complex, and is unpacked into three components: consistency, completeness and plausibility. *Consistency* corresponds to the lack of internal contradictions; for example, a story in which the perpetrator is supposed to be in two places at the same time is patently inconsistent, and thus unacceptable (although what appears to be a contradiction might later be resolved through new evidence). *Completeness* concerns whether a story contains all of its structural elements; for example, a murder story without a motive is incomplete. *Plausibility* concerns how well the story fits with our real-world knowledge: does it conform to our generic understanding of how things and people work? A story that conforms to assumed causal theories is more plausible than one that introduces anomalies – we expect bodies to fall according to the laws of physics, and people to act in service of their goals. Of course, sometimes crimes involve exceptions, so this criterion, like the others, is defeasible.

People use these principles both to evaluate stories and to determine how much confidence they have in a story once selected. A tricky question, not fully addressed in the Story Model, is how these criteria combine and trade off. Stories might differ along various dimensions, and it's not clear how these should be combined, or how they might interact. For example, how does one compare a complete but implausible story versus a plausible but incomplete one? We discuss these questions in more detail below. Note that story evaluation is a holistic process, and does not focus on evaluating evidence at an atomistic level. So we also need some account of how the micro-level evaluation of hypotheses and evidence affects (and is affected by) macro-level episodes and stories.

9.4.2   *Empirical Tests of the Story Model*

Pennington and Hastie have used a variety of materials and methods to test the Story Model. These include simulated videos of real legal trials, interviews, and think-aloud protocols for eliciting people's mental representations and reasoning processes. To give a flavour for these studies, and their key findings, we illustrate with the experiment in Pennington and Hastie (1986).

Participants were sampled from a jury pool and watched a three-hour video of a simulated criminal trial, based on a real American case: *Commonwealth of Massachusetts* v. *Johnson*. The defendant, Frank Johnson, was charged with killing Alan Caldwell with 'deliberate premeditation and malice aforethought'. In the trial, both prosecution and defence accepted that Johnson and Caldwell had argued in their local bar on the day of the incident, and that Caldwell had threatened Johnson with a razor. Later that evening, Johnson returned to the bar. He went outside with Caldwell, and they fought, leading to Johnson stabbing Caldwell with a fishing knife. Caldwell died from the wound. The key facts under dispute included the following: whether or not Johnson intentionally returned home to get his knife, whether Johnson returned to the bar specifically to find Caldwell, whether Caldwell drew out his razor during the fight, and whether Johnson actively stabbed Caldwell or held out his knife in self-defence.

After viewing the trial, participants had to decide between four possible verdicts: not guilty, manslaughter, second-degree murder or first-degree murder (these categories were explained in the judge's instructions at the end of the trial). Crucially, participants were asked to think aloud as they considered the case and made their individual decisions. These think-aloud protocols were transcribed and analyzed in terms of content (e.g., story comments versus verdict comments). Story content was encoded into graphs both at the individual level and at a group level classified by verdict.

Three key empirical findings emerged from these analyses: that people used story structures steeped in causal claims (indeed, 85% of events described in their protocols were causally linked); that people drew numerous inferences beyond the given evidence (only 55% of protocols referred to events in actual testimony; 45% referred to inferred events such as mental states, goals and actions); and that people constructed different stories from the same evidence, and these differences were reflected by correspondingly different verdicts.[12] For example, participants who gave a first-degree murder verdict tended to provide a story that elaborated on the events prior to the stabbing, emphasizing Johnson's anger or humiliation, and his intention to confront and kill Caldwell (see Figure 9.7). In contrast, those who gave a 'not guilty' verdict focused on the altercation itself, spelling out details of how Johnson acted in self-defence. In this story the stabbing was portrayed as a consequence of Caldwell's behaviour rather than a goal-directed action initiated by Johnson.

Overall, the Story Model has gathered strong empirical support, and is widely accepted by legal theorists. It encapsulates the core claim that people use causal explanations to draw inferences from evidence. It also highlights the constructive nature of people's explanations, using their causal knowledge to fill in gaps in the evidence and tell a compelling story. The power of a story to summarize and rationalize a mixed body of evidence is also a potential weakness – the most compelling story is not

---

[12] Later studies showed that people's stories were mediators in their decision-making, and not post hoc rationalizations of their verdicts (e.g., Pennington & Hastie, 1992).

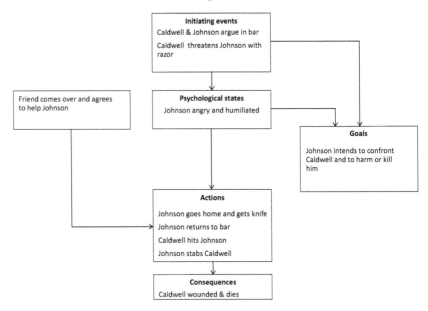

Figure 9.7   Central story for mock jurors choosing first-degree murder.
(Adapted from Pennington & Hastie, 1986)

always the one most likely to be true. Nonetheless, there is strong experimental evidence that people use story structures to organize their evidence
and make decisions.

9.5   Extending the Story Model

The Story Model marks a huge advance in our understanding of juror
decision-making, and is naturally extended to other participators in the
legal process. It also fits with the common notion in the legal literature and
advocacy manuals that lawyers (should) use stories to encapsulate their
theory of a case and persuade the court. There are various areas, however,
where the Story Model could be extended.

9.5.1   Role for Formal Causal Modelling

Central to the Story Model is the use of mental models for causal
reasoning; but these models and inference processes are intuitively
described rather than formally specified. This makes it hard to identify
people's models and evaluate their reasoning against a normative standard.

What makes one model better than another? Given a specific model, what inferences are licensed, and which show inconsistency? How might one improve a model, or the inferences based on this model? These are hard questions, and the Story Model gives no clear-cut answers.

This challenge applies at both the macro-level of story structures, and the micro-level of specific hypotheses and evidence. The Story Model proposes various principles for how people evaluate stories – such as coherence, plausibility and completeness. While these criteria are intuitively appealing, they lack formal specification, so it's unclear how they are quantified and compared across stories, or how they might trade off against each other. It's also unclear how the Story Model captures the relations between story elements and evidence, and, more generally, details about the relation between micro-level and macro-level inference are missing. Without a formal framework for causal representation and inference, it's hard to explain how people construct and evaluate their models, or how these causal models relate to probabilistic inference and reasoning.

When initially developed, the Story Model used ideas from artificial intelligence, such as concept maps, scripts and schemas. A natural move is to formalize the notion of causal network by using the causal modelling framework presented in Chapter 3. Even though people's causal inferences depart from the formal theory in several ways, it provides an indispensable guide to understanding causal cognition (Sloman & Lagnado, 2015).

9.5.1.1 *Modelling Story Structures*

A first step is to translate situation model structures into formal causal networks. For instance, the story structures for the Johnson murder case are readily transformed into causal graphs. We have translated the 'first-degree murder' story into a causal graph (see Figure 9.8). The nodes correspond to events in the case, the directed links to causal relations between these events. Critically, the graph represents the causal relations between key elements of the case. These relations can be probabilistic, to represent our uncertainty about what exactly happened, but they are not *merely* probabilistic: they represent causal processes in the world. Each link from X to Y represents the claim that X causes Y, in the broad sense that X exerts some causal influence on Y.

According to the first-degree murder model, Caldwell threatens Johnson, causing Johnson to be angry and humiliated, which in turn causes him to form the intention to kill or harm Caldwell. Johnson therefore gets his knife and returns to the bar to confront Caldwell. When Caldwell punches Johnson, Johnson intentionally kills him.

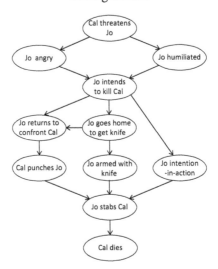

Figure 9.8   Causal model of the 'first-degree' murder story. Jo = Johnson, Cal = Caldwell.
Note the separate nodes for Johnson's 'prior intention' and his 'intention in action'
(See Chapter 10).

The graph represents the key events in the murder story, but many details could be added, and different reasoners are likely to have different models (although from Pennington and Hastie's analyses most of those who chose first-degree murder agreed on the key elements of the story). The graph itself does not specify the functional or probabilistic relations between events; these could be given by probability tables. There are several key functions by which multiple causes combine to influence an effect variable. For example, in the first-degree murder graph, whether Johnson stabs Caldwell depends on three factors: whether Caldwell strikes Johnson, whether Johnson has a knife, and whether Johnson intends to harm or kill Caldwell. Using a *noisy-AND* function would capture the claim that all three factors are needed for Johnson to stab Caldwell. Another common function is the *noisy-OR*, where several causes independently influence the effect variable. For example, the function by which anger and humiliation influence Johnson's intention could be captured using a *noisy-OR* function, whereby each cause independently raises the probability, or an interactive function, if we thought that anger and humiliation combine in a synergistic fashion.

9.5.1.2   *Probabilistic Inference Given a Causal Model*
The causal modelling framework also shows how causal graphs constrain and simplify probabilistic inference (see Chapter 3). For example, in our

graph there are no direct links from anger or humiliation to Johnson stabbing Caldwell. This encodes the assumption that if we know Johnson is intending to kill Caldwell, exactly why (anger or humiliation) does not affect his subsequent actions, and thus will not affect our probabilistic inferences about these actions. But if we thought this was an inadequate model, perhaps because we believe that his anger would have aggravated his reaction to Caldwell, then we could add a direct link from anger to stabbing.

Another key pattern of inference supported by causal models is *explaining away* (see Chapters 3 and 7). Consider the dispute about why Johnson had a knife: he claimed he used the knife for fishing, whereas the prosecution argued he took it because he sought revenge. This dispute can be represented using a common-effect structure:

Fishing → *Knife* ← *Revenge*

Here Johnson's possession of a knife raises the probability of both causes. But suppose we obtain evidence confirming that Johnson is a regular fisher; this gives some support for his claim, and thus decreases the probability that he sought revenge (via explaining away). In contrast, if we obtain evidence that he had never fished in his life, this increases the probability that he acquired the knife for revenge.

By using causal models we can stipulate what probabilistic inferences are mandated, and thus identify sound or biased inference. This capability to link causal and probabilistic inference is crucial in legal contexts.

9.5.1.3 *Counterfactual Reasoning*
A special feature of the causal model framework is that it supports counterfactual inference. For example, on the murder model we can argue that if Caldwell had not threatened Johnson, then Johnson would not have killed Caldwell. Counterfactually intervening to 'stop' the threat would have also stopped Johnson from forming an intention to kill Caldwell. Similarly, we can argue that if Johnson had not had a knife, then he would not have stabbed Caldwell. On this model, intervening to remove the knife will stop the stabbing. However, this counterfactual intervention would not change upstream events:[13] Caldwell would still have argued with Johnson and threatened him, and Johnson would still have wanted revenge.[14]

---

[13] Events causally prior to the event intervened on.
[14] Alternatively, a more elaborate model could allow for the possibility that Johnson gets another weapon with which to attack Caldwell.

One can come up with different and more elaborate versions of events (and thus different causal graphs and possibly different counterfactual inferences). The key point here is not what exact models we use to describe the case, but the capacity of these causal models to support counterfactual reasoning, which is often a critical determinant in legal cases.

9.5.1.4 Generating Story Structures from Causal Knowledge and Intuitive Theories

According to the Story Model people use causal knowledge and abstract episode schemas to construct specific story structures. This fits with recent computational work on how people use intuitive theories of a domain to generate causal models (Gerstenberg & Tenenbaum, 2017; Griffiths & Tenenbaum, 2009; Lake et al., 2017). Applied to the legal domain, the idea would be that people's intuitive theories and knowledge (e.g., about criminal behaviour and social interactions), combined with case-specific information, allow them to generate specific causal situation models (see Chapter 2). Although this has not been empirically tested, it fits with naturalistic studies of investigative reasoning (Innes, 2003), where detectives use generic theories about types of crimes and criminals to help build and test theories about a specific case (see Chapter 5).

9.5.2 Evaluating Hypotheses and Evidence

Another underdeveloped area for the Story Model is the issue of evidence and proof. As well as constructing plausible stories, jurors must evaluate how well the evidence supports these stories, and assess the strength and reliability of the evidence (see Chapter 6; Schum, 2001). Although the Story Model supplies some criteria for story evaluation, these work mainly at a holistic level, and do not concern how well individual items of evidence – such as witness testimony and forensic evidence – support specific elements in the story. Nor does the model explain how the credibility and reliability of sources of evidence are incorporated into people's assessments.

9.5.2.1 Reasoning Competence and Epistemological Stance

Kuhn and colleagues (Kuhn, Weinstock & Flaton, 1994) have developed a broader perspective on juror reasoning that addresses some of these questions. They argue that successful juror reasoning – as in other complex real-world tasks – requires not only constructing stories of what happened, but also evaluating these stories against the evidence. Kuhn proposes a continuum of competence in juror reasoning, from *satisficers* who maintain a single plausible story, to more adept reasoners who engage in *theory–evidence coordination*, assessing how well the evidence confirms or disconfirms multiple theories. Achieving this higher level of competence requires a meta-level perspective: 'to evaluate a theory against evidence implies that the evidence must be reflected on and evaluated, rather than simply assimilated, making possible the recognition of evidence that does not fit the theory' (Kuhn et al., 1994).

Several empirical studies support these claims. Kuhn et al. (1994) presented mock jurors with the same murder trial as above (*Commonwealth* v. *Johnson*), and used post-trial interviews to assess the extent of theory–evidence coordination. As well as giving verdicts and certainty judgments, participants were probed for their awareness of counterevidence and counterarguments to their verdict choices; their ability to consider and discount alternative theories; and the extent to which they reflected on the evidence, 'evaluating it rather than merely drawing on it uncritically'.

Overall, about half of the participants gave extreme verdicts, either first-degree murder or self-defence (not guilty), and the other half gave moderate verdicts, either second-degree murder or manslaughter. Those who showed more competent reasoning gave more moderate verdicts, and were also less confident in these verdicts. In contrast, those who showed less competence, and were thus closer to satisficing, chose more extreme verdicts but with higher confidence. Kuhn et al. suggest that these participants construe the juror's task as establishing 'the truth', and are thus less open to weighing up alternatives, instead seeking to gather evidence to support a singular view of what happened. This story-based focus promotes extreme verdicts because it is easier to generate stories that fit such verdicts than intermediate verdicts (which are also more complex legally). Also, the prosecution and defence will have presented extreme accounts in their opening and closing arguments, and thus set them as default stories.

9.5.2.2 *Normative Status of Theory–evidence Coordination*

Kuhn and colleagues introduce several novel ideas and methods into juror research, including the key distinction between explaining and evaluating (see Chapter 1). They also highlight the complexity inherent in the juror's task, outlining the many sub-tasks required for successful reasoning. Despite the thoroughness of this approach, several questions remain about the nature of evidence evaluation, and the means of assessing people's reasoning competence.

One key question is the normative status of the principles of theory–evidence coordination (TEC). Although reflecting on evidence and engaging in TEC are pre-requisites for successful evidential reasoning, they do not seem sufficient. There's no guarantee that people who fulfil these criteria will thereby display high-quality reasoning. They might still violate principles of logic, probability and causal inference. For example, someone might satisfy the criteria but combine evidence in a sub-optimal way, by committing a probabilistic fallacy; whereas someone else might be less reflective but display sound probabilistic reasoning. Presumably we must include rational principles to assess and criticize reasoners for *how* they judge the evidence (beyond the fact that they use and reflect on it). In short, we need rational principles of evidence evaluation to supplement the criteria for TEC.

The obvious candidate is the Bayesian framework, generally accepted as the normative standard for quantitative evidential reasoning. But the challenge here is to apply this framework to contexts where the relations between hypotheses and evidence are largely qualitative. The feasibility of this is intensely debated in the legal domain, but much of the debate is stymied by an overly narrow construal of probability (Fenton & Lagnado, 2021; see Chapter 6). A crucial point (often overlooked) is that Bayesian reasoning is as much about the structure of inference as exact computation, and thus gives constraints on qualitative as well as quantitative evaluations.

As I argued in Chapter 6, the *causal* framework can help here because it incorporates key issues about the structural relations between variables, such as dependence and conditional independence. These relations provide qualitative constraints on probabilistic reasoning. For example, if a reasoner holds that X and Y are independent, but still insists on updating Y based on knowledge of X, then they are being inconsistent, irrespective of their exact probability estimates about X and Y. Essentially the framework provides normative principles for qualitative reasoning, which are often exactly what is needed in investigative and legal contexts.

Closely related to the normative issue is the question of how we might improve people's reasoning. While TEC captures principles of good practice, these alone seem insufficient, unless bolstered with training in probability and causal reasoning. We want people to fulfil the criteria of TEC, but we also want them to learn normative rules for doing this *consistently* – that is, in conformity to normative principles. This does not mean that people need to build full causal models for all the hypotheses and evidence in a case (which is infeasible for all but the simplest cases). But they should follow probabilistic and causal constraints when evaluating and integrating evidence. Exactly how this training is achieved is an open question, but we discuss some possible routes in Chapter 10.

9.6 Summary

To conclude, let us return to the decision-making in the Sally Clark case. How well does it fit with these cognitive accounts of legal reasoning? The prosecution of Sally Clark exemplifies many of the key elements of the Story Model: the drive for a singular story to account for a complex body of evidence, the use of a prototype story structure, and the heavy use of causal knowledge to explain both the patterns of medical evidence and the behaviour of the key protagonists. The prosecution told a story that centred on the actions of a begrudging and evil mother: the alleged smothering of her babies explained the medical evidence, and her attempts to cover the crimes accounted for the inconsistency in her and her husband's testimony. A stark narrative that is easy to grasp and communicate. Moreover, the court's failure to see the flaws in the statistical evidence, or to properly investigate all the available medical information, suggests a dominating role of story-building over careful evaluation.

The investigative work leading up to the second appeal (and subsequent acquittal) represents a shift from story-focus to evidence evaluation, where a careful examination of the hospital records uncovered new evidence and revealed severe problems with the reliability (and completeness) of the prosecution case. However, the flaws in evidential reasoning went beyond a failure to scrutinize the evidence. Basic probabilistic reasoning errors occurred in court and were likely to have misled the jury in the trial. These went unacknowledged in the first appeal. Hence the crucial need to include normative principles in evidence evaluation – a lesson yet to be fully learnt in the legal domain.

Further, it is not just quantitative statistical thinking that needs to be corrected. Throughout the case the prosecution (and the judges in the first appeal) endorsed poor probabilistic reasoning at the qualitative level. In particular, they presented flawed arguments based on the supposed 'unlikely' similarities between the two deaths. These arguments can also be criticized along Bayesian lines, even without appealing to precise probabilities or computations. In sum, the Sally Clark case highlights the importance of normative standards for evidence evaluation beyond scrutiny of evidence. We also want to criticize flawed statistical arguments and show why they are wrong. And we want to avoid similar errors in future cases.

CHAPTER 10

Idioms for Legal Reasoning[1]

Our object then, specifically, is in essence: To perform the logical (or psychological) process of a conscious juxtaposition of detailed ideas, for the purpose of producing rationally a single final idea. Hence, to the extent that the mind is unable to juxtapose consciously a larger number of ideas, each coherent group of detailed constituent ideas must be reduced in consciousness to a single idea; until the mind can consciously juxtapose them with due attention to each, so as to produce its single final idea.

The Science of Proof, John Henry Wigmore (1937)

10.1 Witness for the Prosecution

Leonard Vole is charged with murdering a rich elderly lady, Miss French. He had befriended her, and visited her regularly at her home, including the night of her death. Miss French had recently changed her will, leaving Vole all her money. She died from a blow to the back of the head. There were various pieces of incriminating evidence: Vole was poor and looking for work; soon after Miss French had changed her will, he visited a travel agent to enquire about luxury cruises; the maid claimed that Vole was with Miss French at the time she was killed; the murderer did not force entry into the house; Vole had blood stains on his cuffs that matched Miss French's blood type.

As befits a good crime story, there were also several pieces of exonerating evidence: the maid admitted that she disliked Vole; she had previously been the sole beneficiary in Miss French's will; Vole's blood type was the same as Miss French's, and thus also matched the blood on his cuffs; Vole claimed that he had cut his wrist slicing ham, and had a scar to prove it. And he had an alibi: Vole's wife, Romaine, was to testify that he had

---

[1] This chapter is more technical than the other chapters and can be skipped by those less interested in the nitty-gritty of modelling legal cases. However, I recommend reading the crime story, and then looking at the proposed Bayes net in Section 10.4.

returned home at 9.30 pm. This would place him far away from the crime scene at the time of Miss French's death. However, during the trial Romaine was called as a witness for the prosecution. Dramatically, she changed her story and testified that Vole had returned home at 10.10 pm, with blood on his cuffs, and had proclaimed: 'I've killed her.'

Just as the case looked hopeless for Vole, a mystery woman gave the defence lawyer a bundle of letters allegedly written by Romaine to her overseas lover (a communist!). In one letter she wrote of her plan to falsely incriminate Vole. This new evidence had a powerful impact on the judge and jury. The key witness for the prosecution was discredited, and Vole was acquitted. After the court case, Romaine revealed to the defence lawyer that she had forged the letters herself. There was no lover overseas. She reasoned that the jury would have dismissed an alibi from a devoted wife; instead, they could be swung by the striking discredit of the prosecution's star witness.

This crime story is a work of fiction, drawn from Agatha Christie's play *Witness for the Prosecution*. The story contains twists and turns beyond a typical crime case; however, it captures the patterns of inference that recur in real-world legal cases. The task of the fact-finder is to pull together all the diverse threads of evidence and reach a singular judgment of innocence or guilt. What makes this task so hard is that the different pieces of evidence are often interrelated. You cannot simply sum up the positive evidence on the one hand, and the negative on the other. The evidence interacts in complex ways. For example, Vole's enquiry about a luxury cruise is not relevant on its own; it becomes relevant because he had recently been written into the old lady's will. Moreover, it strongly suggests he knew she had changed her will. Not only does this give him a motive for the murder, but it also shows that he was lying when he claimed not to know that he stood to benefit from her death.

This is what makes crime stories so fascinating. They cannot be solved simply by tallying the evidence on either side; rather, one must figure out how different parts of the puzzle fit together. Further, the pressure to reach a decisive verdict means that a leaning towards one side or the other is not enough. We must mentally bolster our own version so that it clearly dominates the alternatives – crowding out other possible construals of the case. This compels us to construct a story that is univocal and coherent, and thus likely to fill in gaps left unsupported by the evidence. There is seldom the leisure to tinker away slowly, as in science, accumulating support for each step; instead, one must sketch a picture all in one go, and hope that it captures the essential truths of the case.

Throughout the book we have explored how people attempt to solve these problems, exposing the strengths and weaknesses of human reasoning. I have argued that people's propensity for model-building and storytelling overrides the careful evaluation of evidence. But even when evidence is evaluated, the complexity of the task, combined with the limits of memory and processing, make simplifications inevitable. And by simplifying we can incur biases. How might we improve our reasoning?

Building on the causal modelling perspective, in this chapter I present a novel approach to this challenge (Fenton & Neil, 2018; Fenton, Neil & Lagnado, 2013; Lagnado, Fenton & Neil, 2013). Central to this method is the use of *legal idioms* – causal schemas that represent how evidence is generated and thus underpin common patterns of legal inference. Just as a small number of types of Lego blocks can be used to construct an infinite variety of structures, these idioms are the building blocks for legal reasoning, and can be reused and combined to explain complex bodies of evidence. In contrast to purely probabilistic approaches, legal idioms are based on qualitative causal relations. This allows for consistency in modelling, and also allows us to build models that support what-if and counterfactual reasoning. The idioms correspond to the graphical part of a causal model or Bayes net, and make no precise commitments about the underlying quantitative probabilities. Indeed a key assumption of this approach is that qualitative causal structure is the primary vehicle for representing the world.

10.2   Using Graphical Methods for Legal Reasoning

While causal models and Bayes nets emerged only recently (Pearl, 1988, 2009), the idea of using a graphical method to capture the inferential connections between hypotheses and evidence was explored more than 100 years ago by the legal theorist Wigmore (1913). He identified the need for a 'science of proof' – a principled approach to evaluating a large mass of evidence. He also recognized the limits of human inference in the context of a legal case: people have difficulty juxtaposing more than a few ideas at a time, and usually encounter evidence sequentially, with many interruptions and distractions in the process. Yet to reach a balanced and rational assessment, one must take all the evidence into account, re-evaluating initial evidence as new information is acquired. One needs a global picture of the whole case, but the nature of our minds and the trial process restricts us to seeing only part of the picture at any one instant.

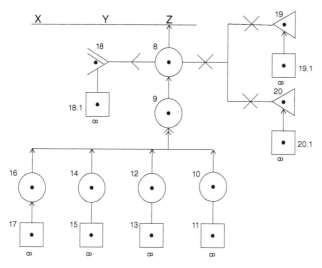

Figure 10.1   Example of a Wigmore chart. Part of a chart for a murder case where *X*, *Y* and *Z* represent the ultimate propositions to be proved. For example, *Z* is the claim that the accused killed the victim, and the network of arrows and shapes beneath *Z* corresponds to the propositions relevant to establishing this claim.
(From Wigmore, 1937)

To address this challenge Wigmore developed his *chart method*, whereby the analyst represents a legal case visually in a large network diagram (see Figure 10.1). Specialized symbols denote the claims and evidence in the case, and arrows represent the inferential links between these elements. The method allows the reasoner to unpack multiple aspects of a claim, to chart alternative explanations and corroborating facts, and to represent factors that affect the credibility and reliability of the evidence. Mapping out all these aspects in a visual graph that can be inspected 'all at once' promotes rational judgments, reducing the risks of omission and bias. Once constructed the chart summarizes the reasoner's own beliefs about the weight of each component, and thus puts them in the best position to assess the net probative force of the evidence.

One central idea behind the method is that despite the infinite variety of possible legal cases, any case can be addressed with only a small set of inferential patterns. Just as a musician can generate an infinite variety of music from a small palette of scales, arpeggios and chords, by combining and reusing these patterns we can chart any legal case. Wigmore also noted that, just as music has an underlying logic of harmony, so too inferential reasoning has a logic of inference.

10.2.1 Status of the System

Wigmore presented the method as an aid to the *rational* appraisal of evidence, but acknowledged that by itself it could not tell us how we *ought* to apportion weight or make a final judgment. Nonetheless the method forces analysts to make their reasoning explicit, to consider each link and element, and ideally to draw out the implications of the totality of evidence. Having a visual depiction of this totality helps us reflect on the complex interrelations between claims and evidence, and overcome our memory and processing limitations. Rather than just enabling us to state pre-formulated arguments, it also acts as a spur to new discoveries, and helps us build a more persuasive case.

In short, the method is not itself a normative system: it does not give us logical rules for reaching judgments of individual probative force, nor for combining these into integrated judgments. But it aims to encourage more considered and rational thinking.

10.2.2 Modern Versions of Wigmore's Method

Wigmore's method was never taken up by legal practitioners, and languished for many years. While the precise method he proposed was overly complex and unmanageable, he laid out several key concepts for evidential reasoning that are still relevant today, and serve as desiderata for any formal analysis of evidence. The chart method has been updated and streamlined by Anderson, Schum and Twining (2005) and Palmer (2011), but is still technically demanding and time consuming, and perhaps best used for training the forensic mind rather than for actual practice (Roberts & Aitken, 2014).

The major shortcoming of the chart method, however, as a guide to *rational reasoning*, is its lack of normative bite. While it yields a method that might improve people's thinking, it cannot guarantee better consistency or accuracy, and gives no normative rules for how we *should* combine or evaluate evidence. So while charting systems give a method to make our judgments more rational – in the sense of being more considered, taking into account all the evidence and assessing its reliability – this by itself is not sufficient for good reasoning. We need normative rules too: guidance for how to maintain consistency, especially when combining our elemental beliefs into larger-scale judgments. And it is exactly these constraints and rules that the causal modelling framework can provide.

10.2.3   Applying Bayes Nets to Legal Reasoning

Like Wigmore charts, Bayes nets represent claims and evidence using nodes, and links between them using directed arrows. Bayes nets, however, have a well-defined formal underpinning: the nodes represent random variables, and links represent probabilistic dependencies between variables. Thus these models can be used both to represent complex interrelations between variables and to compute the impact of evidence: updating the probability of any variable given information on any other variables in the network. Because such updating is carried out using the laws of probability, it is guaranteed to be logically consistent.

Several theorists have applied Bayes nets to legal reasoning (Dawid & Evett, 1997; Edwards, 1991; Kadane & Schum, 2011; Taroni, Biedermann, Bozza, Garbolino & Aitken, 2014). We build on this work, but extend it in various ways.

First, we give causality a more explicit role (see also Chapter 6). Whereas previous work focuses on probabilistic relations, we propose that links are predominantly construed as causal claims.[2] Thus, our Bayes nets are causal models of the *evidence-generating process*: causal models of what happened and of the processes by which evidence is acquired and presented. Indeed, much of the debate in legal fact-finding involves reasoning about cause and effect: whether X did Y, whether Z's testimony is unreliable, whether evidence for A is also evidence against B, whether X would have done A if not for B, and so on. To evaluate such reasoning we need causal norms, not just probability norms. We need a system that respects the constraints of probability theory, but also places constraints on our causal inferences. The causal approach chimes with people's intuitive notions of legal reasoning (Lagnado & Gerstenberg, 2017), and also scenario-based (van Koppen & Mackor, 2020) and explanatory accounts (Allen & Pardo, 2019).

Second, as Wigmore mandated, we must capture the reliability and credibility of evidence. We also give this a causal slant, focusing on the processes that generated the evidence, including causes that might disrupt these processes, such as errors in forensic tests or eyewitness testimony.

Finally, we present a method for modelling full legal cases. Few guidelines exist for how to achieve this scaling-up. A useful starting point is

---

[2] Sometimes links are used to represent definitional, mathematical or conceptual relations. And in certain cases we might use links in a non-causal orientation to simplify inference. But the causal perspective helps us build the skeleton of a model.

given by case analysis and the hierarchy of propositions (Cook, Evett, Jackson, Jones & Lambert, 1998), where propositions are divided into source-level (e.g., blood traces), activity-level (e.g., stabbing, punching) and offence-level (e.g., committing murder). But no clear guidance is given on how to combine these elements into a cohesive structure, nor how to incorporate reliability and credibility.

By introducing a set of legal idioms, which can be reused and combined, we aim to address this challenge.[3] We take advantage of our natural propensity for causal thinking, using our causal knowledge to build the graph structures that underpin inference. Note that the idiom-based approach allows us to add elements to a structure without reworking the previous parts of the model, which is crucial for constructing larger cases in a dynamic fashion.

10.3   The Idiom-Based Approach[4]

10.3.1   The Evidence Idiom

The fundamental building block is the *evidence idiom,* which captures the relation between hypothesis and evidence. In the legal context, a typical hypothesis is a proposition that needs to be proved, such as whether the accused committed the crime in question. Evidence is usually an object or statement gathered during the investigation or presented in court, such as witness testimony or expert report.

We have seen many examples of this idiom throughout the book:

Fractures → X-ray report
Cancer → positive mammogram
Suspect at crime scene → witness statement
Suspect at crime scene → DNA report

The directed link asserts a causal influence from hypothesis to evidence, such that changes to the hypothesis would change the evidence, and thus observing the status of the evidence changes our probability of the hypothesis.

---

[3] For a related approach using object-oriented Bayes nets, see Dawid and Mortera (2020) and Helper, Dawid and Leucari (2007).

[4] This approach is based on joint work with Norman Fenton and Martin Neil (Fenton et al., 2013; Fenton, Neil, Yet & Lagnado, 2020; Fenton & Neil, 2018; Lagnado et al., 2013). A mild warning to the reader – the next sections go into some detail, but you can get a feel for the approach just by looking at the graphs, and skip to Section 10.4 to find out if Vole was guilty or not.

Figure 10.2   Evidence idiom.

Bayes' rule tells us how to update our belief in the hypothesis (H) given evidence (E).[5] In this simple case,[6] the posterior odds for H are a product of its prior odds and the likelihood ratio (LR) for the evidence:

Posterior odds = prior odds × LR

To illustrate, suppose we are investigating whether a suspect was at the crime scene. A shoeprint from the scene matches the suspect's shoes. We use the evidence idiom to construct a two-variable model (see Figure 10.2). Suppose further that the type of shoe is relatively rare, occurring in 1% of the population. We can use this information to assign conditional probabilities to the model:

P(match | suspect at scene) = 1
P(match | suspect not at scene) = .01

We can therefore derive an $LR_{shoeprint} = 1/0.01 = 100$. Thus the shoeprint evidence raises our prior belief in *Suspect at scene* (as measured by our prior odds) by a factor of 100. For instance, if our prior probability is 1/1000 (prior odds of 1:999), we would multiply these odds by 100 to yield a posterior probability of about 1/11 (posterior odds of about 1:10).

This model applies to qualitative judgments too. Even if we lack precise information on which to base our probability judgments, the model still tells us something about how we should update our beliefs given the new evidence. For example, identifying a rare property should boost our prior probability more than a common property.

10.3.1.1   Combining Multiple Items of Evidence
The evidence idiom can be re-used to combine multiple pieces of evidence for the same hypothesis. Each extra item of evidence is added as a separate effect variable. To continue our example, suppose that CCTV shows a man at the crime scene at the time of the crime (see Figure 10.3a). His face is partially occluded, but facial recognition software gives a positive match

---

[5] See the Bayesian updating box in Chapter 3 for more details.
[6] Assuming mutually exclusive and exhaustive hypotheses.

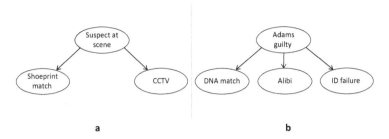

Figure 10.3   Combining multiple items of evidence. (a) Shoeprint and CCTV evidence
that suspect was at crime scene. (b) Adams case with three items of evidence.

to the suspect, with a false-positive probability of 5%. This gives us an LR^7
for the CCTV evidence $= 1/0.05 = 20$.

To combine these two pieces of evidence, assuming they are independent, we simply multiply their individual LRs:

$$LR_{total} = LR_{shoeprint} \times LR_{CCTV} = 100 \times 20 = 2000$$

Therefore, for a prior of $1/1000$ the two items of evidence yield posterior
odds of about 2:1, and thus a posterior probability of about $2/3$. We
started with a prior belief of $1/1000$, so the two pieces of evidence have
increased our belief substantially.

This combination rule applies to both confirming and disconfirming
evidence. When items support the hypothesis, then the probability of the
hypothesis increases, because the odds of the hypothesis are multiplied by
LRs greater than one. When items disconfirm the hypothesis, the probability of the hypothesis decreases, because the odds are multiplied by LRs
less than one. The overall effect of the evidence on the hypothesis depends
on the relative strengths of the individual items of evidence.

The balancing of supporting and disconfirming evidence is particularly
important when quantitative evidence (such as DNA evidence) is pitted
against a less readily quantified item such as witness testimony. The case of
R v. *Adams* highlights the dilemma faced by fact-finders, where an incriminating DNA match was contradicted by the suspect's alibi and the failure of
the victim to identify him (see Dawid, 2002). Using the idiom approach helps
us see how to combine these conflicting pieces of evidence (see Figure 10.3b).[8]

---

[7] Assuming a negligible false-negative rate, such that $P(CCTV \mid$ *suspect at scene*$)$ is approximately equal
to one.

[8] For Bayesian computations for this case see Dawid (2002) and Fenton and Neil (2018).

The evidence idiom thus allows us to deal with both corroborating and conflicting evidence, and captures our basic qualitative intuitions about how these should combine. The probabilistic framework also allows us to combine elements with differing strengths, and integrate quantified evidence such as DNA with qualitative statements.

10.3.2 Alternative Explanations

When one side in a legal dispute presents evidence in support of a hypothesis, a standard riposte is to offer an alternative explanation of that same evidence. This is a hallmark of legal reasoning, and a common practice in everyday arguments. It is also a crucial criterion for rational evidential reasoning: one should strive to consider alternative accounts of the evidence, not only one's favoured hypothesis.

A key distinction here is between hypotheses that are *mutually exclusive* (only one can be true) and hypotheses that are *independent* (both can be true). Both forms are common in legal contexts, but they require slightly different models and entail different patterns of inference. Neglecting these differences can lead to errors (see Chapter 7).

Throughout the book we have seen many cases where competing hypotheses are mutually exclusive:

Murder versus Suicide
Cot death versus Smothering
Intentional versus Accidental killing

The standard approach is to represent each alternative hypothesis as a distinct state of a single variable. For example, in the cliff death (Chapter 1) and jogger death (Chapter 4), murder and suicide are possible states of a single variable that represents the cause of death. In the Sally Clark case (Chapter 9), cot death and smothering are possible states of a variable representing Christopher's death, and also of a separate variable representing Harry's death.

When modelled using a single variable, the evidence idiom is sufficient to capture the competition between exclusive hypotheses.[9] Moreover, if the two hypotheses are also exhaustive (such as murder versus not-murder), their total probability sums to one, and thus if the probability

---

[9] However, sometimes it is better to represent mutually exclusive causes as separate variables, which makes it easier to capture the distinct causal pathways these involve. In such cases extra modelling is required to preserve the mutual exclusivity of the hypotheses (see Fenton et al., 2016).

Figure 10.4   Two alternative causes of the same evidence.

of one increases the other must decrease, and vice-versa. If they are not exhaustive, this zero-sum relation need not hold, because of the other unspecified alternatives.

10.3.2.1   Explaining away Idiom

Sometimes competing hypotheses are independent rather than exclusive. In such cases we use the *explaining away* idiom, representing each alternative with a separate causal variable (see Figure 10.4).

Again many examples occur throughout the book:

> *Handled explosives* → *Test* ← *Playing cards*
> *Cancer* → *Mammogram* ← *Benign cyst*
> *Shot gun* → *GSR* ← *Contamination*
> *Abuse* → *Bruises* ← *Blood disorder*

On this model, it's possible that both hypotheses are true, so finding out the truth about one alternative does not guarantee the falsehood of the other. When either alternative is sufficient to cause the evidence, the structure embodies a distinctive form of inference known as *explaining away* (see Chapter 3). In the absence of any evidence the two alternatives are probabilistically *independent*; but once we find out about the common evidence, they become probabilistically *dependent*, such that getting separate evidence about one cause would reduce the probability of the other – it is explained away.

For example, consider the blood match evidence against Vole in the *Witness for the Prosecution* case. Blood is found on Vole's jacket that matches Miss French's blood type, but it also matches Vole's type. To model this situation we can use the explaining away idiom, with *Blood from French* and *Blood from Vole* as potential sources of the blood on the jacket (see Figure 10.5a).

For simplicity here we assume that we are 100% sure that both French and Vole have the same blood type as the blood found on the jacket (there are no testing errors). This can be relaxed by introducing additional reliability variables (as we see below). Given these assumptions the CPT

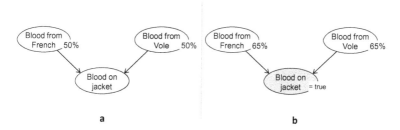

Figure 10.5   Explaining away idiom applied to Vole blood evidence. (a) Prior probabilities for two possible causes. (b) Updated probabilities given evidence of blood on Vole's jacket.

for the evidence variable *–Blood on Jacket* – is straightforward. If either Vole or French (or both) contributed the blood, the probability of seeing the evidence is equal to one. If neither contributed the blood, the probability of seeing the blood on the jacket is low (and it would need to be from someone else with the same blood type).[10]

Assuming priors of 50% for either cause, the model shows us how to update our beliefs given the blood evidence. Both causes rise in probability to 65% (see Figure 10.5b). This illustrates a crucial point: when the opposing side in a legal argument advances an alternative (but independent) explanation for a piece of evidence, this does not (by itself) undermine the probative force of the evidence against the original claim. The blood evidence still counts for the hypothesis that it is Miss French's blood, even if it could have originated from Vole himself. However, equally important, if one can offer some separate evidence for this alternative, then the probability of the original claim *is* reduced (for full details see Chapter 3). Thus, when Vole shows his scar, this reduces the probability that it is Miss French's blood (perhaps not by much).

Note that, although the exact probabilities (for the priors and CPT) affect the magnitude of these changes, the qualitative pattern holds regardless. Separate evidence that supports an alternative explanation (Vole has a scar) will always lower the probability of the target hypothesis (Miss French's blood on the jacket), whatever the probabilities assigned (so long as we don't assign extreme priors of zero or one). Thus, the explaining away idiom captures a basic qualitative pattern of inference, but also has the benefit of yielding precise inferences when the probabilities are available.

[10] This corresponds to a *noisy-OR* function (see Chapter 3).

The explaining away pattern recurs in many contexts in investigative and legal inquiries. And sometimes people get confused with such inferences (see Chapter 7; also Tesic et al., 2020). To make sure we get such inferences right requires a Bayes net model.

10.3.3 Modelling Reliability

Assessing the reliability of evidence is critical to investigative and legal reasoning. How accurate is the witness's report? How rigorous is the forensic testing? Such questions are fundamental to the legal process, and yet it has proved difficult to formalize or systematize the influence that reliability should have on our judgments.

This issue has practical bite. Miscarriages of justice often stem from the prosecution presenting unreliable evidence (cf. Innocence Project;[11] Simon, 2012; Smit et al., 2018), with eyewitness testimony being notoriously unreliable yet often given credence by jurors. Moreover, psychological research suggests that people vary widely in their competence at assessing the reliability of evidence and focus on constructing stories rather than carefully evaluating evidence (see Chapter 9).

The *evidence-reliability* idiom tackles these shortcomings, allowing us to integrate issues of reliability into our beliefs in a coherent and systematic fashion. At a basic level the evidence idiom already incorporates the reliability of an evidential report via the conditional probabilities in the CPT. Thus, when considering forensic tests or eyewitness reports, these probabilities correspond to false-positive and false-negative rates. This idiom suffices in simple cases, but it often proves too crude: for example, when we need to separate out different factors that affect reliability, if we have separate evidence about the source's reliability, or if the reliability of one piece of evidence is linked to other pieces.

To address these challenges the evidence-reliability idiom introduces a 'reliability' node as a causal parent of the evidential report node (see Figure 10.6).[12]

Formally, the reliability node modulates the degree to which the evidence report is an accurate reflection of the true status of the hypothesis. In the limiting case, with a fully reliable test or witness, the evidence report would be true when the hypothesis is true, and false when the hypothesis

---

[11] www.innocenceproject.org

[12] See Bovens and Hartmann (2003) for a similar approach to modelling reliability in epistemology and philosophy of science.

Figure 10.6   Evidence-reliability idiom.

is false. However, in reality tests and witnesses are always fallible to some degree. At the opposite extreme, a fully unreliable test would deliver an evidence report that is independent of the truth of the hypothesis. Most tests lie between these two extremes, and a crucial part of evidential reasoning is gathering information and evidence to establish evidence reliability. Indeed, in the justice system the oral presentation and the cross-examination of witnesses are designed for this purpose.

To show how the reliability idiom works, consider the example of a burglar alarm on a car. We show the model and its CPT in Figure 10.7a. A fully reliable alarm would sound only when the car is broken into. This is represented in the left-hand side of the CPT, where *P(alarm | break-in, reliable)* = 1, *P(alarm | no break-in, reliable)* = 0. A fully unreliable alarm would sound with some probability, independent of whether or not there is a break-in. This is represented in the right-hand side of the CPT. Here we assume[13] the probability of a fully unreliable alarm sounding on any particular night is 50%: *P(alarm | break-in, not reliable)* = *P(alarm | no break-in, not reliable)* = 0.5.

To fully parameterize the model, we must assign priors for break-in and the reliability of the alarm. We might have base-rate statistics for these priors, but here suppose that the chance of a break-in (on any particular night) is 1% and the prior for the alarm being reliable is 95%. We can now use this model for a range of inferences.

Suppose the alarm sounds. How should we update our belief in a break-in? The model tells us that the probability of a break-in rises from 1% to about 28%, while the probability that the alarm is reliable drops from 95% to about 28% (see Figure 10.7b). A false alarm is more likely than a true break-in. This captures the fact that the alarm being unreliable is a more plausible explanation for the alarm sounding than a break-in.

Clearly the exact updating depends on the probabilities used in the model. But this does not mean that the model cannot be usefully applied

---

[13] This assumption is not crucial to the argument here – in a later example we show how the idiom works when this probability is varied.

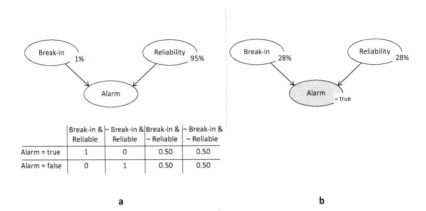

	Break-in & Reliable	~ Break-in & Reliable	Break-in & ~ Reliable	~ Break-in & ~ Reliable
Alarm = true	1	0	0.50	0.50
Alarm = false	0	1	0.50	0.50

a   b

Figure 10.7   Alarm model. (a) Model with priors and CPT for *Alarm*. (b) Updated model given evidence of alarm sounding.

even without precise probabilities – we will often have rough estimates of the priors and strengths of the alternative explanations which will allow us to draw approximate conclusions.

The evidence-reliability idiom captures an archetypal pattern that recurs in a vast number of contexts beyond law. In medical contexts it clarifies a commonly misunderstood pattern of inference (see Chapter 4): when a disease is rare, and the test for the disease is not fully reliable, then in most cases a positive test is more likely to be due to an unreliable test than a true reflection of the target hypothesis.

One notable feature of the idiom is that – although prior to knowing the status of the evidence report, the two hypotheses (for example, the break-in and the reliability of the alarm) are probabilistically independent – once we know the status of the report (the alarm sounds), the two hypotheses become dependent, and compete to explain the evidence. This is another example of explaining away.

This idiom also shows how the relevance of one piece of evidence can vary according to what other evidence is presented. Suppose we have a new piece of evidence about the reliability of the car alarm: for instance, that it has recently been tested and declared in good working order. This is clearly relevant to the inferences we draw when knowing that the alarm has sounded; the probability of a break-in given the alarm is now higher. By contrast, in a situation where we have no knowledge about whether the alarm has sounded, evidence about the car alarm's reliability would not change our belief in the probability of a break-in. This emphasizes the

Figure 10.8   Model of independent witnesses of the same event.

conditionality of relevance (see Chapter 6), but also shows how the idiom naturally captures these subtleties.

10.3.3.1   Modelling Multiple Testimonies
One strength of using the evidence-reliability idiom is that it can be applied to contexts with multiple testimonies about the same events. In such cases, corroborating (or conflicting) testimonies not only tell us about the target events, but also about the reliabilities of the witnesses. For example, consider a case where a house has been burgled. Three neighbours report seeing a man run away from the premises (see Pilditch, Lagator & Lagnado, 2021). None of the neighbours saw his face, but they all state he was wearing a hoodie. We can represent this example by using a separate evidence-reliability idiom for each witness (see Figure 10.8).

The witnesses give their testimonies separately and know nothing about the other witness reports; therefore we can treat them as independent. With no additional information about the witnesses, we assume that they each have the same initial reliability, and that each report is characterized by the same CPT. Here a reliable witness would be fully accurate in their report, whereas an unreliable witness would simply guess. Moreover, in this example we assume that the witness guesses an item of clothing in rough proportion to the base-rate occurrence of that clothing. This means that the probability of a witness guessing hoodie is roughly equal to the base-rate of hoodies. We set this at 50% for now.

The model shows us how to update our belief given each new piece of testimony (shown in Figure 10.9a). As intuitively expected, each testimony raises the probability that the man was in fact wearing a hoodie, and also raises the reliability of each individual witness. This shows the strength of corroborating evidence, and also the diminishing effect as extra witnesses are added (such that the final witness adds less than the second witness).

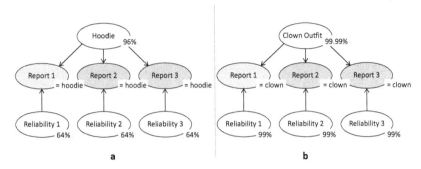

Figure 10.9   Belief updating when all three witnesses report the same thing. (a) For the common outfit (hoodie). (b) For the rare outfit (clown costume).

We can also use this model to explore a trickier question. How does this case compare with one where the descriptions given by witnesses are unusual rather than common? For example, what if they all report seeing a man in a clown's outfit? While intuitively one might expect corroborating testimonies to have a stronger effect, one also needs to factor in the lower prior for this outfit. Let's assume that the prior for a clown outfit is 1%. We model this example in Figure 10.9b.

In the clown outfit case, the corroboration indeed has a stronger effect, and, despite starting from a much lower prior (1% versus 50%), by the third testimony the probability of a clown outfit has overtaken the corresponding probability of a hoodie. Moreover, the probability of the witnesses being reliable is much higher (99%) than in the hoodie case (64%). This makes good sense – the agreement of three witnesses is more impressive when the event reported is rare rather than common.

By using the evidence-reliability idiom we thus show how corroboration boosts witness reliability, and more so when witnesses report surprising (low prior) events. Without using the model it would be difficult to work out when the corroborative boost overcomes the low prior. Indeed, people find this kind of inference difficult, and seem to underestimate the value of corroborating witnesses for a surprising versus common event (Pilditch, Lagator & Lagnado, 2021).

10.3.3.2   Reliability Unpacked

So far we have used a single generic reliability variable to model the possibility that an evidence source is inaccurate. However, the concept of reliability is broad, and there are several ways in which a source of evidence

Figure 10.10   Eyewitness testimony unpacked.

might be unreliable. Moreover, factors can disrupt the reliability of an evidence report at different points in the measuring process (see Chapter 6). For example, an eyewitness might be unreliable due to poor viewing conditions, memory interference or an intention to mislead.

To capture such situations we need finer-grained analyses of the causal processes linking the target events and the evidence report, also including alternative causal factors that might disrupt these processes. We can achieve this by reusing and combining the idioms introduced so far. While the principles of construction are the same for any type of evidence, each can involve distinctive factors. We illustrate by looking at examples from eyewitness testimony and forensic trace evidence.

10.3.3.3   Modelling Witness Testimony

Eyewitness testimony is a critical source of evidence, but it is notoriously fallible, as shown by a large body of empirical research (Wells & Olson, 2003) and many legal cases where eyewitness testimony has been discredited. The idiom-based approach helps us model a wide variety of eyewitness contexts, incorporating the key factors that underpin or undermine reliability.

To take a prototypical example, which we introduced in Chapter 6, suppose an eyewitness testifies in court that she saw the suspect leave the crime scene on the night of the crime. We might start with the simple evidence-reliability idiom, but this gives a coarse representation, and does not identify the separate factors that might undermine the testimony. Instead we can unpack the process from the purported events to the testimony presented in court (see Figure 10.10).

First, we consider the causal factors present at the time of the alleged events. These include external conditions, such as viewing conditions (was the scene poorly lit, was the witness far away, was her line of sight occluded?), perceptual capabilities of the eyewitness (such as her eyesight) and so on. Such factors influence whether (and how well) the witness encoded the claimed events, and are modelled as enhancing or disrupting causes of the putative sighting.

Next, the witness is usually required to identify the suspect from photos or a line-up. Here various factors can affect the witness's recall, each with the potential to induce bias. Aside from the passage of time and intervening events weakening the memory traces, several other factors can intrude in the identification process. Especially relevant are techniques used by the police to secure an identification (Simon, 2012; Wells & Olson, 2003), such as (biased) instructions to the witness, the make-up of the line-up, the presentation format and so on. These elements can be modelled as alternative or interfering causes of the witness's recall. To the extent that the defence can provide evidence that these factors were present, this should reduce the probability that the suspect's recall is accurate.

Finally, we need to take into account the *veracity* of the witness; in particular, the possibility that the witness is intentionally giving a false report. There are various reasons why a witness might lie – perhaps to protect the suspect or to incriminate someone else, or due to a general dislike or distrust of the police and legal system. These possibilities can be fleshed out according to the details of the case, and represented as extra variables in the model (we will see some examples in Section 10.3.8). By making these factors explicit in the model, they can be linked to (and supported by) other items of evidence. For example, if it is known that the witness is a colleague or friend of the suspect, this could undermine the witness's credibility (or, if they report something that incriminates the suspect, it might actually boost their credibility).

Note that a witness might be honest (or dishonest) irrespective of how well they have encoded or recalled the information. This is modelled by the lack of a link from veracity to the other disrupting factors. This further underlines the importance of representing sources of error separately.

Questions of veracity go beyond cases of eyewitness testimony, and loom large in many contexts where witnesses give testimony, especially when the suspect is presenting their own account. These questions raise several subtle inferential issues, which we discuss in Section 10.3.8.

Representing separate components of reliability allows us to clarify how different pieces of evidence might impact on different aspects of a witness's reliability. For example, in court an eyewitness report might be contested on the grounds that the witness is dishonest or inaccurate (or possibly both).

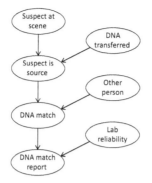

Figure 10.11   DNA evidence unpacked.

Each issue requires a different kind of evidence. Whereas evidence of dishonesty might come from a poor character reference, evidence of inaccuracy might come from eye-test results. Analyzing reliability into sub-components also allows us to capture additional probabilistic links that might be disguised at a coarser level of representation.

10.3.3.4   Modelling Forensic Trace Evidence

Modelling the reliability of trace evidence also requires separating out different potential sources of error. Again, idioms can be used to give a finer-grained analysis at different stages in the evidential process. For example, suppose that a forensic expert reports that the suspect's DNA matches a trace found at the crime scene. The inference from the reported match to the claim that it's the suspect's DNA involves several steps, and introduces several possibilities for error (see the model in Figure 10.11; see also Chapters 4 and 6):

- The report of a match might be due to an error in the lab DNA testing. This is captured using the evidence-reliability idiom.
- The suspect's DNA profile might match the DNA trace found at the scene, even though the trace actually comes from another person. This requires the suspect to share his DNA profile with this other person. This possibility is represented as an alternative state of the variable *Suspect is source of DNA,* and the probability this leads to the suspect matching the trace is given by the random match probability (RMP) encoded in the CPT for variable *Suspect DNA matches trace.*
- The suspect's DNA might be found at the crime scene even though the suspect wasn't actually there: it might have been transferred by another

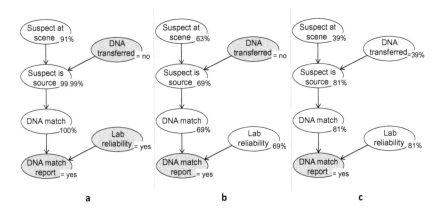

Figure 10.12   Updating the DNA model. (a) Model without allowing for possibility of transfer or lab error. (b) Model allowing for lab error. (c) Model allowing for both transfer and lab error. Note the RMP is contained in the CPT for DNA match, so we don't use the 'Other person' variable here.

person, or placed there to frame the suspect. Such possibilities are represented as alternative causes of the suspect's DNA being at the crime scene.

This model allows us to assess the influence of each of these alternative possibilities on the probative value of a DNA match. For example, suppose we have an RMP of 1/million, and the lab testing reliability is 99%, and there is a 1% probability of transferred DNA. Let's compare three cases:

(1)   No consideration of the possibility of lab testing errors or transferred DNA
(2)   Possibility of lab testing errors
(3)   Possibility of lab testing errors and transferred DNA

We use a prior that the suspect was at the crime scene of 1%. Given the match evidence, the posterior probability that he was at the scene rises to about 91% if we don't factor in the possibility of lab testing errors or planting (case 1 – see Figure 10.12a). If we include the possibility of a lab error, this reduces to about 63% (case 2 – see Figure 10.12b). Finally, including the possibility of planting too reduces it to about 39% (case 3 – see Figure 10.12c).

These results clearly show the crucial importance of taking into account possible errors in DNA testing. Even with an extremely low RMP, lab testing error rates substantially reduce the probative force of a DNA match

(Koehler, 2011). In our example it reduced our probability of the suspect being at the scene from 91% to 39%. Indeed the modelling of trace match evidence is sometimes even more complicated, with various other potential sources of error (see Fenton & Neil, 2018). These complex cases can also be captured by repeated use of the idioms.

In both the eyewitness and trace evidence examples we have shown how to use idioms to model finer-grained aspects of evidence reliability. These are generic examples, and specific cases will require attention to different factors. And sometimes it is unnecessary to unpack the process too much; a lot will depend on what other evidence might be available to support the model. No single template will cover all cases, but by reusing and combining the idioms we can model a broad variety of cases.

All the idioms considered so far involve variables that are downstream effects of the crime event. However, two of the main elements in a crime investigation – opportunity and motive – are pre-conditions or precursors to a crime, and thus (on a causal view) should be modelled as causes rather than effects of the crime event.[14] Both elements introduce novel considerations into the modelling and analysis of evidence.

10.3.4 Modelling Opportunity

Opportunity is a prerequisite for most crimes, including typical cases of assault, robbery, rape and murder. If someone was not at the crime scene at the time of the incident, then they could not have committed the crime. Opportunity is often contested, particularly in whodunit cases where the identity of the perpetrator is the central issue. The suspect denies being at the crime scene, and the prosecution seeks to prove that they were there. In keeping with our causal perspective, we model opportunity as a cause of the crime – not as a sufficient cause, but as a pre-condition (see Figure 10.13). The opportunity hypothesis is also the cause of evidence about the suspect's whereabouts, such as witness testimony or trace evidence.

Modelling opportunity helps us tackle one of the most controversial issues in applying Bayesian approaches in legal contexts – where do our priors come from, and aren't they too subjective and arbitrary? These are

[14] There are exceptions to this rule, where modelling opportunity or motive works better if we go against the causal direction and model them as child nodes of the crime node. However, care must be taken not to introduce any unwarranted dependencies. Also, at a broader level we can see the link from crime to motive evidence as shortcuts that hide the 'true' causal structure, whereby both crime and evidence of motive are common effects of a hidden motive node.

Figure 10.13   Basic opportunity model.

tricky questions, but the notion of an opportunity prior provides a first step towards addressing them (Fenton, Lagnado, Dahlman, & Neil, 2019).

10.3.4.1   *The Opportunity Prior*

When the police suspect someone of a crime, one of the first questions they ask is where the suspect was at the time of the crime. This question is very diagnostic: if the suspect can show he was elsewhere, then he is ruled out of the frame. If, however, the police can show he was at the crime scene, then he is ruled into a relatively small set of possible perpetrators.

Establishing opportunity is thus critical at the investigative phase. But the same logic applies at later stages of the legal process, in particular when the suspect is charged with the crime, and we must evaluate the strength of evidence against him. Information about the suspect's whereabouts in relation to the crime scene provides a starting point for building a case, before other evidence is presented. A key point, frequently neglected in formal analyses of evidence, is that case-specific information allows us to assess the probative value of opportunity evidence.

Consider an idealized case first. Suppose we know that only five people were in a room when a crime was committed – for instance, an item of jewellery is stolen from a small boutique. Before considering any other information, the only rational (and fair) judgment is to assign each person a probability of $1/5$ of committing the theft. More generally, for n people in the room, each is assigned a probability of $1/n$. Note this doesn't mean that we think each person has an equal propensity to commit the crime, but just that given our current state of knowledge (ignorance), we should assign an equal probability to each potential perpetrator; anything else would be illogical and unfair.

This logic can be generalized to many types of crime. Here we focus on crimes committed by a single perpetrator, and which require the perpetrator to be physically present at the crime scene at the time of the crime. If the suspect is one of n people who was close enough (in space and time) to have committed the crime, then we assign probability $1/n$.

The ease of estimating n depends on what is known about the location and time of the crime. For a crime committed at a solitary place and during a brief time window, we can safely assume there was only a small number of possible perpetrators. By contrast, a crime in a busy high street will include a far larger number of people. Often it will be possible to get a rough estimate or establish reasonable upper bounds for n. Most of the cases examined in this book allow for estimates with sensible bounds.

A crucial point here is that we are estimating the number of people who were *actually* at the crime scene at the critical time, not the number of people who *could have been* there. Thus even if we don't know who the other people are (and might never discover this), we can still assign our suspect, who was definitely at the crime scene, a probability of $1/n$. In other words, even if many individuals *could have* been one of the other $n - 1$ at the crime scene, our suspect has probability $1/n$ regardless.

This analysis does not simply see opportunity as a necessary condition for guilt. Instead it can set a reasonable (and fair) initial probability – informed by the spatiotemporal circumstances of the case, but before considering other evidence. In cases where the suspect's presence at the crime scene is uncontested, this is a major advantage because we can set the prior at $1/n$. For example, in a murder case where a man was accused of killing his wife, the fact that he was definitely with her when she was violently killed – and it was established that at most only three other people were in the vicinity – justifies an initial probability of about $1/4$ based on this opportunity information (Fenton et al., 2020).

In many cases, however, the suspect denies being at the crime scene at the time of the crime. To apply our analysis to these contexts we introduce the notion of the *extended crime scene,* which is based on the closest proven location and time for the suspect from which he could still have got to the crime scene to commit the crime. This can include a location before or after the crime was committed. For example, it might be accepted that the suspect was at a location two miles from the crime scene, one hour after the crime took place. We use this location and time to generate the extended crime scene, which will cover all people who were in the area at most two miles from the crime and at most one hour after the crime. This gives us the number of possible perpetrators N, which includes the suspect. Based on this extended crime scene we assign a probability for the suspect committing the crime of n/N (as there are n people at the crime scene).

Estimating the number of people in the extended crime scene can be difficult, especially if the agreed locations and times are distant from the

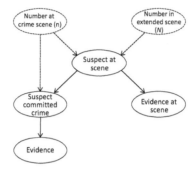

Figure 10.14   The opportunity prior idiom. Note that dashed lines show that prior values
are derived from *n* and *N* via a binomial transformation.
(See Fenton et al., 2019, for details)

crime scene. But in many cases (including most of those considered in this book) we can set reasonable upper limits on *N*, and thus reasonable lower bounds on the prior probability of the suspect being at the crime scene. Moreover, we can accommodate uncertainty in these estimates by using distributions rather than point values for *n* and *N*.

These opportunity priors can be incorporated into our crime model, allowing us to initialize the model with sensible prior probabilities, and then update given new evidence. We show the key opportunity idiom in Figure 10.14, with separate 'prior value' variables for the number of people at the crime scene (*n*) and the number of people in the extended crime scene (*N*).

- The prior probability for the node *Suspect at crime scene* is determined by the number of people at the crime scene *n* and the number at the extended crime scene *N*, such that the prior is *n/N*.
- The prior probability for the node *Suspect committed crime* is determined by whether the suspect is at the crime scene, and the number of people at the crime scene such that:

  ○ If *Suspect at crime scene = true,* then the probability *Suspect committed crime* is $1/n$
  ○ If *Suspect at crime scene = false,* then the probability *Suspect committed crime* is 0

Let's use an example to show how the model works (see Figure 10.15). A woman is suspected of stealing a bag from a bar. The theft took place at 9 pm, and about 10 people were in the bar at that time. The woman denies being in the bar, but admits that she was at a pub one mile from the bar at 9.30 pm. The extended crime scene therefore includes all people one mile

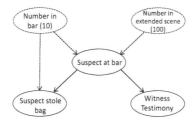

Figure 10.15   Opportunity model for bar theft.

or less from the bar in that 30-minute window, which is estimated as roughly 100. Thus we have $n = 10$ and $N = 100$.

This gives us priors for the model:

Prior probability for *Suspect at bar* $= n/N = 10\%$
Prior probability for *Suspect stole bag* $= 1\%$

Using our model, we can update these probabilities as new evidence arrives. For example, suppose an eyewitness claims that he saw the suspect at the bar at 9 pm. We assume the witness is fairly reliable (in a fuller model we could use the reliability idiom, and add evidence about his reliability).

Updating the model based on this new evidence:

Posterior probability for *Suspect at bar* $= 99\%$
Posterior probability for *Suspect stole bag* $= 8\%$

So despite now being confident that the suspect was at the bar at 9 pm, she is just one of about 10 people who could have stolen the bag.

In sum, the opportunity prior helps us incorporate crucial information about the spatiotemporal location of the suspect in relation to the crime scene – something that detectives do intuitively. The analysis quantifies the value of this information, rather than simply concluding that the suspect 'might' have been at the crime scene. It also shows us how to combine opportunity with other evidence in the case. There is plenty of scope to debate the numbers, and sometimes priors will be extremely low. But some inferential edge, however small, is better than none.

10.3.5   Modelling Motive

Establishing a motive is often crucial in investigative reasoning, helping the police to understand a crime, identify a suspect and build a compelling case against them. While motive itself rarely needs to be proved in a legal

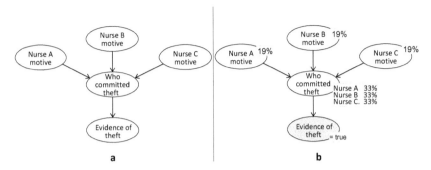

Figure 10.16 Three nurses motive model. (a) The basic model. (b) Updated with evidence of theft.

case, it nonetheless plays a key role in the trial too. Making sense of the 'why' that lies behind the crime, by identifying the drivers and reasons for the defendant's actions, allows for a coherent and often compelling explanation. Evidence of motive is indirectly evidence of the suspect's intentions and thus also whether their actions were premeditated.

Like opportunity, motive is a precursor to the criminal act, and therefore also modelled as one of its causes. In the simplest case we can model motive as a direct parent of the crime variable. Consider a legal case where three nurses (A, B, C) are suspected of stealing drugs from the hospital storeroom. They were the only three workers with access to the storeroom. To keep things simple, we assume that only one of them could have stolen the drugs. The police discover that nurse A has a record of drug addiction. How should we change our beliefs about who stole the drugs?

The motive model is shown in Figure 10.16a. As well as separate nodes to represent whether each nurse has a motive, we have a common-effect node that represents who stole the drugs (A, B, C or no theft). We also have a child node (effectively an evidence node) that tells us whether or not a theft has occurred. We assume that nurses are more likely to steal drugs if they have an addiction than if they don't, and that the prior of addiction is low (we set it at 10% for each nurse).

Once we know a theft has occurred, but before we know about motive, each nurse has an equal probability of 33% of stealing the drugs (see Figure 10.16b). Once we find out that nurse A has a motive, her probability increases to 66% (see Figure 10.17a). If we then discover that neither nurse B nor C has a motive, nurse A's probability increases to 71% (see Figure 10.17b).

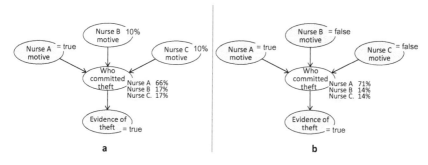

Figure 10.17   Updated model based on motive evidence. (a) When nurse A has motive. (b) When we also know that neither nurse B nor C has motive.

Note that before we enter the evidence that a theft has occurred, the knowledge of one nurse having a motive does not affect the probability of the other nurses having a motive (these causes are independent). However, conditional on evidence that a theft has occurred, the probability of motive increases for all nurses; then, knowing that nurse A has a motive slightly reduces the probability of the other nurses having a motive via explaining away.

We have kept the example simple, but it is naturally extended to more suspects, and where evidence of motive is unreliable. Also we can explore the effect of different priors and strength of motives. The model so far glosses over some important distinctions between the notions of motive, intention and premeditation, which can also be captured in the Bayes net approach.

10.3.5.1   *Motive, Intentions and Premeditation*
Distinguishing motive from intention is a mainstay of legal discourse: while intention is a critical element to be proved in certain crimes, motive is deemed irrelevant. For example, the law of murder requires the mental element of intent, but it does not take motive into account, and thus does not differentiate between a revenge killing and a mercy killing (Herring, 2014).

Nonetheless, motive and intention are closely related, with motive often cast as a cause of intentional action, and thus potentially evidence for an intention. We can model this by adding a separate node for intention, and thus allowing evidence of motive to support inferences about intention, since both are common effects of motive (see Figure 10.18). This extension is germane when no direct evidence about the suspect's intention is

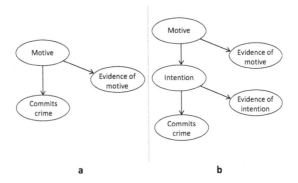

Figure 10.18   Modelling motive and intention. (a) Simple model with direct link from motive to crime. (b) Expanded model with intention as an intermediate variable between motive and crime.

available. For example, a wife charged with murdering her husband looks more guilty when it is discovered that the husband was having an affair.

Another important distinction is between an intention just prior to an action – an *intention-in-action* – and a *prior intention* to do something, formed in advance of the intended action (Searle & Willis, 1983). The two are often causally connected: X hatches a plan to kill Y, generating a sequence of actions that culminate in the final deadly act. But someone can also act intentionally without a prior plan or intention, such as when X kills Y spontaneously in a fit of rage.

Often critical in a murder case is establishing a causal link from the prior intention – via the planned activity it generates – to the intention-in-action, just before the crime is committed. This causal pathway can be used to confirm that the action was premeditated. For example, in the murder case discussed in Chapter 6, Emile Gourbin was shown to have planned the murder of his fiancée Marie Latelle because he had set the clocks forward the night before her death, to fabricate an alibi (see Figure 10.19).

A third distinction is between motive as a fact versus motive as a mental state (Wigmore 1913). The former is a cause of the latter, and each factor might require separate evidence. For example, Emile's alleged motive for killing Marie was her decision to break off their engagement. To support this claim one might need evidence that Marie indeed decided to break off the engagement (the motive fact), and that Emile was suitably upset by this decision that he planned to kill her (the motive as mental state leading to a prior intention to kill). The latter step is often hard to establish because it involves inferring a mental state.

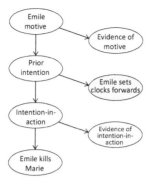

Figure 10.19 Modelling Emile Gourbin's motive and intention for killing Marie Latelle.

We have reviewed three key distinctions: motive versus intention, prior intention versus intention-in-action, motive as fact versus mental state. All three are at play in the first-degree murder case discussed in Chapter 9, in which the defendant Johnson was charged with killing Caldwell 'with deliberate premeditation and malice aforethought'. The prosecution alleged that Johnson, angry and humiliated after Caldwell had threatened him, formed a plan to kill Caldwell. To achieve this goal Johnson returned home to get a knife, and then confronted Caldwell, stabbing him to death (see Figure 10.20).

Constructing a causal model of a case is a valuable method for charting the interrelations between motives, intentions and actions, and clarifying the impact of different pieces of evidence. While such analyses are usually conducted implicitly and intuitively, Bayesian networks force us to make our arguments explicit and open to scrutiny. We need not model every nuance in the case – indeed this would be impossible – but we should strive to separate out propositions for which there is separate evidence, and ideally build a causal pathway from motives to intentions through to the final actions.

10.3.6 Character and Propensity

Common sense tells us that a person's previous conduct is often useful for inferring their current conduct. But in legal contexts admitting a defendant's previous convictions is often disallowed, on the grounds that it might prejudice the fact-finder against the defendant. However, rules on admissibility of previous convictions have been relaxed somewhat, with the constraint that they be suitably related to the charge under consideration.

Figure 10.20   Model of fight between Johnson and Caldwell.[15]

We sidestep the legal debate and show how character evidence can be modelled and combined with other evidence.[16]

In the legal context the defendant's character is typically assessed in terms of previous convictions. It helps to separate the evidence used to assess character from the person's character itself: the former is only a noisy indicator of the latter, and there might be other evidence for someone's character besides their actual convictions. Construed in this way, character refers to a propensity or tendency of the person, a latent cause of their overt criminal behaviour. Thus, we model propensity as a common cause of the defendant's previous convictions and of the crime they are currently accused of (see Figure 10.21).

The notion of propensity is also usefully broken down into subtypes corresponding to different types of crime – homicide, assault, burglary and so on – and allowing for some overlap, such that the propensity for one type of crime might be correlated with a propensity for another type (see Redmayne, 2015).

Crime statistics help us quantify the strength of relation between propensity and probability of re-offending, which can vary across types of crime. By using such data to parameterize our networks we can evaluate the probative force of propensity evidence and see how it combines with other evidence.

---

[15] This model is slightly simplified compared with the model presented in Chapter 9, but this model includes nodes to represent the evidence.

[16] For discussion of character evidence see Redmayne (2015), who makes a strong case for its probative value and admission in trial.

Figure 10.21 Modelling propensity.

Because propensity is modelled as a cause of the crime hypothesis, the crucial parameters are the conditional probabilities of offending – with versus without previous convictions. Indeed, as Redmayne stresses, we are mainly concerned with *comparative propensity* – how much does knowledge of the suspect's prior convictions raise the probability that he committed the crime compared to no convictions? Moreover, we should not use propensity evidence alone, but see how it magnifies the probability of guilt when combined with other evidence.

To illustrate, we show the effect of previous convictions in a model that includes both propensity and opportunity. We use a propensity variable with three levels (high, medium, low) and an evidence-of-propensity variable with three states (high, medium, low), corresponding to the suspect's previous convictions for burglary.[17] For illustrative purposes we assume a prior distribution of high (1%), medium (19%), low propensity (80%), assuming that only a small number of people have a high propensity for burglary;[18] we use an opportunity prior of 1/100: the suspect is one of a hundred people who could have committed the burglary (but the key issue to be shown does not depend on these numbers).

When the suspect has no prior convictions, the probability he committed the crime is close to the prior at 1% (see Figure 10.22a). However, if the suspect has a high number of prior convictions, then the probability rises to about 22% (see Figure 10.22b).

The key point here is that character evidence, as well as motive and opportunity, can be included in our models. The exact numbers can

---

[17] The same points can be shown using binary variables, but using three levels adds a degree of realism. More finer-grained models are possible, which take into account more gradations, and also the nature of the offence. For relevant base rates see Redmayne (2015).

[18] These numbers could be refined using official crime statistics.

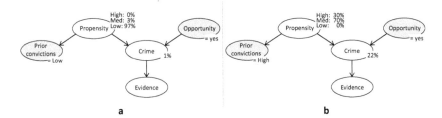

Figure 10.22   Updated propensity model for (a) low prior convictions and
(b) high prior convictions.

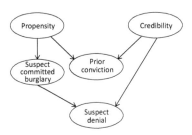

Figure 10.23   Prior convictions as evidence of both propensity and low credibility.

sometimes be derived from sources such as crime statistics. But it is the
comparative inferences that are crucial here.

Evidence of character can speak to both propensity and credibility. For
example, suppose a defendant charged with burglary has previous convictions for burglary. These convictions can be used to show that he has the
propensity to steal, and/or to show he is an unreliable witness (Redmayne,
2015). This dual use of character evidence is neatly captured in a Bayes net
(see Figure 10.23).

This model allows us to separate out the two different routes by
which character evidence impacts on our overall belief in the defendant's guilt – via an increase in his propensity to commit the crime, and
via a decrease in the reliability of his claim that he did not commit the
crime.[19]

---

[19] Note that I have oriented the arrow from credibility to prior convictions, assuming that his lack of
credibility was an influencing factor in his committing previous burglaries. But this link could be re-
oriented if one assumed that his previous burglaries led to him becoming less credible. The 'real'
causality might go either or both ways.

10.3.7 Dependent Evidence

So far we have assumed that items of evidence are independent (more precisely, that items are conditionally independent given the target hypothesis). This assumption makes it easier to assess the impact of multiple pieces of evidence and is a common default in evidential reasoning (see Chapter 4). However, sometimes items of evidence are dependent, and it is critical to model this pattern when assessing the overall probative force of the evidence. The simplest way to capture such a dependency is to add a direct link between the two related items (see Figure 10.24).

On this model, the status of evidence item 1 depends both on the target hypothesis and the status of evidence item 2, with the exact functional relation given by the CPT for item 1. This means that the extent to which item 1 changes the probability of the hypothesis is modulated by item 2. If this dependency is not acknowledged, there is a severe risk of overestimating the value of item 1, and thus overestimating the posterior probability of the hypothesis.

Consider a legal example where the target hypothesis is whether suspect X was present at the crime scene. Two pieces of evidence are presented to support this hypothesis: a reported match between fingerprints found at the crime scene and those of the suspect (item 1), and an eyewitness report placing the suspect at the scene (item 2).

Let's look at two cases:

- Case A (*independent evidence*): the fingerprint expert did not know about the eyewitness report when she analyzed the fingerprints and completed her report. Therefore there is no causal link from the eyewitness report to her report.
- Case B (*dependent evidence*): the fingerprint expert knew about the eyewitness report, and this influenced her judgment that the fingerprints match the suspect. Therefore there is a causal link from the eyewitness report to her report.

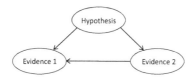

Figure 10.24 Dependence between two items of evidence.

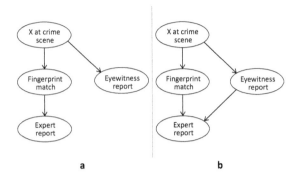

Figure 10.25   Models of (a) independent versus (b) dependent evidence.

The two cases yield different models (see Figure 10.25). We use these models to see how the evidential dependency in case B changes the probative value of the fingerprint match, and consequently the posterior probability of the hypothesis given both items of evidence.

The CPTs for the nodes *Eyewitness report and Fingerprint match* are the same in both models. We assume that the eyewitness has an accuracy of 90%; and that if X was at the crime scene the probability of his fingerprints being left is 90%, whereas if he was not at the scene this probability is only 1%.

In case A the expert report has an accuracy of 90%. The critical difference is for the expert report in case B. Crucially, the expert is influenced by the eyewitness report: she is more likely to report a match if she knows the eyewitness gave a positive ID (and would be less likely if she knew the ID was negative). The CPT used in this example reflects this qualitative pattern.[20]

The models show us how to update our beliefs. For example, with a prior of 10% that X was at the crime scene, for case A receiving both items of evidence gives a posterior of 88% (see Figure 10.26a), whereas for case B the posterior is 69% (see Figure 10.26b). Thus, the dependence between items in case B has reduced the impact of the expert report.

Suppose you are a decision-maker receiving the evidence but not knowing about the dependency between the expert and eyewitness reports. If you assumed independence, as is the common default, you would overestimate the probative force of the expert report, and thus overestimate

---

[20]   The CPT for *Expert report* in case B is:
   P(*expert report* | *match, eyewitness*) = 0.95
   P(*expert report* | *match, ~eyewitness*) = 0.6
   P(*expert report* | *~match, eyewitness*) = 0.4
   P(*expert report* | *~match, ~eyewitness*) = 0.05
   Note that any probabilities matching this qualitative pattern will give similar results.

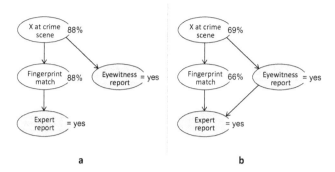

Figure 10.26 The difference in updating the models given (a) independent and (b) dependent evidence.

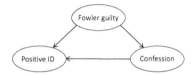

Figure 10.27 Dependence between positive ID and confession evidence.

the posterior probability that X was at the crime scene. Situations with dependent evidence can get more complex – such as when witnesses collude, or share information from a common source, and such cases demand more complex modelling (see also Pilditch et al., 2020).

Nonetheless, even this simple dependent-evidence model can correct serious inferential errors. For example, in a death penalty case (see Mosteller, 2015), Elrico Fowler was convicted of murder on the basis of two supposedly independent pieces of evidence: an eyewitness identification and Fowler's confession (later retracted). But it turned out that these items were not independent: the eyewitness had been unsure of the identification, and only gave a positive ID when told that Fowler had confessed (see Figure 10.27). Modelling these items correctly would reduce the overall probative value of the evidence (perhaps below the threshold for a murder conviction).

10.3.8 Modelling Deception

Legal cases often hinge upon witness credibility: is the eyewitness telling the truth when he accuses the defendant? Is the defendant telling the truth when she proclaims her innocence? These are thorny questions to answer, requiring careful evaluation of witness testimony. We have introduced the evidence-reliability idiom as a general-purpose tool for modelling witness credibility, but the issue of veracity raises several additional subtleties.

The heart of the problem is that testimony offered by a witness, if honestly given, tells us one thing; but, if dishonestly given, it tells us something quite different. Thus, if a witness claims that she saw the accused at the crime scene – and she is in fact telling the truth – we should raise our belief in the accused's guilt; but if the witness is lying, we should not raise our belief – indeed perhaps we should lower it. But if we don't know for sure whether the witness is telling the truth or lying, how should we update our beliefs given her testimony? Moreover, the content of her testimony (what it is about) is also relevant to the witness's credibility: if what she reports is implausible, or does not fit with what else we know, we might assign her lower credibility.

So we are faced with two unknowns – the honesty of the witness and the truth of what she says – and need to juggle these to draw sensible inferences from her evidence. The problem is that we rarely know for sure whether witnesses are telling the truth. We might have information to suggest they are generally dishonest, or have a strong motive to be dishonest on this occasion. But exactly how we take this into account to assess the impact of their testimony is a complicated inferential task.

Adding to the problem is a strategic dimension. Witnesses who seek to mislead their audience will adopt a strategy that takes into account how they expect the audience to respond. A sophisticated liar has a model of her audience, which will shape what she says; but in turn a sophisticated audience uses a model of what they think the witness believes about them, and so on. Furthermore, a sophisticated liar might best persuade an audience by selective rather than wholesale lying (lying just enough to convince the audience, but not too much to allow for refutation). We don't have space to explore all these nuances here, but we will show how the idiom-based approach can start to capture some of these subtleties.

10.3.8.1 Selective versus Non-selective Strategies

A key distinction is between *non-selective* versus *selective* lying strategies. To illustrate, suppose someone knows the truth status of a hypothesis, and wants to mislead their audience. A *non-selective strategy* would be to state the opposite of the truth: if the hypothesis is true, state that it is false, and if it is false, state that it is true. Such a strategy might be used if a witness's goal is to mislead the audience, whatever the truth of the hypothesis. For example, suppose the police are pursuing a suspect through a busy network of streets, and don't know which turning the suspect has taken, left or

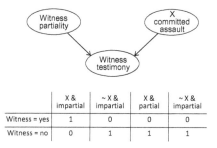

	X & impartial	~X & impartial	X & partial	~X & impartial
Witness = yes	1	0	0	0
Witness = no	0	1	1	1

Figure 10.28 Deception model with CPT for witness testimony.

right. They ask a bystander – who happens to be an accomplice of the suspect, and thus wants to mislead the police. If the suspect has turned right, the bystander will say left, and vice-versa.

In contrast, suppose that a witness only wants to mislead the audience if the hypothesis is false. Then a selective strategy is appropriate. For example, a witness might want to convince the police of the suspect's innocence (perhaps they are close friends). If the suspect is guilty, she will say he's innocent; if he's innocent she will (honestly) say he is innocent. One implication of this strategy is that she always says the suspect is innocent, whatever the actual truth. More generally, a *selective strategy* is to lie about evidence that goes against one's hypothesis, but to tell the truth about evidence that supports it.

Both types of strategy can be modelled using the evidence-reliability idiom, with the differences captured in their CPTs. However, as noted above, the real problem is that we don't know whether the witness is a liar (selective or non-selective), and this uncertainty needs to be incorporated into the model. This introduces another layer of complexity. Here we focus on the selective strategy, since it is more common in investigative and legal contexts, but a similar approach can be used for the non-selective strategy (see Mocke, Pilditch & Lagnado, 2020).

Suppose a youth X is accused of assault in a nightclub. The police plan to interview witnesses to the assault; some of these are friends of the suspect (and thus likely to be partial) and some are strangers (and thus likely to be impartial), but the police don't know who is who. We model this set-up using the evidence-reliability idiom, with two parental cause nodes – the hypothesis that X is guilty of the assault and the credibility of the witness – and a specialized CPT that captures how these causes interact to determine the witness's testimony (see Figure 10.28).

To keep things simple we assume that impartial witnesses will accurately report what they saw, whereas partial witnesses will lie selectively: that is, if

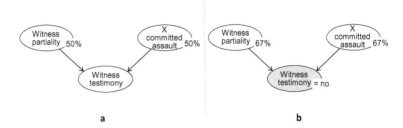

Figure 10.29   Deception model. (a) Prior probabilities. (b) Updated probability given
witness testifies it was not suspect X.

X committed the assault, they will falsely report that he didn't; if X did not commit the assault, they will correctly report that he didn't. Either way we assume a partial witness will report that X did not commit the crime.

These assumptions are captured in the CPT for the witness testimony node; they are readily made probabilistic, but to show the logic of the model it is easiest to keep the relations deterministic. We assume uniform priors for whether X committed the assault, and for whether the witness is partial (for example, half of the witnesses are friends of X). The prior probabilities are shown in Figure 10.29a.

The first witness is interviewed (without the police knowing if he is partial or impartial), and he testifies that X did not commit the assault. What should we conclude? Does his testimony change our probability that X is guilty? Does it change our probability that the witness is partial?

Intuitively, the testimony should lower our belief that X committed the assault: there is a 50% chance the witness is impartial and thus correctly testifies that X didn't do it. However, updating the probability that the witness is partial or impartial is trickier. It is tempting to reason that if his testimony lowers the probability of X's guilt, then he's more likely to be impartial. But the Bayes net reveals that the witness is actually more likely to be partial (see Figure 10.29b).

This might seem counter-intuitive, but on reflection it makes sense. Before the testimony is given there are four possible states (and by assumption these are equally probable):

- X is guilty, and witness is impartial
- X is guilty, and witness is partial
- X is not guilty, and witness is impartial
- X is not guilty, and witness is partial

Figure 10.30   Deception model with separate evidence.

When the witness testifies that X did not commit the assault, we can rule out one possibility – that X is guilty *and* that the witness is impartial – leaving three possible states:

- X is guilty, and witness is partial
- X is not guilty, and witness is impartial
- X is not guilty, and witness is partial

X is guilty in one of these three states, therefore:

> Probability X is guilty $= 1/3$

However, the witness is partial in two of these three states, therefore:

> Probability that witness is partial $= 2/3$

By keeping the example simple – perfect accuracy of witness and uniform priors – we can do these computations by hand, but anything more complex requires a Bayes net.

The model is naturally extended to include additional evidence. For example, suppose that police find a new witness whom they know to be impartial, with an accuracy of 90%. The new model and updated probabilities are shown in Figure 10.30. The new evidence decreases the probability of X's guilt to 5%, and increases the probability that the previous witness was impartial to 47%. But note that this latter probability remains below its prior of 50%. Indeed, even if we were certain that X was not guilty, the probability of the witness being impartial stays at its prior. This is due to explaining away – his testimony is fully explained by the fact that X did not commit the crime.

Even with a simplified example the inferences surrounding deception are subtle, and people are likely to go astray without a formal framework to help them (Mocke et al., 2020; Pilditch, Fries & Lagnado, 2019). A key challenge is to model our uncertainty about the witness's credibility, and make rational inferences. Our intuitive judgments here can only take us so far because we need to draw conclusions based on several unknowns.

10.3.9   Alibi Idiom

An alibi is often critical evidence in a legal case. For most crimes – including assault, rape, robbery and most types of murder – if the defendant can show they were not present at the crime scene at the time of the incident, then they cannot be guilty. Hence the crucial importance for the prosecution to establish opportunity. However, a solid alibi is often hard to provide, because people spend a fair proportion of their time on their own or with friends, relatives or colleagues. This is especially true for crimes committed late at night: 'where else would law-abiding citizens be at 3am but in bed with their spouse?' (Martin, 1967). Such alibi providers are often treated with suspicion, due to their vested interest in protecting the accused.

Alibi evidence raises several inferential challenges: how much weight should an alibi be given if the provider is impartial versus partial? How does one deal with conflicting statements between alibi witnesses and other witnesses? What if an alibi is contradicted by physical evidence? Here again we cannot cover all the complexities, but the idiom-based approach can shed light on these questions.

We will focus on the key differences between impartial versus partial alibi providers, and how beliefs about guilt should change when an alibi is discredited. This latter issue is of legal relevance, because jurors are commonly warned against drawing 'adverse inferences' when a defendant is found to be lying. We will show under what conditions such inferences are rationally licensed.

Impartial witnesses, such as strangers or bystanders, usually have no reason to lie, although they can still make mistakes in their testimony (due to memory lapses, etc.). In contrast, partial witnesses, such as relatives or friends, are more likely to be motivated to lie to protect the suspect. We can capture this using a *Credibility* variable,[21] such that a witness motivated to lie is not credible (*Credibility* = false), whereas a witness not motivated to lie is credible (*Credibility* = true). When motivated to lie the witness will provide an alibi irrespective of whether the suspect was with them or not.

---

[21] To keep things simple, here we ignore other aspects of credibility, and focus on whether the alibi witness has a motive to lie; we also assume that a partial witness automatically has a motive to lie. A more complex model could be constructed to capture other issues affecting credibility and its relation to deception. Also note that the *Credibility* variable corresponds to the *Witness partiality* variable used in the deception model.

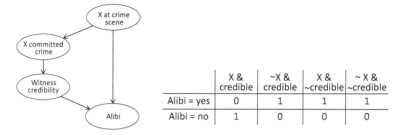

	X & credible	~X & credible	X & ~credible	~X & ~credible
Alibi = yes	0	1	1	1
Alibi = no	1	0	0	0

Figure 10.31 Alibi idiom model with CPT for alibi node. Note that this CPT is effectively the same as that used for the deception model in the previous example.

In addition, what makes alibi evidence distinctive is that the alibi provider's credibility can itself depend on whether or not the suspect committed the crime. If the suspect is guilty, the witness is more likely to be motivated to lie (and thus not credible), especially if it is the suspect alone who provides the alibi. As we shall see, this extra dependency has serious implications for how beliefs are revised when someone's alibi is discredited.

We use the *alibi idiom* to model cases where the alibi witness's credibility is affected by whether the suspect is guilty, adding a direct link from the crime hypothesis to the alibi witness's credibility (see Figure 10.31). This link corresponds to the assumption that the witness is less likely to be credible if the suspect is guilty rather than innocent. The CPT for the alibi testimony incorporates selective lying, such that a non-credible witness will state that the suspect was not at the crime scene irrespective of the truth.

We can use this idiom to explore the situation where a suspect gives an alibi that is subsequently contradicted by other evidence. Suppose that the suspect is accused of assault, which took place late at night in a quiet alleyway. The suspect claims he was at home several miles away at the time of the crime. The police have access to CCTV footage, which they will examine to see if the suspect was in the vicinity of the crime scene. We use the opportunity idiom, alibi idiom and evidence-reliability idiom to construct the Bayes net (see Figure 10.32).

We assume that if the suspect was at the crime scene, he would have been one of only two people with the opportunity to commit the crime. We also assume that if he is guilty, he is 9 times more likely to be motivated to lie (and hence non-credible) than if he is innocent.[22]

---

[22] Note that these assumptions can be varied without affecting the key points to be demonstrated. I encourage the interested reader to download the alibi model and explore different probabilities.

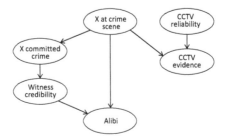

Figure 10.32   Alibi model combined with CCTV evidence.

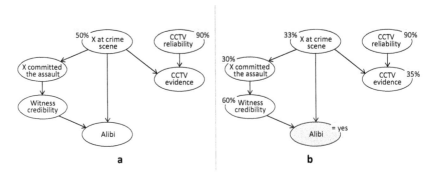

Figure 10.33   Alibi model. (a) With prior probabilities. (b) Updated probabilities when suspect gives alibi.

We assume a prior of 50% that the suspect was at the crime scene, and a prior of 90% that the CCTV evidence is reliable (see Figure 10.33a). The probability he committed the assault is 25%. Next, we enter the alibi evidence, which lowers the probability that the suspect was at the crime scene from 50% to 33%. At this point the probability he committed the assault is 30%, and the probability that he is credible is 60% (see Figure 10.33b).

Finally, we enter the CCTV evidence, which shows the suspect at the crime scene close to the time of the assault. This substantially raises the probability that he was at the crime scene, from 33% to 90%. The probability that he committed the assault jumps up from 30% to 81%, and his credibility falls to 9% (see Figure 10.34a).

Crucially, the CCTV evidence affects the probability of guilt along two separate routes: (1) it raises the probability that he was at the crime scene and (2) it contradicts his alibi and, via explaining away, shows that he is highly likely to be lying.

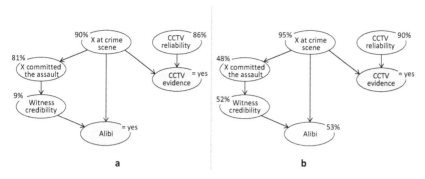

Figure 10.34   Alibi model. (a) Updated probabilities with alibi and CCTV evidence. (b) Updated probabilities with CCTV only.

To see the impact of the alibi discredit, we can look at the model without the alibi evidence (see Figure 10.34b). With only the CCTV evidence, but no alibi evidence, the probability that he is at the scene is 95%, but the probability of guilt is lower at 48%. Giving a false alibi statement is much worse for the suspect than giving none!

This finding supports the common intuition that a suspect who is shown to be lying in their testimony is more likely to be guilty. Of course, in an actual case we would need to look for other reasons why the suspect might lie about his whereabouts. Perhaps he was having an affair, or committing an even worse crime. This is why the judge instructs the jury about adverse inferences – telling them to consider (and rule out) alternative accounts for the lies. The model can handle this by adding alternative possible causes of the witness's credibility. The modelling approach forces us to make these factors explicit, and helps us assess their impact on our other judgments. If alternative explanations are very implausible, then the inference from lying to guilt is supported.

One final complication – the viability of a link from guilt to credibility depends on the knowledge or beliefs of the witness. If the alibi witness is the suspect, we can assume he knows whether or not he is guilty, and this justifies the link. However, in cases where the alibi witness does not know whether the suspect is guilty, this link is less plausible. For example, consider a mother who gives her son an alibi, but does not know if he is guilty of the crime. In such a case we should remove the link from guilt to credibility (see Figure 10.35).

Here we use a prior for the mother's credibility of 10%, but keep all other parameters the same as in the previous model. While the probability

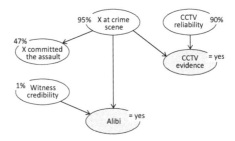

Figure 10.35   Model with alibi and CCTV, but alibi provider does not know whether suspect is guilty.

that the suspect was at the crime scene remains high at 95%, the probability he committed the crime is much lower at 47%. Indeed it is virtually the same as in the case where no alibi is given. This shows that the mother's discredited alibi does not support an additional inference about guilt (her lie is not diagnostic of the suspect's guilt) because there is no direct link from guilt to credibility. This example demonstrates how the impact of a discredited alibi depends on what the alibi provider knows about the suspect's guilt. Again the model helps clarify what inferences are licensed.

10.3.10   Summary

We have finished our tour of the idioms. They capture the key schemas used in investigative reasoning, and can be combined and re-used to model larger cases. Alongside the idioms, we can model additional causal structure to flesh out the hypotheses presented by prosecution and defence. This connects up the disparate pieces of evidence to give a coherent narrative-like structure to the model. While Bayes nets are not bound to represent causal relations, using causal knowledge is often crucial for getting the structure right, and gives a principled way of building up larger structures. It also resonates with our claims that to properly evaluate evidence we must model the causal processes and mechanisms that generate that evidence (see Chapter 6).

10.4   Putting It All Together

To show how the idioms can be used to model a whole case, we return to the *Witness for the Prosecution*. To recap, Leonard Vole is accused of murdering

Miss French, and the prosecution case looks strong, with blood matching that of Miss French found on Vole's jacket, the maid placing Vole with Miss French at the time of the crime, and Vole's wife saying that Vole had confessed to her that he had committed the murder. Vole also stood to gain a large sum from Miss French's will. The defence case argues that the blood on Vole's jacket could have come from Vole himself, and that the maid is not an impartial witness, having been written out of the will in favour of Vole. But the pivotal moment in the case is when Vole's wife's testimony is dramatically undermined at the last minute, resulting in Vole's acquittal.

Using the idioms, we construct a Bayes net that covers the key evidence in the case (see Figure 10.36). It is helpful to divide the model into four main parts:

Opportunity. We use the opportunity prior idiom that draws on two estimates – the number of people actually in the area when the crime took place (n), and the number of people in the extended crime scene based on Vole's agreed location (N). These two numbers allow us to set the prior that Vole had opportunity (n/N) and the conditional probability for his committing the crime given he was present (and before we consider other evidence).

For the current model we use $n = 5$, to reflect the fact that the crime took place at a well-defined time during the night in a quiet area, and $N = 100$ (because Vole admitted he was at the house earlier that evening). These numbers could be represented as distributions rather than point values, and their impact on the probability of guilt assessed using sensitivity analysis (Fenton et al., 2020).

Evidence about opportunity. We use the evidence-reliability idiom to represent the maid's testimony, taking into account her dislike for Vole (given that she had previously been the sole benefactor in the will). We use the alibi evidence idiom to represent Vole's testimony that he was not present at the time of the crime, with his credibility being modulated by whether or not he committed the crime (hence the direct link from crime to credibility).

Motive. We represent motive as precursor to the crime. The main alleged motive was that Vole knew he was in the will, and stood to inherit a huge fortune; also the fact that he was poor and unemployed is taken into account as an enhancing factor. We also use the evidence idiom to include the fact (undisputed) that Vole was enquiring about luxury cruises.

Blood evidence. To model the blood evidence we use the explaining away idiom, with two competing (but not exclusive) causes of the blood found on Vole's jacket: either it came from Miss French or from Vole himself (or both). Crucial here is that although the blood on the jacket was the same

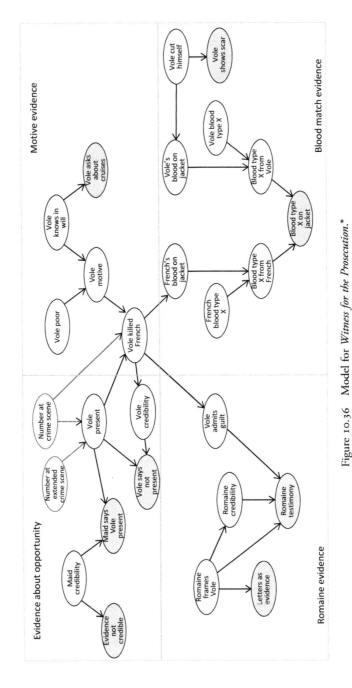

Figure 10.36 Model for *Witness for the Prosecution*.*

* The full model can be downloaded from www.explainingtheevidence.com. I used priors of 90% for the maid's credibility, 10% for Romaine wanting to frame Vole, and 10% for Vole cutting himself.

Table 10.1 *Updating the* Witness for the Prosecution *model.*

	Probability Vole is guilty (%)
Prior (using opportunity prior with $n = 5$, $N = 100$)	5
Prosecution evidence	
Motive evidence (*Vole poor* = true, *Vole asks about cruises* = true)	7
Maid testifies Vole was present	46
Blood type on jacket matches French (*French blood type X* = true, *Jacket blood type X* = true)	87
Romaine testifies Vole admitted guilt	97
Defence evidence	
Vole testifies he was not present	97
Evidence that maid is not credible	85
Blood type on jacket matches Vole (*Vole blood type X* = true)	71
Vole shows scar	58
Letters as evidence of that Romaine wants to frame Vole	21

type as Miss French's, Vole also had the same blood type. To avoid over-complicating the model we assume that the blood type testing was 100% accurate, but the possibility of error is easily introduced using the evidence-reliability idioms for each blood test. Also note that we assume that the blood type is rare (1/100) rather than common (in the original story it was blood type o – relatively common – but nowadays forensic testing is much more powerful).

Romaine testimony. We represent Romaine's testimony using the evidence-reliability idiom, with the added twist that her credibility might also depend on her supposed desire to frame Vole.

10.4.1 Updating the Model

We can now see how the model updates the probability that Vole is guilty as each item of evidence is presented. We use a presentation sequence that mimics the trial, where prosecution evidence is presented before defence evidence.[23] As our model uses Bayesian updating, the final probability will be the same irrespective of the order of evidence; but we learn much from seeing how the probabilities change as individual items are presented. The sequence of probability updates is shown in Table 10.1.

[23] But note that in an actual trial, cross-examination of witnesses takes place after each witness gives evidence, so discrediting of a witness can occur then too.

Using the opportunity prior we start at 5%. The motive evidence increases this to 7%. The maid's testimony that Vole was present boosts this to 46%, showing the importance of opportunity. The blood match evidence increases this up to 87%, showing its significance. The final item of prosecution evidence, Romaine's testimony, drives the probability over 95%, which for many people would be enough for a guilty verdict.

Next we look at the defence evidence. Vole's testimony that he was not present counts for little: he would say that, wouldn't he? However, evidence undermining the maid's testimony brings the probability of guilt down to 85% – again showing the relevance of opportunity. Finding that Vole's blood type also matches the blood on the jacket reduces the probability to 71%, and his production of the scar on his wrist decreases it further to 58%. Finally, when the letters are revealed, compromising Romaine's testimony, the probability falls to 21%.

Irrespective of the exact numbers, the model captures the rise and fall of the case against Vole, showing how the evidence can interact in a subtle but intuitively reasonable fashion.

While the use of probabilities is essential for running the models, specific numbers are not essential for grasping the key patterns of inference, which are often qualitative in nature. We can try out a range of parameters and see how our inferences change. Indeed, we can explore how sensitive our conclusions are to the specific probabilities we have used (aptly named *sensitivity analysis*). For example, we could explore how much our conclusions about Vole's guilt change if we vary the priors and other conditional probabilities in the model.[24]

10.5   Practical Aspects

While the idiom-based approach can be used to model an entire legal case, this is often not necessary or even desirable. Sometimes it is enough to focus on key parts of a case – such as the forensic evidence – where the logic imposed by the Bayes net approach is crucial for drawing correct inferences. Thus, we might concentrate our analysis of the Vole case on the blood evidence component, which rationally integrates the rarity of the blood type. Likewise, in a case that hinges on DNA evidence, it might suffice to analyze only this part of the case. By taking advantage of the modularity

---

[24] For more details about the use of sensitivity analysis in modelling crime cases, see Fenton et al. (2020) and Smit, Lagnado, Morgan and Fenton (2016).

inherent in Bayes nets, we can often isolate pivotal components of a case, and focus our analysis of one or two of these parts of the network. This process works well when our aim is to expose and correct faulty reasoning.

For example, in Figure 10.37 we show a partial model of the Barry George case (see Chapters 5 and 7). We have used the idioms to represent the key hypotheses, the evidence and its reliability. However, in Chapter 7 we only applied a quantitative analysis to one component: the GSR evidence and its two potential causes. But this was enough to suggest that, contrary to what was argued in the appeal, the GSR evidence did have some probative weight, and should not have been judged irrelevant.

Furthermore, in some cases it is best to create separate models for prosecution and defence accounts, rather than trying to integrate these into one complete model. This is particularly useful when the two opposing accounts disagree on key issues, and present different hypotheses and different bodies of evidence. Capturing both accounts in a single network is difficult and can undermine the clarity of the Bayes net analysis. Keeping the accounts separate can make explicit comparison more difficult, but problems or weaknesses inherent to either case are more likely to be exposed, which could be a critical factor in deciding between the accounts (see Neil et al., 2019, for an approach to this problem).

Finally, returning to a common concern about the modelling of legal cases: where do the numbers come from? While we need probabilities to run a model, we should not get too fixated on the exact numbers. Often our focus is on qualitative or comparative inferences: is this piece of evidence stronger than that piece? Do these two opposing pieces of evidence balance out, or does one dominate? What happens to competing hypotheses when one is confirmed? Is this witness more credible than that one? Does the possibility of deception undermine the evidence altogether?

Here it is the logic of inference that is critical, not the precise calculations. We can try out a range of values, and still draw vital conclusions. Moreover, there is often information that can help us refine our probability judgments. For example, we can draw on crime statistics to help quantify issues of propensity and character (Redmayne, 2015), or spatio-temporal information about the crime and the location of possible suspects to help quantify opportunity. We can also attain empirical data about the accuracy of different types of forensic tests and even about the accuracy of eyewitnesses. By combining qualitative and quantitative evidence Bayes nets allow us to take advantage of all available information.

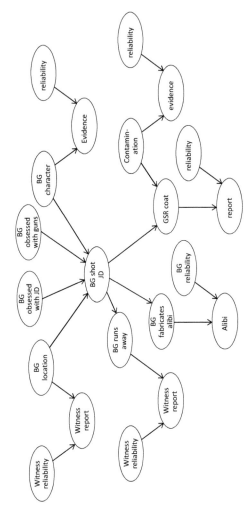

Figure 10.37   Model of the Barry George case.

10.6   Where and When Should We Use Bayes Nets?

Where and when might Bayes nets be used? Potentially at various stages in the legal process:

- *Investigative phase* – by investigators and forensic scientists to help organize and draw inferences from complex evidence; also as a guide for searching for new evidence and identifying gaps in their accounts; helping to build an evidential case for prosecution.
- *Decisions to prosecute* – by the CPS to help make decisions about whether there is sufficient evidence to charge a suspect.
- *Case preparation* – by prosecution and defence teams when building a case for the trial, identifying the logic of arguments; quantifying the value of forensic evidence.
- *In court* – to provide visual depictions of forensic evidence, helping to overcome jury misunderstanding of complex probabilistic arguments.
- *Post trial* – in appeals, inquests and enquiries, to deal with arguments about misinterpretation of complex evidence.

The idea of using Bayes nets in court is controversial. Indeed in an appeal judgment UK judges explicitly criticized the use of Bayes' rule:

> the attempt to determine guilt or innocence on the basis of a mathematical formula, applied to each separate piece of evidence, is simply inappropriate to the jury's task. Jurors evaluate evidence and reach a conclusion not by means of a formula, mathematical or otherwise, but by the joint application of their individual common sense and knowledge of the world to the evidence before them. (*R* v. *Adams,* 1996)

However, this statement needs to be put in context. It was given in response to an attempt by the defence to explain Bayes' rule to the jury in the rape case *R* v. *Adams*. In the first trial an expert statistician used illustrative probabilities, but encouraged the jury to substitute their own estimates. Adams was found guilty; but he appealed on the basis that the judge had misdirected the jury on the use of Bayes' rule. In the second trial the defence expert again tried to show jurors how to apply Bayes' rule, even giving them calculators to compute probabilities themselves (see Lynch & McNally, 2003). Needless to say this attempt also failed.[25]

Nonetheless, complex probabilistic evidence such as DNA is routinely used in court, and we must strive to help jurors understand it. Perhaps

---

[25] As we have seen in Chapter 4, a raft of psychological research confirms that people struggle with such computations.

Bayes nets could help? They go beyond simply applying a formula, and graphically display the causal relations between evidence and hypotheses. This suggests two possibilities. First, when forensic scientists and lawyers prepare their arguments, or in a pre-trial meeting, they could use Bayes nets to help them understand the evidence and make logically consistent inferences. This process might also suggest ways for them to present their arguments in court. Second, the visual side of Bayes nets could be used to help explain these inferences to the jury – building on people's intuitive sense of causality to help them follow the probabilistic reasoning, without requiring that they do the computations themselves.

10.6.1   Bayes Nets for Training

Where I see the best use for Bayes nets, however, is as a training tool. Forensic scientists, lawyers and judges could benefit from such training, if only to understand what inferences should be drawn from DNA evidence, and to avoid common fallacies. As noted above, building Bayes nets forces you to be clear about your assumptions, and helps you think about alternative explanations and consider evidence reliability; it also allows you to explore different possible scenarios and the impact of different priors and conditional probabilities. These are all essential skills for evaluating evidence.

We don't yet know how readily legal decision-makers could learn to use Bayes nets, or if this training would improve their reasoning. But there are some promising signs. For example, in a series of studies we successfully trained lay people to use Bayes nets to solve complex probability problems (Cruz et al., 2020). These problems centred on investigative cases, and required people to reason about complex bodies of evidence. In particular, participants had to combine evidence of differing weight and reliability, to make explaining away inferences, to allow for the possibility of deception, to deal with dependent evidence, and to avoid zero-sum thinking. Even after just a few hours of training, participants who used the Bayes net software gave substantially more correct answers relative to controls who only received general instructions about evidential reasoning. The benefits of such training would not be restricted to the legal context. We expect similar gains in other areas where evidential reasoning is key, including intelligence analysis, medicine, politics and finance.

10.7 Bayes Nets as a Thinking Tool

The idiom-based approach is not a magic bullet to solve a crime. It does not replace the need for human judgment, but it supports and encourages careful thinking. By constructing formal models we sharpen our reasoning: clarifying the logic and structure of our arguments, identifying gaps and presuppositions, and making our assumptions explicit and open to scrutiny.

Crucially, we can use these *formal models* to help us build and explore our own *mental models*. Here there is a division of labour between our own judgments, which we use to construct the models, and the computational algorithms of the Bayes net program, which allow us to perform calculations. But the tool does not merely ensure consistent computations; it can draw out implications that go beyond our intuitions, even contradicting our expectations. For example, as shown above, how we ought to assess the credibility of multiple witnesses is not obvious, especially when there is the possibility of deception. The Bayes nets give us answers that might initially look counterintuitive, but on reflection make good sense. We have learned something new about the consequences of our assumptions.

In contrast, sometimes Bayesian computations lead to conclusions that fit poorly with strongly held beliefs; and once we identify the assumptions that underpin these conclusions, we might decide to revise our models instead. For example, we might have made assumptions about independence that on reflection (and given the output of the model) do not fit the situation we seek to model.

This interplay between building a model and checking the model's outputs against our intuitions is key – using the modelling tool as a means to explore and test our ideas. In a similar vein, the modelling supports 'what-if' thinking, allowing us to check the feasibility of different lines of argument and the consequences of different suppositions. Using the model to externalize our reasoning helps us take a metacognitive stance to our reasoning, and allows us to reflect on our models and assumptions. This back and forth between model building and testing seems a critical feature of evidence evaluation.

In short, we suggest that causal Bayes nets serve as a tool for thinking – allowing us to explore and reflect on our assumptions about the world, while keeping our inferences consistent with the laws of probability. The tool does not replace the need for human judgment, but it makes our judgments more rigorous and reflective.

10.8 Summary

In this chapter I presented an idiom-based approach to modelling legal cases using Bayes nets. I argued that these idioms provide the building blocks for reasoning about larger legal cases, and showed how they can capture a range of common issues, including questions of reliability, opportunity, motive and dependent evidence. I emphasized that more important than the exact numbers is the structure of the inferences that these models capture. I also discussed when and where such an approach might be used, and argued that primarily it could be used as a training tool to improve inferential reasoning.

CHAPTER 11

Causal Reasoning in a Time of Crisis

Throughout this book I have used legal cases to explore how people reason about evidence. I have selected controversial cases to show why good reasoning matters, and how flawed inferences can lead to miscarriages of justice. In all these cases we were (fortunately) at some distance from the action, watching from afar with no direct involvement in the events that unfolded. But my premise was that these legal examples also provide a compelling model for reasoning in everyday contexts – situations where the quality of our inferences has an impact on our own daily lives.

My initial plan for this final chapter was to flesh out this argument, showing how the main themes in this book apply to everyday situations. But then the covid-19 crisis struck,[1] and my plans changed. Here was a global disaster that confronted us all, one where we were forced to reason about entirely novel things, in the face of high uncertainty, and where our decisions affected our own and other people's well-being. Even staying home doing nothing was a consequential action. Hence my new plan is to show how key messages of this book – from both psychology and formal modelling – apply to problems faced during the coronavirus crisis.

11.1 Explaining versus Evaluating

One of the main themes in the book is that we are causal thinkers – we reason about the world by building and manipulating mental models. These models allow us to predict, to plan, to decide and to ask what if. We are driven to explain things – whether it's a biological process (such as the pathology of a disease) or a social process (such as people's reactions to its spread). But the problems we face are often complex and challenging, with intricate webs of causes and effects. Inevitably we must simplify

---

[1] At the time of writing the covid-19 virus has spread around the world, with over 100 million cases and over 3 million deaths.

things, sacrificing fidelity for efficiency. This allows us to make 'good enough' models, but can also lead to flawed inferences. Throughout the book we have seen the dangers of oversimplified models in investigative and legal contexts.

But constructing models is not sufficient for good reasoning. We need to evaluate our models against the evidence. This adds another layer of complexity, requiring us to assess how well the evidence supports our models, and to assess the reliability of the evidence itself, pulling it all together to reach a final judgment. To make things even more difficult, information often comes from unreliable sources with their own vested interests. Unsurprisingly even experts struggle to evaluate models here, and once again simplifying strategies are needed.

In short, we are quick to jump to causal claims but less capable at evaluating the evidence for these claims, especially in complex and uncertain situations. With this theme as background, I will take a selective look at reasoning in the coronavirus crisis.

11.2 The Flexibility of Causal Thinking

One advantage of causal thinking is its flexibility: it allows us to adapt our decision-making to changes in our environment. By knowing the causes behind the things we observe, we can better anticipate and deal with change. Our rapid responses to the crisis showcased this capability. None of us had encountered a global pandemic before or experienced such abrupt changes to our daily lives. But despite this, we rapidly adapted our thinking to the novel circumstances, constructing new models and reusing old ones to suit new purposes. Experts in epidemiology built models of the new disease: how it spreads and affects people, and how it might be contained, treated and eventually eliminated. Governments devised new strategies to fight the virus: lockdowns, track and trace systems, and new forms of public messaging. This is not to say these strategies were well-conceived or successful; but they were novel responses nonetheless, built from prior causal knowledge.

As lay people we were forced to rethink many of our day-to-day routines, designing new ways to help us solve a host of new problems. For example, we changed how we work, socialize and travel in order to minimize our risks of catching the virus. We also became armchair experts in public health, discussing concepts such as infection rates and herd immunity, and debating the pros and cons of lockdowns, mask-wearing and social distancing. Again it's not that we fully mastered these arguments; but we were quick to assimilate them into our planning and decision-making.

Our ingenuity at building new mental models does not of course guarantee success. Many ideas fail and need to be revised; but without the initial impetus we would have no chance of dealing with the changing landscape. Our causal invention allows us to go beyond past experience, creating novel models to fit the new situations that confront us.

How is this achieved? In Chapter 2 I argued that we possess model-building systems – intuitive theories, scripts and schemas – to help us construct mental models tailored to the new situations we face, sometimes using knowledge accrued in one domain to help construct new models for a novel context. These models embody causal claims, and thus support various forms of inference, allowing us to predict and diagnose, and to mentally try out ideas before we act. But our success depends heavily on the quality of our models and assumptions.

11.2.1   Diagnostic Reasoning Using Causal Models

To take an example that affects us all – the problem of diagnosis. Suppose you develop a fever and a cough, and you have recently visited friends with young children, one of whom was sneezing a lot. How likely is it that you have the virus? This is a tricky question because covid-19 causes a wide range of symptoms, many of which are also caused by other ailments such as colds, flus and allergies. Moreover, your chance of being exposed to the virus depends on many factors, such as your own contacts and the contacts of the people you are visiting too. Perhaps your friend's child caught the virus at school? Or maybe she's allergic to cats?

Diagnosis is a causal question – we seek the cause (or causes) of our symptoms, in order to explain and treat our condition. To achieve this we need to represent the interrelations between risk factors, diseases and symptoms. Whether explicitly or implicitly, we must construct a causal model. While covid-19 is a new virus, we can draw on our prior knowledge about other viruses to help build a plausible model. We already know that viruses are spread by infected individuals and that their severity depends on various risk factors, and in turn that infection causes a variety of symptoms. We might not know the exact details, but even at this stage we have a skeletal structure to build on.[2]

---

[2] This is very similar to our use of idioms in Chapter 10 to build models of legal cases. In particular, we separated causes of the crime event – such as opportunity, motive and propensity – and effects of the crime event – such as witness testimony and forensic evidence.

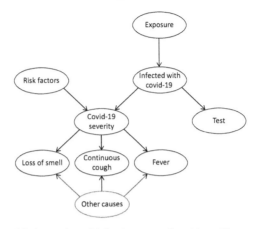

Figure 11.1 Simplified causal model for diagnosis of covid-19. Note: we show just three symptoms (based on the NHS app), but a wide range of symptoms is readily included.

Based on this generic structure we can build a model tailored to the specifics of covid-19, including its typical symptoms and risk factors (see Figure 11.1).[3] Here we take the perspective of a lay person, who uses information from media and public health sources, but this can be adapted to represent a model held by a medical expert, or even an AI diagnostic system (Richens et al., 2020).

The causal model supports various forms of reasoning. We can reason forwards from causes to effects: if you are young and infected you are likely to have mild or possibly no symptoms; backwards from effects to causes: if you have lost your sense of smell your chances of having the virus jump up; and more complex patterns: if you test positive but have been isolating and show no symptoms, then you might doubt the reliability of the test. We can also use the model to envisage tests of alternative hypotheses: if my symptoms are caused by an allergy rather than covid, then taking anti-allergy pills should reduce them; but if this doesn't work, then the probability I have covid increases.

We can re-use the basic template to create a larger model, for example, to reason about your friend's child and her likelihood of having covid, based on her symptoms and exposure. Our models can also be updated as we get new information about the risk factors and symptoms: for instance, loss of smell was not recognized straight away, but is now a key diagnostic

---

[3] Recent empirical studies suggest that people draw out very similar models (Leone, Kleinberg & Lagnado, 2021; Liefgreen & Lagnado, 2021), and can use these models for various forms of reasoning.

sign, and is easily added to the model without disrupting other links. Likewise, obesity is now considered a significant risk factor, so it can be added alongside factors such as age, sex and ethnicity.

Note that when building models we face a trade-off between the level of detail we include and how useful the model is for inference. Too much complexity can make reasoning intractable, but oversimplifying risks missing out crucial factors or links. In our current model, we have omitted many symptoms, and have not included links between risk factors and exposure, or risk factors and other causes. A more sophisticated model might have separate risk factors for disease severity and exposure; also, we might want to model interactions between symptoms, and expand the model to capture different stages of the infection (Fenton, Neil, Osman & McLachlan, 2020).

11.3 Danger of Spurious Causal Inferences

Causal inference is crucial for handling novelty and change, but it also has its dangers. Our propensity for inferring causes often outstrips the evidence. We leap too quickly to singular causes while ignoring alternative explanations. The early stages of the covid-19 crisis saw many examples of hasty causal inferences. Strong claims were made without clear knowledge of the pathology of the virus, or the conditions under which it was spreading. Even experts jumped to causal claims that over-reached the evidence, many of which were retracted once the evidence was properly scrutinized.

Problems occur when we are unable to conduct experimental studies and only have observational data to go on. Here the dangers of inferring spurious causation are rife. Take the problem of confounding, where an apparent causal relation between two variables disappears once we take into account the operation of a common cause. For example, an early claim in the covid crisis was that ibuprofen should not be given to covid sufferers because it worsened their symptoms (Sodhi & Etminan, 2020). But in the absence of controlled experiments this relationship could be due to confounding – such that patients with more severe infections were more likely to be given ibuprofen (see Figure 11.2), making it look as if ibuprofen had a negative effect.

Less well documented, but equally dangerous, is collider bias (Pearl & McKenzie, 2018), where two independent causes of an outcome become correlated if we condition on a common outcome.[4] It's tempting to infer a

[4] This pattern, where independent causes become correlated given a common effect, was discussed in Chapter 3. For example, in the barn fire example, two possible causes of the fire (lightning or a dropped match) become negatively correlated conditioning on fire. For example, knowing that

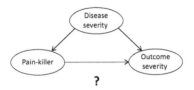

Figure 11.2   Causal model of confounding. Model showing how the putative effect of ibuprofen on covid outcomes might be confounded by disease severity.

causal relation between these two factors, but the correlation can be explained by the fact that they compete to explain the observed outcome. A potent form of collider bias arises when our dataset is a non-random sample from the population of interest, created by selecting participants according to specific factors, and thus inducing non-causal associations between these factors (Griffith et al., 2020).

Consider the striking claim that smoking reduces the severity of covid-19. This claim was made several times early in the covid crisis, based on observational studies revealing a negative correlation between smoking and covid severity (Williamson et al., 2020). It was counterintuitive, flying in the face of medical evidence that smoking aggravates respiratory conditions. But it was pursued as a plausible hypothesis with some researchers exploring whether nicotine might have a preventative effect on covid sufferers (Miyara et al., 2020).

An alternative explanation is that the correlation is due to collider bias (see Figure 11.3). Crucially, the studies were not based on a random sampling from the general population. Instead early on in the crisis they mainly tested either health workers or patients with severe covid symptoms. Given that health workers are less likely to smoke than the general population, this can induce a negative correlation between smoking and covid severity, despite there being no such link (and possibly the opposite link) in the general population (Fenton, 2020; Griffith et al., 2020). Both non-smokers and those with severe symptoms are over-represented in the dataset, whereas smokers are under-represented.

Note at this stage we cannot rule out a preventative effect of smoking (although other evidence suggests it is an aggravating factor). But the negative correlation in the data clearly admits of an alternative account

---

lightning has occurred would reduce the probability of a dropped match – even though these factors are not causally connected. Psychological research suggests that people sometimes find this pattern of inference difficult (Rehder & Waldmann, 2017; Rottman & Hastie, 2014; Tesic et al., 2020).

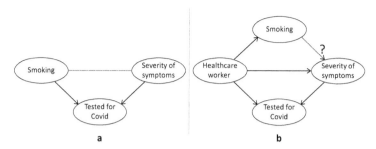

Figure 11.3   Models of collider bias. (a) Simple causal model showing how smoking and covid severity can become negatively correlated when conditioning on patients tested, because smokers and those with mild or no symptoms are under-represented. (b) More realistic model including health worker status as an explicit variable.[5]

in terms of collider bias. Here then is another example where people jump to a possible causal link without evaluating the evidence carefully.

Even more difficult are situations with a wide range of possible risk factors, and a complex and unknown web of causes and effects between these factors and the disease outcomes. For example, many studies in the UK showed an effect of ethnicity on disease severity, with Black and Asian minorities showing a heightened risk of severe covid outcomes. While the statistical relationship seemed robust, even when controlling for confounding factors – such as age, sex, occupation and housing – experts struggled to identify the underlying reasons. Various different causal mechanisms were proposed, ranging from genetic factors to social conditions, but evidential support for any singular mechanism was lacking.

Here again experts, media and the public all looked for simple causal explanations, but the real causal mechanisms are likely to be complex, and hard to identify given the restriction to observational studies and the threat of non-causal associations.

11.4   What-Ifs and Counterfactuals

Addressing what-if questions is crucial for deciding what actions to take, especially under conditions of high uncertainty. The covid crisis raised many such questions: What happens if we lockdown, close schools or

[5] Note that health workers are less likely to be smokers, but are also more likely to suffer severe symptoms than the general population. These relations are captured by direct causal links in the model. The dashed link from smoking to severity corresponds to the induced negative correlation. See Fenton (2020) for full details of the models.

impose social distancing? What if I wear a mask, visit my grandmother or take a bus to work? These questions require us to envisage what will happen if we take specific actions, often under conditions never experienced before. Here again causal models are vital; they allow us to explore the effects of new interventions.

In the book I have argued that people address such questions by mentally simulating their own causal models; this is akin to how a computational model simulates possible scenarios, except that human simulation is far cruder and more idealized. We saw how in legal cases people often need to simplify their models and inferences, raising the danger of flawed judgments. The covid crisis presents a host of similar challenges, and shows how predicting the future is fraught with difficulties, even for experts. Here the complexity of prediction can overwhelm our limited processing capacity.

In particular, individual reasoners, using their own mental models, struggle to simulate complex systems with many interacting elements, or to capture dynamics such as exponential growth, feedback loops and time delays (Osman, 2011; Sterman, 1989, 2010). All these factors are at play when trying to predict the spread of the virus. For example, consider the challenge of predicting the effects of risky individual actions, such as socializing when one knows one has symptoms, and when the consequences will be delayed and hard to identify. One's actions propagate through a complicated network of causes and effects, and depend on what other people do and on complex and 'invisible' dynamics of how the virus spreads. Inevitably, we must use hugely simplified models of these complex processes if we are to simulate events at all.[6]

Another threat to what-if reasoning is our tendency to take an 'inside' view when making scenario-based forecasts – focusing on the specifics of the situation at hand and failing to take an 'outside' view by placing this case in the context of similar cases (Kahneman & Lovallo, 1993; Kahneman & Tversky, 1982b). Here we risk the *planning fallacy*, underestimating how long we will take to complete a project because we only focus on the factors we think might interrupt our current project and ignore broader information from similar projects (Buehler et al., 1994).

---

[6] Despite their use of sophisticated computational modelling and large datasets, expert modellers faced similar challenges. During the crisis they sought to predict the effects of large-scale interventions on the numbers of covid cases and deaths in the general population. This required not only modelling the disease but also people's social behaviour, including how they would respond to public messaging. Faced with such complexity and uncertainty, experts had to make many simplifying assumptions, with different approaches producing very different predictions.

During the crisis many committed this fallacy. For example, the UK government repeatedly made grand predictions about the speed and quality of their policies, such as providing personal protective equipment, robust testing, and a 'world-beating' track and trace system, which all proved overblown.[7] The flaw here is to over-focus on the single case, and fail to incorporate information from past performance into future predictions.

A more general problem is that the inside view is sometimes all we have, especially in novel circumstances with no prior track record to help us calibrate our predictions. At best we can try out various models and simulate different scenarios before deciding on a specific course of action.[8] But this still leaves us with the problem of combining or weighting different scenarios, and the temptation of simply going with our best guess.

Despite all these pitfalls, what-if thinking is a prerequisite for prediction in novel circumstances. Better to have an imperfect vision of the future than none at all.

11.4.1   Counterfactuals and Causation

Counterfactual reasoning involves a special kind of what-if thinking: instead of predicting the future, we look backwards at what might have been. This is crucial for deciding what caused what. Suppose I have a headache. I take some allergy pills, and a few hours later my headache has gone. Would I still have had the headache if I hadn't taken the pills? Was it the pills that alleviated my headache? Causal models are a prerequisite for this kind of inference. We need to construct an alternative version of the world, where we change the events or actions in question, and see whether things would have been different. Sometimes this is relatively easy to work out, as in the allergy example, but it is often more difficult.

Consider a harder question: did the UK government's delay in imposing a lockdown[9] cause extra deaths from covid? Here we must consider a counterfactual where the UK locked down earlier. Would there have been fewer deaths? Calculating this is non-trivial; it inherits the difficulties of what-if predictions, requiring many simplifying assumptions. One group

---

[7] But perhaps they eventually learned from their mistakes because the UK vaccine roll-out was better than predicted.

[8] One advantage for expert computational modelling is that they can run their models thousands of times, under varying conditions, capturing to some extent the uncertainty in how things might play out. The outputs of different models can also be combined to create consensus predictions.

[9] Here we refer to the first major lockdown in the UK, which occurred on 23 March 2020.

of experts used what-if modelling to address this counterfactual, estimating that deaths would have been halved;[10] but this remains a contentious issue.

An important difference between predictions and counterfactuals is that in evaluating the latter we can use a degree of hindsight: taking account of things that happened after the prediction (but were unknown at the time). For example, the UK public complied with the initial lockdown measures, which suggests they would also have complied with an even earlier lockdown. So in evaluating the counterfactual we might assume that compliance would still be high (at least early on).[11] But we can't transport everything that actually happened into our counterfactual model; in particular, we don't hold fixed things that might be changed by our imagined intervention (i.e., downstream effects), such as the number of infected people. After all, these are the possible changes we are interested in. The general question of what events of the actual world we should transport over to our counterfactual world is tricky and depends on our causal models.

Different causal models can support very different counterfactual conclusions. A stark example is the debate between public health experts and sceptics about the efficacy of preventative measures such as lockdowns. The dispute is neatly captured by the graphic in Figure 11.4, which plots covid cases against time. The graph compares predictions if prevention measures are taken (flattening the curve) versus business as usual (a steep rise in cases), and it also predicts that if measures are relaxed, cases will rise again.

We can use causal models to capture both positions. According to the public health view, the crisis was very severe, and the outcomes would have been much worse if we had not taken preventative actions (see Figure 11.5a). In causal model language – if we imagine the counterfactual where we do not act, we will infer a much higher rate of death.

In contrast, the sceptics give a very different interpretation. On their view the crisis was not as severe as claimed, and the forecasts were overblown, as shown by the lower number of deaths (see Figure 11.5b). The preventative actions were therefore unnecessary and did not make a

[10] www.theguardian.com/world/2020/jun/10/uk-coronavirus-lockdown-20000-lives-boris-johnson-neil-ferguson

[11] It's possible to question this assumption – perhaps compliance depends on people's perceptions of danger, which in turn depend on how many fatalities have been reported. An earlier lockdown might have had less compliance because there were fewer fatalities at that point. This again highlights the subtleties of counterfactual thinking.

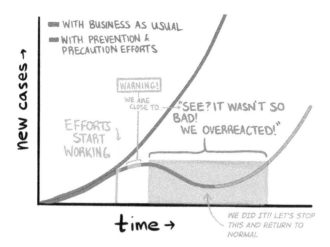

Figure 11.4 Graphic depicting the consensus public health view shortly after the first lockdowns were imposed. The annotations show how lockdown sceptics might interpret the actual line.
(Created by Ethan Lee @scienergetic)

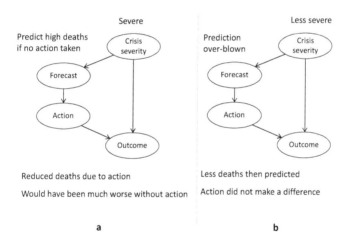

Figure 11.5 Competing counterfactual models. (a) Public health view that outcomes would have been much worse without preventative actions; (b) Sceptic view that preventative actions did not make a difference, and predictions were overblown.

big difference to the outcome – we would have seen similar numbers of deaths irrespective (and the actions had other bad side-effects).

Moreover, each view makes a different prediction for the future. Once measures are relaxed, and a second wave is possible, the public health view predicts severe outcomes if we don't introduce preventative actions again, whereas the sceptic argues that things aren't so bad, and new preventative actions will be ineffective.[12]

The debate should now shift to how well the evidence supports these opposing models, by drawing on a range of arguments and data. But often the proponents simply reassert their position without securing new evidence to support it (or selectively citing evidence to confirm their position). The key point here is that formulating the causal models is a crucial step in the evaluative process, but we also need evidence to help discriminate between models.

11.5 Gathering and Interpreting Evidence

People are often ill-equipped for the difficult task of evaluating evidence, and similar misunderstandings are repeated in many domains, including legal and medical reasoning. These problems range from misconstruing the results of evidential tests to more subtle biases in the way we select and interpret evidence. The covid crisis highlights many of these issues. Testing is a critical factor in dealing with any virus – to identify who is infected, to track the spread of the virus and to estimate its incidence in the population. Yet poor testing strategies have bedevilled many government responses to the pandemic.

One oversight is to assume that tests are fully accurate, and thus that a test result perfectly indicates someone's actual infected status. In a legal context this is akin to conflating a witness report of a fact with the fact itself (see Chapters 6 and 10). But no tests are infallible, and indeed covid testing procedures (especially early in the crisis) had high error rates compared with other standard tests. But even once we acknowledge that tests are not 100% reliable, confusion remains as to what false-positive or false-negative rates actually mean, with non-experts such as politicians and the media clearly confused.

As we have shown in this book, people often overestimate the impact of a positive test, even when given statistical information about error rates and disease incidence (see Chapter 4). For example, if someone is randomly tested for a rare disease, and tests positive, people often infer the person has the disease. But in fact, given a low incidence of the disease, the result is more likely to be a false positive (even for fairly accurate tests). These studies reflect the difficulties people have with probabilistic

---

[12] Looks like we might be locked in this cycle of arguments for a while!

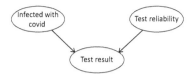

Figure 11.6   Model for inferring covid status given a test result (using the evidence-reliability idiom – see Chapter 10 for details).

computations, and highlight the need for careful risk communication. To capture the issue of test reliability we can apply a simple causal model – the evidence-reliability idiom (see Figure 11.6), which we introduced in Chapter 10. This model helps clarify what inferences to draw from test results, and indeed presenting information to people in a causal format can improve their inferences from test results (see Chapter 4).

11.5.1   Confirmatory Strategies

Throughout the book we have seen how legal investigations can be derailed by poor search strategies. The same issues arise in investigating the pandemic. Let's consider one well-known problem, *confirmation bias,* which occurs when people seek evidence to confirm their own expectations or favoured position. The term actually covers various strategies for gathering and interpreting evidence. In Chapter 8, I argued that confirmation bias has good, bad and ugly sides, and indeed we see all of these facets in the covid crisis. For example, most testing strategies focus on people with symptoms or high risk of exposure, so we are more likely to find positive cases than if testing purely at random. Pragmatically this makes good sense, since we should prioritize finding those more likely to be infected in order to treat them and avoid further spread. But such a test strategy has its drawbacks. It means that we might miss a significant class of cases, such as asymptomatic carriers, and also that we cannot get an accurate picture of the proportion infected in the general population. Indeed, despite 10 months of testing after the pandemic had started, we still didn't know how prevalent the virus was in the UK.

In fact the proper analysis of the impact of testing strategies – and what testing data can tell us about the spread, incidence and fatality rate of the virus – is very complicated. We must model the complex processes by which evidence is acquired and analyzed (see also Chapter 6). One approach is to use the causal modelling framework, and the idiom-based method presented in Chapter 10 can be adapted for these purposes (see Fenton et al., 2020).

People also show biases in selecting what evidence to present to support an argument, whether in court, in parliament or in media debates. For example, discussions about the success or failure of government actions often involve comparisons with other countries (such as in the debate between public health and sceptics noted in Section 11.4.1), but these are often cherry-picked to suit an agenda, rather than to present a balanced evaluation.

Finally, we have seen in Chapter 9 that people sometimes confuse explanations for evidence, assuming that an explanation *is* evidence (Kuhn, 1989, 2001). In the covid crisis, policy-makers frequently claimed that they were 'following the evidence', but based their decisions on causal claims with no solid evidence. For example, the concept of 'behavioural fatigue' was cited as a reason to avoid locking down too early, but while this notion sounds plausible it had no evidence to back it up (Harvey, 2020). It was an explanation masquerading as evidence.

11.6   Competing Narratives

The covid crisis sparked many polarized debates, even among experts with access to the same data and evidence. We saw sharp disagreement about the costs and benefits of lockdowns, the feasibility of herd immunity, the utility of mask wearing, the efficacy of different testing strategies and modelling approaches. Despite the manifest uncertainty, proponents expressed high confidence in their views, judiciously selecting from equivocal evidence.

Here there is a strong parallel with adversarial legal cases, where opposing parties – prosecution and defence – present vastly different versions of events, marshalling and selecting evidence to support their positions. As we saw in Chapter 9, stories are a central device to explain and persuade, and in the pandemic advocates too used narratives to convince policy-makers and the public.

As lay people witnessing these debates, our role is similar to jurors in a court case. We face the same basic challenge – to make sense of a confusing and contradictory body of facts, claims and counterclaims. We must decide between competing stories, and ultimately take decisions with consequences for ourselves and society. To deal with this challenge, we too use narratives to interpret evidence and fill gaps in our knowledge, with the danger that compelling stories can edge out the truth. We are also susceptible to one-sidedness, with the mind striving for a single coherent perspective (Holyoak & Simon, 1999; Simon et al., 2004).

11.6.1 The Blame Game

Narratives also help us play the blame game. Who was responsible for the initial spread of the virus? For the excessive deaths in the UK? For the delays and mistakes in track and trace systems? For the mishandling of preventative measures? None of these questions have simple answers. We need to assess complicated systems of cause and effect at many levels – individuals, groups, institutions – with interacting elements unfolding across time. How do we decide whom to blame?

We face a dual problem here: which version of events do we accept and how do we distribute blame among its elements? (Or perhaps we should weight our blame according to our degree of belief in each version?). For example, consider the question of who is to blame for initial spread of the virus. The dominant narrative is that it started when the virus jumped from bat to human at a wet market in Wuhan, and that Chinese authorities were slow to acknowledge the problem, thus failing to halt the global spread. Others claim the virus leaked from a lab in Wuhan, or – even more conspiratorially – that the virus was deliberately released.

Deciding between these versions is already a tricky inference task, but even if we agree on one version, how do we allocate blame among the many contributing factors? It seems too simplistic to single out the bat or even the wet market. Should we look for more systemic causes, such as institutional practices and broader environmental issues? And what role should be accorded to the Chinese government's failure to act swiftly and stamp it out? Or how quickly other governments restricted travel from China?

Similar questions arose in Chapter 3 when we discussed the causes of the Chicago fire. It seems myopic to blame Mrs O'Leary when failures by the emergency service were critical for the fire spreading throughout the city.

To make matters worse – when assigning blame we must also consider intention and foresight. Were an agent's actions intentional, negligent or accidental? Were they aware of the consequences of their actions? Not only do we need a model of what happened, but also a model of what people thought was going to happen. These are complex issues. Stories and narratives offer us a path through the thicket; they give us a single unifying account and help us identify agents to blame (cf. Chapter 9). But again they run the risk of oversimplifying and distorting a complex reality.

Finally, in several chapters we have discussed how to improve our reasoning. No silver bullet exists, but a range of approaches is possible.

For Kuhn (1989, 2001) the crucial step is metacognition – getting us to reflect on our reasoning, and to co-ordinate theory and evidence (see Chapter 9). This paves the way for us to move from the allure of a single story, to entertaining and evaluating multiple versions of reality.

These are necessary steps, but perhaps not sufficient. I have argued that we also need to appreciate the basics of causal and probabilistic inference (as presented in Chapters 3 and 10). We need not become experts in building formal causal models, but we should see how these principles apply to real-world cases, even without exact numbers. It's the qualitative structure of our reasoning that is crucial. However, if we do seek a deeper understanding of a complex system – such as identifying the risk factors for covid, or building a diagnostic system – the tools of causal modelling can give us a clearer insight and help avoid pitfalls.

But ultimately the key benefit of any such tool is how we then embed its insights into our own thinking. We might not be able to build a complex causal model of the risk factors for covid, but even if we learn to watch out for confounded and spurious causal claims, we will have progressed a few steps forward.

11.7   Final Conclusions

I started the book with the puzzle of how we are able to tackle and possibly solve crime mysteries (real or fictional). To address this question, we needed to uncover the cognitive principles that underpin our ability to reason. Through the book I have argued that we have a special capacity for creating and manipulating mental models, allowing us to draw inferences from uncertain evidence and to explain complex events. However, I have also exposed the difficulties we face in evaluating these models against the evidence. Our use of crude but flexible models can explain both our strengths and weaknesses in evidential reasoning. I have introduced formal causal modelling, which provides a benchmark to show us how well we are doing, and how we might improve. Based on this framework I presented a method to help us model complex legal cases. But the key message is that we need to think carefully about our model building and try to calibrate our models to the evidence.

In this final chapter I aimed to show the generality of these ideas, by applying them to our thinking during the coronavirus crisis. Indeed I believe that they apply in most spheres of enquiry, wherever we must interpret and reason with evidence.

Of course, in our daily lives we are unlikely to draw up a Bayes net to solve a problem (although it can help!); but many of the principles discussed in this book still apply. We should avoid jumping to causal claims on sparse data, try to consider alternative explanations, scrutinize what evidence we have and look for better evidence, assess our sources of information (are they biased or partial?), and aim to weight and balance things before drawing firm conclusions. Even day-to-day problems can rapidly become hard to manage, so we must accept that simplifications are inevitable, but watch out for oversimplified and distorted inferences. We need to take a meta-level view of our own reasoning practices.

While writing this book there has been an explosion of interest in AI, largely due to the amazing success of deep-learning algorithms at tasks such as image recognition, analyzing protein folding and playing games such as Go (Botvinick et al., 2019). However, getting an AI system to solve crimes still seems a long way off, precisely because of the difficulty in formalizing common-sense reasoning (Marcus & Davis, 2019). Nonetheless formal tools such as Bayes nets can already offer valuable assistance when we seek to evaluate complex legal cases. We cannot replace real investigators, judges and jurors, but anything that improves our quality of reasoning is a good thing.

Finally, since writing this book I now see every crime drama in a new light – as a tangled web of causes and effects crying out for a Bayes net analysis. While I don't wish a similar curse upon you, I hope that the ideas in this book might inspire you next time you try to solve a murder mystery.

References

Achinstein, P. (2001). *The book of evidence*. New York: Oxford University Press.

Alicke, M. D., Mandel, D. R., Hilton, D. J., Gerstenberg, T., & Lagnado, D. A. (2015). Causal conceptions in social explanation and moral evaluation: A historical tour. *Perspectives on Psychological Science, 10*(6), 790–812.

Allen, R. J., & Pardo, M. S. (2019). Relative plausibility and its critics. *The International Journal of Evidence & Proof, 23*(1–2), 5–59.

Anderson, J. R. (1996). ACT: A simple theory of complex cognition. *American Psychologist, 51*(4), 355.

Anderson, T., Schum, D., & Twining, W. (2005). *Analysis of evidence*. New York: Cambridge University Press.

Austerweil, J. L., & Griffiths, T. L. (2011). A rational model of the effects of distributional information on feature learning. *Cognitive Psychology, 63*(4), 173–209.

Bales, R. (2002). *The great Chicago fire and the myth of Mrs. O'Leary's cow*. Jefferson, NC: McFarland.

Banks, D. L., Kafadar, K., Kaye, D. H., & Tackett, M. (Eds.). (2020). *Handbook of forensic statistics*. Boca Raton, FL: CRC Press.

Barbey, A. K., & Sloman, S. B. (2007). Base-rate respect: From ecological rationality to dual processes. *Behavioral and Brain Sciences, 30*(3), 241–254.

Baron, R. A. (2004). The cognitive perspective: A valuable tool for answering entrepreneurship's basic 'why' questions. *Journal of Business Venturing, 19*(2), 221–239.

Barrett, E. C. (2009). *The interpretation and exploitation of information in criminal investigations* [Unpublished doctoral dissertation]. University of Birmingham.

Battaglia, P. W., Hamrick, J. B., & Tenenbaum, J. B. (2013). Simulation as an engine of physical scene understanding. *Proceedings of the National Academy of Sciences, 110*(45), 18327–18332.

Bayes, T. (1763). An essay towards solving a problem in the doctrine of chances. *Philosophical Transactions of the Royal Society of London, 53* (53), 370–418.

Bechlivanidis, C., Lagnado, D. A., Zemla, J. C., & Sloman, S. (2017). Concreteness and abstraction in everyday explanation. *Psychonomic Bulletin & Review, 24*(5), 1451–1464.

Beer, I., Ben-David, S., Chockler, H., Orni, A., & Trefler, R. (2012). Explaining counterexamples using causality. *Formal Methods in System Design, 40*(1), 20–40.

Bennett, W. L., & Feldman, M. S. (1981). *Reconstructing reality in the courtroom.* Alameda, CA: Tavistock.

Bentham, J. (1843). *The works of Jeremy Bentham* (Vol. 6). Edinburgh: W. Tait.

Bes, B., Sloman, S., Lucas, C. G., & Raufaste, É. (2012). Non-Bayesian inference: Causal structure trumps correlation. *Cognitive Science, 36*(7), 1178–1203.

Bilton, M. (2012). *Wicked beyond belief: The hunt for the Yorkshire ripper.* New York: Harper.

Bingham, T. (2006). Assessing contentious eyewitness evidence: A judicial review. In A. Heaton-Armstrong, E. Shepherd, G. Gudjonsson, & D. Wolchover (Eds.), *Witness testimony: Psychological, investigative and evidence perspectives* (2nd ed., pp. 327–345). Oxford: Oxford University Press.

Botvinick, M., Ritter, S., Wang, J. X., Kurth-Nelson, Z., Blundell, C., & Hassabis, D. (2019). Reinforcement learning, fast and slow. *Trends in Cognitive Sciences, 23*(5), 408–422.

Bovens, L., & Hartmann, S. (2002). Bayesian networks and the problem of unreliable instruments. *Philosophy of Science, 69*(1), 29–72.

(2003). *Bayesian epistemology.* Oxford University Press, on demand.

Bramley, N. R., Dayan, P., Griffiths, T. L., & Lagnado, D. A. (2017). Formalizing Neurath's ship: Approximate algorithms for online causal learning. *Psychological Review, 124*(3), 301–338.

Brem, S. K., & Rips, L. J. (2000). Explanation and evidence in informal argument. *Cognitive Science, 24*(4), 573–604.

Buck, U., Naether, S., Räss, B., Jackowski, C., & Thali, M. J. (2013). Accident or homicide – Virtual crime scene reconstruction using 3D methods. *Forensic Science International, 225*(1–3), 75–84.

Buehler, R., Griffin, D., & Ross, M. (1994). Exploring the 'planning fallacy': Why people underestimate their task completion times. *Journal of Personality and Social Psychology, 67*(3), 366–381.

Carey, S. (1995). On the origin of causal understanding. In D. Sperber, D. Premack, & A. J. Premack (Eds.), *Symposia of the Fyssen Foundation. Causal cognition: A multidisciplinary debate* (pp. 268–308). Oxford: Clarendon Press/Oxford University Press.

Cartwright, N., & Hardie, J. (2012). *Evidence-based policy: A practical guide to doing it better.* New York: Oxford University Press.

Chi, M. T., De Leeuw, N., Chiu, M. H., & LaVancher, C. (1994). Eliciting self-explanations improves understanding. *Cognitive Science, 18*(3), 439–477.

Chisum, W. J., & Turvey, B. E. (2011). *Crime reconstruction.* Cambridge, MA: Academic Press.

Coenen, A., Nelson, J. D., & Gureckis, T. M. (2018). Asking the right questions about the psychology of human inquiry: Nine open challenges. *Psychonomic Bulletin and Review, 74*, 1–41.

Conan Doyle, A. (1891). A scandal in Bohemia. *The adventures of Sherlock Holmes* (pp. 5–29).

(1892). Silver blaze. *Strand Magazine.*

Cook, R., Evett, I. W., Jackson, G., Jones, P. J., & Lambert, J. A. (1998). A hierarchy of propositions: Deciding which level to address in casework. *Science & Justice, 4*(38), 231–239.

Cornish, D. B., & Clarke, R. V. (1987). Understanding crime displacement: An application of rational choice theory. *Criminology, 25*(4), 933–948.

(Eds.). (2014). *The reasoning criminal: Rational choice perspectives on offending.* New Brunswick: Transaction Publishers.

Craik, K. J. W. (1952). *The nature of explanation.* Cambridge: Cambridge University Press.

Crisp, A., & Feeney, A. (2009). Causal conjunction fallacies: The roles of causal strength and mental resources. *Quarterly Journal of Experimental Psychology, 62*(12), 2320–2337 .

Crown Court Compendium (2020). Part I: Jury and Trial Management and Summing Up. Judicial College (England and Wales). www.judiciary.uk/wp-content/uploads/2020/12/Crown-Court-Compendium-Part-I-December-2020-amended-01.02.21.pdf

Crupi, V., Tentori, K., & Gonzalez, M. (2007). On Bayesian measures of evidential support: Theoretical and empirical issues. *Philosophy of Science, 74*, 229–252.

Cruz, N., Connor Desai, S., Dewitt, S., Hahn, U., Lagnado, D., Liefgreen, A., ... Tesic, M. (2020). Widening access to Bayesian problem solving. *Frontiers in Psychology, 11*, 660.

Curley, L. J., Munro, J., Lages, M., MacLean, R., & Murray, J. (2020). Assessing cognitive bias in forensic decisions: A review and outlook. *Journal of Forensic Sciences, 65*(2), 354–360.

Danks, D. (2014). *Unifying the mind: Cognitive representations as graphical models.* Cambridge, MA: MIT Press.

(2018). Privileged (default) causal cognition: A mathematical analysis. *Frontiers in Psychology, 9*, 498.

Dawid, A. P. (2000). Causal inference without counterfactuals. *Journal of the American Statistical Association, 95*(450), 407–424.

(2002). Bayes's theorem and weighing evidence by juries. In *Proceedings of the British Academy* (Vol. 113, pp. 71–90). Oxford: Oxford University Press.

(2005). Statistics on trial. *Significance, 2*(1), 6–8.

(2021). The tale wags the DAG. In R. Dechter, H. Geffner, and J. Halpern (Eds.), *Probabilistic and causal inference: The works of Judea Pearl.* New York: Association for Computing Machinery.

Dawid, A. P., & Evett, I. W. (1997). Using a graphical method to assist the evaluation of complicated patterns of evidence. *Journal of Forensic Science, 42* (2), 226–231.

Dawid, A. P., & Mortera, J. (2020). Bayesian networks in forensic science. In D. Banks, K. Kafadar, D. H. Kaye, & M. Tackett (Eds.), *Handbook of forensic statistics* (pp. 165–197). Boca Raton, FL: CRC Press.

Dennis, I. H. (2007). *The law of evidence.* London: Sweet & Maxwell.

Dennis, M. J., & Ahn, W. (2001). Primacy in causal strength judgments. *Memory & Cognition, 29*, 152–164.

Denrell, J. (2005). Selection bias and the perils of benchmarking. *Harvard Business Review, 83*(4), 114–119.

Denrell, J., & March, J. G. (2001). Adaptation as information restriction: The hot stove effect. *Organization Science, 12*(5), 523–538.

Devine, D. J. (2012). *Jury decision making: The state of the science* (Vol. 8). New York: New York University Press.

Devroye, L. (2006). Nonuniform random variate generation. *Handbooks in Operations Research and Management Science, 13*, 83–121.

Dewitt, S., Fenton, N., Liefgreen, A., & Lagnado, D. A. (2020). Propensities and second order uncertainty: A modified taxi cab problem. *Frontiers in Psychology, 11*, 503233.

Dewitt, S., Lagnado, D. A., & Fenton, N. (2018). Updating prior beliefs based on ambiguous evidence. In C. Kalish, M. Rau, J. Zhu, & T. T. Rogers (Eds.), *Proceedings of the 40th Annual Conference of the Cognitive Science Society* (pp. 2047–2052). Austin, TX: Cognitive Science Society.

Dostoevsky, F. (1866/1957). *Crime and punishment* (C. Garnett, Trans.). London: Folio Society.

Dougherty, M. R., Gettys, C. F., & Thomas, R. P. (1997). The role of mental simulation in judgments of likelihood. *Organizational Behavior and Human Decision Processes, 70*(2), 135–148.

Dror, I. E. (2018). Biases in forensic experts. *Science, 360*(6386), 243.

Dror, I. E., & Charlton, D. (2006). Why experts make errors. *Journal of Forensic Identification, 56*(4), 600.

Dror, I. E., Morgan, R. M., Rando, C., & Nakhaeizadeh, S. (2017). The bias snowball and the bias cascade effects: Two distinct biases that may impact forensic decision making [Letter to the editor]. *Journal of Forensic Sciences, 62* (3), 832–833.

Edwards, W. (1991). Influence diagrams, Bayesian imperialism, and the Collins case: An appeal to reason. *Cardozo Law Review, 13*, 1025.

Eggleston, R. (1978). Wigmore, fact-finding and probability. *Monash University Law Review, 15*(3), 370–382.

Evans, J. S. B. (1989). *Bias in human reasoning: Causes and consequences.* Brighton: Erlbaum.

(2007). *Hypothetical thinking: Dual processes in reasoning and judgement.* London: Psychology Press.

Fenton, N. (2014). Assessing evidence and testing appropriate hypotheses. *Science and Justice, 54*(6), 502–504.

(2020). A note on 'Collider bias undermines our understanding of COVID-19 disease risk and severity' and how causal Bayesian networks both expose and resolve the problem. *arXiv preprint arXiv:2005.08608.*

Fenton, N., Lagnado, D., Dahlman, C., & Neil, M. (2019). The opportunity prior: A proof-based prior for criminal cases. *Law, Probability and Risk, 18*(4), 237–253.

Fenton, N., Lagnado, D., Hsu, A., Berger, D., & Neil, M. (2014). Response to 'On the use of the likelihood ratio for forensic evaluation: Response to Fenton et al.'. *Science Justice, 54*(4), 319–320.

Fenton, N., & Neil, M. (2018). *Risk assessment and decision analysis with Bayesian networks*. New York: Chapman and Hall/CRC.

Fenton, N., Neil, M., & Lagnado, D. A. (2013). A general structure for legal arguments about evidence using Bayesian networks. *Cognitive Science, 37*(1), 61–102.

Fenton, N., Neil, M., Lagnado, D., Marsh, W., Yet, B., & Constantinou, A. (2016). How to model mutually exclusive events based on independent causal pathways in Bayesian network models. *Knowledge-based Systems, 113*, 39–50.

Fenton, N., Neil, M., Yet, B., & Lagnado, D. A. (2020). Analyzing the Simonshaven case using Bayesian networks. *Topics in Cognitive Science, 12* (4), 1092–1114.

Fenton, N. E., & Lagnado, D. A. (2021). Bayesianism: Objections and rebuttals. In G. Tuzet, C. Dahlman, & A. Stein (Eds.), *Philosophical foundations of evidence law*. Oxford University Press.

Fenton, N. E., Neil, M., Osman, M., & McLachlan, S. (2020). COVID-19 infection and death rates: The need to incorporate causal explanations for the data and avoid bias in testing. *Journal of Risk Research, 23*(7–8), 862–865.

Fiedler, K. (2000). Beware of samples! A cognitive-ecological sampling approach to judgment biases. *Psychology Review, 107*(4), 659–676.

Fiedler, K., Brinkmann, B., Betsch, T., & Wild, B. (2020). A sampling approach to biases in conditional probability judgments: Beyond base rate neglect and statistical format. *Journal of Experimental Psychology: General, 129*(3), 399.

Fiedler, K., & Juslin, P. (2006). Taking the interface between mind and environment seriously. In K. Fiedler & P. Juslin (Eds.), *Information sampling and adaptive cognition* (pp. 3–29). Cambridge: Cambridge University Press.

Fiedler, K., Walther, E., Freytag, P., & Plessner, H. (2002). Judgment biases in a simulated classroom – A cognitive-environmental approach. *Organizational Behavior and Human Decision Processes, 88*(1), 527–561.

Fischhoff, B., Slovic, P., & Lichtenstein, S. (2013). Fault trees. *Judgment and Decision Making, 124*, 330–344.

Flavell, J. H. (1979). Metacognition and cognitive monitoring: A new area of cognitive–developmental inquiry. *American Psychologist, 34*(10), 906.

Forster, E. M. (1927/1955). *Aspects of the novel*. New York: Harcourt.

Friedman, R. D. (1987). Route analysis of credibility and hearsay. *Yale Law Journal, 96*(4), 1.

Garrett, B. (2011). *Convicting the innocent*. Cambridge, MA: Harvard University Press.

Gentner, D., & Stevens, A. L. (Eds.). (1983). *Mental models*. Hillsdale, NJ: Lawrence Erlbaum.

Gerstenberg, T., Goodman, N. D., Lagnado, D. A., & Tenenbaum, J. B. (2021). A counterfactual simulation model of causal judgments for physical events. *Psychological Review*. https://doi.org/10.1037/rev0000281

Gerstenberg, T., & Tenenbaum, J. B. (2017). Intuitive theories. In M. R. Waldmann (Ed.), *Oxford library of psychology. The Oxford handbook of causal reasoning* (pp. 515–547). New York: Oxford University Press.

Gettys, C. F., Kelly III, C., & Peterson, C. R. (1973). The best guess hypothesis in multistage inference. *Organizational Behavior and Human Performance, 10* (3), 364–373.

Gigerenzer, G., & Todd, P. (1999). *Simple heuristics that make us smart*. New York: Oxford University Press.

Gill, R. D., Fenton, N., Neil, M., & Lagnado, D. A. (2020). *Statistical issues in Serial Killer Nurse cases* [Unpublished manuscript].

Gillies, D., & Gillies, D. A. (2000). *Philosophical theories of probability*. London: Psychology Press.

Glymour, C. (2001). *The mind's arrows: Bayes nets and graphical causal models in psychology*. Cambridge, MA: MIT Press.

(2003). Learning, prediction and causal Bayes nets. *Trends in Cognitive Sciences, 7*(1), 43–48.

Goodman, N. D., Ullman, T. D., & Tenenbaum, J. B. (2011). Learning a theory of causality. *Psychological Review, 118*(1), 110.

Gopnik, A., Glymour, C., Sobel, D. M., Schulz, L. E., Kushnir, T., & Danks, D. (2004). A theory of causal learning in children: Causal maps and Bayes nets. *Psychological Review, 111*(1), 3–32.

Gopnik, A., & Schulz, L. (Eds.). (2007). *Causal learning: Psychology, philosophy, and computation*. New York: Oxford University Press.

Gopnik, A., & Wellman, H. M. (2012). Reconstructing constructivism: Causal models, Bayesian learning mechanisms, and the theory theory. *Psychological Bulletin, 138*(6), 1085.

Gorman, R., Charney, E., Holtzman, N., & Roberts, K. (1985). A successful city-wide smoke detector giveaway program. *Pediatrics, 75*(1), 14–18.

Griffith, G. J., Morris, T. T., Tudball, M. J., Herbert, A., Mancano, G., Pike, L., ... Hermani, G. (2020). Collider bias undermines our understanding of COVID-19 disease risk and severity. *Nature Communications, 11*(1), 1–12.

Griffiths, T. L. (2020). Understanding human intelligence through human limitations. *Trends in Cognitive Sciences, 24*(11), 873–883.

Griffiths, T. L., Lieder, F., & Goodman, N. D. (2015). Rational use of cognitive resources: Levels of analysis between the computational and the algorithmic. *Topics in Cognitive Science, 7*(2), 217–229.

Griffiths, T. L., & Tenenbaum, J. B. (2009). Theory-based causal induction. *Psychological Review, 116*(4), 661–716.

Hacking, I. (1975). *The emergence of probability*. New York: Cambridge University Press.

Hahn, U. (2020). Argument quality in real world argumentation. *Trends in Cognitive Sciences, 24*(5), 363–374.

Hahn, U., & Harris, A. J. (2014). What does it mean to be biased: Motivated reasoning and rationality. In *Psychology of learning and motivation* (Vol. 61, pp. 41–102). New York: Academic Press.

Halpern, J. (2016). *Actual Causality*. Cambridge, MA: MIT Press.

Halpern, J. Y., & Pearl, J. (2005). Causes and explanations: A structural-model approach. Part I: Causes. *The British Journal for the Philosophy of Science, 56* (4), 843–887.

Hanson, N. R. (1958). *Patterns of discovery: An inquiry into the conceptual foundations of science.* Cambridge, UK: Cambridge University Press.

Harvey, N. (2020). Behavioral fatigue: Real phenomenon, naïve construct, or policy contrivance? *Frontiers in Psychology, 11,* 589892.

Hayes, B. K., Hawkins, G. E., & Newell, B. R. (2016). Consider the alternative: The effects of causal knowledge on representing and using alternative hypotheses in judgments under uncertainty. *Journal of Experimental Psychology: Learning, Memory, and Cognition, 42*(5), 723.

Hayes, B. K., Hawkins, G. E., Newell, B. R., Pasqualino, M., & Rehder, B. (2014). The role of causal models in multiple judgments under uncertainty. *Cognition, 133*(3), 611–620.

Hayes, B. K., Ngo, J., Hawkins, G. E., & Newell, B. R. (2018). Causal explanation improves judgment under uncertainty, but rarely in a Bayesian way. *Memory & Cognition, 46*(1), 112–131.

Hegarty, M. (2004). Mechanical reasoning by mental simulation. *Trends in Cognitive Sciences, 8*(6), 280–285.

Heider, F. (1958). *The psychology of interpersonal relations.* Hoboken, NJ: Wiley.

Heller, K. J. (2006). The cognitive psychology of circumstantial evidence. *Michigan Law Review, 105,* 241.

Hempel, C. G. (1965). *Aspects of scientific explanation.* New York: Free Press.

Hepler, A. B., Dawid, A. P., & Leucari, V. (2007). Object-oriented graphical representations of complex patterns of evidence. *Law, Probability and Risk, 6* (1–4), 275–293.

Herring, J. (2014). *Criminal law: Text, cases, and materials.* New York: Oxford University Press.

Hogarth, R. M., & Einhorn, H. J. (1992). Order effects in belief updating: The belief-adjustment model. *Cognitive Psychology, 24*(1), 1–55.

Hogarth, R. M., Lejarraga, T., & Soyer, E. (2015). The two settings of kind and wicked learning environments. *Current Directions in Psychological Science, 24*(5), 379–385.

Hogarth, R. M., & Soyer, E. (2011). Sequentially simulated outcomes: Kind experience versus nontransparent description. *Journal of Experimental Psychology: General, 140*(3), 434.

Holyoak, K. J., & Simon, D. (1999). Bidirectional reasoning in decision making by constraint satisfaction. *Journal of Experimental Psychology: General, 128*(1), 3.

Horst, S. (2016). *Cognitive pluralism.* Cambridge, MA: MIT Press.

Howson, C., & Urbach, P. (2006). *Scientific reasoning: The Bayesian approach.* Chicago, IL: Open Court Publishing.

Icard, T. (2016). Subjective probability as sampling propensity. *Review of Philosophy and Psychology, 7,* 863–903.

Innes, M. (2003). *Investigating murder: Detective work and the police response to criminal homicide.* Clarendon Studies in Criminology. Oxford: Oxford University Press.

(2007). Investigation order and major crime inquiries. In T. Newburn, T. Williamson, & A. Wright (Eds.), *Handbook of Criminal Investigation* (pp. 255–276). London: Taylor & Francis.

Johnson, S. G., Merchant, T., & Keil, F. C. (2020). Belief digitization: Do we treat uncertainty as probabilities or as bits? *Journal of Experimental Psychology: General, 149*(8), 1417–1434.

Johnson-Laird, P. N. (1983). *Mental models: Towards a cognitive science of language, inference, and consciousness.* Cambridge, MA: Harvard University Press.

(2006). *How we reason.* New York: Oxford University Press.

(2010). Mental models and human reasoning. *Proceedings of the National Academy of Sciences, 107*(43), 18243–18250.

Kadane, J. B., & Schum, D. A. (2011). *A probabilistic analysis of the Sacco and Vanzetti evidence* (Vol. 773). Hoboken, NJ: Wiley.

Kahneman, D. (2011). *Thinking, fast and slow.* New York: Farrar, Straus and Giroux.

Kahneman, D., & Lovallo, D. (1993). Timid choices and bold forecasts: A cognitive perspective on risk taking. *Management Science, 39*(1), 17–31.

Kahneman, D., & Tversky, A. (1982a). The simulation heuristic. In D. Kahneman, P. Slovic, & A. Tversky (Eds.), *Judgment under uncertainty: Heuristics and biases* (pp. 201–208). New York: Cambridge University Press.

(1982b). Variants of uncertainty. *Cognition, 11*(2), 143–157.

Kassin, S., Dror, I., & Kukucka, J. (2013). The forensic confirmation bias: Problems, perspectives, and proposed solutions. *Journal of Applied Research in Memory and Cognition, 2*(1), 42–52.

Keil, F. C. (2003). Folk science: Coarse interpretations of a complex reality. *Trends in Cognitive Sciences, 7*, 368–373.

(2006). Explanation and understanding. *Annual Review of Psychology, 57*, 227–254.

Klayman, J. (1995). Varieties of confirmation bias. In J. Busemeyer, R. Hastie, & D. L. Medin (Eds.), *Decision making from a cognitive perspective* (pp. 365–418). New York: Academic Press.

Klayman, J., & Ha, Y. W. (1987). Confirmation, disconfirmation, and information in hypothesis testing. *Psychological Review, 94*(2), 211–228.

Klein, G. A. (1999). Applied decision making. In P. A. Hancock (Ed.), *Handbook of perception and cognition series. Human performance and ergonomics* (2nd ed., pp. 87–107). New York: Academic Press.

(2008). Naturalistic decision making. *Human Factors, 50*(3), 456–460.

(2017). *Sources of power: How people make decisions* (Anniversary ed.). Cambridge, MA: MIT Press.

Klein, G., Moon, B., & Hoffman, R. R. (2006). Making sense of sensemaking 2: A macrocognitive model. *IEEE Intelligent Systems, 21*(5), 88–92.

Klein, G., Phillips, J. K., Rall, E. L., & Peluso, D. A. (2007). A data-frame theory of sensemaking. In R. R. Hoffman (Ed.), *Expertise out of context: Proceedings of the Sixth International Conference on Naturalistic Decision Making* (pp. 113–155). Hillsdale, NJ: Lawrence Erlbaum.

Koehler, J. J. (2011). If the shoe fits they might acquit: The value of forensic science testimony. *Journal of Empirical Legal Studies, 8,* 21–48.

(2016). Communicating probabilistic forensic evidence in court. In A. Jamieson & S. Bader (Eds.), *A guide to forensic DNA profiling.* Hoboken, NJ: Wiley.

Koehler, J. J., Chia, A., & Lindsey, S. (1995). The random match probability (RMP) in DNA evidence: Irrelevant and prejudicial? *Jurimetrics, 35,* 201–219.

Koslowski, B. (1996). *Theory and evidence: The development of scientific reasoning.* Cambridge, MA: MIT Press.

Krynski, T. R., & Tenenbaum, J. B. (2007). The role of causality in judgment under uncertainty. *Journal of Experimental Psychology: General, 136*(3), 430–450.

Kuhn, D. (1989). Children and adults as intuitive scientists. *Psychological Review, 96*(4), 674.

(1991). *The skills of argument.* Cambridge: Cambridge University Press.

(2000). Metacognitive development. *Current Directions in Psychological Science, 9,* 178–181.

(2001). How do people know?. *Psychological Science, 12,* 1–8.

(2008). *Education for thinking.* Cambridge, MA: Harvard University Press.

(2012). The development of causal reasoning. *Wiley Interdisciplinary Reviews: Cognitive Science, 3.* doi:10.1002/wcs.1160

(2017). *Building our best future: Thinking critically about ourselves and our world.* Blacksburg, VA: Wessex.

Kuhn, D., Weinstock, M., & Flaton, R. (1994). How well do jurors reason? Competence dimensions of individual variation in a juror reasoning task. *Psychological Science, 5,* 289–296.

Lagnado, D. A., Fenton, N., & Neil, M. (2013). Legal idioms: A framework for evidential reasoning. *Argument & Computation, 4*(1), 46–63.

Lagnado, D. A., & Gerstenberg, T. (2017). Causation in legal and moral reasoning. In M. R. Waldmann (Ed.), *Oxford library of psychology. The Oxford handbook of causal reasoning* (pp. 565–601). New York: Oxford University Press.

Lagnado, D. A., Gerstenberg, T., & Zultan, R. (2013). Causal responsibility and counterfactuals. *Cognitive Science, 37*(6), 1036–1073.

Lagnado, D. A., Waldmann, M. R., Hagmayer, Y., & Sloman, S. A. (2007). Beyond covariation: Cues to causal structure. In A. Gopnik & L. Schulz (Eds.), *Causal learning: Psychology, philosophy, and computation* (pp. 154–172). New York: Oxford University Press.

Laird, J. E. (2012). *The Soar cognitive architecture.* Cambridge, MA: MIT Press.

Lakatos, I., Worrall, J., & Zahar, E. (Eds.). (1976). *Proofs and refutations: The logic of mathematical discovery.* Cambridge: Cambridge University Press.

Lake, B., Ullman, T., Tenenbaum, J., & Gershman, S. (2017). Building machines that learn and think like people. *Behavioral and Brain Sciences, 40,* E253.

Laplace, P. S. (1812/1951). *Philosophical essay on probability.* New York: Dover.

Leone, C., Kleinberg, S., & Lagnado, D. (2021). Mitigating collider bias in the evaluation of causal claims. [unpublished manuscript].

Lichtenstein, S., Slovic, P., Fischhoff, B., Layman, M., & Combs, B. (1978). Judged frequency of lethal events. *Journal of Experimental Psychology: Human Learning and Memory, 4*(6), 551.

Lieder, F., & Griffiths, T. L. (2020) Resource-rational analysis: Understanding human cognition as the optimal use of limited computational resources. *Behavioral and Brain Sciences, 43*(e1), 1–60.

Lieder, F., Griffiths, T. L., & Hsu, M. (2018). Overrepresentation of extreme events in decision making reflects rational use of cognitive resources. *Psychological Review, 125*(1), 1.

Liefgreen, A., Pilditch, T., & Lagnado, D. (2020). Strategies for selecting and evaluating information. *Cognitive Psychology, 123*, 101332.

Liefgreen, A., Yousif, S. R., Keil, F. C., & Lagnado, D. A. (2020). I don't know if you did it, but I know why: A 'motive' preference at multiple stages of the legal–investigative process. In S. Denison, M. Mack, Y. Yu, & B. C. Armstrong (Eds.), *Proceedings of the 42nd Annual Conference of the Cognitive Science Society* (pp. 1123–1129). Austin, TX: Cognitive Science Society.

Liefgreen, A. and Lagnado, D. (2021). The role of causal models in evaluating simple and complex legal explanations. In Proceedings of the 43rd Annual Meeting of the Cognitive Science Society. Austin, TX: Cognitive Science Society.

Lipton, P. (2004). *Inference to the best explanation.* London: Taylor & Francis.

Lombrozo, T. (2012). Explanation and abductive inference. In K. J. Holyoak & R. G. Morrison (Eds.), *Oxford library of psychology. The Oxford handbook of thinking and reasoning* (pp. 260–276). New York: Oxford University Press.

Lynch, M., & McNally, R. (2003). 'Science', 'common sense', and DNA evidence: A legal controversy about the public understanding of science. *Public Understanding of Science, 12*(1), 83–103.

Mandel, D. R., & Navarrete, G. (2015). Improving Bayesian reasoning: What works and why? *Frontiers in Psychology, 6*, 1872.

Marcus, G., & Davis, E. (2019). *Rebooting AI: Building artificial intelligence we can trust.* New York: Vintage.

Martin, G. A. (1967). Closing argument to the jury for the defense in criminal cases. *Journal of Criminal Law, Criminology and Political Science, 58*, 2–17.

Martire, K. A., Kemp, R. I., Watkins, I., Sayle, M. A., & Newell, B. R. (2013). The expression and interpretation of uncertain forensic science evidence: Verbal equivalence, evidence strength, and the weak evidence effect. *Law and Human Behavior, 37*(3), 197–207.

McCoy, M. L., Nunez, N., & Dammeyer, M. M. (1999). The effect of jury deliberations on jurors' reasoning skills. *Law and Human Behavior, 23*(5), 557–575.

McGrayne, S. B. (2011). *The theory that would not die: How Bayes' rule cracked the enigma code, hunted down Russian submarines, and emerged triumphant from two centuries of controversy.* New Haven, CT: Yale University Press.

McKenzie, C. R. (2004). Hypothesis testing and evaluation. In D. J. Koehler & N. Harvey (Eds.), *Blackwell handbook of judgment and decision making* (pp. 200–219). Hoboken, NJ: Wiley-Blackwell.

(2006). Increased sensitivity to differentially diagnostic answers using familiar materials: Implications for confirmation bias. *Memory & Cognition, 34*(3), 577–588.

McNair, S., & Feeney, A. (2015). Whose statistical reasoning is facilitated by a causal structure intervention? *Psychonomic Bulletin & Review, 22*(1), 258–264.

Mercier, H., & Sperber, D. (2011). Why do humans reason? Arguments for an argumentative theory. *The Behavioral and Brain Sciences, 34*, 57–74.

(2017). *The enigma of reason.* Cambridge, MA: Harvard University Press.

Mierley, M. C., & Baker, S. P. (1983). Fatal house fires in an urban population. *Journal of the American Medical Association, 249*(11), 1466–1468.

Mill, J. S., (1869). *On liberty.* London: Longman, Roberts & Green.

Miyara, M., Tubach, F., Pourcher, V., Morelot-Panzini, C., Pernet, J., & Harochei, J. (2020). Low rate of daily active tobacco smoking in patients with symptomatic COVID-19. *Oeios.* doi:10.32388/WPP19W.3

Mocke, P., Pilditch, T., & Lagnado, D. (2020). *How to catch a liar: A Bayesian approach to laypeople's reasoning about deception* [Unpublished manuscript].

Morgan, R. M. (2017). Conceptualising forensic science and forensic reconstruction. Part I: A conceptual model. *Science and Justice, 57*(6), 455–459.

Morris, M. W., & Larrick, R. P. (1995). When one cause casts doubt on another: A normative analysis of discounting in causal attribution. *Psychological Review, 102*(2), 331.

Mosteller, R. P. (2015). Pernicious inferences: Double counting and perception and evaluation biases in criminal cases. *Howard Law Journal, 58*, 365–396.

Murrie, D. C., Gardner, B. O., Kelley, S., & Dror, I. E. (2019). Perceptions and estimates of error rates in forensic science: A survey of forensic analysts. *Forensic Science International, 302*, 109887.

Neil, M., Fenton, N., Lagnado, D., & Gill, R. (2019). Modelling competing legal arguments using Bayesian model comparison and averaging. *Artificial Intelligence and Law, 27.* doi:10.1007/s10506-019-09250-3

Neisser, U. (1976). *Cognition and reality: Principles and implications of cognitive psychology.* New York: W. H. Freeman/Times Books/Henry Holt.

Nelson, J. D. (2005). Finding useful questions: On Bayesian diagnosticity, probability, impact, and information gain. *Psychological Review, 112*(4), 979–999.

Nickerson, R. S. (1998). Confirmation bias: A ubiquitous phenomenon in many guises. *Review of General Psychology, 2*(2), 175–220.

Nisbett, R. E., & Ross, L. (1980). *Human inference: Strategies and shortcomings of social judgment.* Upper Saddle River, NJ: Prentice-Hall.

Oaksford, M., & Chater, N. (2007). *Bayesian rationality: The probabilistic approach to human reasoning.* New York: Oxford University Press.

OIG. (2006). A review of the FBI's handling of the Brandon Mayfield case. Office of the Inspector General, Oversight & Review Division, US Department of Justice.

Oldroyd, D. R. (1986). *The arch of knowledge: An introductory study of the history of the philosophy and methodology of science.* London: Methuen.

Operskalski, J. T., & Barbey, A. K. (2016). Risk literacy in medical decision-making. *Science, 352*(6284), 413–414.

Ormerod, T. C., Barrett, E., & Taylor, P. J. (2008). Investigative sense-making in criminal contexts. In J. M. C. Schraagen (Ed.), *Proceedings of the Seventh International NDM Conference, Amsterdam, the Netherlands, June 2005* (pp. 81–102).

Osman, M. (2011). *Controlling uncertainty: Decision making and learning in complex worlds.* Hoboken, NJ: Wiley.

Palmer, A. (2011). Why and how to teach proof. *Sydney Law Review, 33,* 563.

Pearl, J. (1988). Probabilistic *reasoning in intelligent systems: Networks of plausible inference.* San Francisco, CA: Morgan-Kaufmann.

(2009). *Causality: Models, reasoning, and inference* (2nd ed.). New York: Cambridge University Press.

(2011). The algorithmization of counterfactuals. *Annals of Mathematics and Artificial Intelligence, 61*(1), 29–39.

(2018). Theoretical impediments to machine learning with seven sparks from the causal revolution [Keynote speech]. WSDM, Feb. 5–9, 2018, Marina Del Ray, CA. arXiv:1801.04016.

Pearl, J., Glymour, M., & Jewell, N. P. (2016). *Causal inference in statistics: A primer.* Chichester: Wiley.

Peirce, C. S. (1931). *Collected papers.* Cambridge, MA: Harvard University Press.

Pennington, N., & Hastie, R. (1986). Evidence evaluation in complex decision making. *Journal of Personality and Social Psychology, 51*(2), 242–258.

(1988). Explanation-based decision making: Effects of memory structure on judgment. *Journal of Experimental Psychology: Learning, Memory, and Cognition, 14*(3), 521–533.

(1992). Explaining the evidence: Tests of the Story Model for juror decision making. *Journal of Personality and Social Psychology, 62*(2), 189–206.

Perfect, T. J., & Schwartz, B. L. (Eds.). (2002). *Applied metacognition.* Cambridge, UK: Cambridge University Press.

Pilditch, T. D., Fenton, N., & Lagnado, D. (2019). The zero-sum fallacy in evidence evaluation. *Psychological Science, 30,* 250–260.

Pilditch, T. D., Fries, A., & Lagnado, D. (2019). Deception in evidential reasoning: Wilful deceit or honest mistake? In A. Goel, C. Seifert, & C. Freska, (Eds.), *Proceedings of the 41st Annual Conference of the Cognitive Science Society* (pp. 931–937). Austin, TX: Cognitive Science Society.

Pilditch, T. D., Hahn, U., Fenton, N., & Lagnado, D. (2020). Dependencies in evidential reports: The case for informational advantages. *Cognition, 204,* 104343.

Pilditch, T. D., Lagator, S., & Lagnado, D. (2021). Strange but true: Corroboration and base rate neglect. *Journal of Experimental Psychology: Learning, Memory, and Cognition, 47*(1), 11–28.

Pilditch, T. D., Liefgreen, A., & Lagnado, D. A. (2019). Zero-sum reasoning in information selection. In A. Goel, C. Seifert, & C. Freska, (Eds.), *Proceedings of the 41st Annual Conference of the Cognitive Science Society* (pp. 938–943). Austin, TX: Cognitive Science Society.

Poe, E. A. (1841/2012). *'The Murders in the Rue Morgue' and other tales.* London: Penguin Classics.

Poletiek, F. H. (2001). *Essays in cognitive psychology. Hypothesis-testing behaviour.* London: Psychology Press.

Popper, K. R. (1959). *The logic of scientific discovery.* New York: Basic Books.

Radvansky, G. A., & Zacks, J. M. (2014). *Event cognition.* New York: Oxford University Press.

Redmayne, M. (2015) *Character in the criminal trial.* Oxford: Oxford University Press.

Rehder, B. (2017). Concepts as causal models: Induction. In M. R. Waldmann (Ed.), *Oxford library of psychology. The Oxford handbook of causal reasoning* (pp. 377–413). New York: Oxford University Press.

Rehder, B., & Waldmann, M. R. (2017). Failures of explaining away and screening off in described versus experienced causal learning scenarios. *Memory & Cognition, 45*(2), 245–260.

Richens, J. G., Lee, C. M., & Johri, S. (2020). Improving the accuracy of medical diagnosis with causal machine learning. *Nature Communications, 11*(1), 1–9.

Roberts, P., & Zuckerman, A. (2010). *Criminal evidence.* New York: Oxford University Press.

Robertson, P., & Aitken, C. (2014). *The logic of forensic proof: Inferential reasoning in criminal evidence and forensic science.* (Communicating and Interpreting Statistical Evidence in the Administration of Criminal Justice.) Guidance for Judges, Lawyers, Forensic Scientists and Expert Witnesses, Practitioner Guide. Royal Statistical Society. https://rss.org.uk/news-publications/our-research/

Roese, N. J., & Vohs, K. D. (2012). Hindsight bias. *Perspectives on Psychological Science, 7*(5), 411–426.

Rogers, T. T., & McClelland, J. L. (2004). *Semantic cognition: A parallel distributed processing approach.* Cambridge, MA: MIT Press.

Rossmo, D. K. (2008). *Criminal investigative failures.* Boca Raton, FL: CRC Press.

Rossmo, K., & Pollock, J. (2019). Confirmation bias and other systemic causes of wrongful convictions: A sentinel events perspective. *Northeastern University Law Review, 11*(2), 790–835.

Rottman, B. M., & Hastie, R. (2014). Reasoning about causal relationships: Inferences on causal networks. *Psychological Bulletin, 140*(1), 109–139.

(2016). Do people reason rationally about causally related events? Markov violations, weak inferences, and failures of explaining away. *Cognitive Psychology, 87*, 88–134.

Royce, C. S., Hayes, M. M., & Schwartzstein, R. M. (2019). Teaching critical thinking: A case for instruction in cognitive biases to reduce diagnostic errors and improve patient safety. *Academic Medicine, 94*(2), 187–194.

Rozenblit, L., & Keil, F. (2002). The misunderstood limits of folk science: An illusion of explanatory depth. *Cognitive Science, 26*(5), 521–562.

Rule, J. S., Tenenbaum, J. B., & Piantadosi, S. T. (2020). The child as hacker. *Trends in Cognitive Sciences, 24*(11), 900–915.

Rumelhart, D. E. (1975). Notes on a schema for stories. In D. G. Bobrow & A. Collins (Eds.), *Representation and understanding* (pp. 211–236). New York: Academic Press.

Rusconi, P., & Mckenzie, C. (2013). Insensitivity and oversensitivity to answer diagnosticity in hypothesis testing. *Quarterly Journal of Experimental Psychology, 66*(12), 2443–2464.

Saks, M. J., & Koehler, J. J. (2005). The coming paradigm shift in forensic identification science. *Sciences, 309*(5736), 892–895.

Sanborn, A. N., & Chater, N. (2016). Bayesian brains without probabilities. *Trends in Cognitive Sciences, 20*(12), 883–893.

Schank, R. C., & Abelson, R. P. (1977). *Scripts, plans, goals, and understanding: An inquiry into human knowledge structures.* Mahwah, NJ: Lawrence Erlbaum.

Scherr, K. C., Redlich, A. D., & Kassin, S. M. (2020). Cumulative disadvantage: A psychological framework for understanding how innocence can lead to confession, wrongful conviction, and beyond. *Perspectives on Psychological Science, 15*(2), 353–383.

Schofield, D. (2016). The use of computer generated imagery in legal proceedings. *Digital Evidence & Electronic Signature Law Review, 13*, 3.

Schum, D. A. (2001). *The evidential foundations of probabilistic reasoning.* Evanston, IL: Northwestern University Press.

(2009). A science of evidence: Contributions from law and probability. *Law, Probability and Risk, 8*(3), 197–231.

Searle, J. R., & Willis, S. (1983). *Intentionality: An essay in the philosophy of mind.* Cambridge University Press.

Semmler, C., Dunn, J., Mickes, L., & Wixted, J. T. (2018). The role of estimator variables in eyewitness identification. *Journal of Experimental Psychology: Applied, 24*(3), 400.

Shaler, R. C. (2011). *Crime scene forensics: A scientific method approach.* London: Taylor & Francis.

Shengelia, T., & Lagnado, D. (2020). Are jurors intuitive statisticians? Bayesian causal reasoning in legal contexts. *Frontiers in Psychology, 11*, 5519262.

Shepard, R. N. (1978). The mental image. *American Psychologist, 33*(2), 125.

Simon, D. (2012). *In doubt: The psychology of the criminal justice process.* Cambridge, MA: Harvard University Press.

Simon, D., Snow, C. J., & Read, S. J. (2004). The redux of cognitive consistency theories: Evidence judgments by constraint satisfaction. *Journal of Personality and Social Psychology, 86*(6), 814–837.

Simon, H. A. (1956). Rational choice and the structure of the environment. *Psychological Review, 63*(2), 129–138.

Skov, R. B., & Sherman, S. J. (1986). Information-gathering processes: Diagnosticity, hypothesis-confirmatory strategies, and perceived hypothesis confirmation. *Journal of Experimental Social Psychology, 22*(2), 93–121.

Sloman, S. (2005). *Causal models: How people think about the world and its alternatives*. New York: Oxford University Press.

Sloman, S., & Lagnado, D. (2015). Causality in thought. *Annual Review of Psychology, 66*, 223–247.

Sloman, S. A., & Fernbach, P. M. (2018). *The knowledge illusion: Why we never think alone*. New York: Riverhead.

Smit, N. M., Lagnado, D. A., Morgan, R. M., & Fenton, N. E. (2016). Using Bayesian networks to guide the assessment of new evidence in an appeal case. *Crime Science, 5*(1), 1–12.

Smit, N. M., Morgan, R. M., & Lagnado, D. (2018). A systematic analysis of misleading evidence in unsafe rulings in England and Wales. *Science & Justice, 58*(2), 128–137.

Sodhi, M., & Etminan, M. (2020). Safety of ibuprofen in patients with COVID-19: Causal or confounded?. *Chest, 158*(1), 55–56.

Stapleton, J. (2008). Choosing what we mean by causation in the law. *Missouri Law Review, 73*, 433.

Stephen, J. F. (1876). *A digest of the law of evidence* (12th ed.). London: Macmillan.

(1948). *A digest of the law of evidence* (1st ed.). London: Macmillan.

Sterman, J. D. (1989). Modeling managerial behavior: Misperceptions of feedback in a dynamic decision making experiment. *Management Science, 35*(3), 321–339.

(2010). *Business dynamics*. New York: Irwin/McGraw-Hill.

Stone, J. V. (2013). *Bayes' rule: A tutorial introduction to Bayesian analysis*. Sebtel Press.

Strevens, M. (2008). *Depth: An account of scientific explanation*. Cambridge, MA: Harvard University Press.

Stuhlmüller, A., & Goodman, N. D. (2014). Reasoning about reasoning by nested conditioning: Modeling theory of mind with probabilistic programs. *Cognitive Systems Research, 28*, 80–99.

Taroni, F., Biedermann, A., Bozza, S., Garbolino, P., & Aitken, C. (2014). *Bayesian networks for probabilistic inference and decision analysis in forensic science*. Hoboken, NJ: Wiley.

Tenenbaum, J. B., Griffiths, T. L., & Niyogi, S. (2007). Intuitive theories as grammars for causal inference. In A. Gopnik & L. Schulz (Eds.), *Causal learning: Psychology, philosophy, and computation* (pp. 301–322). New York: Oxford University Press.

Tenenbaum, J. B., Kemp, C., Griffiths, T. L., & Goodman, N. D. (2011). How to grow a mind: Statistics, structure, and abstraction. *Science, 331*(6022), 1279–1285.

Tentori, K., Crupi, V., & Russo, S. (2013). On the determinants of the conjunction fallacy: Probability versus inductive confirmation. *Journal of Experimental Psychology: General, 42*(1), 235.

Tetlock, P. E. (2002). Social functionalist frameworks for judgment and choice: Intuitive politicians, theologians, and prosecutors. *Psychological Review, 109*(3), 451.

Tetlock, P. E., & Gardner, D. (2016). *Superforecasting: The art and science of prediction*. New York: Random House.

Thomas, N. J. T., (2020). Mental imagery. In E. N. Zalta (Ed.), *The Stanford encyclopedia of philosophy* (Fall 2020 edition). https://plato.stanford.edu/archives/fall2020/entries/mental-imagery/

Thompson, W. C. (2011). What role should investigative facts play in the evaluation of scientific evidence?. *Australian Journal of Forensic Sciences, 43* (2–3), 123–134.

Trabasso, T., & Sperry, L. L. (1985). Causal relatedness and importance of story events. *Journal of Memory and Language, 24*(5), 595–611.

Tversky, A., & Kahneman, D. (1973). Availability: A heuristic for judging frequency and probability. *Cognitive Psychology, 5*(2), 207–232.

(1981). The framing of decisions and the psychology of choice. *Science, 21*(1), 453–58.

(1982). Causal schemas in judgments under uncertainty. In D. Kahneman, P. Slovic, & A. Tversky (Eds.), *Judgment under uncertainty: Heuristics and biases* (pp. 117–128). New York: Oxford University Press.

(1983). Extensional versus intuitive reasoning: The conjunction fallacy in probability judgment. *Psychological Review, 90*(4), 293–315.

Twining, W. (1985). *Theories of evidence: Bentham and Wigmore*. London: Weidenfeld & Nicolson.

Ullman, T. D., Spelke, E., Battaglia, P., Tenenbaum, J. B. (2017). Mind games: Game engines as an architecture for intuitive physics. *Trends in Cognitive Sciences, 21*(9), 649–665.

van Koppen, P. J., & Mackor, A. R. (2020). A scenario approach to the Simonshaven case. *Topics in Cognitive Science, 12*(4), 1132–1151.

Vul, E., Goodman, N., Griffiths, T. L., Tenenbaum, J. B. (2014). One and done? Optimal decisions from very few samples. *Cognitive Science, 38*(2014), 599–637.

Waldmann, M. R. (1996). Knowledge-based causal induction. *Psychology of Learning and Motivation, 34*, 47–88.

(Ed.). (2017). *Oxford library of psychology. The Oxford handbook of causal reasoning*. New York: Oxford University Press.

Waskin, M. (1985). *Mrs O'Leary's comet: Cosmic causes of the great Chicago fire*. Chicago, IL: Academy Chicago Publishers.

Wason, P. C. (1960). On the failure to eliminate hypotheses in a conceptual task. *Quarterly Journal of Experimental Psychology, 12*: 129–140.

Weick, K. (1995). *Sensemaking in organisations*. London: SAGE.

Weinstock, M. (1999). *Epistemological understanding and argumentive competence as foundations of juror reasoning skill* [Unpublished doctoral dissertation]. Teachers College, Columbia University.

Weinstock, M., & Cronin, M. A. (2003). The everyday production of knowledge: Individual differences in epistemological understanding and juror-reasoning skill. *Applied Cognitive Psychology, 17*(2), 161–181.

Wells, G. L. (1992). Naked statistical evidence of liability: Is subjective probability enough? *Journal of Personality and Social Psychology, 62*(5), 739–752.

Wells, G. L., & Gavanski, I. (1989). Mental simulation of causality. *Journal of Personality and Social Psychology*, *56*(2), 161–169.

Wells, G. L., & Olson, E. A. (2003). Eyewitness testimony. *Annual Review of Psychology*, *54*(1), 277–295.

Wigmore, J. H. (1913). The problem of proof. *Illinois Law Review*, *8*(2), 77–103. (1937). *The science of proof: As given by logic, psychology and general experience and illustrated judicial trials* (3rd ed.). Boston, MA: Little, Brown.

Williamson, E. J., Walker, A. J., Bhaskaran, K., Bacon, S., Bates, C., Morton, C. E., ... Goldacre, B. (2020). Factors associated with COVID-19-related death using OpenSAFELY. *Nature*, *584*(7821), 430–436.

Woodward, J. (2003). *Making things happen: A theory of causal explanation.* New York: Oxford University Press.

Wortley, R., & Sidebottom, A. (2017). Deterrence and rational choice theory. In *The Encyclopedia of Juvenile Delinquency and Justice* (pp. 1–6). Wiley Online Library. https://doi.org/10.1002/9781118524275.ejdj0131

Wykes, A. (1964). *The complete illustrated guide to gambling.* London: Aldus Books.

Yaniv, I., & Foster, D. P. (1995). Graininess of judgment under uncertainty: An accuracy-informativeness trade-off. *Journal of Experimental Psychology: General*, *124*(4), 424–432.

Yardley, E., & Wilson, D. (2016). In search of the 'angels of death': conceptualising the contemporary nurse healthcare serial killer. *Journal of Investigative Psychology and Offender Profiling*, *13*(1), 39–55.

Zsambok, C. E., & Klein, G. (Eds.). (2014). *Naturalistic decision making.* London: Psychology Press.

Zwaan, R. A. (1999). Situation models: The mental leap into imagined worlds. *Current Directions in Psychological Science*, *8*(1), 15–18.

Zwaan, R. A., & Radvansky, G. A. (1998). Situation models in language comprehension and memory. *Psychological Bulletin*, *123*(2), 162–185.

Index

Page numbers in *italics* relate to Figures and Tables.

abductive inference. *see* explaining (abductive inference)
alibi (idiom and modelling), 250–254, *251–252, 254*
alternative explanations idiom, 219–220. *see also* competing causes and explanations
evaluating alternative stories, 199–201, 206–207
artificial intelligence (AI) systems, 203, 268, 281
assumptions, and inference
causal graph construction, 65–67
hydraulic assumption, 159, 170
prosecutor's fallacy, 190, 196
rarity assumption, 177
zero-sum assumption. *see* zero-sum assumption
availability heuristic, 100–102, *101*
backwards reasoning. *see* diagnostic (backwards) inference
barn fire, modelling. *see also* Great Chicago fire
causal graphs, *38*, 38, 46–48
conditional probability tables (CPT), *40–44*, 40–44, *43–44*, 45
inference, 49–56, *49*, *49–50*, *51*, *55–56*, *56*, 61–62, *61*, 71–72

Barrett, E., 129–130
base-rate neglect, 78–82, 107, 109, 170
Bayes nets. *see* causal Bayes nets
Bayes' rule, 42, 50, 75, 80, 217
Bayesian inference and updating, 42–43, 49, 51, 54–55, 66, 72, 257–258. *see also* probabilities and probabilistic approaches
and evidence idiom, 217–219
as mentally challenging, 80, 82, 84, 208
behaviour modelling, 20–21
Bes, B., 84–86, *86*
bias
base-rate neglect, 78–82, 107, 109, 170
cognitive bias, 181–182

collider bias, 269–271, *271*
heuristics and biases framework, 77–78
in polygraph test validity studies, 107
in sampling, failure to recognize and correct, 106–108
in sampling, selection bias, 106
in witness testimony, 141
blood evidence, 210, 220–221, 255–257
Bramley, N. R., 104–105
Byrne, Caroline, 2. *see also* cliff death (crime case)

case construction, 4, 125–126, 129. *see also* crime (case) narratives
causal Bayes nets
causal Markov condition, 64
qualitative component. *see* causal graphs/ models (formal)
quantitative component. *see* conditional probability tables (CPT)
utility as thinking tool, 263
utility as training tool, 262
utility during the legal process, 261–262
causal chains
in causal graphs, 46–47, 146–147
vs common causes in explanation-based hypothesis, 85
causal graphs/models (formal). *see also* causal Bayes nets
and actual causation, 69–72
background conditions, 39
causal chain structure, 46–47, 146–147
causal relations vs. probabilistic dependence in, 63–65
common cause structure, 47, 56, 147
common effect structure. *see* common effect structure, in causal graph
defined, 35
definition of causality in, 38–39, 46, 146
direct and indirect causes, 37–38, 145–146

causal graphs/models (formal). (cont.)
  evidential test selection (judgment task), *164*
  extending, 68–70, *68–69*
  granularity, 39
  and human judgment, 78–84
  idiom-based approach. *see* idiom-based
    approach
  and independent vs. dependent evidence,
    243–245, *243–245*
  inference. *see* inference
  intention in, *237–239*, *237–239*, *239*
  and legal reasoning (general principles),
    215–216
  links, 37
  motive in, 235–239, *235–239*, *237–239*
  opportunity in, 231–235, *231–235*, *234–235*,
    255
  practical aspects, 258–259
  propensity in, 239–242, *241–242*
  pruning, 91–94, *93*, 159
  vs purely probabilistic models, 53–54
  and relevance of evidence, 145–149
  and reliability and credibility of evidence,
    151–154
  sensitivity analysis, 67
  and story model, 202–206, *204*
  and strength of evidence, 149–151
  structural causal models, 59–60
  summary, 63
  utility and importance, 35–36, 72–73
  variables. *see* variables, in causal graphs
  Wigmore charts, 212–214, *213*
causal models (in general), defined, 35
causal models (mental). *see also* mental models
    and simulations; stories and narratives
  abstraction (simplification). *see* simplified
    mental models
  coordinating theory and evidence, 109–110
  defined, 35, 75
  explanatory function, 22
  heuristics. *see* heuristics
  and independent vs. dependent evidence,
    82–84, *83*, 94
  and intuitive probability judgments, 78–87,
    89–90
  intuitive theories. *see* intuitive theories
  key characteristics, 19–20
  latent causes, 26
  normative inference, 167–170, 176,
    208–209
  and positive test strategy, 110, 178
  and prediction, 20
  revision and flexibility, 77–78, 105, 125,
    165–171, *169*, 266–269
  specific. *see* specificity of mental models

causality, formal definition, 38–39, 46, 146
CCTV footage evidence, 177, 217–218,
    251–253, 251–253, *253–254*
chains, causal. *see* causal chains
character evidence. *see* propensity (modelling)
Chater, N., 175–177
child abuse (case), 112, *114*, 115–120, *119*, 176
  judgment task (model updating), 165–171,
    167–169
Christie, Agatha, *Witness for the Prosecution*,
    210–211, 220–221, *221*, 254–258, *256–257*
chronology (of crime), and evidence, 126–128.
    see also spatiotemporal frameworks of
    mental models
circumstantial evidence, 7
Clark, Sally (miscarriage of justice), 94, 185–192
  analysis of stories and causal reasoning,
    192–197, 209
cliff death (crime case), 1–11
  appeal, 13
  evidence, 2–3, 5–9
  stories and causal explanations, 1–2, 5
  trial, 6–11
cognitive bias, 181–182
collider bias, 269–271, *271*
combination functions, in conditional
    probability tables (CPT), 44–45
common causes. *see also* confounding
  assumed (naïve Bayes model), 94
  vs causal chains in explanation-based
    hypothesis, 85
  in causal graphs, 47, 56, 147
  and relevance, 147
common effect structure, in causal graph, 47–48,
    147–149, 147–149, *149*
  explosives handling scenario, *163*
  Jill Dando (murder case), *161–162*
  mammogram (judgment task), *81*, 81
competing causes and explanations, 157–159,
    278–280
  alternative explanations idiom. *see* alternative
    explanations idiom
  hydraulic assumption, 159, 170
  simplification strategies, 165
  zero-sum assumption. *see* zero-sum
    assumption
computer modelling
  analogy with mental modelling, 16–17, 25
  vs animation, 18
  fight (shooting) (crime case), 14–16, *15*, 18
conditional probability tables (CPT), 39–40. *see
    also* causal graphs/models (formal)
  and alibi idiom model, *251*
  challenges with populating, 149
  combination functions, 44–45

and deception model, *247*
and general-level or specific causal knowledge
and factors, 149–151
in larger models, 46–48
with multiple causes, 41–45, *43–44*
with simple cause-effect link, *40–41*, 40–41, *43*
confessions, 141, 245
confirmation bias, 30, 172–173
and confirmatory strategies (overview), *173*,
173, 277–278
and evaluating evidence, 180–183
and presenting evidence, 183–185
and searching for evidence, 174–180
confounding. *see also* common causes
de-confounding, and interventional inference,
56–57, 57
factors, 56–57, 269
and sampling in mental models, 106
conjunction error, 96–97
corroborating testimonies, 225–226, *226*
counterfactual inference, 58–63
and actual causation, 71–72
barn fire, 61–62
covid-19 crisis, 273–276, *275*
fight (shooting) (crime case), 19
Great Chicago fire, 69
mental models and, 19–20, 78, 205–206
Sally Clark appeal (miscarriage of justice), 196
covid-19 crisis
causal models, *268*, *270–271*
competing narratives and blame game,
278–279
confirmatory strategies, 277–278
danger of spurious causal inferences, 269–271
diagnostic inference, 267–269, *268*
flexibility of causal thinking, 266–267
public health view, *274–276*, 274–276
test reliability, 276–277, *277*
what-ifs and counterfactuals, 271–276
Craik, Kenneth, 16
credibility of witness evidence. *see* reliability and
credibility of witness evidence
crime (case) narratives, 128–129. *see also* case
construction
crime typologies, 128–129
cross-contamination of evidence
forensic evidence (cognitive bias), 180–181,
243–245
forensic evidence (physical contamination), 148
mitigation strategies, 183
witness evidence, 181–182, *182*

Dando, Jill (murder case), 123–126, 129,
156–157, 160–162, *161–162*, 184,
259

data-frame theory
abductive inference in, 118–119
child abuse (case), *114*, 115–118
cognitive operations in sensemaking, 116–117
data and frame interplay in, *115*, 115–116
and expert reasoning, 121, 130
functional goals and sensemaking, 117–118
key claims and terminology, 113–115, *114*
Dawid, P., 215, 218
deception (modelling), 245–249, *247–249*
selective vs. non-selective lying strategies,
246–247
de-confounding, and interventional inference,
56–57, *57. see also* common causes. *see also*
confounding
dependent evidence
formal causal models, 243–245, *243–245*
mental causal models, 82–84, *83*, 94
diagnostic (backwards) inference, 50–51, *50*
in child abuse (judgment task) model, *168*
in covid-19 crisis, 267–269, *268*
vs predictive inference in explanation-based
hypothesis, 85
simulation in, 89–90
skills, relative weakness, 77–78, 85, 89–90
diagnosticity of test outcomes, 175, 276–277,
277. see also evidence-reliability idiom
direct and indirect causes
in causal graphs, 37–38, 145–146
and intuitive probability judgments, 85
disconfirming evidence, 30, 136, *173*, 218
DNA match evidence, 91–94, 143, 147–148,
149, 152–153, 181, 218
modelling reliability of, *218*, 229–231, *230*
do-operator, 54, *57. see also* interventional
inference
Dror, I., 181
drug test evidence, 152

episode schemas, 197–198, 206. *see also* story
model
evaluating
by experts, 131
vs explaining, 11–13, 265–266, 280
importance, 30–31
as reasoning about the evidence, 12–13
and stories, 199–201, 206–207
Evans, J., 178
evidence
blood evidence, 210, 220–221, 255–257
and case narrative, 125–126, 192–194
and causal reasoning, 68, 93–94, 109–110,
139–144, 195–196
character evidence. *see* propensity (modelling)
and chronology of crime, 126–128

evidence (cont.)
  circumstantial evidence, 7
  combining multiple items (evidence idiom),
    216–219, 216–219, *218*, 255
  cross-contamination. *see* cross-contamination
    of evidence
  disconfirming evidence, 30, 136, *173*, 218
  DNA match evidence. *see* DNA match evidence
  drug test evidence, 152
  evaluation and alternative stories, 199–201,
    206–207
  evaluation and confirmation bias, 180–183
  evaluation by experts, 131
  fingerprint evidence, 172, 180–181, 243–244,
    244
  gunshot residue (GSR) evidence, 156–157,
    160–162, *161–162*
  hair analysis evidence, 143
  idioms. *see* evidence idiom. *see* evidence-
    reliability idiom
  and illusion of explanatory depth, 25
  independent vs. dependent, and cross-
    contamination, 180–183, *182*
  independent vs. dependent, and formal causal
    models, 243–245, *243–245*
  independent vs. dependent, and mental causal
    models, 82–84, *83*, 94
  opportunity, *231–235*, 231–235, *234–235*,
    255
  presenting, and confirmation bias, 183–185
  as relational and contextual, 133–134
  relevance, 135–136, 138, 145–149
  reliability and credibility. *see* evidence-
    reliability idiom; reliability and credibility
    of witness evidence; reliability of physical
    evidence
  searching for, and confirmation bias, 174–180
  shoeprint evidence, 217
  'soft' and 'hard' evidence, 126
  strength. *see* strength of evidence
  as tangible objects or evidentiary facts, 134–135
  tests and test selection. *see* tests and test
    selection
  theory–evidence coordination (TEC),
    206–209
  witness evidence. *see* witnesses and witness
    evidence
evidence idiom, *216–219*, 216–219, *218*,
  255
evidence-reliability idiom, 217–255, *223*, 257. *see
  also* reliability and credibility of witness
  evidence; reliability of physical evidence
  and multiple testimonies, 225–226, *225–226*,
    226
  and test reliability, *277*, 277

evidential test selection. *see* tests and test selection
expert reasoning and decision-making
  and data-frame theory, 121, 130
  evidence evaluation, 130–131
  experimental studies of police detectives,
    129–130
  fieldwork studies of police detectives, 122–129
  lines of enquiry, 126
  in self-solvers, 122–123, *123*
  in whodunits, *123–124*, 123–129
expert witnesses, 6, 8–9, 144, 187–188, 192,
  196–197
  misconduct, 191
explaining (abductive inference). *see also* stories
    and narratives
  and data-frame theory, 118–119
  vs evaluating, 11–13, 265–266, 280
  as reasoning from the evidence, 12, 201–202
explaining away (intercausal reasoning), 52, *52*,
  168, 205, 220–222, *221*, 224, 249
explanation-based hypothesis, 84–87, *86*
explosives handling (scenario), 162–164, *163*
extended crime scene, 233–235, 255
extremity preference, in test selection, 178–179
eyewitness testimony
  cross-contamination (cognitive bias), 181, *182*
  modelling, *227–229*, 227–229
  reliability, 7–8, 25, 222, 227–229, *227–229*

Fenton, N., 212, 231
Fielder, K., 106–107
fight (shooting) (crime case), 14–16
  causal mental models, 19, 22–24, 26, 28–29, 90
  computer modelling and reconstruction,
    14–16, *15*, 18
  fingerprint evidence, 172, 180–181, 243–244,
    244
forensic process (pruning example), 91–94,
  91–94, *92–93*
forwards reasoning. *see* predictive inference
frame theory. *see* data-frame theory
frames. *see* data-frame theory
frontrunner preference, in test selection, 179

George, Barry. *see* Dando, Jill (murder case)
Gerstenberg, T., 26
Great Chicago fire, 32
  causal models, *65–69*, 65–69, *67–68*, 69–70
  stories and causal explanations, 32–34
Grenfell Tower fire, 58–59
gunshot residue (GSR) evidence, 156–157,
  160–162, *161–162*

hair analysis evidence, 143
Hastie, R., 200–201, *202*

Hayes, B. K., 82
heuristics. *see also* simplified mental models
  availability heuristic, 100–102, *101*
  heuristics and biases framework, 77–78
  mental simulation as, 78–87
  reframing, 76–77
hierarchical knowledge, in intuitive theories, 26–28, *27*, 29
'hindsight' bias, 66
Hogarth, R. M., 107–108
hydraulic assumption, 159, 170

idiom-based approach, 216, 254
  in Agatha Christie play, 254–258, *256–257*
  alibi idiom, 250–254, *252*, *254*
  alternative explanations. *see* alternative explanations idiom
  evidence idiom, 216–219, *216–219*, *218*, 255
  evidence reliability idiom. *see* evidence-reliability idiom
  explaining-away idiom, 52, *52*, *168*, 205, 220–222, *221*, 224, 249
  opportunity idiom, *231–235*, 231–235, *235*, 255
  opportunity prior idiom, 232–235, *234*
  practical aspects, 258–259
illusion of explanatory depth, 24–25
inference
  abductive inference. *see* explaining (abductive inference)
  and assumptions. *see* assumptions, and inference
  and prior probabilities. *see* prior probabilities, and inference
  and witness reliability assessment, 141
  Bayesian. *see* Bayesian inference and updating
  by experts. *see* expert reasoning and decision-making
  counterfactual. *see* counterfactual inference
  dangers of outstripping available evidence, 269–271
  diagnostic. *see* diagnostic (backwards) inference
  idioms. *see* idiom-based approach
  intercausal reasoning (explaining away), 52, *52*, *168*, 205, 220–222, *221*, 224, 249
  interventional. *see* interventional inference
  normative, 167–170, 176, 208–209
  Pearl's 3-level hierarchy (overview), 48, *49*
  predictive. *see* predictive inference
  what-if inference. *see* what-if inferences (suppositional reasoning)

Innes, M., 122, *123–124*, 125, 128–129
intention
  modelling, 237–239, *237–239*, *239*
  prior, 238–239
  vs motive, 237–238
intention-in-action, 238–239
intercausal reasoning (explaining away), 52, *52*, *168*, 205, 220–222, *221*, 224, 249
interventional inference, *52*, 53–56, *56*, 78
  and actual causation, 71–72
  counterfactual inference. *see* counterfactual inference
  for de-confounding. *see* de-confounding, and interventional inference
  in investigative and legal contexts, 57–59
intuitive judgments of probabilities, 78–87, 89–90
intuitive theories
  dangers of (confirmation bias). *see* confirmation bias
  key characteristics of, 26–29
  and scaling up, 29
iterative looping, 28–29, 125

jogger, shooting (crime case), 74–75, 89, 158
Johnson-Laird, P., 16
jury decisions
  cliff death (crime case), 11
  and evidence omission/mis-presentation, 196
  and illusion of explanatory depth, 25
  and metacognition, 110, 207
  quality of reasoning, 110, 206–207
  story model. *see* story model
  utility of Bayes nets, 261–262
  and witness credibility, 140
just-in-time mental models, 117

Kahneman, D., 77–78, 87, 96–97, *101*, 101–102
Klayman, J., 176–177
Klein, G., *114*
Koehler, J. J., 91
Krynski, T. R., 78–82, *79*, *81*
Kuhn, D., 109–110, 206–207

Lagnado, D. A., 163–165, 179, 225–226
latent causes, 26
Lieder, F., 103
Liefgreen, A., 179
likelihood framework, 136–139
lines of enquiry, 126
line-ups (bias), 141, 228
links, in causal graphs, 37
  pruning, 91–94, *93*, 159
Locard, Edmond, 132–133, 144

Madrid terrorist attack. *see* Mayfield, Brandon
  (miscarriage of justice)
mammogram (judgment task), *79*, 79–82, *81*,
  82–84, *83*
  naïve sampling in, 107
Markov condition, causal, 64
Mayfield, Brandon (miscarriage of justice), 172,
  180–181
McKenzie, C., 180
Meadow, Roy, 187–191
mental models and simulations. *see also* stories
  and narratives
  abstraction (simplification). *see* simplified
    mental models
  analogy with computer models, 16–17, 25
  behaviour modelling, 20–21
  causality. *see* causal models (mental)
  confirmation bias. *see* confirmation bias
  and data frame theory, 116–117
  ease of simulation as proxy for probability,
    89–90
  generic and specific models and scenarios, 17
  heuristics. *see* heuristics
  intuitive theories. *see* intuitive theories
  key research, 16–17
  metacognition. *see* metacognition
  model refinement, 28–29, 125
  modelling systems, 17, 25–26, 29
  sampling. *see* sampling, in mental models
  vs. simple imagery, 17–19
  simulation in diagnostic inference, 89–90
  simulations and specificity, 98–99, 165
  simulations as heuristic vs. basic mechanism
    for thinking, 87–89
  simulations in expert inference, 130
  spatiotemporal frameworks, 21–22, 127–128
  specificity. *see* specificity of mental models
  utility-weighted model, 103
  what-ifs, 53, 271–273
metacognition, 76, 109–110
  'blind spot' (cognitive bias), 181–182
  in jury decisions, 110, 207
  'metacognitive myopia' in sampling bias,
    107–108
meta-level decisions, and confirmatory
  strategies, 4
miscarriages of justice, 13, 143. *see also* Mayfield,
  Brandon (miscarriage of justice). *see also*
  Clark, Sally (miscarriage of justice)
models. *see* computer modelling. *see* story model.
  see eyewitness testimony: modelling. *see*
  motive:modelling. *see* intention:modelling.
  see propensity (modelling). *see* deception
  (modelling). *see* alibi (idiom and
  modelling). *see* opportunity (idiom and

modelling). *see* causal graphs/models
  (formal). *see* causal models (mental). *see*
  mental models and simulations
modular interventions, 55. *see also* interventional
  inference
motive
  as fact vs. mental state, 238
  vs. intention, 237–238
  modelling, *235–239*, 235–239, *237–239*
murder investigations
  in Agatha Christie play, 210–211, 220–221,
    221, 254–258, *256–257*
  fieldwork studies of police detectives,
    122–129
  Jill Dando, 123–126, 129, 156–157,
    160–162, *161–162*, 184, 259
  jogger, shooting, 74–75, 89, 158
  Marie Latelle, 132–135, 139, 147, 238
  self-solvers, 122–123, *123*
  whodunits, 123–129, *123–124*, 231

naïve Bayes model, 94
naïve sampling, 106–108
narratives. *see* stories and narratives
naturalistic decision-making (NDM), 113
Neil, M., 212, 231
noisy-AND function, 45, 204
noisy-OR function, 44–45, 52, 66, 204. *see also*
  explaining away (intercausal reasoning)
normative inference, 167–170, 176, 208–209. *see*
  also Bayesian inference and updating

Oaksford, M., 176–177
opportunity (idiom and modelling), 231–235,
  231–235, *234–235*, 255

Pearl, J., 32, 46, 48, *49*, 54, 60–61
Pennington, N., 200–201, *202*
Pilditch, T., 163–164, 225–226
planning fallacy, 272–273
polygraph tests, bias in validity studies,
  107
positive test strategy, 175–178, 180
predictions. *see also* counterfactual inference
predictive inference, 48–50, *50*, *51*
  and causal modelling, 20
  vs. diagnostic inference in explanation-based
    hypothesis, 85
pre-emption, 72
prior convictions. *see* propensity (modelling)
prior intention, 238–239
prior probabilities, and inference, 66–67, 150
  base rate neglect, 78–82, 107, 109, 170
  opportunity, *231–235*, 231–235, *234–235*, 255

probabilities and probabilistic approaches. *see also* Bayesian inference and updating
  availability heuristic, 100–102, *101*
  challenges associated with, 137–139, 196
  conditional probability tables. *see* conditional probability tables (CPT)
  intuitive judgments, 78–87, 89–90
  prior probabilities. *see* prior probabilities, and inference
prosecutor's fallacy, 190, 196
  and relevance of evidence, 135–136, 138
  in Sally Clark case (miscarriage of justice), 189–191, 193–195
  and strength of evidence, 136–139
probability tables. *see* conditional probability tables (CPT)
probative value of evidence. *see* relevance of evidence; strength of evidence
profiling, 21. *see also* behaviour modelling
propensity (modelling), 239–242, *241–242*
prosecutor's fallacy, 190, 196
pruning networks (simplification strategy), 91–94, *93*, 159

rarity assumption, 177
reconstruction, 16. *see also* computer modelling
  fight (shooting) (crime case), 14–16, *15*, 18
Redmayne, M., 240–242
relevance of evidence, 135–136, 138, 145–149
reliability and credibility of witness evidence, 139–140. *see also* evidence-reliability idiom; expert witnesses
  alibi evidence, 7, *251–252*, 253–254, *254*
  causal models approach, *153–154*, 153–154
  credibility vs. reliability, 139
  deception. *see* deception (modelling)
  evaluation of, 140–142, 196–197
  eyewitness evidence, 8
  eyewitness testimony, 7, 25, 222, 227–229, *227–229*
  multiple testimonies, 6, 225–226, *225–226*, *226*
  multiple witnesses, 7
reliability of physical evidence, 126, 142–144, 151–153, 157. *see also* evidence-reliability idiom
  modelling forensic trace evidence, *226*, 229–231, *230*
sampling, in mental models, 75–76, 99–100
  availability heuristic, 100–102, *101*
  confounding effects, 106
  and model revision, 104–105
  new sampling approaches, 102–103
  sampling from internal models, 103–104
  sampling the mind, 100–105

sampling the world, 105–108
  selection bias, 106
  and 'wicked' environments, 107–108

'satisficers' (level of reasoning competence), 206–207
scenarios. *see* specificity of mental models
Schum, D., 134, 140
selection bias, in sampling, 106
self-solvers (murder investigations), 122–123, *123*
sensemaking, 121
  by experts. *see* expert reasoning and decision-making
  data-frame theory. *see* data-frame theory
sensitivity analysis, 67
Shengelia, T., 165
shoeprint evidence, 217
shooting
  fight (crime case). *see* fight (shooting) (crime case)
  Jill Dando, 123–126, 129, 156–157, 160–162, *161–162*, 184, 259
  jogger (crime case), 74–75, 89, 158
SIDS (sudden infant death syndrome). *see* Clark, Sally (miscarriage of justice)
simplified mental models, 19–20, 22–25. *see also* heuristics; sampling, in mental models
  assuming independence of evidence, 94, 194–195
  benefits of simplification, 23–24, 39, 88, 170–171
  and competing causes, 165
  conjunction error, 96–97
  dangers of simplification, 24–25, 75, 94, 194–195, 269–271
  and data-frame theory, 116
  pruning networks, 91–94, *93*, 159
  singular models, 90–91, 269
simulations, mental. *see* mental models and simulations
singular mental models (simplification strategy), 90–91, 269
situation models. *see* specificity of mental models
Sloman, S., 84–86, *86*
spatiotemporal frameworks of mental models, 21–22, 127–128
specificity of mental models, 75, 197
  benefits of specific models, 95, 97–99
  dangers of specific models, 95–97
  and mental simulation, 98–99, 165
Stephen, J. F., 135, 145
stories and narratives. *see also* case construction; explaining (abductive inference)
  alternative explanations idiom. *see* alternative explanations idiom

stories and narratives. (cont.)
  cliff death (crime case), 1–2, 5
  competing stories. *see* competing causes and
    explanations
  crime (case) narratives, 128–129
  evidence and, 125–126, 192–194
  Great Chicago fire, 32–34
  Sally Clark case (miscarriage of justice),
    192–194
  Story Model. *see* Story Model
Story Model, 197
  empirical tests, 200–202, *202*
  and formal causal models, 202–206, *204*
  story structure, 197–200, *198–199*
strength of evidence
  and admissibility, 136
  causal model approach, 149–151
  physical evidence, 93–94, 130, 136–137
  probabilistic approaches, 136–139
  witness evidence, 34, 136, 150
structural causal models, 60
suppositional reasoning. *see* what-if inferences
    (suppositional reasoning)
Sutcliffe, Peter (Yorkshire Ripper), 95–96

temporal properties of mental models. *see*
    spatiotemporal frameworks of mental models
Tenenbaum, J. B., 78–82, *79, 81*
tests and test selection
  diagnosticity of outcomes, 175, 276–277, *277*
  extremity preference, 178–179
  frontrunner preference, 179
  judgment task, 164
  positive test strategy, 175–178, 180
theory–evidence coordination (TEC),
    206–209
triggering events, causing larger event, 33–34
Tversky, A., 77–78, 87–89, 96–97, *101*, 101–102

utility-weighted model, 103

variables, in causal graphs, 36–37
  endogenous and exogenous variables, 46
  parent and child variables, 37–38
  probability distributions. *see* conditional
    probability tables (CPT)
  pruning, 91–94, *93*, 159

Wason 2-4-6 task, 176
what-if inferences (suppositional reasoning), 53,
    271–273. *see also* counterfactual inference
whodunits (murder investigations), *123–124*,
    123–129, 231
'wicked' environments, and sampling,
    107–108
Wigmore charts, 212–214, *213*
Wigmore, J. H., 212–214
witnesses and witness evidence
  alibi, 250–254, *251–252, 254*
  collusion, 94
  confessions, 141, 245
  corroborating testimonies, 225–226,
    226
  cross-contamination of evidence, 181–182,
    182
  deception. *see* deception (modelling)
  expert witnesses. *see* expert witnesses
  eyewitness testimonies. *see* eyewitness
    testimony
  reliability and credibility. *see* reliability and
    credibility of witness evidence
Woodward, J., 22, 38

Yorkshire Ripper (Peter Sutcliffe), 95–96

zero-sum assumption, 159–162
  in lay reasoning, 162–165, 170

Lightning Source UK Ltd.
Milton Keynes UK
UKHW022138191021
392506UK00010B/162